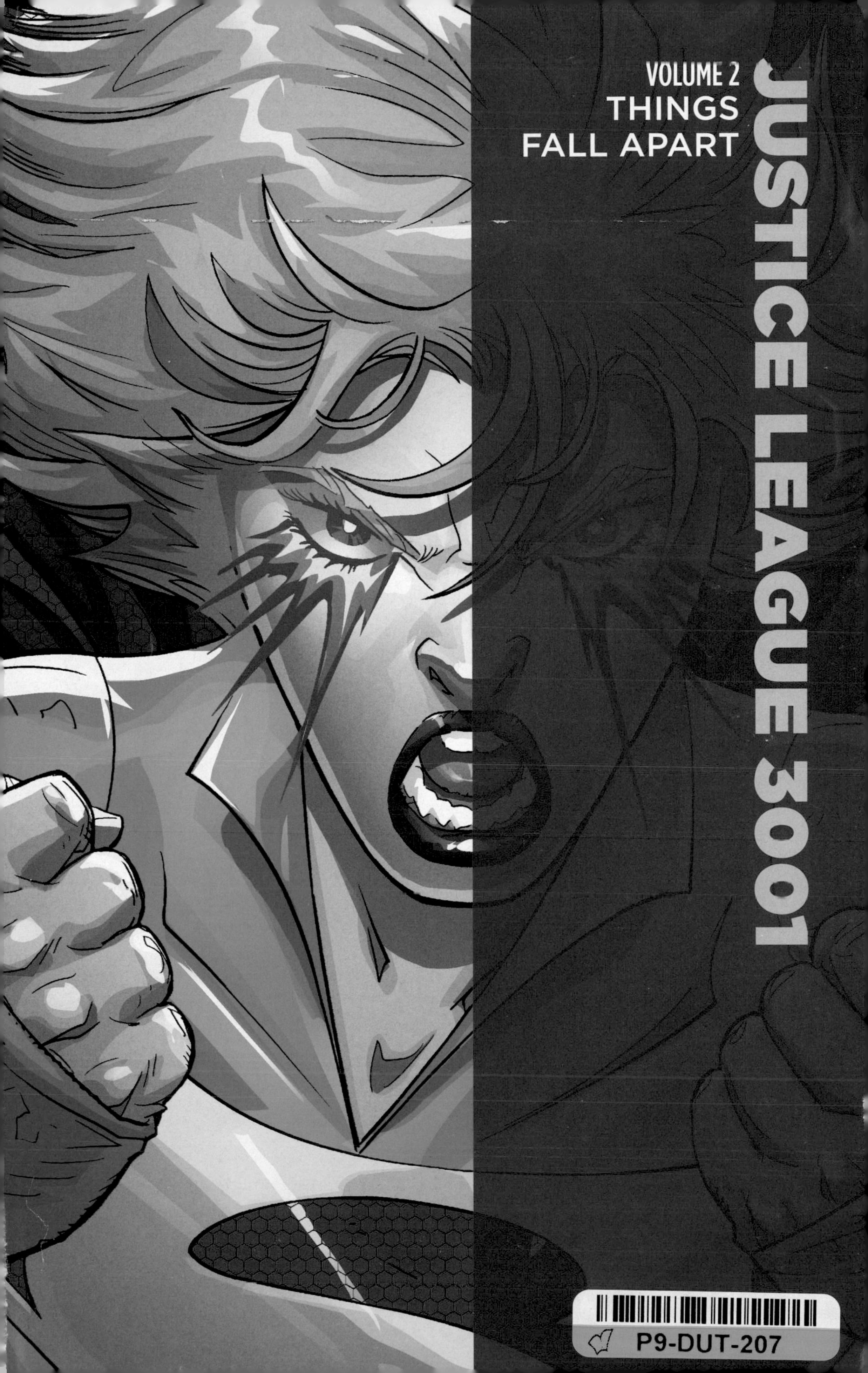
VOLUME 2
THINGS
FALL APART
JUSTICE LEAGUE 3001

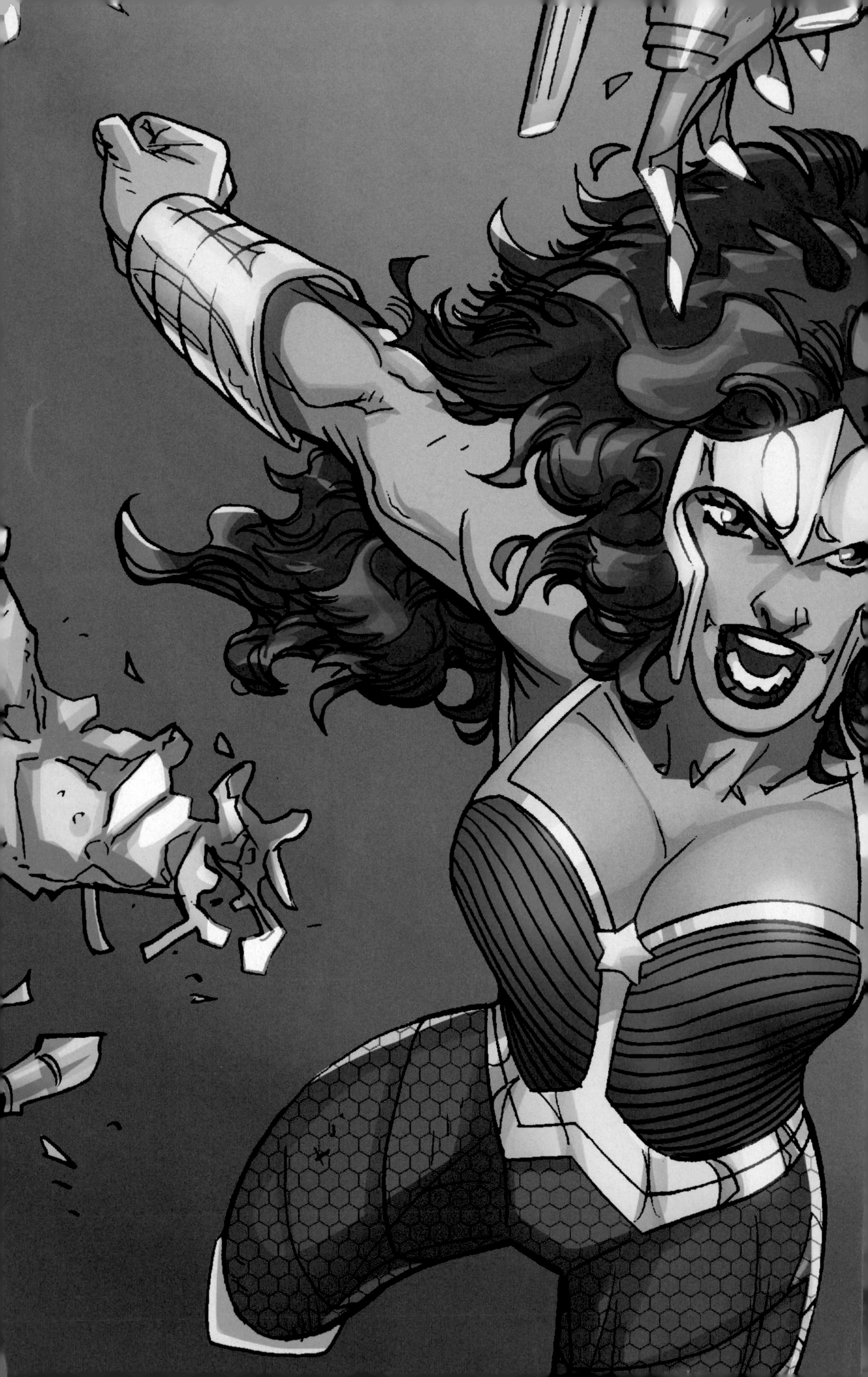

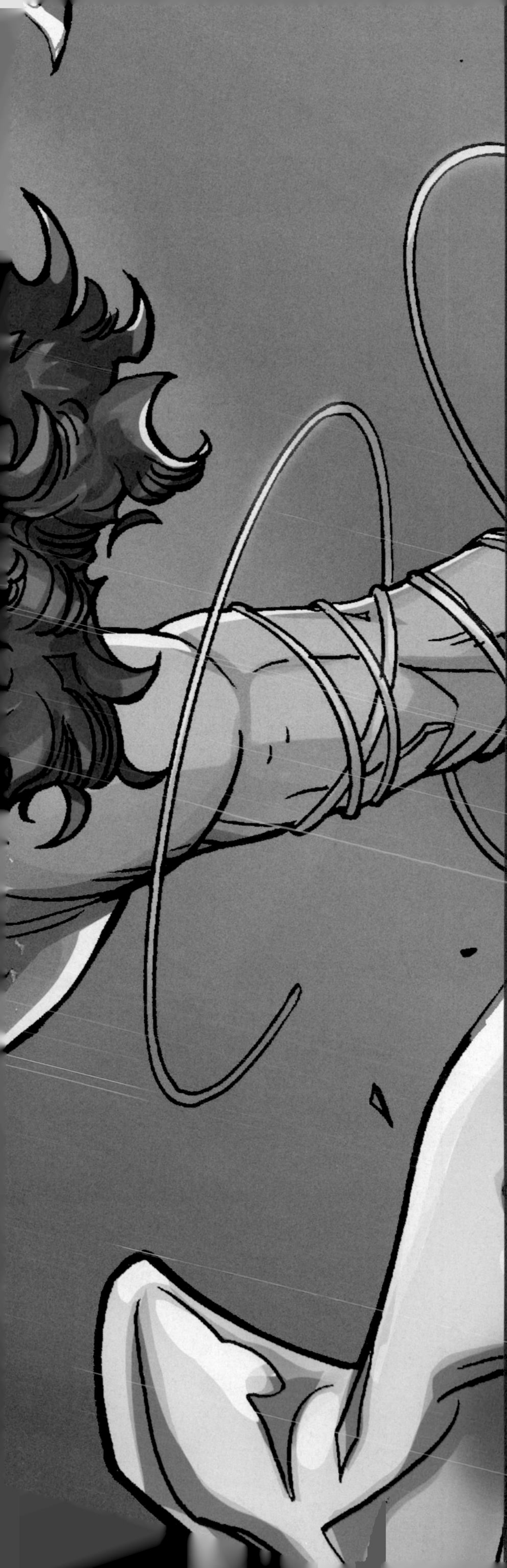

JUSTICE LEAGUE 3001

VOLUME 2
THINGS FALL APART

WRITTEN BY
KEITH GIFFEN
J.M. DeMATTEIS

ART BY
SCOTT KOLINS
COLLEEN DORAN
CHRIS BATISTA
WAYNE FAUCHER
ANDY OWENS
TIMOTHY GREEN II

COLOR BY
HI-FI

LETTERS BY
ROB LEIGH
MARILYN PATRIZIO
TRAVIS LANHAM
SAL CIPRIANO

COLLECTION COVER ART BY
SCOTT KOLINS & HI-FI

SUPERMAN CREATED BY
JERRY SIEGEL &
JOE SHUSTER

SUPERGIRL BASED ON
THE CHARACTERS CREATED BY
JERRY SIEGEL &
JOE SHUSTER
BY SPECIAL ARRANGEMENT
WITH THE JERRY SIEGEL FAMILY

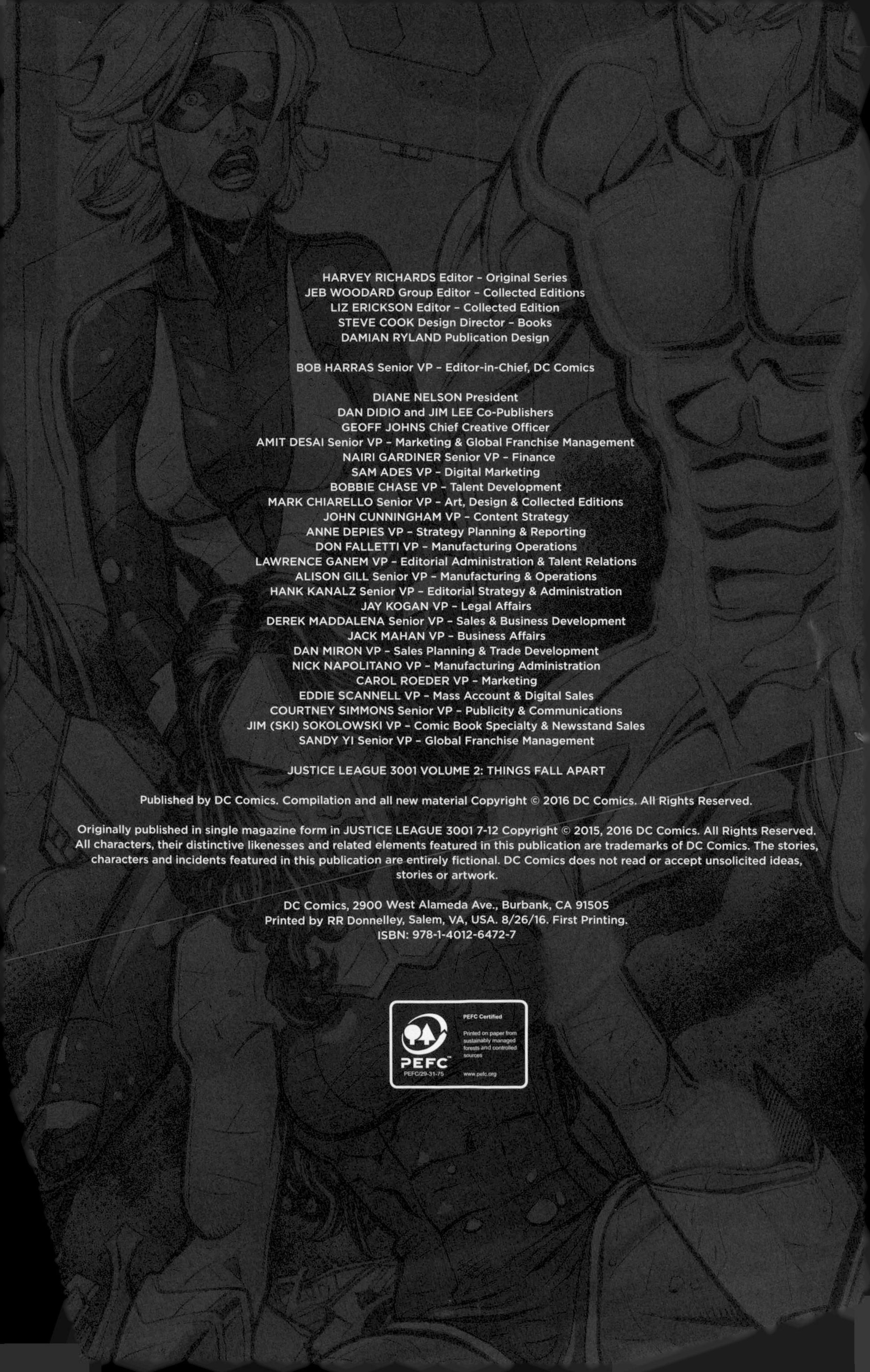

HARVEY RICHARDS Editor - Original Series
JEB WOODARD Group Editor - Collected Editions
LIZ ERICKSON Editor - Collected Edition
STEVE COOK Design Director - Books
DAMIAN RYLAND Publication Design

BOB HARRAS Senior VP - Editor-in-Chief, DC Comics

DIANE NELSON President
DAN DIDIO and JIM LEE Co-Publishers
GEOFF JOHNS Chief Creative Officer
AMIT DESAI Senior VP - Marketing & Global Franchise Management
NAIRI GARDINER Senior VP - Finance
SAM ADES VP - Digital Marketing
BOBBIE CHASE VP - Talent Development
MARK CHIARELLO Senior VP - Art, Design & Collected Editions
JOHN CUNNINGHAM VP - Content Strategy
ANNE DEPIES VP - Strategy Planning & Reporting
DON FALLETTI VP - Manufacturing Operations
LAWRENCE GANEM VP - Editorial Administration & Talent Relations
ALISON GILL Senior VP - Manufacturing & Operations
HANK KANALZ Senior VP - Editorial Strategy & Administration
JAY KOGAN VP - Legal Affairs
DEREK MADDALENA Senior VP - Sales & Business Development
JACK MAHAN VP - Business Affairs
DAN MIRON VP - Sales Planning & Trade Development
NICK NAPOLITANO VP - Manufacturing Administration
CAROL ROEDER VP - Marketing
EDDIE SCANNELL VP - Mass Account & Digital Sales
COURTNEY SIMMONS Senior VP - Publicity & Communications
JIM (SKI) SOKOLOWSKI VP - Comic Book Specialty & Newsstand Sales
SANDY YI Senior VP - Global Franchise Management

JUSTICE LEAGUE 3001 VOLUME 2: THINGS FALL APART

DC Comics, 2900 West Alameda Ave., Burbank, CA 91505
Printed by RR Donnelley, Salem, VA, USA. 8/26/16. First Printing.
ISBN: 978-1-4012-6472-7

PEFC Certified
Printed on paper from sustainably managed forests and controlled sources
PEFC
PEFC/29-31-75
www.pefc.org

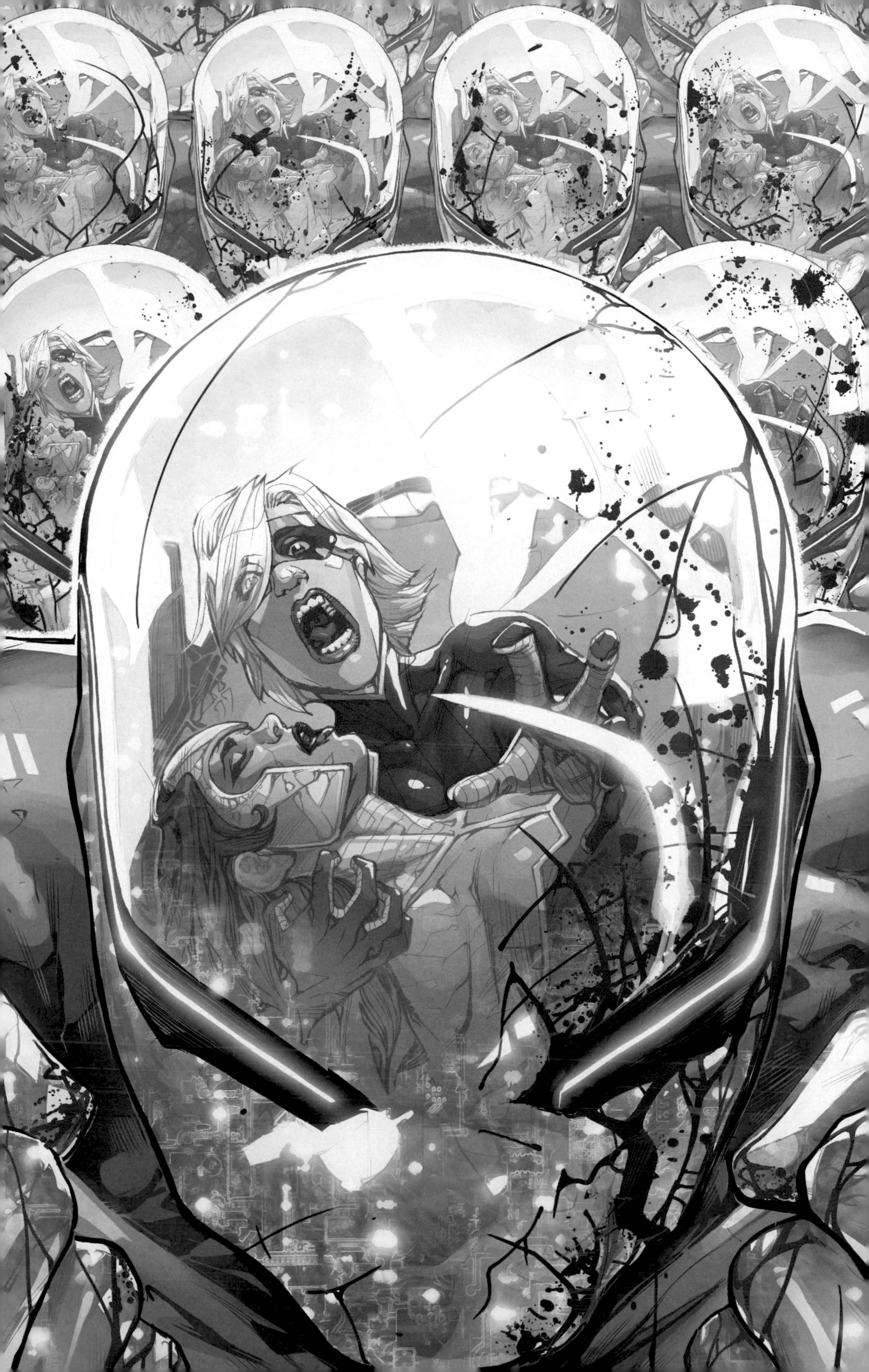

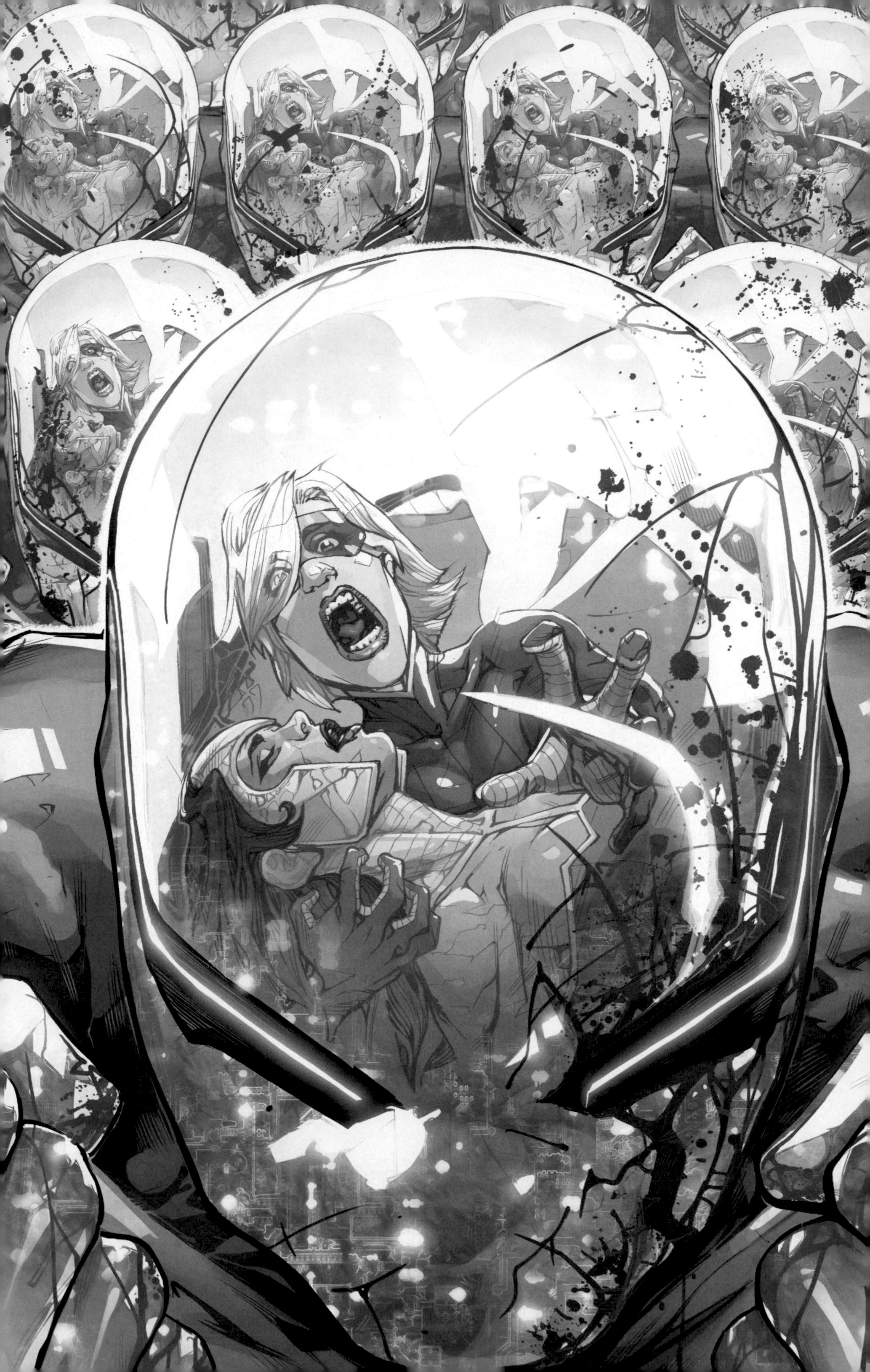

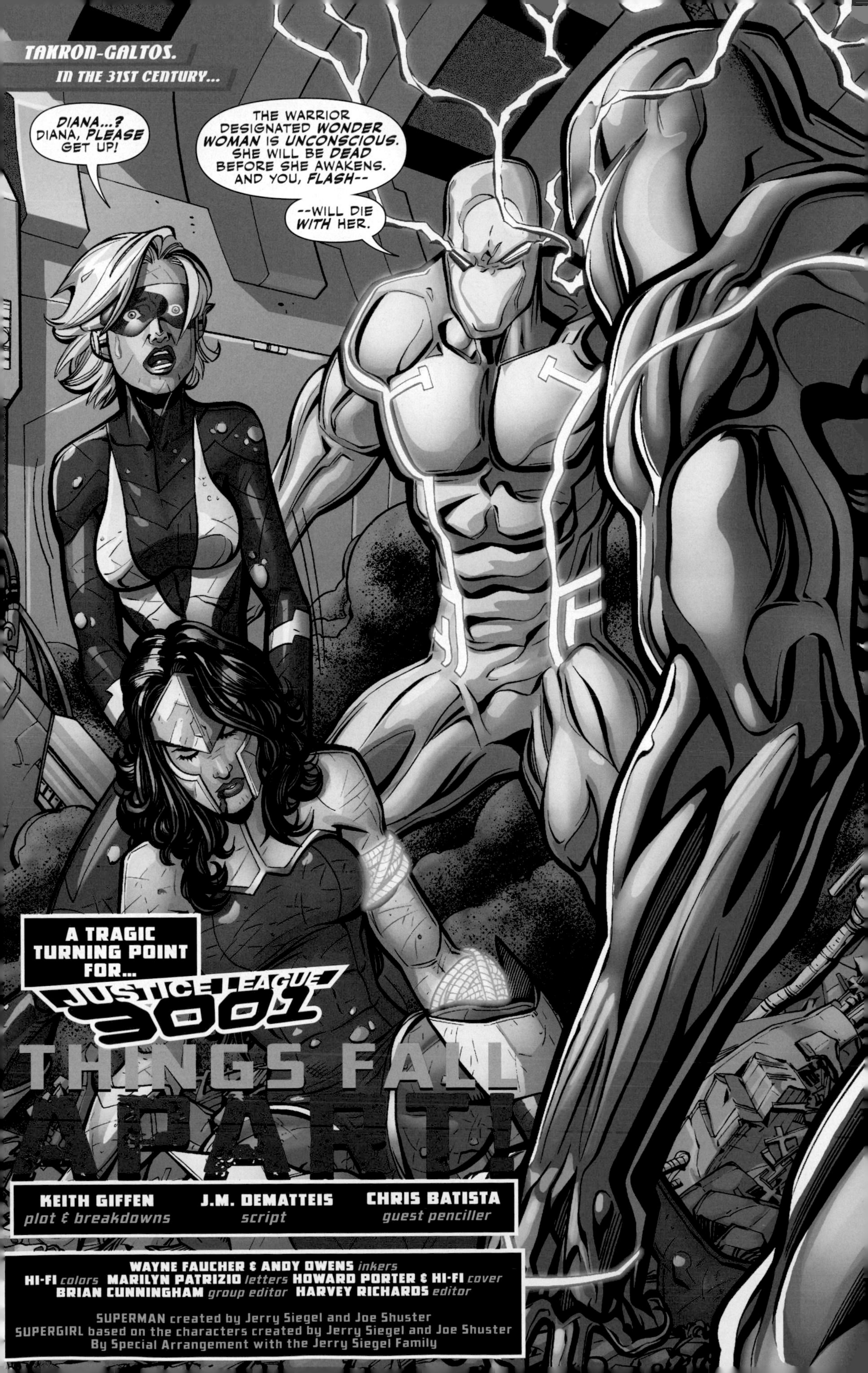
TAKRON-GALTOS.
IN THE 31ST CENTURY...
DIANA...? DIANA, PLEASE GET UP!
THE WARRIOR DESIGNATED WONDER WOMAN IS UNCONSCIOUS. SHE WILL BE DEAD BEFORE SHE AWAKENS. AND YOU, FLASH--
--WILL DIE WITH HER.
A TRAGIC TURNING POINT FOR...
JUSTICE LEAGUE 3001
THINGS FALL APART!
KEITH GIFFEN plot & breakdowns
J.M. DEMATTEIS script
CHRIS BATISTA guest penciller
WAYNE FAUCHER & ANDY OWENS inkers
HI-FI colors MARILYN PATRIZIO letters HOWARD PORTER & HI-FI cover
BRIAN CUNNINGHAM group editor HARVEY RICHARDS editor
SUPERMAN created by Jerry Siegel and Joe Shuster
SUPERGIRL based on the characters created by Jerry Siegel and Joe Shuster
By Special Arrangement with the Jerry Siegel Family

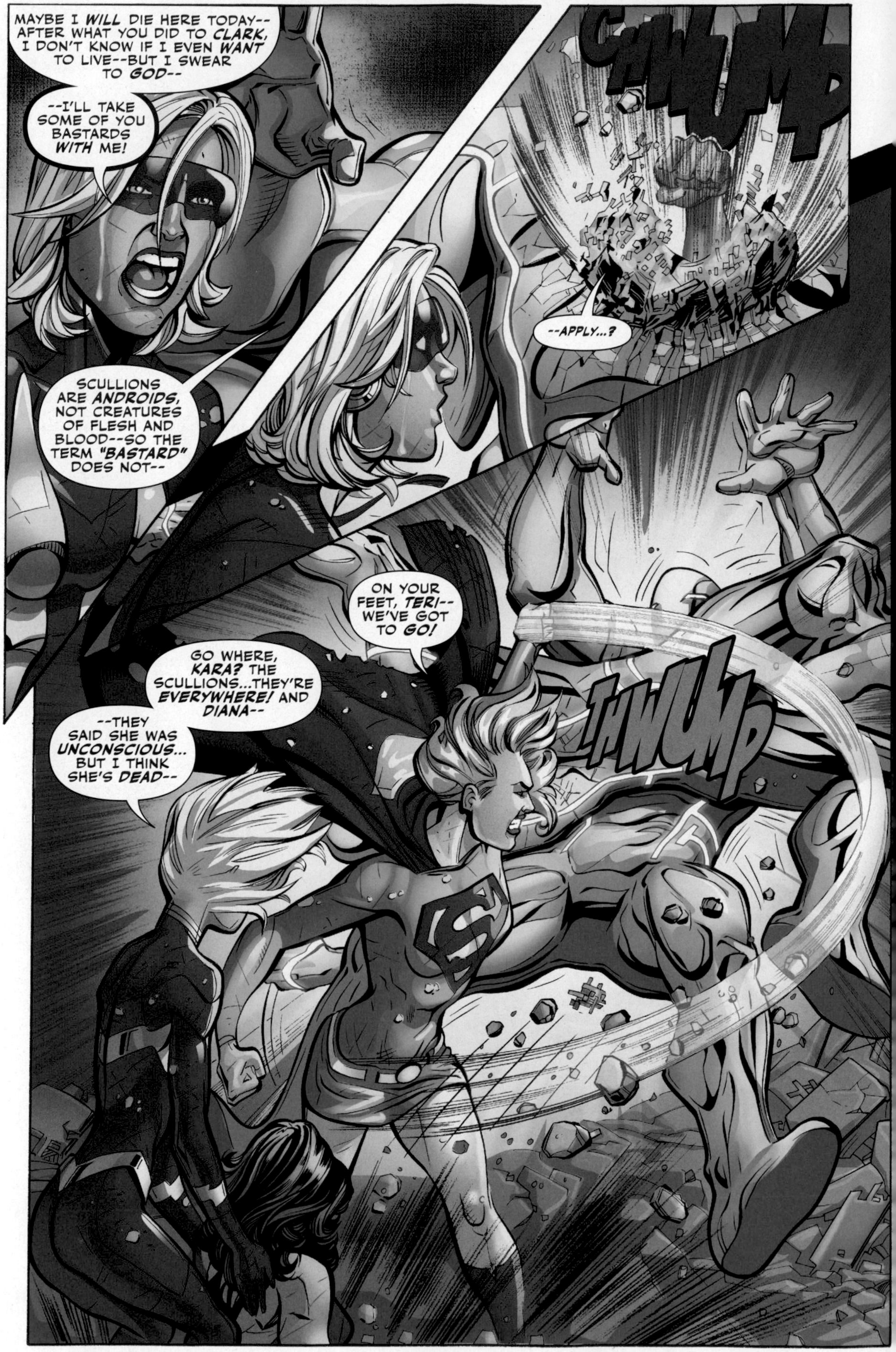
MAYBE I WILL DIE HERE TODAY--AFTER WHAT YOU DID TO CLARK, I DON'T KNOW IF I EVEN WANT TO LIVE--BUT I SWEAR TO GOD--
--I'LL TAKE SOME OF YOU BASTARDS WITH ME!
CHWUMP
SCULLIONS ARE ANDROIDS, NOT CREATURES OF FLESH AND BLOOD--SO THE TERM "BASTARD" DOES NOT--
--APPLY...?
ON YOUR FEET, TERI--WE'VE GOT TO GO!
GO WHERE, KARA? THE SCULLIONS...THEY'RE EVERYWHERE! AND DIANA--
--THEY SAID SHE WAS UNCONSCIOUS... BUT I THINK SHE'S DEAD--
THWUMP

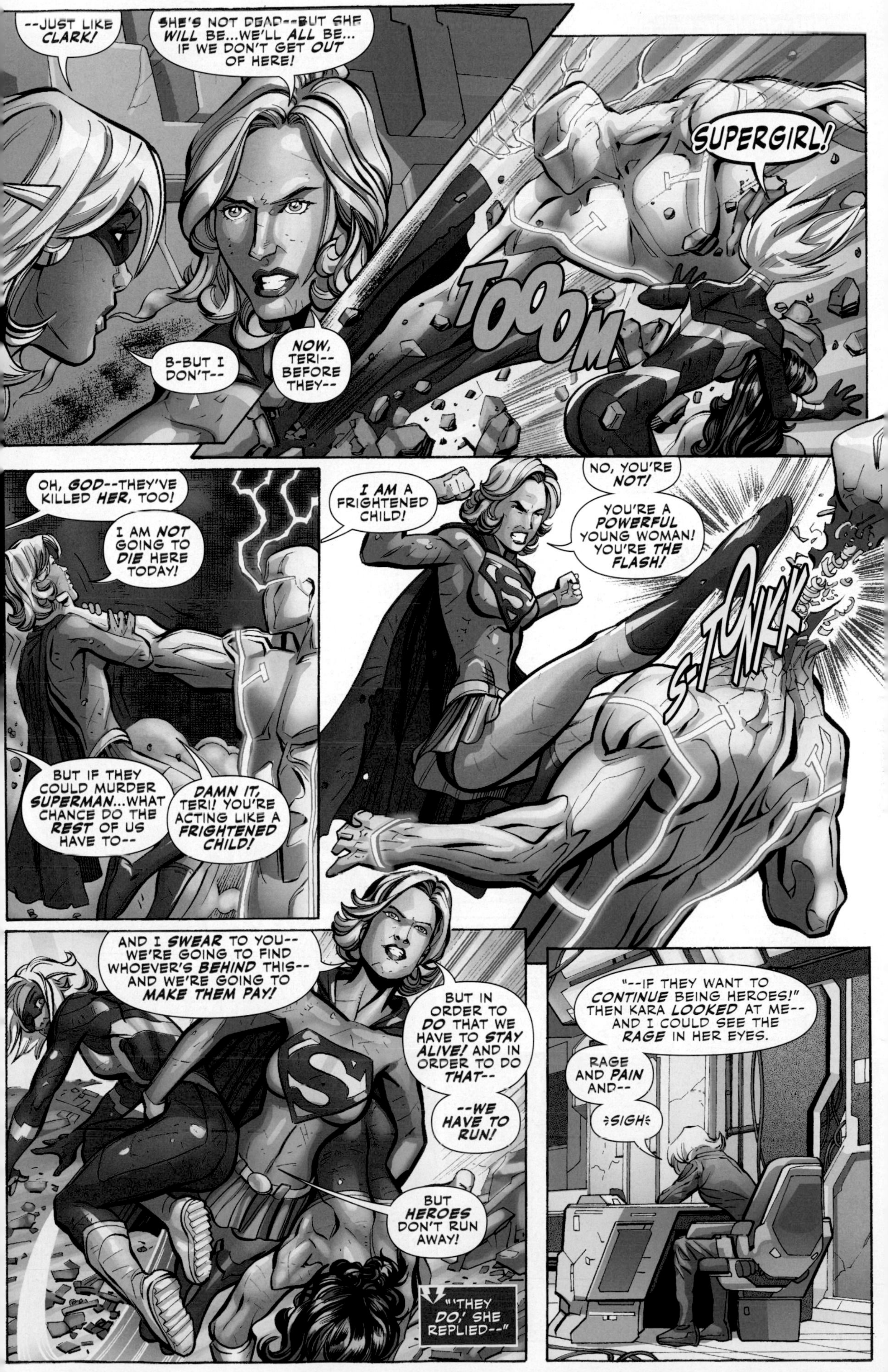
--JUST LIKE CLARK!
SHE'S NOT DEAD--BUT SHE WILL BE...WE'LL ALL BE... IF WE DON'T GET OUT OF HERE!
B-BUT I DON'T--
NOW, TERI--BEFORE THEY--
TOOOOM
SUPERGIRL!
OH, GOD--THEY'VE KILLED HER, TOO!
I AM NOT GOING TO DIE HERE TODAY!
BUT IF THEY COULD MURDER SUPERMAN...WHAT CHANCE DO THE REST OF US HAVE TO--
DAMN IT, TERI! YOU'RE ACTING LIKE A FRIGHTENED CHILD!
I AM A FRIGHTENED CHILD!
NO, YOU'RE NOT!
YOU'RE A POWERFUL YOUNG WOMAN! YOU'RE THE FLASH!
S-TONKK
AND I SWEAR TO YOU--WE'RE GOING TO FIND WHOEVER'S BEHIND THIS--AND WE'RE GOING TO MAKE THEM PAY!
BUT IN ORDER TO DO THAT WE HAVE TO STAY ALIVE! AND IN ORDER TO DO THAT--
--WE HAVE TO RUN!
BUT HEROES DON'T RUN AWAY!
"'THEY DO,' SHE REPLIED--"
"--IF THEY WANT TO CONTINUE BEING HEROES!" THEN KARA LOOKED AT ME--AND I COULD SEE THE RAGE IN HER EYES.
RAGE AND PAIN AND--
SIGH

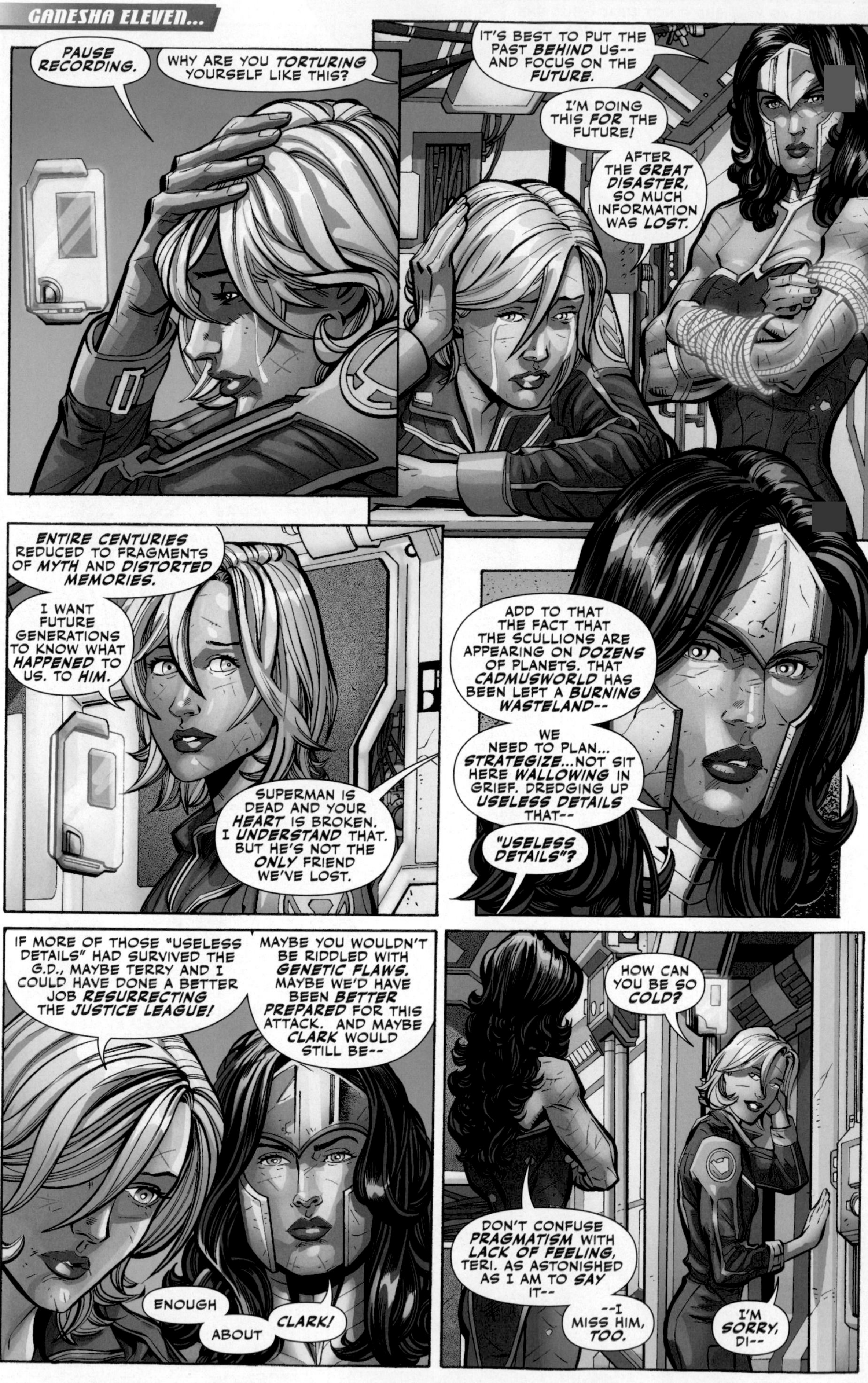
GANESHA ELEVEN...
PAUSE RECORDING.
WHY ARE YOU TORTURING YOURSELF LIKE THIS?
IT'S BEST TO PUT THE PAST BEHIND US-- AND FOCUS ON THE FUTURE.
I'M DOING THIS FOR THE FUTURE!
AFTER THE GREAT DISASTER, SO MUCH INFORMATION WAS LOST.
ENTIRE CENTURIES REDUCED TO FRAGMENTS OF MYTH AND DISTORTED MEMORIES.
I WANT FUTURE GENERATIONS TO KNOW WHAT HAPPENED TO US. TO HIM.
SUPERMAN IS DEAD AND YOUR HEART IS BROKEN. I UNDERSTAND THAT. BUT HE'S NOT THE ONLY FRIEND WE'VE LOST.
ADD TO THAT THE FACT THAT THE SCULLIONS ARE APPEARING ON DOZENS OF PLANETS. THAT CADMUSWORLD HAS BEEN LEFT A BURNING WASTELAND--
WE NEED TO PLAN... STRATEGIZE...NOT SIT HERE WALLOWING IN GRIEF. DREDGING UP USELESS DETAILS THAT--
"USELESS DETAILS"?
IF MORE OF THOSE "USELESS DETAILS" HAD SURVIVED THE G.D., MAYBE TERRY AND I COULD HAVE DONE A BETTER JOB RESURRECTING THE JUSTICE LEAGUE!
MAYBE YOU WOULDN'T BE RIDDLED WITH GENETIC FLAWS. MAYBE WE'D HAVE BEEN BETTER PREPARED FOR THIS ATTACK. AND MAYBE CLARK WOULD STILL BE--
ENOUGH
ABOUT
CLARK!
HOW CAN YOU BE SO COLD?
DON'T CONFUSE PRAGMATISM WITH LACK OF FEELING, TERI. AS ASTONISHED AS I AM TO SAY IT--
--I MISS HIM, TOO.
I'M SORRY, DI--

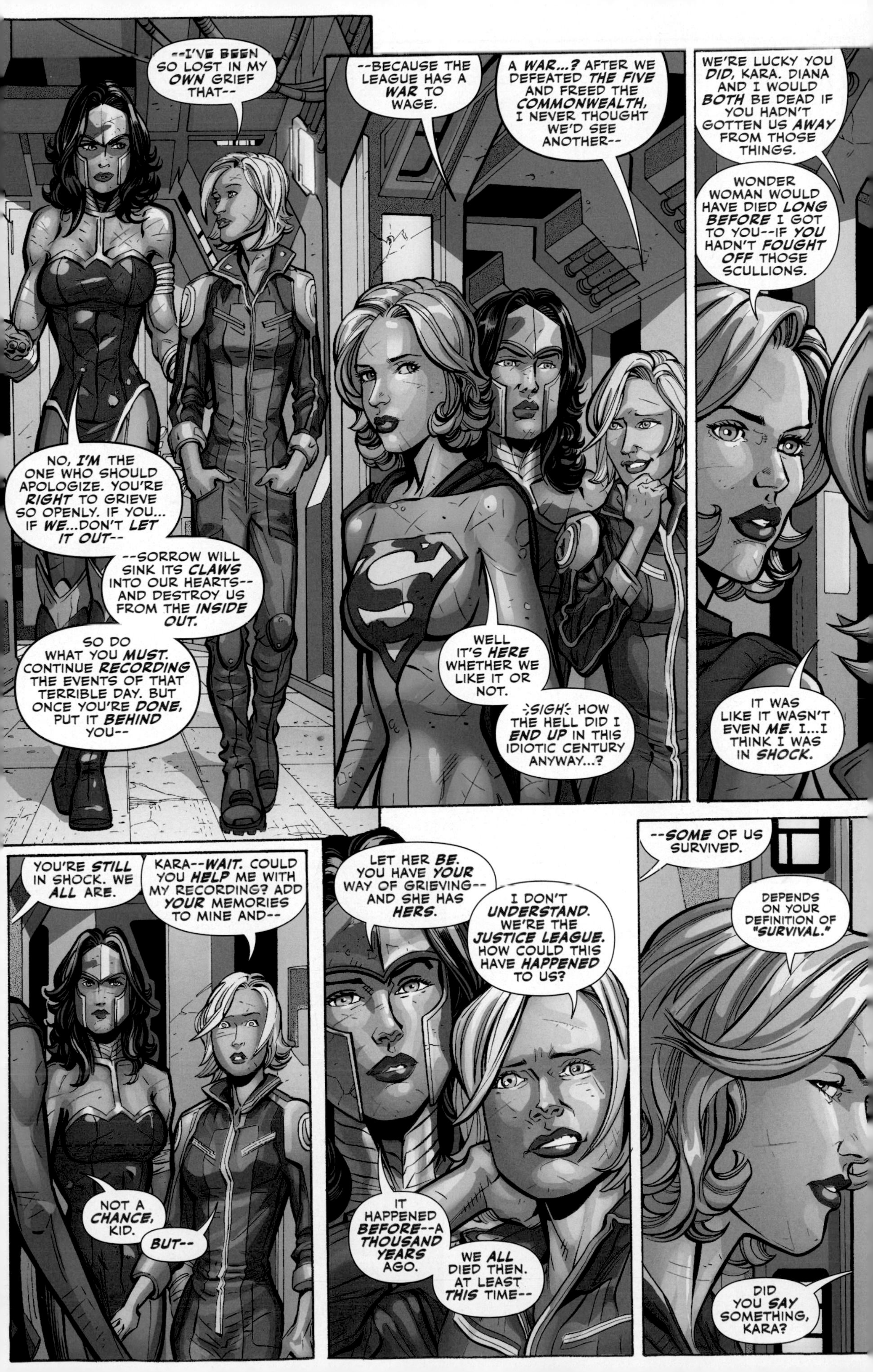
--I'VE BEEN SO LOST IN MY OWN GRIEF THAT--
NO, I'M THE ONE WHO SHOULD APOLOGIZE. YOU'RE RIGHT TO GRIEVE SO OPENLY. IF YOU... IF WE...DON'T LET IT OUT--
--SORROW WILL SINK ITS CLAWS INTO OUR HEARTS--AND DESTROY US FROM THE INSIDE OUT.
SO DO WHAT YOU MUST. CONTINUE RECORDING THE EVENTS OF THAT TERRIBLE DAY. BUT ONCE YOU'RE DONE, PUT IT BEHIND YOU--
--BECAUSE THE LEAGUE HAS A WAR TO WAGE.
A WAR...? AFTER WE DEFEATED THE FIVE AND FREED THE COMMONWEALTH, I NEVER THOUGHT WE'D SEE ANOTHER--
WELL IT'S HERE WHETHER WE LIKE IT OR NOT.
-SIGH- HOW THE HELL DID I END UP IN THIS IDIOTIC CENTURY ANYWAY...?
WE'RE LUCKY YOU DID, KARA. DIANA AND I WOULD BOTH BE DEAD IF YOU HADN'T GOTTEN US AWAY FROM THOSE THINGS.
WONDER WOMAN WOULD HAVE DIED LONG BEFORE I GOT TO YOU--IF YOU HADN'T FOUGHT OFF THOSE SCULLIONS.
IT WAS LIKE IT WASN'T EVEN ME. I...I THINK I WAS IN SHOCK.
YOU'RE STILL IN SHOCK. WE ALL ARE.
KARA--WAIT. COULD YOU HELP ME WITH MY RECORDING? ADD YOUR MEMORIES TO MINE AND--
NOT A CHANCE, KID.
BUT--
LET HER BE. YOU HAVE YOUR WAY OF GRIEVING--AND SHE HAS HERS.
I DON'T UNDERSTAND. WE'RE THE JUSTICE LEAGUE. HOW COULD THIS HAVE HAPPENED TO US?
IT HAPPENED BEFORE--A THOUSAND YEARS AGO.
WE ALL DIED THEN. AT LEAST THIS TIME--
--SOME OF US SURVIVED.
DEPENDS ON YOUR DEFINITION OF "SURVIVAL."
DID YOU SAY SOMETHING, KARA?

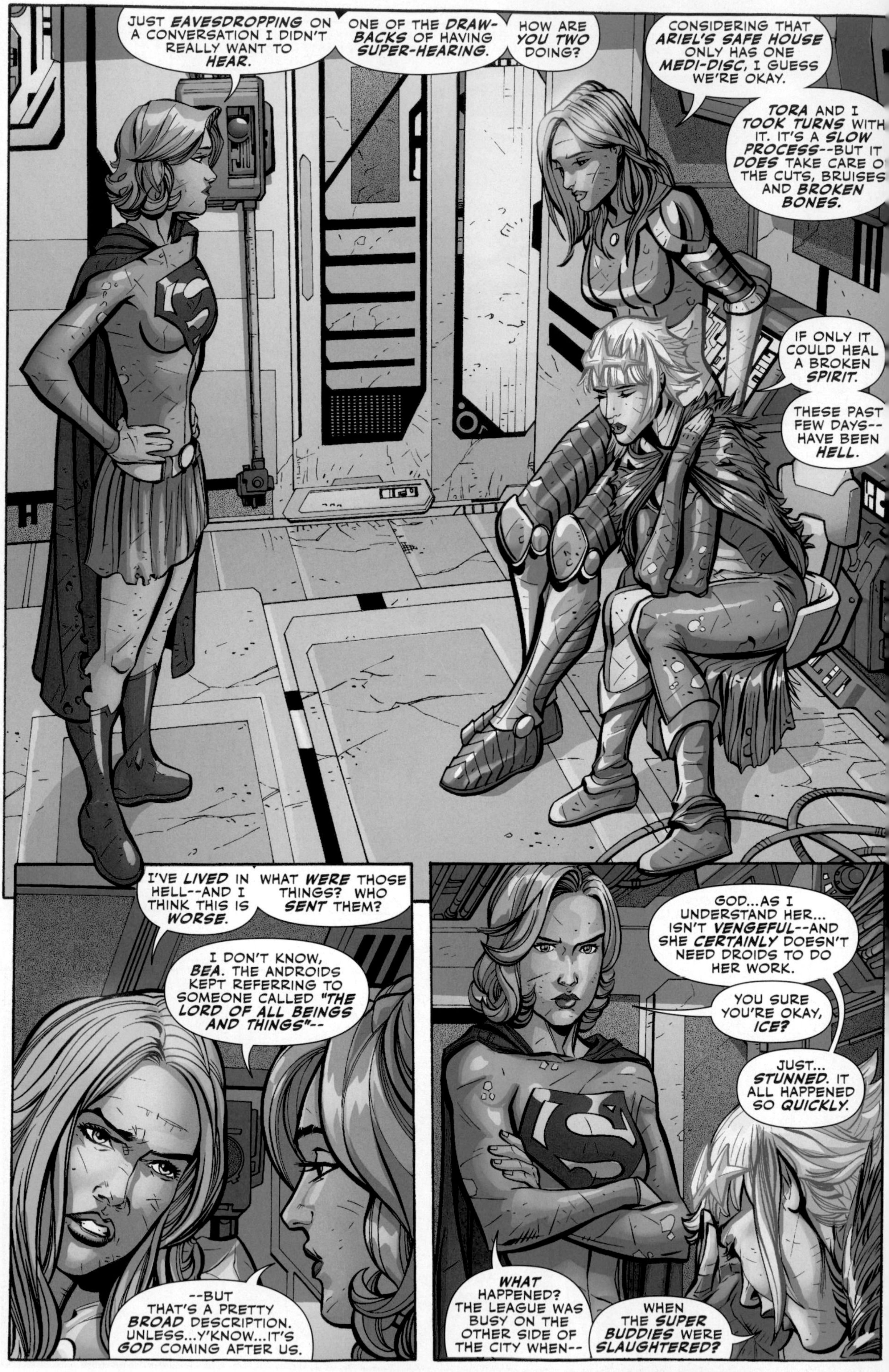
JUST EAVESDROPPING ON A CONVERSATION I DIDN'T REALLY WANT TO HEAR.
ONE OF THE DRAWBACKS OF HAVING SUPER-HEARING.
HOW ARE YOU TWO DOING?
CONSIDERING THAT ARIEL'S SAFE HOUSE ONLY HAS ONE MEDI-DISC, I GUESS WE'RE OKAY.
TORA AND I TOOK TURNS WITH IT. IT'S A SLOW PROCESS--BUT IT DOES TAKE CARE OF THE CUTS, BRUISES AND BROKEN BONES.
IF ONLY IT COULD HEAL A BROKEN SPIRIT.
THESE PAST FEW DAYS--HAVE BEEN HELL.
I'VE LIVED IN HELL--AND I THINK THIS IS WORSE.
WHAT WERE THOSE THINGS? WHO SENT THEM?
I DON'T KNOW, BEA. THE ANDROIDS KEPT REFERRING TO SOMEONE CALLED "THE LORD OF ALL BEINGS AND THINGS"--
--BUT THAT'S A PRETTY BROAD DESCRIPTION. UNLESS...Y'KNOW...IT'S GOD COMING AFTER US.
GOD...AS I UNDERSTAND HER... ISN'T VENGEFUL--AND SHE CERTAINLY DOESN'T NEED DROIDS TO DO HER WORK.
YOU SURE YOU'RE OKAY, ICE?
JUST... STUNNED. IT ALL HAPPENED SO QUICKLY.
WHAT HAPPENED? THE LEAGUE WAS BUSY ON THE OTHER SIDE OF THE CITY WHEN--
WHEN THE SUPER BUDDIES WERE SLAUGHTERED?

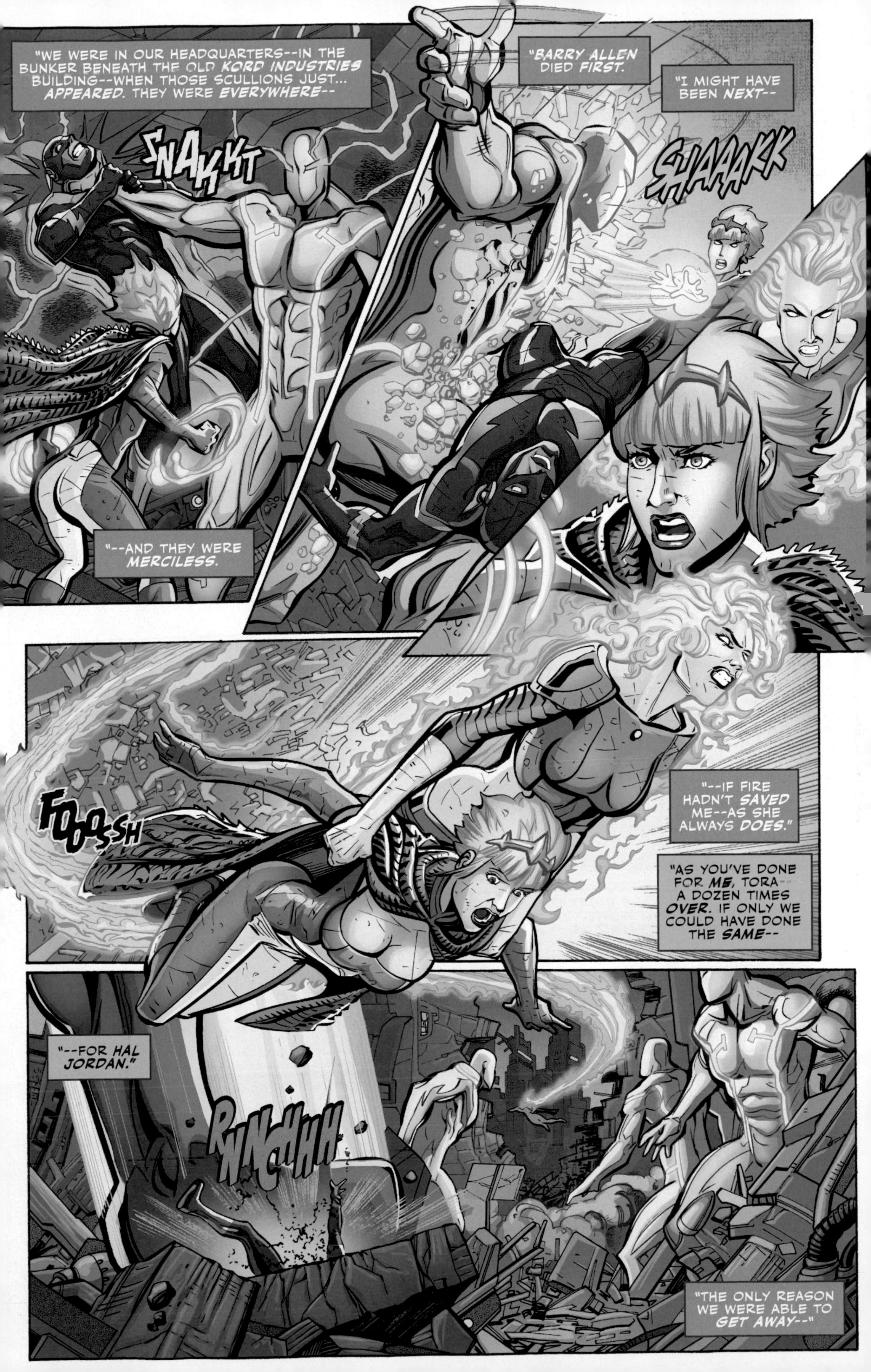
"WE WERE IN OUR HEADQUARTERS--IN THE BUNKER BENEATH THE OLD KORD INDUSTRIES BUILDING--WHEN THOSE SCULLIONS JUST... APPEARED. THEY WERE EVERYWHERE--
SNAKKT
"--AND THEY WERE MERCILESS.
"BARRY ALLEN DIED FIRST.
"I MIGHT HAVE BEEN NEXT--
SHAAAKK
FOOOSSH
"--IF FIRE HADN'T SAVED ME--AS SHE ALWAYS DOES."
"AS YOU'VE DONE FOR ME, TORA-- A DOZEN TIMES OVER. IF ONLY WE COULD HAVE DONE THE SAME--
"--FOR HAL JORDAN."
RMMCHHH
"THE ONLY REASON WE WERE ABLE TO GET AWAY--"

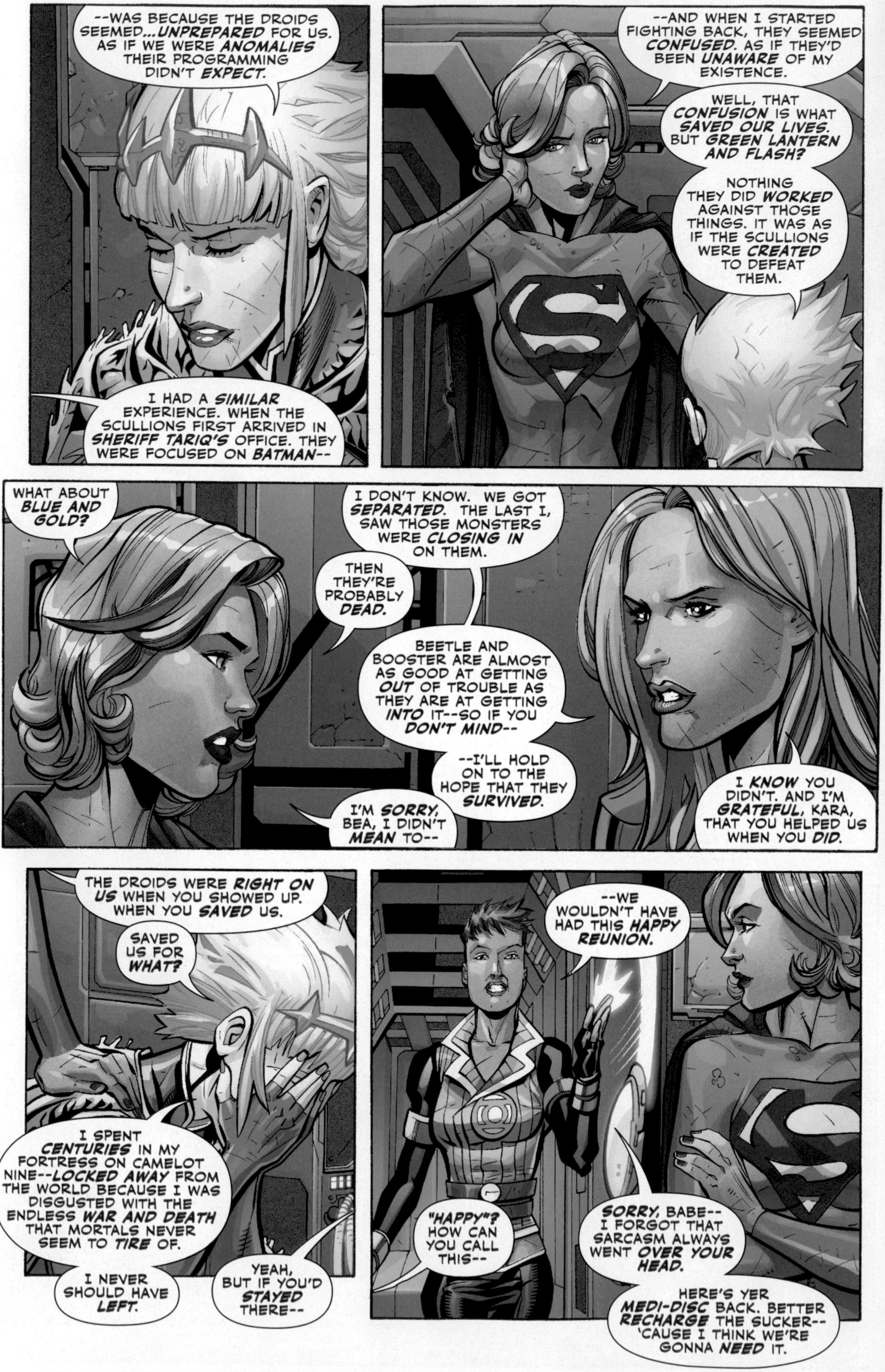
--WAS BECAUSE THE DROIDS SEEMED...UNPREPARED FOR US. AS IF WE WERE ANOMALIES THEIR PROGRAMMING DIDN'T EXPECT.
I HAD A SIMILAR EXPERIENCE. WHEN THE SCULLIONS FIRST ARRIVED IN SHERIFF TARIQ'S OFFICE. THEY WERE FOCUSED ON BATMAN--
--AND WHEN I STARTED FIGHTING BACK, THEY SEEMED CONFUSED. AS IF THEY'D BEEN UNAWARE OF MY EXISTENCE.
WELL, THAT CONFUSION IS WHAT SAVED OUR LIVES. BUT GREEN LANTERN AND FLASH?
NOTHING THEY DID WORKED AGAINST THOSE THINGS. IT WAS AS IF THE SCULLIONS WERE CREATED TO DEFEAT THEM.
WHAT ABOUT BLUE AND GOLD?
I DON'T KNOW. WE GOT SEPARATED. THE LAST I, SAW THOSE MONSTERS WERE CLOSING IN ON THEM.
THEN THEY'RE PROBABLY DEAD.
BEETLE AND BOOSTER ARE ALMOST AS GOOD AT GETTING OUT OF TROUBLE AS THEY ARE AT GETTING INTO IT--SO IF YOU DON'T MIND--
--I'LL HOLD ON TO THE HOPE THAT THEY SURVIVED.
I'M SORRY, BEA, I DIDN'T MEAN TO--
I KNOW YOU DIDN'T. AND I'M GRATEFUL, KARA, THAT YOU HELPED US WHEN YOU DID.
THE DROIDS WERE RIGHT ON US WHEN YOU SHOWED UP. WHEN YOU SAVED US.
SAVED US FOR WHAT?
I SPENT CENTURIES IN MY FORTRESS ON CAMELOT NINE--LOCKED AWAY FROM THE WORLD BECAUSE I WAS DISGUSTED WITH THE ENDLESS WAR AND DEATH THAT MORTALS NEVER SEEM TO TIRE OF.
I NEVER SHOULD HAVE LEFT.
YEAH, BUT IF YOU'D STAYED THERE--
--WE WOULDN'T HAVE HAD THIS HAPPY REUNION.
"HAPPY"? HOW CAN YOU CALL THIS--
SORRY, BABE--I FORGOT THAT SARCASM ALWAYS WENT OVER YOUR HEAD.
HERE'S YER MEDI-DISC BACK. BETTER RECHARGE THE SUCKER--'CAUSE I THINK WE'RE GONNA NEED IT.

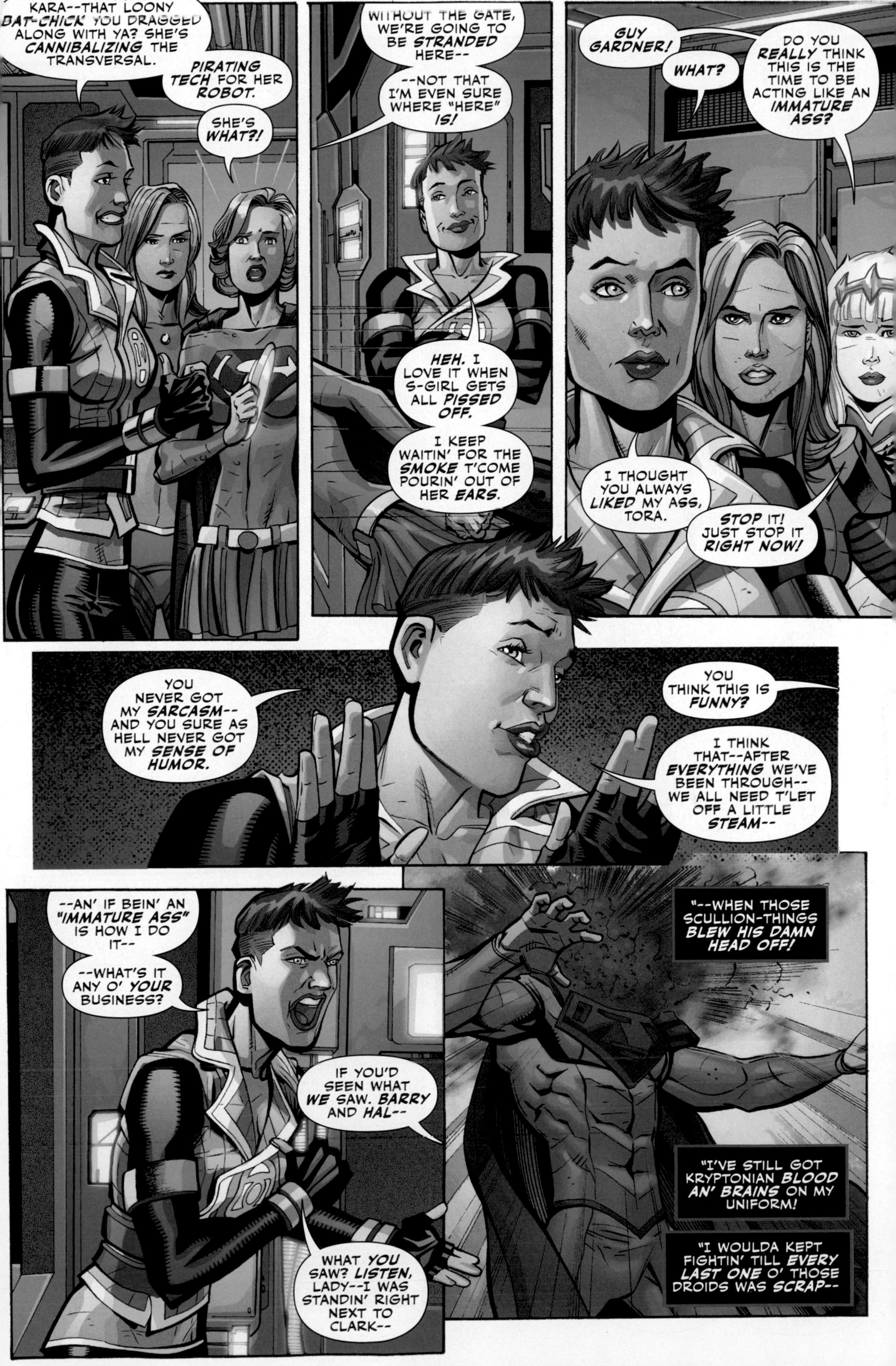
BY THE WAY, KARA--THAT LOONY BAT-CHICK YOU DRAGGED ALONG WITH YA? SHE'S CANNIBALIZING THE TRANSVERSAL.
PIRATING TECH FOR HER ROBOT.
SHE'S WHAT?!
WITHOUT THE GATE, WE'RE GOING TO BE STRANDED HERE--
--NOT THAT I'M EVEN SURE WHERE "HERE" IS!
HEH. I LOVE IT WHEN S-GIRL GETS ALL PISSED OFF.
I KEEP WAITIN' FOR THE SMOKE T'COME POURIN' OUT OF HER EARS.
GUY GARDNER!
WHAT?
DO YOU REALLY THINK THIS IS THE TIME TO BE ACTING LIKE AN IMMATURE ASS?
I THOUGHT YOU ALWAYS LIKED MY ASS, TORA.
STOP IT! JUST STOP IT RIGHT NOW!
YOU NEVER GOT MY SARCASM-- AND YOU SURE AS HELL NEVER GOT MY SENSE OF HUMOR.
YOU THINK THIS IS FUNNY?
I THINK THAT--AFTER EVERYTHING WE'VE BEEN THROUGH-- WE ALL NEED T'LET OFF A LITTLE STEAM--
--AN' IF BEIN' AN "IMMATURE ASS" IS HOW I DO IT--
--WHAT'S IT ANY O' YOUR BUSINESS?
IF YOU'D SEEN WHAT WE SAW. BARRY AND HAL--
WHAT YOU SAW? LISTEN, LADY--I WAS STANDIN' RIGHT NEXT TO CLARK--
"--WHEN THOSE SCULLION-THINGS BLEW HIS DAMN HEAD OFF!
"I'VE STILL GOT KRYPTONIAN BLOOD AN' BRAINS ON MY UNIFORM!
"I WOULDA KEPT FIGHTIN' TILL EVERY LAST ONE O' THOSE DROIDS WAS SCRAP--

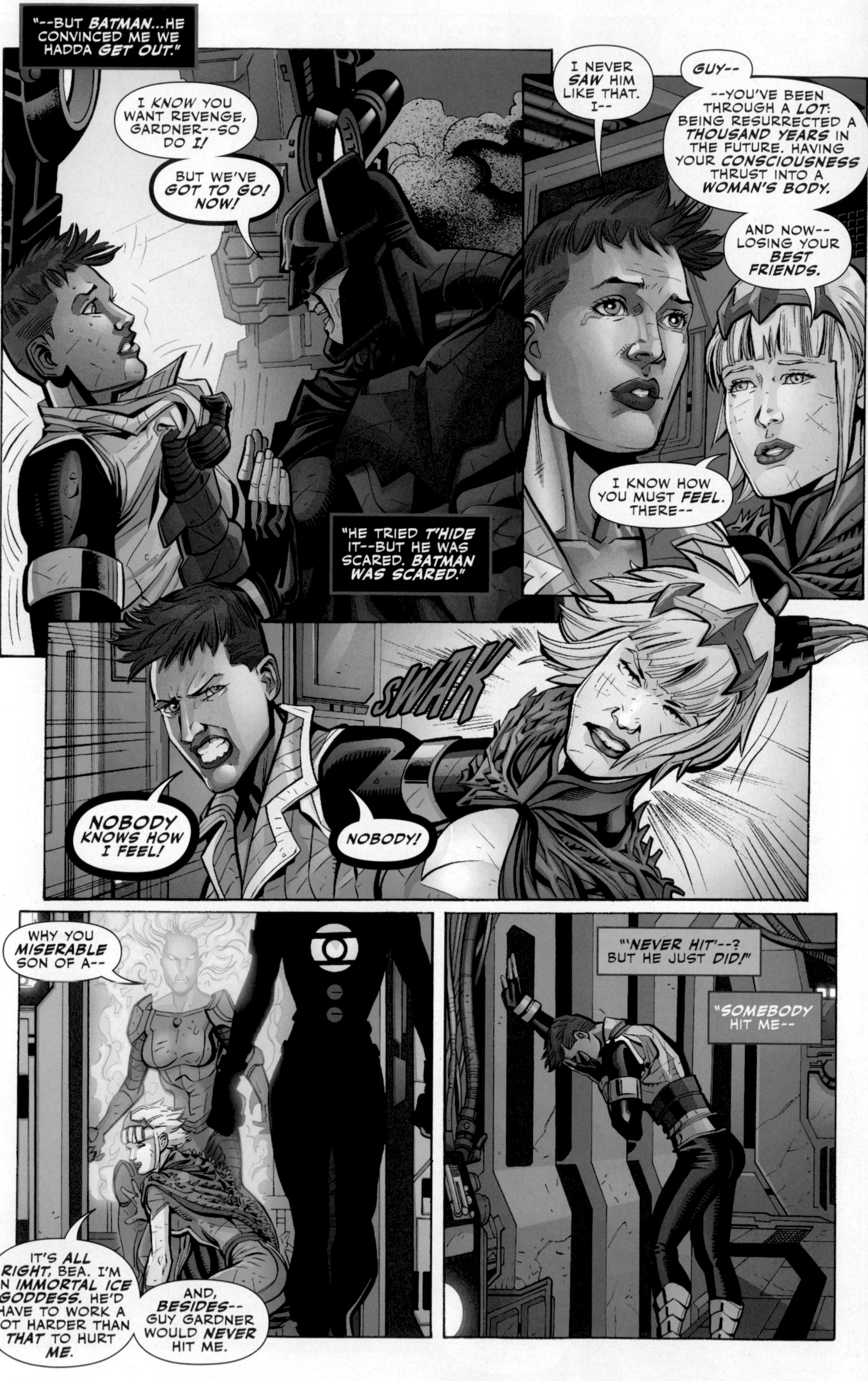
"--BUT BATMAN...HE CONVINCED ME WE HADDA GET OUT."
I KNOW YOU WANT REVENGE, GARDNER--SO DO I!
BUT WE'VE GOT TO GO! NOW!
"HE TRIED T'HIDE IT--BUT HE WAS SCARED. BATMAN WAS SCARED."
I NEVER SAW HIM LIKE THAT. I--
GUY--
--YOU'VE BEEN THROUGH A LOT: BEING RESURRECTED A THOUSAND YEARS IN THE FUTURE. HAVING YOUR CONSCIOUSNESS THRUST INTO A WOMAN'S BODY.
AND NOW--LOSING YOUR BEST FRIENDS.
I KNOW HOW YOU MUST FEEL. THERE--
SWAK
NOBODY KNOWS HOW I FEEL!
NOBODY!
WHY YOU MISERABLE SON OF A--
IT'S ALL RIGHT, BEA. I'M AN IMMORTAL ICE GODDESS. HE'D HAVE TO WORK A LOT HARDER THAN THAT TO HURT ME.
AND, BESIDES--GUY GARDNER WOULD NEVER HIT ME.
"'NEVER HIT'--? BUT HE JUST DID!"
"SOMEBODY HIT ME--

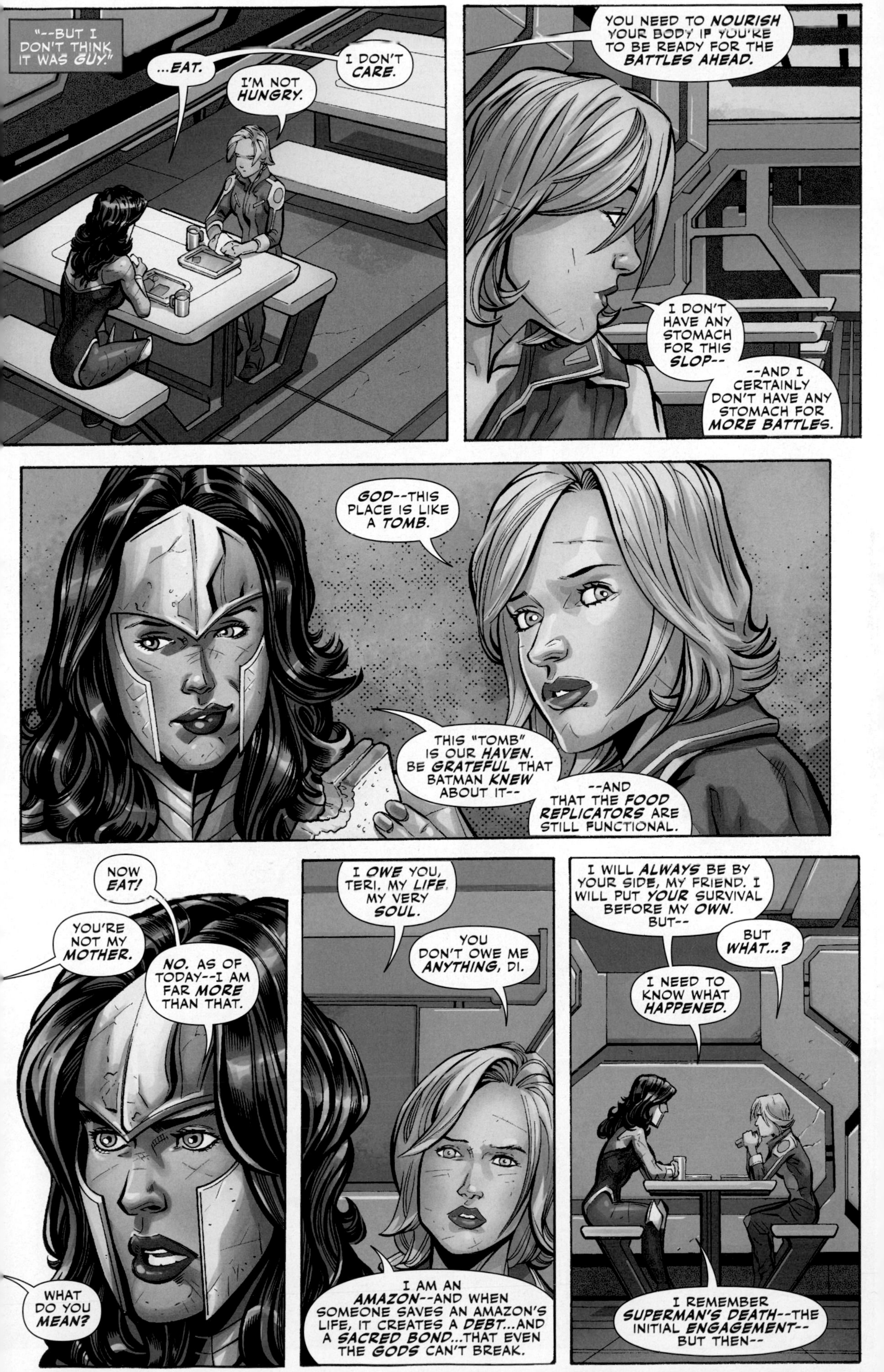
"--BUT I DON'T THINK IT WAS GUY."
...EAT.
I'M NOT HUNGRY.
I DON'T CARE.
YOU NEED TO NOURISH YOUR BODY IF YOU'RE TO BE READY FOR THE BATTLES AHEAD.
I DON'T HAVE ANY STOMACH FOR THIS SLOP--
--AND I CERTAINLY DON'T HAVE ANY STOMACH FOR MORE BATTLES.
GOD--THIS PLACE IS LIKE A TOMB.
THIS "TOMB" IS OUR HAVEN. BE GRATEFUL THAT BATMAN KNEW ABOUT IT--
--AND THAT THE FOOD REPLICATORS ARE STILL FUNCTIONAL.
NOW EAT!
YOU'RE NOT MY MOTHER.
NO. AS OF TODAY--I AM FAR MORE THAN THAT.
WHAT DO YOU MEAN?
I OWE YOU, TERI. MY LIFE. MY VERY SOUL.
YOU DON'T OWE ME ANYTHING, DI.
I AM AN AMAZON--AND WHEN SOMEONE SAVES AN AMAZON'S LIFE, IT CREATES A DEBT...AND A SACRED BOND...THAT EVEN THE GODS CAN'T BREAK.
I WILL ALWAYS BE BY YOUR SIDE, MY FRIEND. I WILL PUT YOUR SURVIVAL BEFORE MY OWN. BUT--
BUT WHAT...?
I NEED TO KNOW WHAT HAPPENED.
I REMEMBER SUPERMAN'S DEATH--THE INITIAL ENGAGEMENT--BUT THEN--

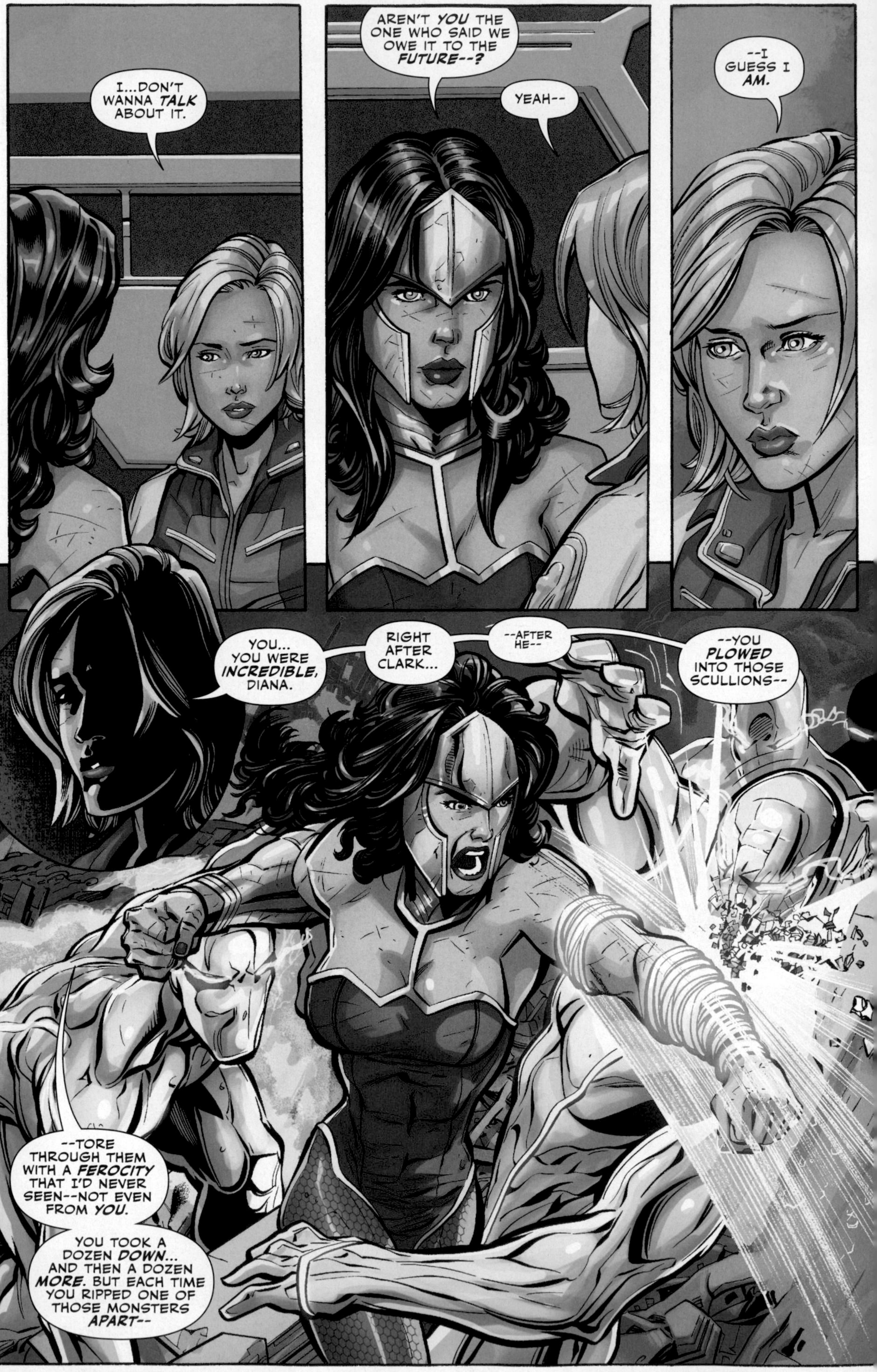
I...DON'T WANNA *TALK* ABOUT IT.
AREN'T *YOU* THE ONE WHO SAID WE OWE IT TO THE *FUTURE*--?
YEAH--
--I GUESS I *AM.*
YOU... YOU WERE *INCREDIBLE,* DIANA.
RIGHT AFTER CLARK...
--AFTER HE--
--YOU *PLOWED* INTO THOSE SCULLIONS--
--TORE THROUGH THEM WITH A *FEROCITY* THAT I'D NEVER SEEN--NOT EVEN FROM *YOU.*
YOU TOOK A DOZEN *DOWN*... AND THEN A DOZEN *MORE.* BUT EACH TIME YOU RIPPED ONE OF THOSE MONSTERS *APART*--

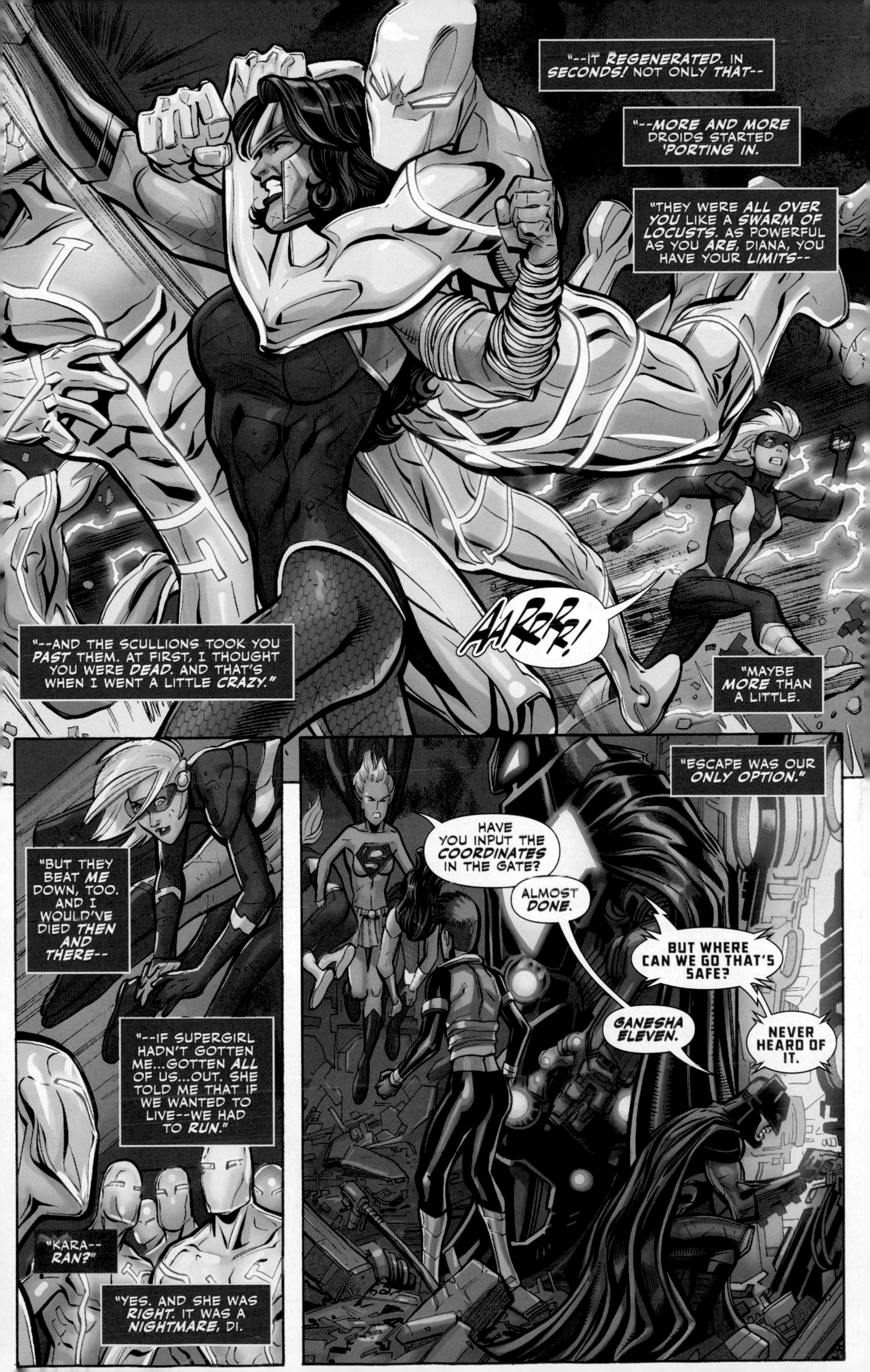
"--IT REGENERATED. IN SECONDS! NOT ONLY THAT--
"--MORE AND MORE DROIDS STARTED 'PORTING IN.
"THEY WERE ALL OVER YOU LIKE A SWARM OF LOCUSTS. AS POWERFUL AS YOU ARE, DIANA, YOU HAVE YOUR LIMITS--
"--AND THE SCULLIONS TOOK YOU PAST THEM. AT FIRST, I THOUGHT YOU WERE DEAD. AND THAT'S WHEN I WENT A LITTLE CRAZY."
AARRRR!
"MAYBE MORE THAN A LITTLE.
"BUT THEY BEAT ME DOWN, TOO. AND I WOULD'VE DIED THEN AND THERE--
"--IF SUPERGIRL HADN'T GOTTEN ME...GOTTEN ALL OF US...OUT. SHE TOLD ME THAT IF WE WANTED TO LIVE--WE HAD TO RUN."
"KARA--RAN?"
"YES. AND SHE WAS RIGHT. IT WAS A NIGHTMARE, DI.
"ESCAPE WAS OUR ONLY OPTION."
HAVE YOU INPUT THE COORDINATES IN THE GATE?
ALMOST DONE.
BUT WHERE CAN WE GO THAT'S SAFE?
GANESHA ELEVEN.
NEVER HEARD OF IT.

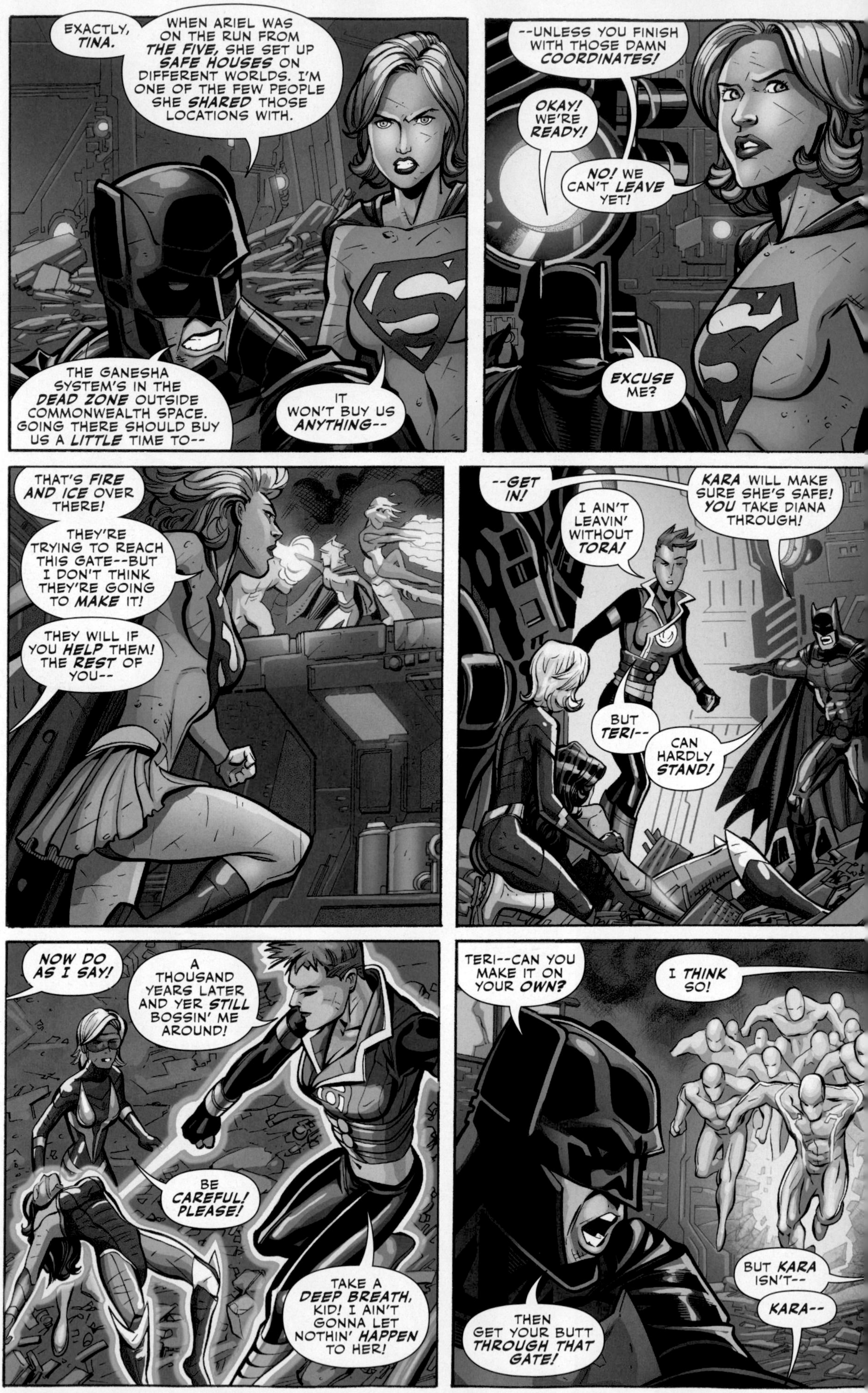
EXACTLY, TINA.
WHEN ARIEL WAS ON THE RUN FROM THE FIVE, SHE SET UP SAFE HOUSES ON DIFFERENT WORLDS. I'M ONE OF THE FEW PEOPLE SHE SHARED THOSE LOCATIONS WITH.
THE GANESHA SYSTEM'S IN THE DEAD ZONE OUTSIDE COMMONWEALTH SPACE. GOING THERE SHOULD BUY US A LITTLE TIME TO--
IT WON'T BUY US ANYTHING--
--UNLESS YOU FINISH WITH THOSE DAMN COORDINATES!
OKAY! WE'RE READY!
NO! WE CAN'T LEAVE YET!
EXCUSE ME?
THAT'S FIRE AND ICE OVER THERE!
THEY'RE TRYING TO REACH THIS GATE--BUT I DON'T THINK THEY'RE GOING TO MAKE IT!
THEY WILL IF YOU HELP THEM! THE REST OF YOU--
--GET IN!
KARA WILL MAKE SURE SHE'S SAFE! YOU TAKE DIANA THROUGH!
I AIN'T LEAVIN' WITHOUT TORA!
BUT TERI--
CAN HARDLY STAND!
NOW DO AS I SAY!
A THOUSAND YEARS LATER AND YER STILL BOSSIN' ME AROUND!
BE CAREFUL! PLEASE!
TAKE A DEEP BREATH, KID! I AIN'T GONNA LET NOTHIN' HAPPEN TO HER!
TERI--CAN YOU MAKE IT ON YOUR OWN?
I THINK SO!
THEN GET YOUR BUTT THROUGH THAT GATE!
BUT KARA ISN'T--
KARA--

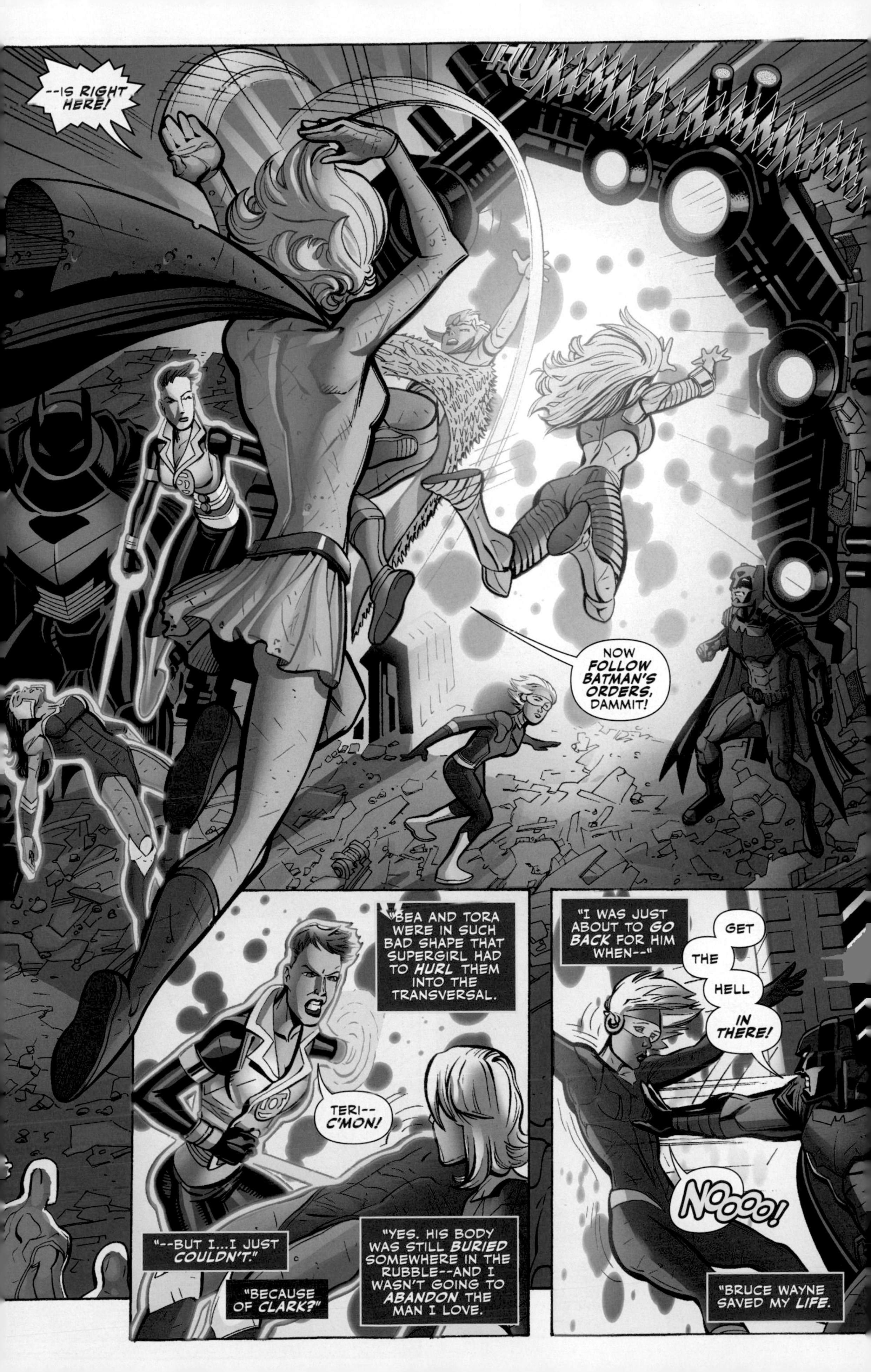
--IS RIGHT HERE!
NOW FOLLOW BATMAN'S ORDERS, DAMMIT!
"BEA AND TORA WERE IN SUCH BAD SHAPE THAT SUPERGIRL HAD TO HURL THEM INTO THE TRANSVERSAL.
TERI-- C'MON!
"--BUT I...I JUST COULDN'T."
"BECAUSE OF CLARK?"
"YES. HIS BODY WAS STILL BURIED SOMEWHERE IN THE RUBBLE--AND I WASN'T GOING TO ABANDON THE MAN I LOVE.
"I WAS JUST ABOUT TO GO BACK FOR HIM WHEN--"
GET THE HELL IN THERE!
NOOOO!
"BRUCE WAYNE SAVED MY LIFE.

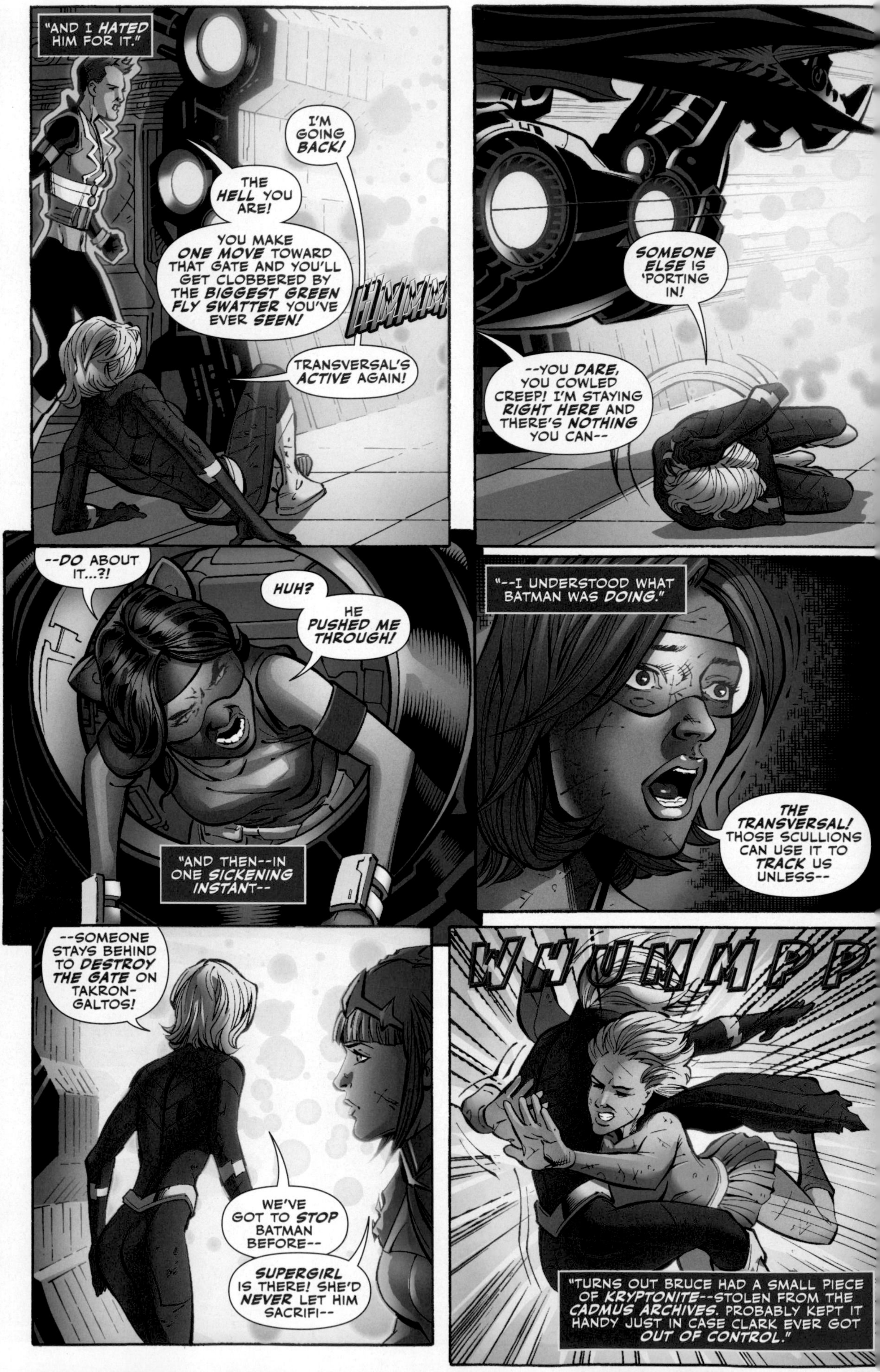
"AND I HATED HIM FOR IT."
I'M GOING BACK!
THE HELL YOU ARE!
YOU MAKE ONE MOVE TOWARD THAT GATE AND YOU'LL GET CLOBBERED BY THE BIGGEST GREEN FLY SWATTER YOU'VE EVER SEEN!
HMMMM
TRANSVERSAL'S ACTIVE AGAIN!
SOMEONE ELSE IS 'PORTING IN!
--YOU DARE, YOU COWLED CREEP! I'M STAYING RIGHT HERE AND THERE'S NOTHING YOU CAN--
--DO ABOUT IT...?!
HUH?
HE PUSHED ME THROUGH!
"AND THEN--IN ONE SICKENING INSTANT--
"--I UNDERSTOOD WHAT BATMAN WAS DOING."
THE TRANSVERSAL! THOSE SCULLIONS CAN USE IT TO TRACK US UNLESS--
--SOMEONE STAYS BEHIND TO DESTROY THE GATE ON TAKRON-GALTOS!
WE'VE GOT TO STOP BATMAN BEFORE--
SUPERGIRL IS THERE! SHE'D NEVER LET HIM SACRIFI--
WHUMMPP
"TURNS OUT BRUCE HAD A SMALL PIECE OF KRYPTONITE--STOLEN FROM THE CADMUS ARCHIVES. PROBABLY KEPT IT HANDY JUST IN CASE CLARK EVER GOT OUT OF CONTROL."

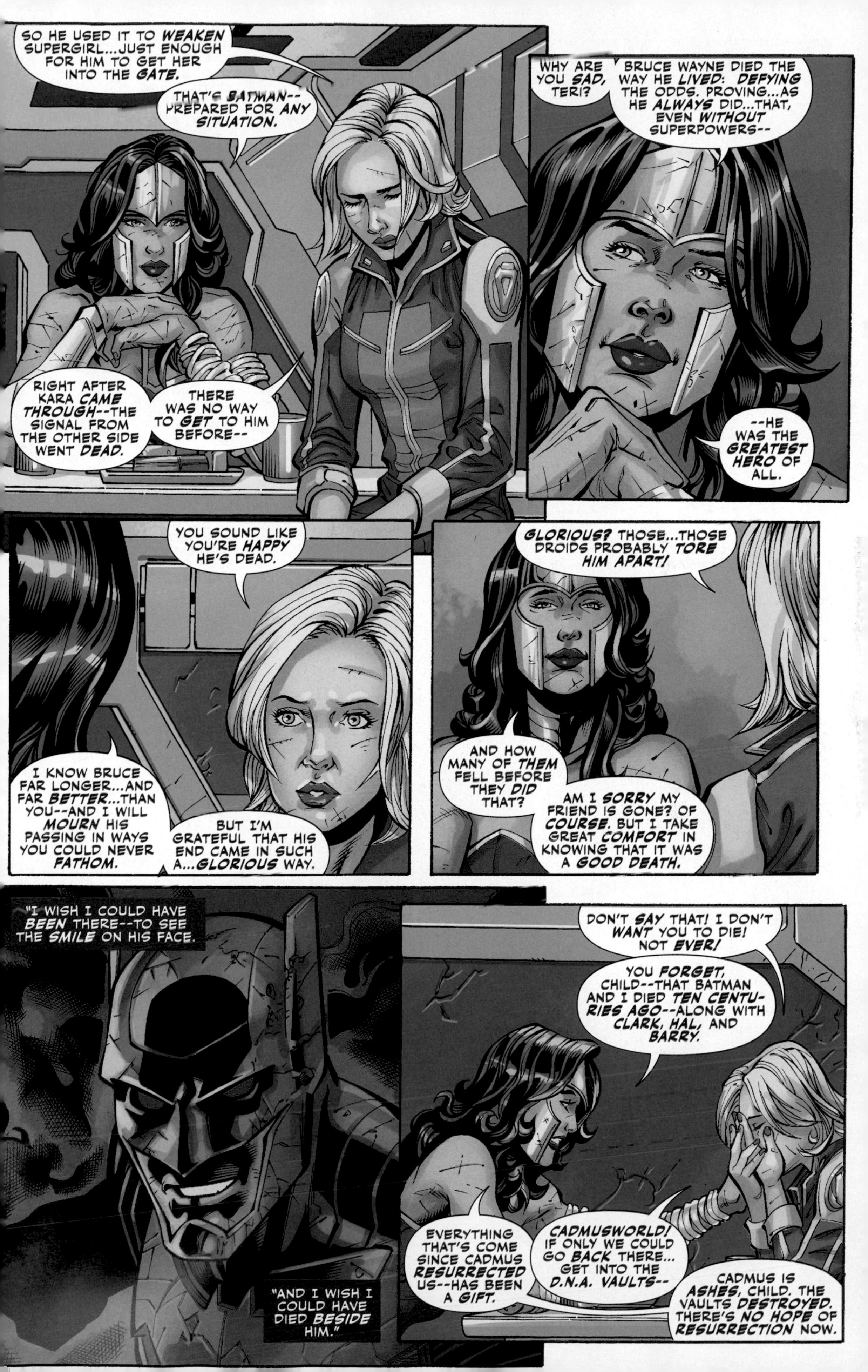
SO HE USED IT TO WEAKEN SUPERGIRL...JUST ENOUGH FOR HIM TO GET HER INTO THE GATE.
THAT'S BATMAN--PREPARED FOR ANY SITUATION.
RIGHT AFTER KARA CAME THROUGH--THE SIGNAL FROM THE OTHER SIDE WENT DEAD.
THERE WAS NO WAY TO GET TO HIM BEFORE--
WHY ARE YOU SAD, TERI?
BRUCE WAYNE DIED THE WAY HE LIVED: DEFYING THE ODDS. PROVING...AS HE ALWAYS DID...THAT, EVEN WITHOUT SUPERPOWERS--
--HE WAS THE GREATEST HERO OF ALL.
YOU SOUND LIKE YOU'RE HAPPY HE'S DEAD.
I KNOW BRUCE FAR LONGER...AND FAR BETTER...THAN YOU--AND I WILL MOURN HIS PASSING IN WAYS YOU COULD NEVER FATHOM.
BUT I'M GRATEFUL THAT HIS END CAME IN SUCH A...GLORIOUS WAY.
GLORIOUS? THOSE...THOSE DROIDS PROBABLY TORE HIM APART!
AND HOW MANY OF THEM FELL BEFORE THEY DID THAT?
AM I SORRY MY FRIEND IS GONE? OF COURSE. BUT I TAKE GREAT COMFORT IN KNOWING THAT IT WAS A GOOD DEATH.
"I WISH I COULD HAVE BEEN THERE--TO SEE THE SMILE ON HIS FACE.
"AND I WISH I COULD HAVE DIED BESIDE HIM."
DON'T SAY THAT! I DON'T WANT YOU TO DIE! NOT EVER!
YOU FORGET, CHILD--THAT BATMAN AND I DIED TEN CENTURIES AGO--ALONG WITH CLARK, HAL, AND BARRY.
EVERYTHING THAT'S COME SINCE CADMUS RESURRECTED US--HAS BEEN A GIFT.
CADMUSWORLD! IF ONLY WE COULD GO BACK THERE... GET INTO THE D.N.A. VAULTS--
CADMUS IS ASHES, CHILD. THE VAULTS DESTROYED. THERE'S NO HOPE OF RESURRECTION NOW.

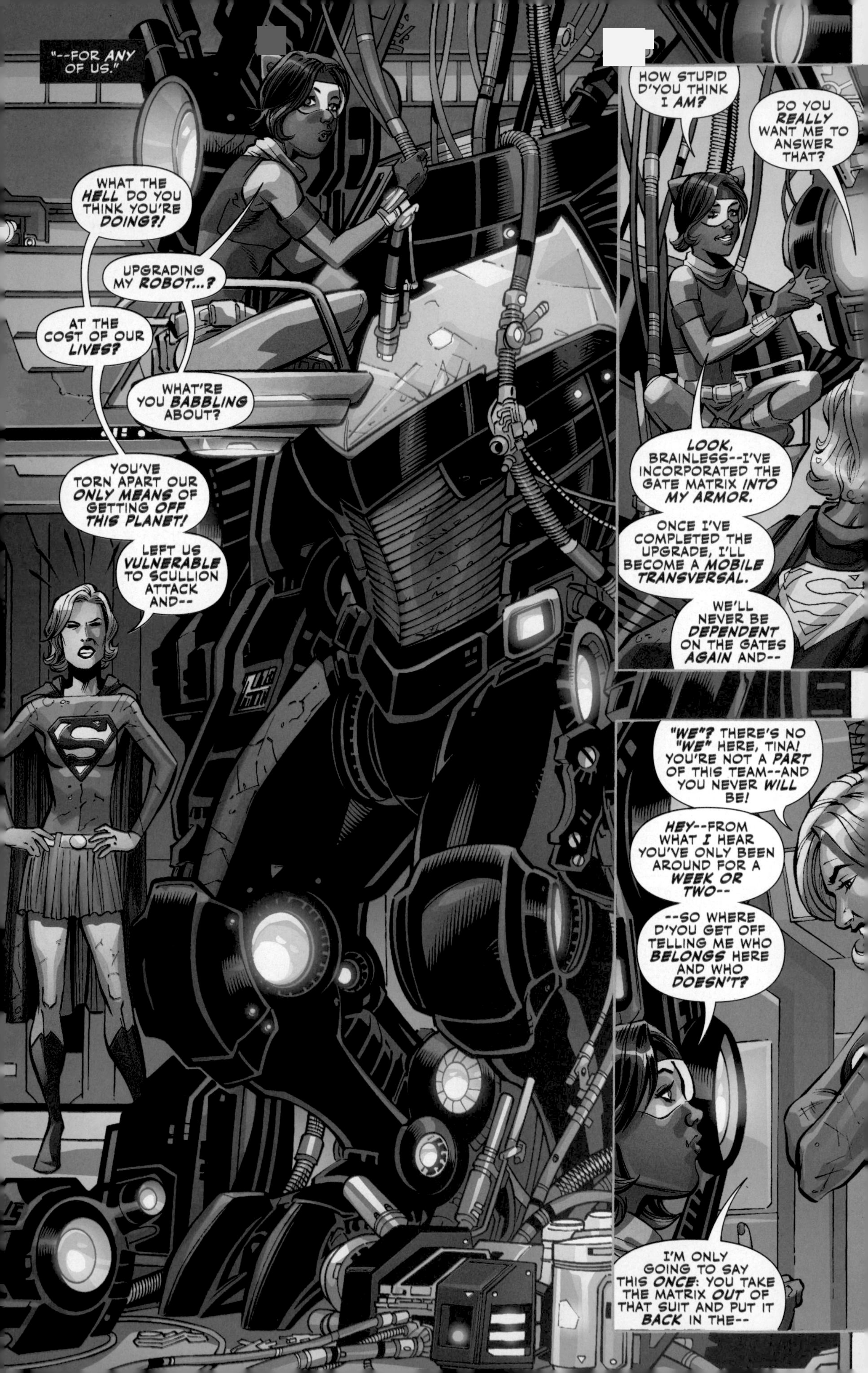
"--FOR ANY OF US."
WHAT THE HELL DO YOU THINK YOU'RE DOING?!
UPGRADING MY ROBOT...?
AT THE COST OF OUR LIVES?
WHAT'RE YOU BABBLING ABOUT?
YOU'VE TORN APART OUR ONLY MEANS OF GETTING OFF THIS PLANET!
LEFT US VULNERABLE TO SCULLION ATTACK AND--
HOW STUPID D'YOU THINK I AM?
DO YOU REALLY WANT ME TO ANSWER THAT?
LOOK, BRAINLESS--I'VE INCORPORATED THE GATE MATRIX INTO MY ARMOR.
ONCE I'VE COMPLETED THE UPGRADE, I'LL BECOME A MOBILE TRANSVERSAL.
WE'LL NEVER BE DEPENDENT ON THE GATES AGAIN AND--
"WE"? THERE'S NO "WE" HERE, TINA! YOU'RE NOT A PART OF THIS TEAM--AND YOU NEVER WILL BE!
HEY--FROM WHAT I HEAR YOU'VE ONLY BEEN AROUND FOR A WEEK OR TWO--
--SO WHERE D'YOU GET OFF TELLING ME WHO BELONGS HERE AND WHO DOESN'T?
I'M ONLY GOING TO SAY THIS ONCE: YOU TAKE THE MATRIX OUT OF THAT SUIT AND PUT IT BACK IN THE--

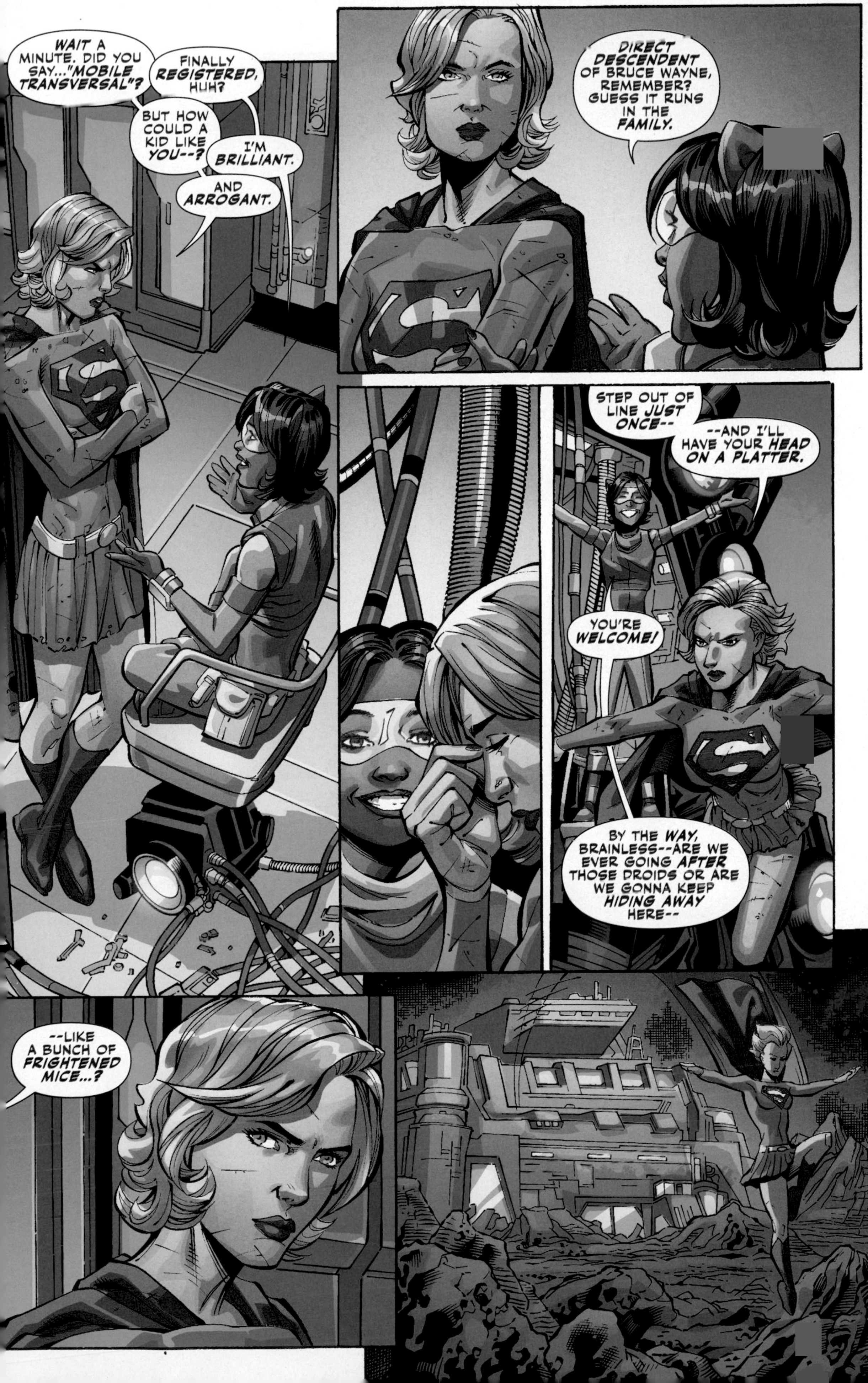

WAIT A MINUTE. DID YOU SAY..."MOBILE TRANSVERSAL"?
FINALLY REGISTERED, HUH?
BUT HOW COULD A KID LIKE YOU--?
I'M BRILLIANT.
AND ARROGANT.
DIRECT DESCENDENT OF BRUCE WAYNE, REMEMBER? GUESS IT RUNS IN THE FAMILY.
STEP OUT OF LINE JUST ONCE--
--AND I'LL HAVE YOUR HEAD ON A PLATTER.
YOU'RE WELCOME!
BY THE WAY, BRAINLESS--ARE WE EVER GOING AFTER THOSE DROIDS OR ARE WE GONNA KEEP HIDING AWAY HERE--
--LIKE A BUNCH OF FRIGHTENED MICE...?

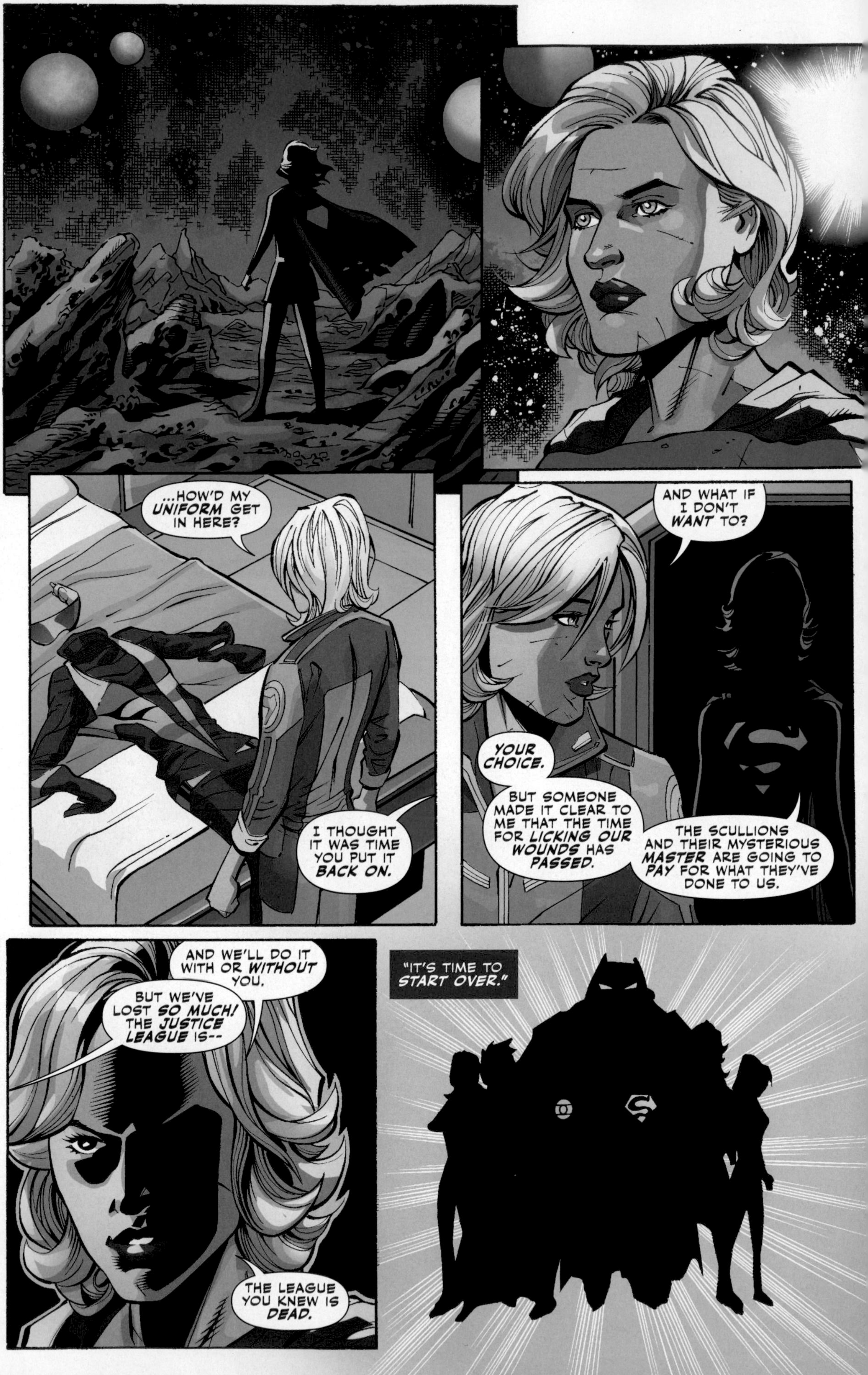

...HOW'D MY UNIFORM GET IN HERE?
I THOUGHT IT WAS TIME YOU PUT IT BACK ON.
AND WHAT IF I DON'T WANT TO?
YOUR CHOICE.
BUT SOMEONE MADE IT CLEAR TO ME THAT THE TIME FOR LICKING OUR WOUNDS HAS PASSED.
THE SCULLIONS AND THEIR MYSTERIOUS MASTER ARE GOING TO PAY FOR WHAT THEY'VE DONE TO US.
AND WE'LL DO IT WITH OR WITHOUT YOU.
BUT WE'VE LOST SO MUCH! THE JUSTICE LEAGUE IS--
THE LEAGUE YOU KNEW IS DEAD.
"IT'S TIME TO START OVER."

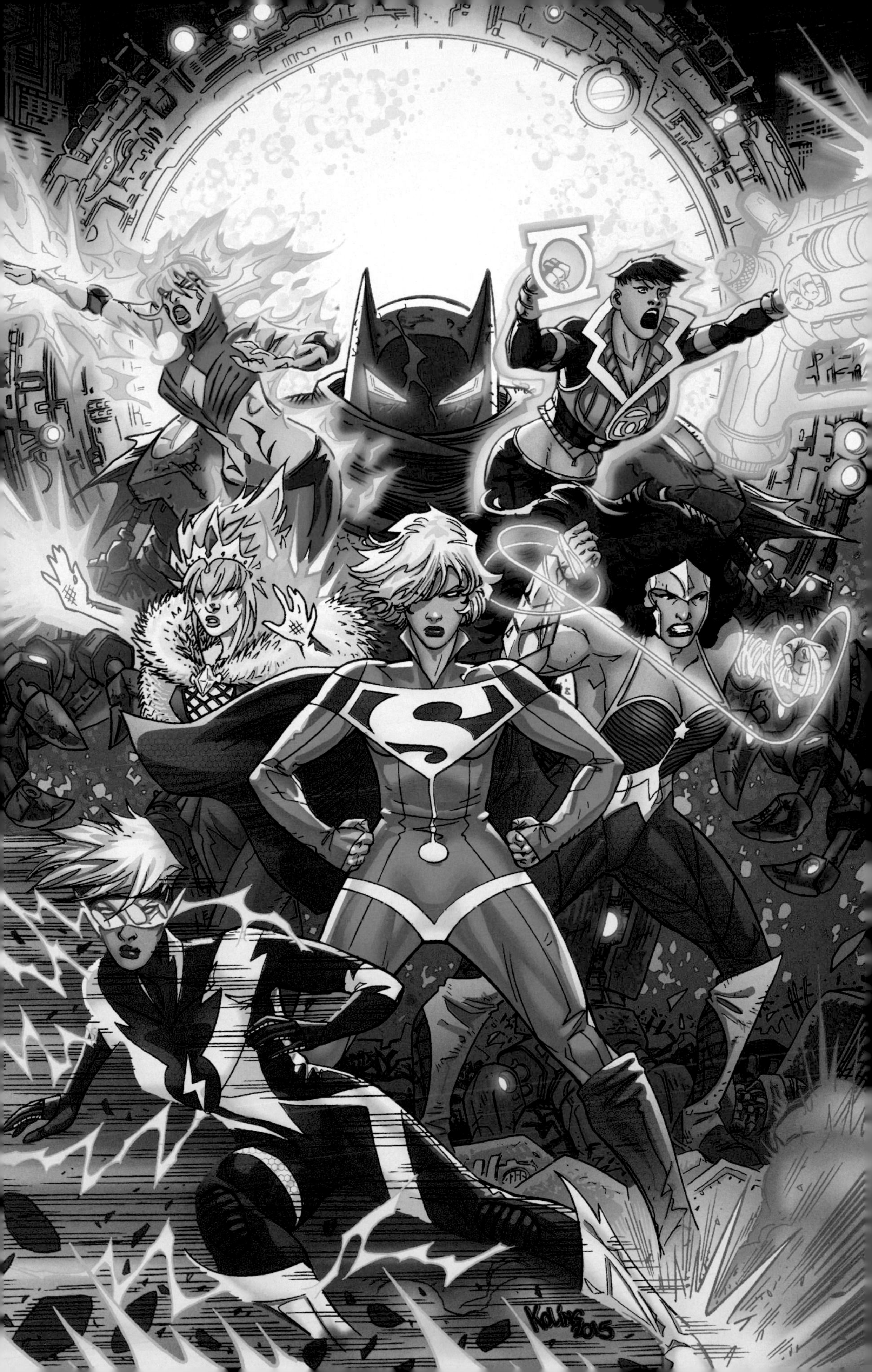
Kolins 2015

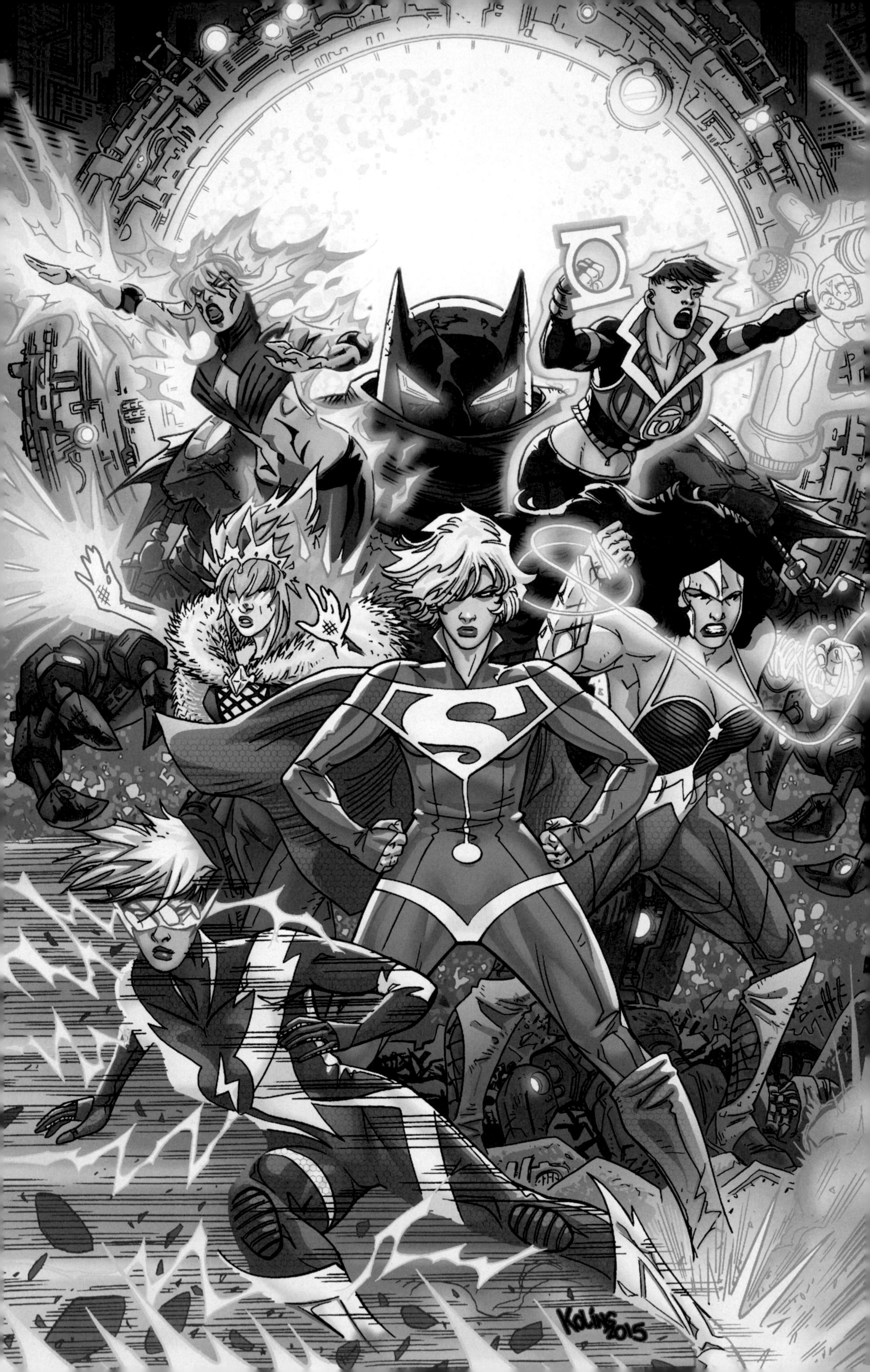
KOLINS 2015

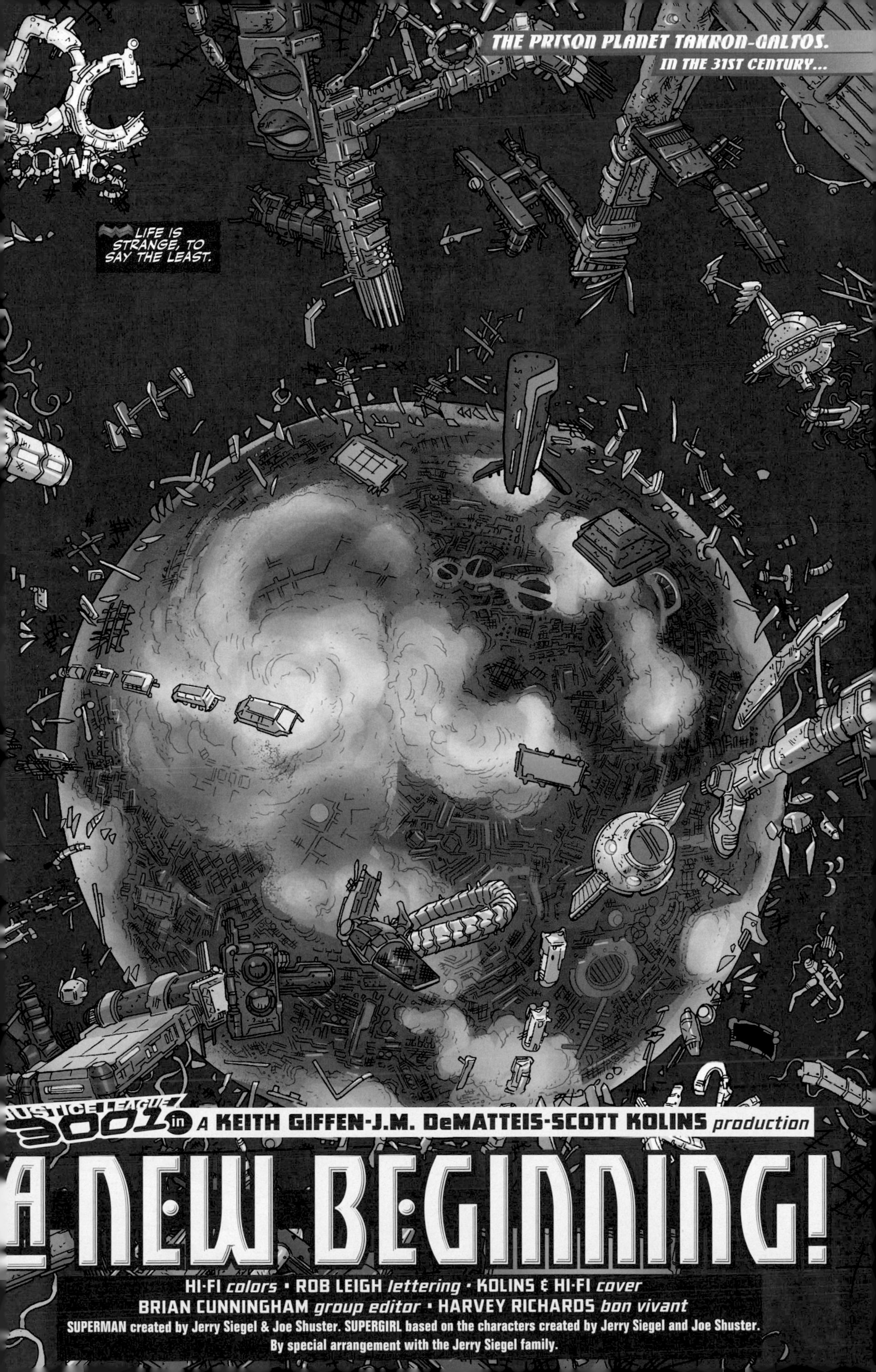
DC COMICS
THE PRISON PLANET TAKRON-GALTOS.
IN THE 31ST CENTURY...
LIFE IS STRANGE, TO SAY THE LEAST.
JUSTICE LEAGUE 3001 in A KEITH GIFFEN-J.M. DeMATTEIS-SCOTT KOLINS production
A NEW BEGINNING!
HI-FI colors • ROB LEIGH lettering • KOLINS & HI-FI cover
BRIAN CUNNINGHAM group editor • HARVEY RICHARDS bon vivant
SUPERMAN created by Jerry Siegel & Joe Shuster. SUPERGIRL based on the characters created by Jerry Siegel and Joe Shuster.
By special arrangement with the Jerry Siegel family.

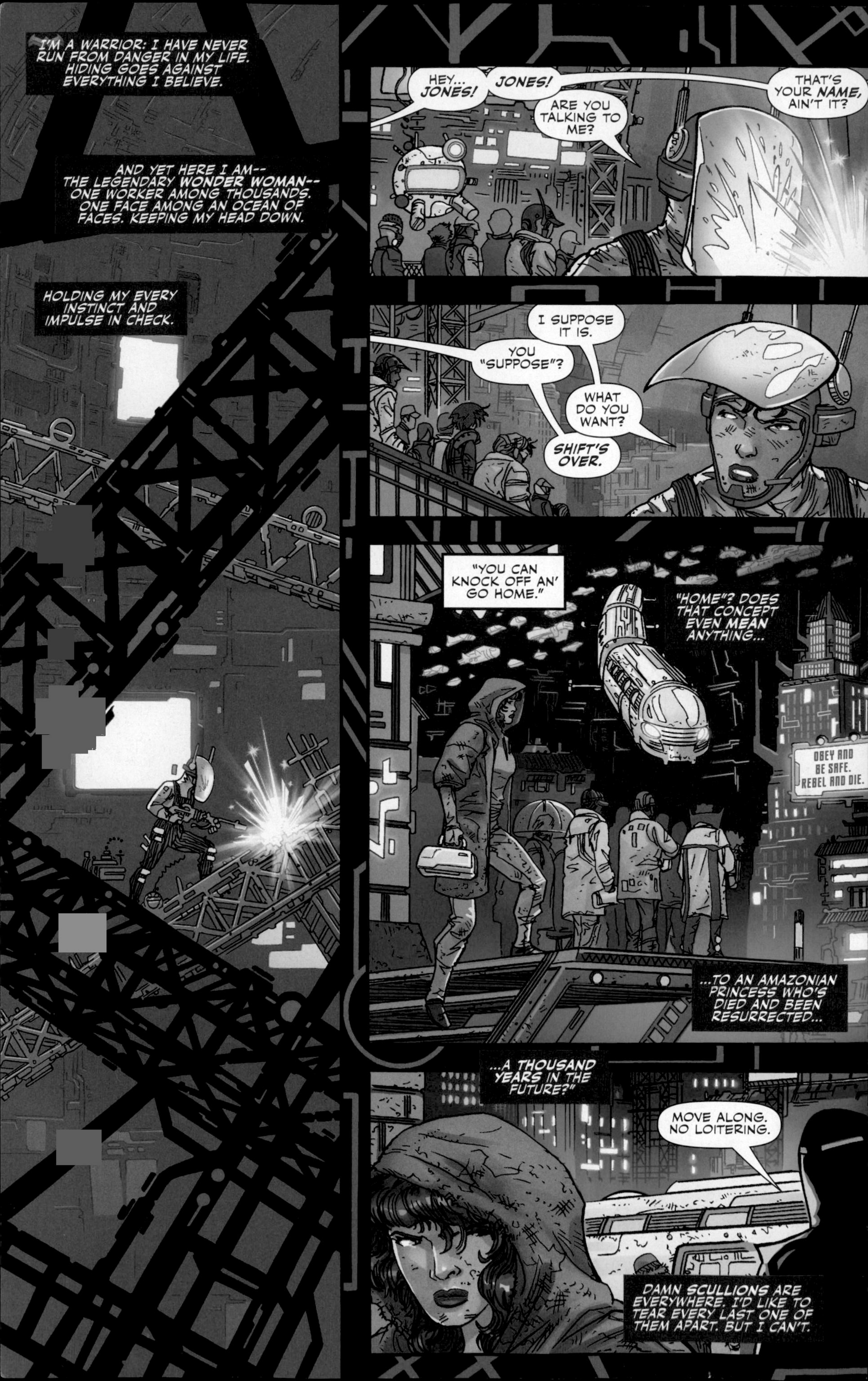
I'M A WARRIOR: I HAVE NEVER RUN FROM DANGER IN MY LIFE. HIDING GOES AGAINST EVERYTHING I BELIEVE.
AND YET HERE I AM-- THE LEGENDARY WONDER WOMAN-- ONE WORKER AMONG THOUSANDS. ONE FACE AMONG AN OCEAN OF FACES. KEEPING MY HEAD DOWN.
HOLDING MY EVERY INSTINCT AND IMPULSE IN CHECK.
HEY... JONES!
JONES!
ARE YOU TALKING TO ME?
THAT'S YOUR NAME, AIN'T IT?
I SUPPOSE IT IS.
YOU "SUPPOSE"?
WHAT DO YOU WANT?
SHIFT'S OVER.
"YOU CAN KNOCK OFF AN' GO HOME."
"HOME"? DOES THAT CONCEPT EVEN MEAN ANYTHING...
OBEY AND BE SAFE. REBEL AND DIE.
...TO AN AMAZONIAN PRINCESS WHO'S DIED AND BEEN RESURRECTED...
...A THOUSAND YEARS IN THE FUTURE?"
MOVE ALONG. NO LOITERING.
DAMN SCULLIONS ARE EVERYWHERE. I'D LIKE TO TEAR EVERY LAST ONE OF THEM APART. BUT I CAN'T.

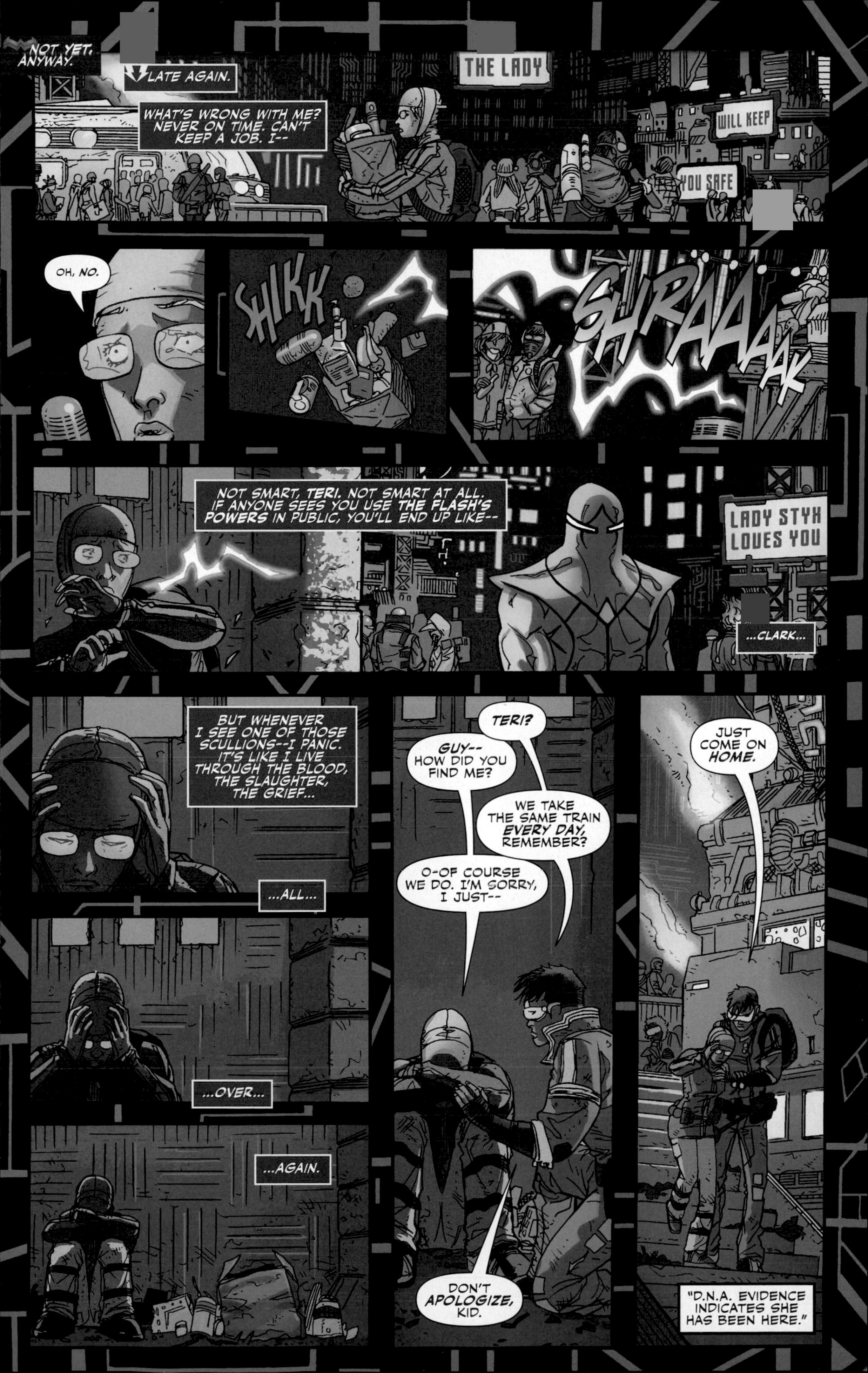

NOT YET. ANYWAY.
LATE AGAIN.
WHAT'S WRONG WITH ME? NEVER ON TIME. CAN'T KEEP A JOB. I--
THE LADY
WILL KEEP
YOU SAFE
OH, NO.
SHIKK
SHRAAAAAK
NOT SMART, TERI. NOT SMART AT ALL. IF ANYONE SEES YOU USE THE FLASH'S POWERS IN PUBLIC, YOU'LL END UP LIKE--
LADY STYX LOVES YOU
...CLARK...
BUT WHENEVER I SEE ONE OF THOSE SCULLIONS--I PANIC. IT'S LIKE I LIVE THROUGH THE BLOOD, THE SLAUGHTER, THE GRIEF...
...ALL...
...OVER...
...AGAIN.
TERI?
GUY-- HOW DID YOU FIND ME?
WE TAKE THE SAME TRAIN EVERY DAY, REMEMBER?
O-OF COURSE WE DO. I'M SORRY, I JUST--
DON'T APOLOGIZE, KID.
JUST COME ON HOME.
"D.N.A. EVIDENCE INDICATES SHE HAS BEEN HERE."

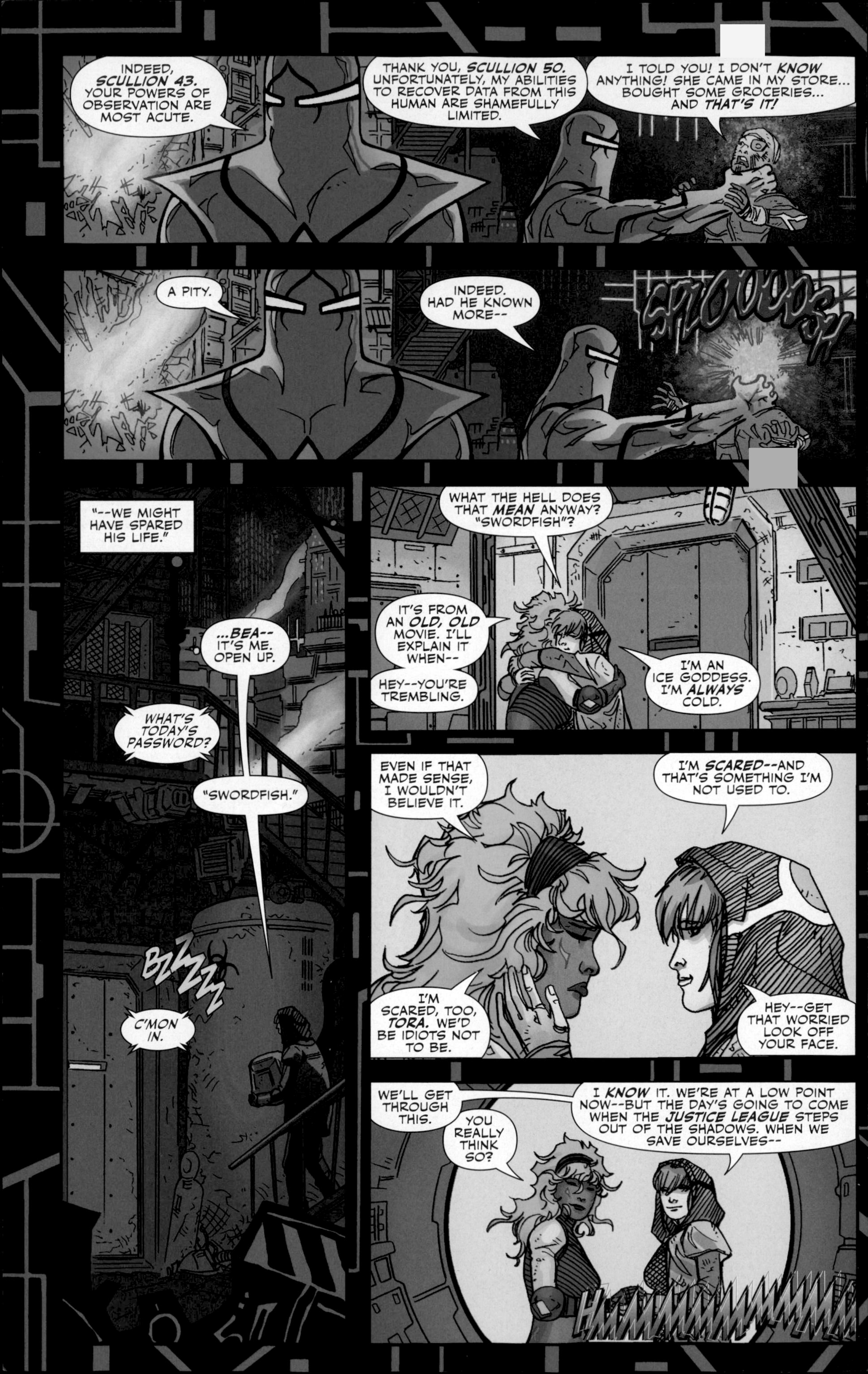
INDEED, SCULLION 43. YOUR POWERS OF OBSERVATION ARE MOST ACUTE.
THANK YOU, SCULLION 50. UNFORTUNATELY, MY ABILITIES TO RECOVER DATA FROM THIS HUMAN ARE SHAMEFULLY LIMITED.
I TOLD YOU! I DON'T KNOW ANYTHING! SHE CAME IN MY STORE... BOUGHT SOME GROCERIES... AND THAT'S IT!
A PITY.
INDEED. HAD HE KNOWN MORE--
SPLOOOSH
"--WE MIGHT HAVE SPARED HIS LIFE."
...BEA-- IT'S ME. OPEN UP.
WHAT'S TODAY'S PASSWORD?
"SWORDFISH."
BZZZZ
C'MON IN.
WHAT THE HELL DOES THAT MEAN ANYWAY? "SWORDFISH"?
IT'S FROM AN OLD, OLD MOVIE. I'LL EXPLAIN IT WHEN--
HEY--YOU'RE TREMBLING.
I'M AN ICE GODDESS. I'M ALWAYS COLD.
EVEN IF THAT MADE SENSE, I WOULDN'T BELIEVE IT.
I'M SCARED--AND THAT'S SOMETHING I'M NOT USED TO.
I'M SCARED, TOO, TORA. WE'D BE IDIOTS NOT TO BE.
HEY--GET THAT WORRIED LOOK OFF YOUR FACE.
WE'LL GET THROUGH THIS.
YOU REALLY THINK SO?
I KNOW IT. WE'RE AT A LOW POINT NOW--BUT THE DAY'S GOING TO COME WHEN THE JUSTICE LEAGUE STEPS OUT OF THE SHADOWS. WHEN WE SAVE OURSELVES--

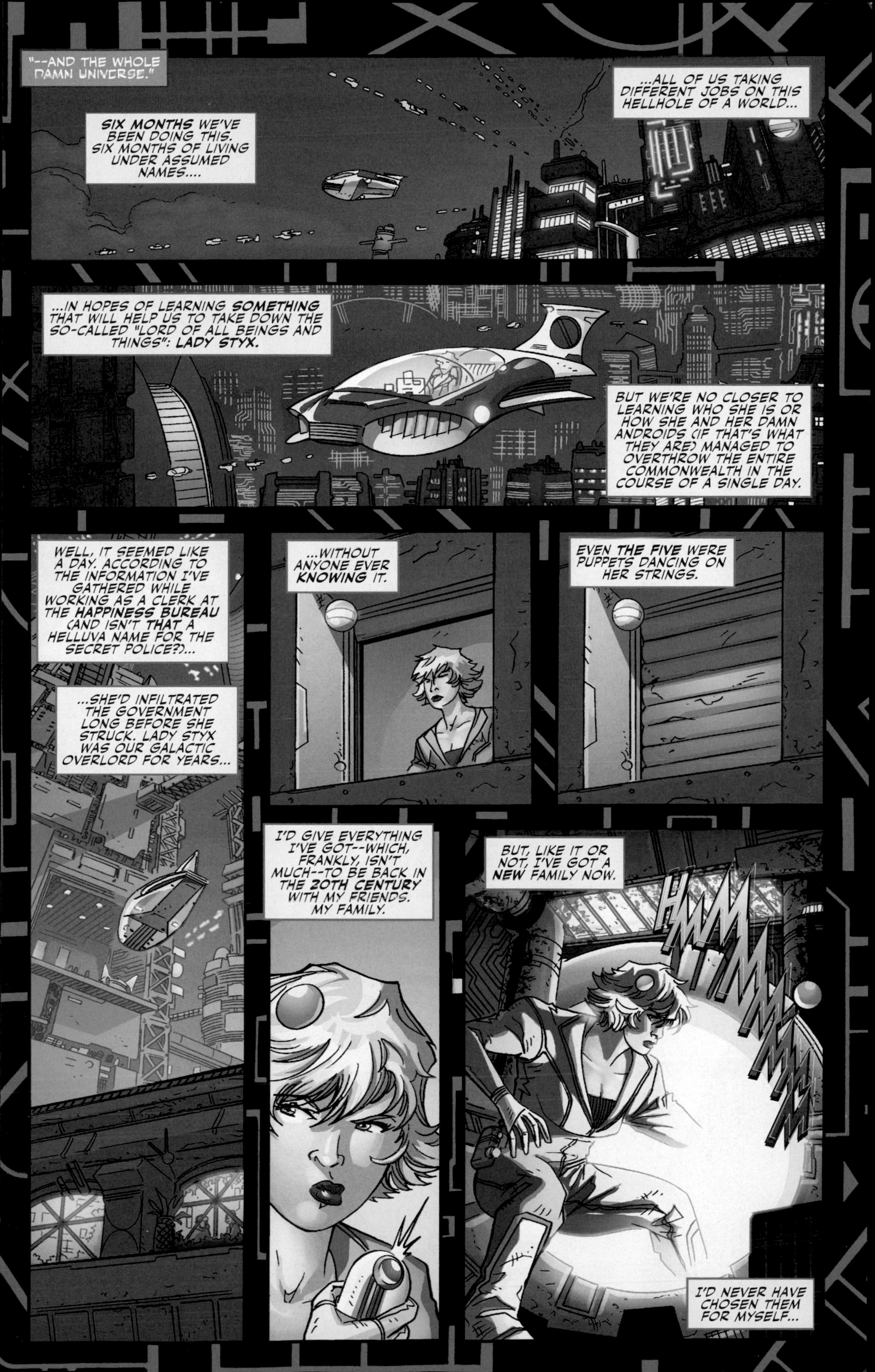
"--AND THE WHOLE DAMN UNIVERSE."
SIX MONTHS WE'VE BEEN DOING THIS. SIX MONTHS OF LIVING UNDER ASSUMED NAMES....
...ALL OF US TAKING DIFFERENT JOBS ON THIS HELLHOLE OF A WORLD...
...IN HOPES OF LEARNING SOMETHING THAT WILL HELP US TO TAKE DOWN THE SO-CALLED "LORD OF ALL BEINGS AND THINGS": LADY STYX.
BUT WE'RE NO CLOSER TO LEARNING WHO SHE IS OR HOW SHE AND HER DAMN ANDROIDS (IF THAT'S WHAT THEY ARE) MANAGED TO OVERTHROW THE ENTIRE COMMONWEALTH IN THE COURSE OF A SINGLE DAY.
WELL, IT SEEMED LIKE A DAY. ACCORDING TO THE INFORMATION I'VE GATHERED WHILE WORKING AS A CLERK AT THE HAPPINESS BUREAU (AND ISN'T THAT A HELLUVA NAME FOR THE SECRET POLICE?)...
...SHE'D INFILTRATED THE GOVERNMENT LONG BEFORE SHE STRUCK. LADY STYX WAS OUR GALACTIC OVERLORD FOR YEARS...
...WITHOUT ANYONE EVER KNOWING IT.
EVEN THE FIVE WERE PUPPETS DANCING ON HER STRINGS.
I'D GIVE EVERYTHING I'VE GOT--WHICH, FRANKLY, ISN'T MUCH--TO BE BACK IN THE 20TH CENTURY WITH MY FRIENDS. MY FAMILY.
BUT, LIKE IT OR NOT, I'VE GOT A NEW FAMILY NOW.
HMMMMMMM
I'D NEVER HAVE CHOSEN THEM FOR MYSELF...

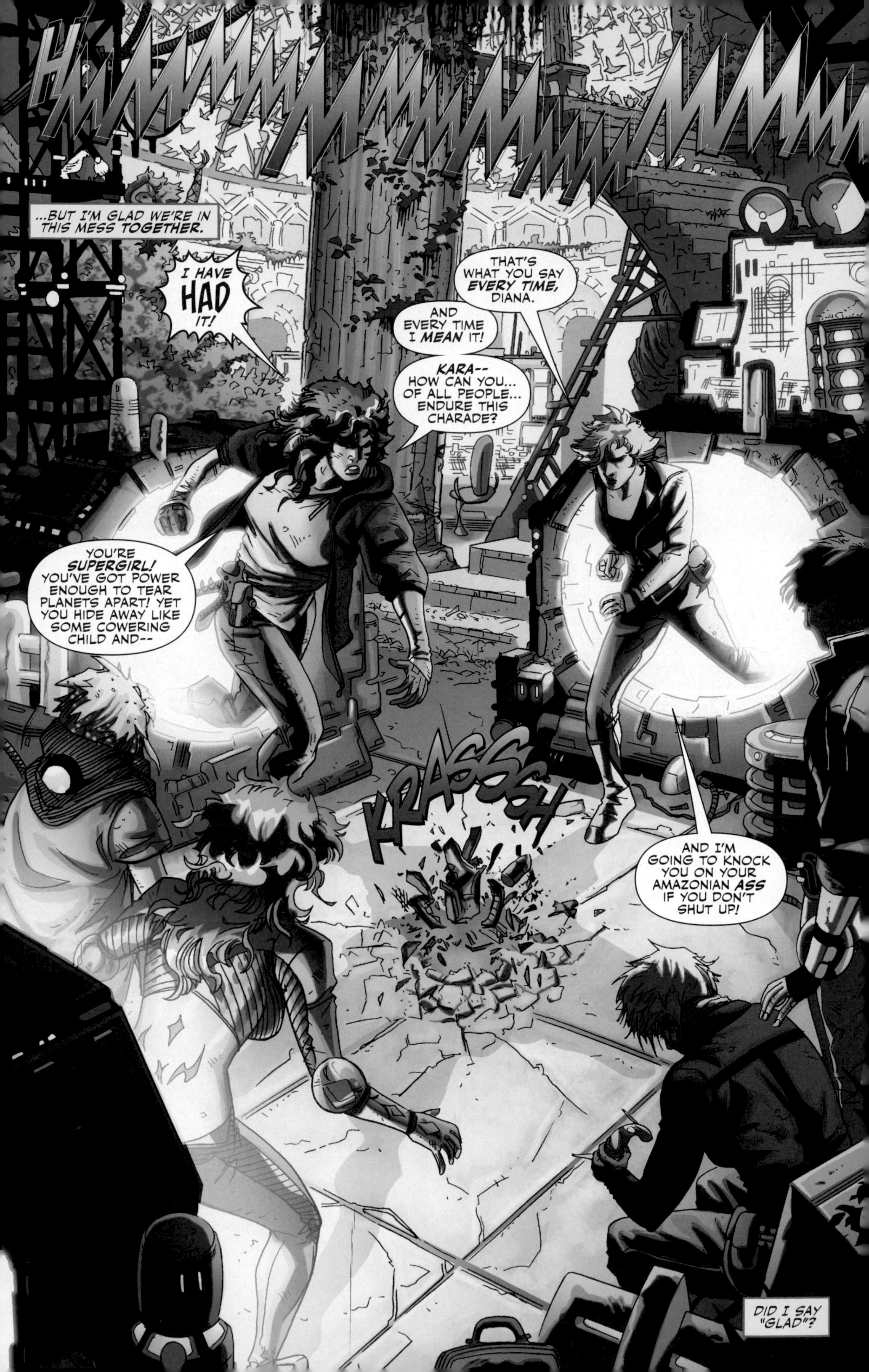
HMMMMMMMMMMMMMMMMM
...BUT I'M GLAD WE'RE IN THIS MESS TOGETHER.
I HAVE HAD IT!
THAT'S WHAT YOU SAY EVERY TIME, DIANA.
AND EVERY TIME I MEAN IT!
KARA-- HOW CAN YOU... OF ALL PEOPLE... ENDURE THIS CHARADE?
YOU'RE SUPERGIRL! YOU'VE GOT POWER ENOUGH TO TEAR PLANETS APART! YET YOU HIDE AWAY LIKE SOME COWERING CHILD AND--
KRASSSH
AND I'M GOING TO KNOCK YOU ON YOUR AMAZONIAN ASS IF YOU DON'T SHUT UP!
DID I SAY "GLAD"?

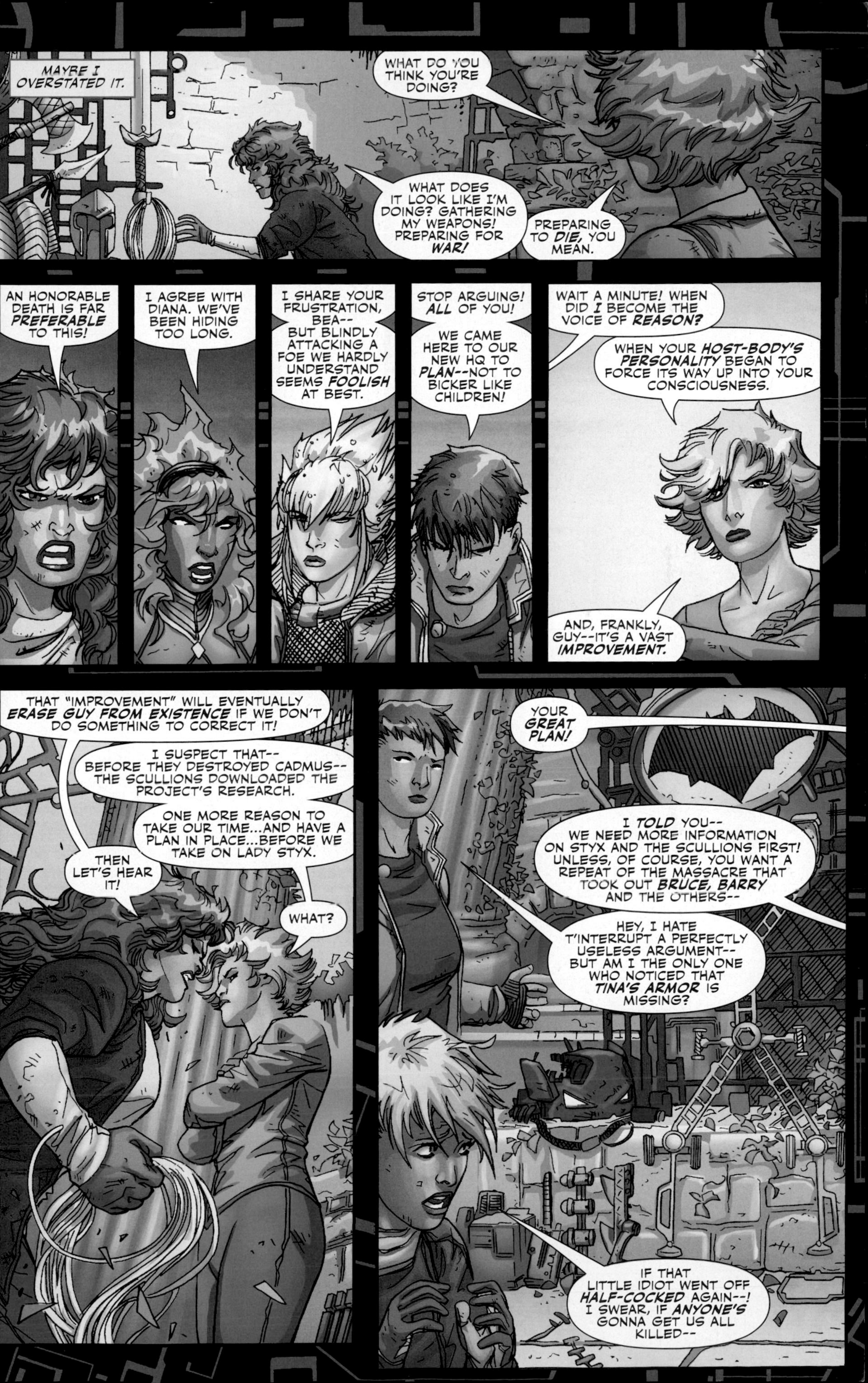

MAYBE I OVERSTATED IT.
WHAT DO YOU THINK YOU'RE DOING?
WHAT DOES IT LOOK LIKE I'M DOING? GATHERING MY WEAPONS! PREPARING FOR WAR!
PREPARING TO DIE, YOU MEAN.
AN HONORABLE DEATH IS FAR PREFERABLE TO THIS!
I AGREE WITH DIANA. WE'VE BEEN HIDING TOO LONG.
I SHARE YOUR FRUSTRATION, BEA--
BUT BLINDLY ATTACKING A FOE WE HARDLY UNDERSTAND SEEMS FOOLISH AT BEST.
STOP ARGUING! ALL OF YOU!
WE CAME HERE TO OUR NEW HQ TO PLAN--NOT TO BICKER LIKE CHILDREN!
WAIT A MINUTE! WHEN DID I BECOME THE VOICE OF REASON?
WHEN YOUR HOST-BODY'S PERSONALITY BEGAN TO FORCE ITS WAY UP INTO YOUR CONSCIOUSNESS.
AND, FRANKLY, GUY--IT'S A VAST IMPROVEMENT.
THAT "IMPROVEMENT" WILL EVENTUALLY ERASE GUY FROM EXISTENCE IF WE DON'T DO SOMETHING TO CORRECT IT!
I SUSPECT THAT-- BEFORE THEY DESTROYED CADMUS-- THE SCULLIONS DOWNLOADED THE PROJECT'S RESEARCH.
ONE MORE REASON TO TAKE OUR TIME...AND HAVE A PLAN IN PLACE...BEFORE WE TAKE ON LADY STYX.
THEN LET'S HEAR IT!
WHAT?
YOUR GREAT PLAN!
I TOLD YOU-- WE NEED MORE INFORMATION ON STYX AND THE SCULLIONS FIRST! UNLESS, OF COURSE, YOU WANT A REPEAT OF THE MASSACRE THAT TOOK OUT BRUCE, BARRY AND THE OTHERS--
HEY, I HATE T'INTERRUPT A PERFECTLY USELESS ARGUMENT-- BUT AM I THE ONLY ONE WHO NOTICED THAT TINA'S ARMOR IS MISSING?
IF THAT LITTLE IDIOT WENT OFF HALF-COCKED AGAIN--! I SWEAR, IF ANYONE'S GONNA GET US ALL KILLED--

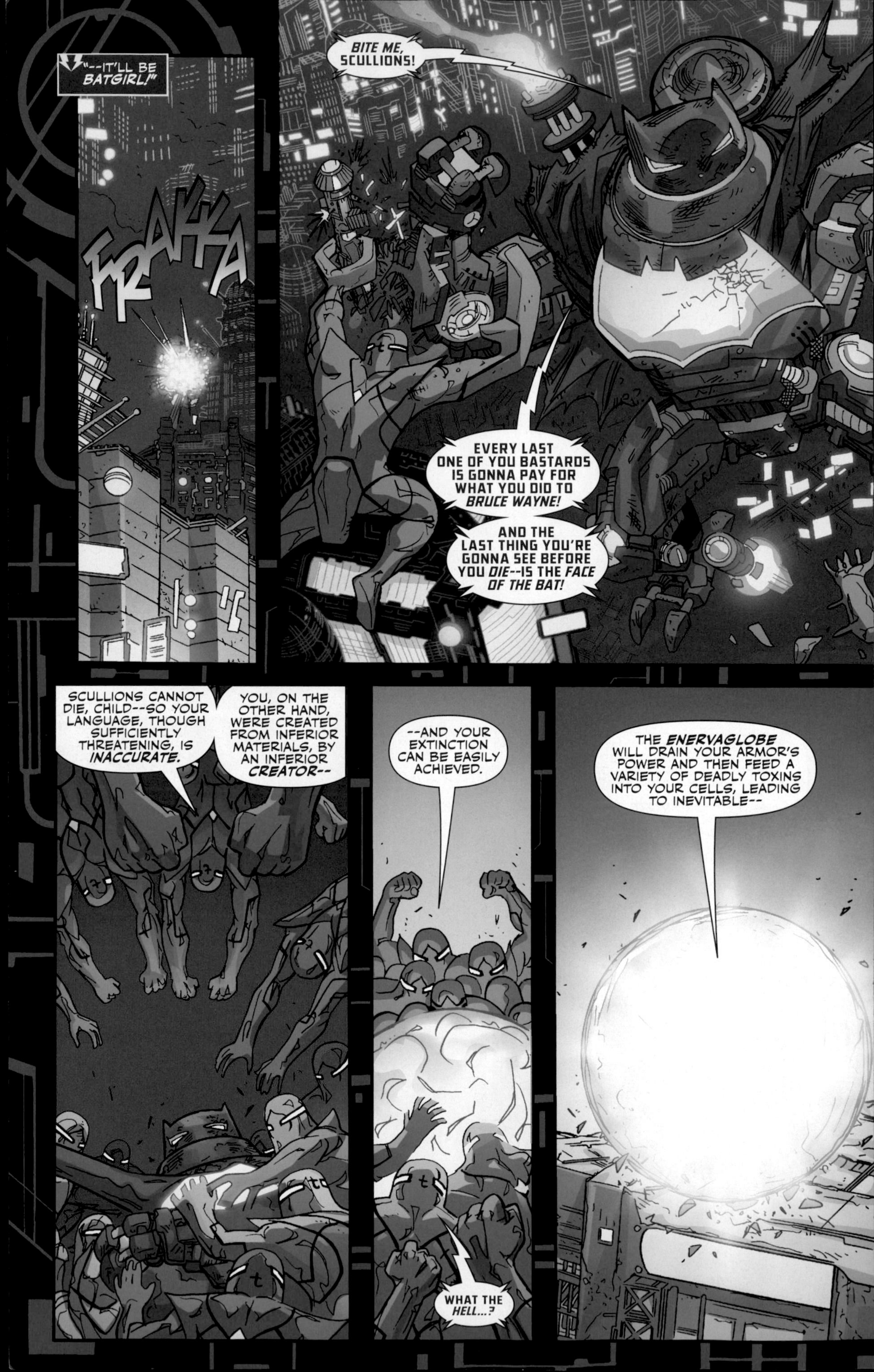
"--IT'LL BE BATGIRL!"
FRAKKA
BITE ME, SCULLIONS!
EVERY LAST ONE OF YOU BASTARDS IS GONNA PAY FOR WHAT YOU DID TO BRUCE WAYNE!
AND THE LAST THING YOU'RE GONNA SEE BEFORE YOU DIE--IS THE FACE OF THE BAT!
SCULLIONS CANNOT DIE, CHILD--SO YOUR LANGUAGE, THOUGH SUFFICIENTLY THREATENING, IS INACCURATE.
YOU, ON THE OTHER HAND, WERE CREATED FROM INFERIOR MATERIALS, BY AN INFERIOR CREATOR--
--AND YOUR EXTINCTION CAN BE EASILY ACHIEVED.
WHAT THE HELL...?
THE ENERVAGLOBE WILL DRAIN YOUR ARMOR'S POWER AND THEN FEED A VARIETY OF DEADLY TOXINS INTO YOUR CELLS, LEADING TO INEVITABLE--

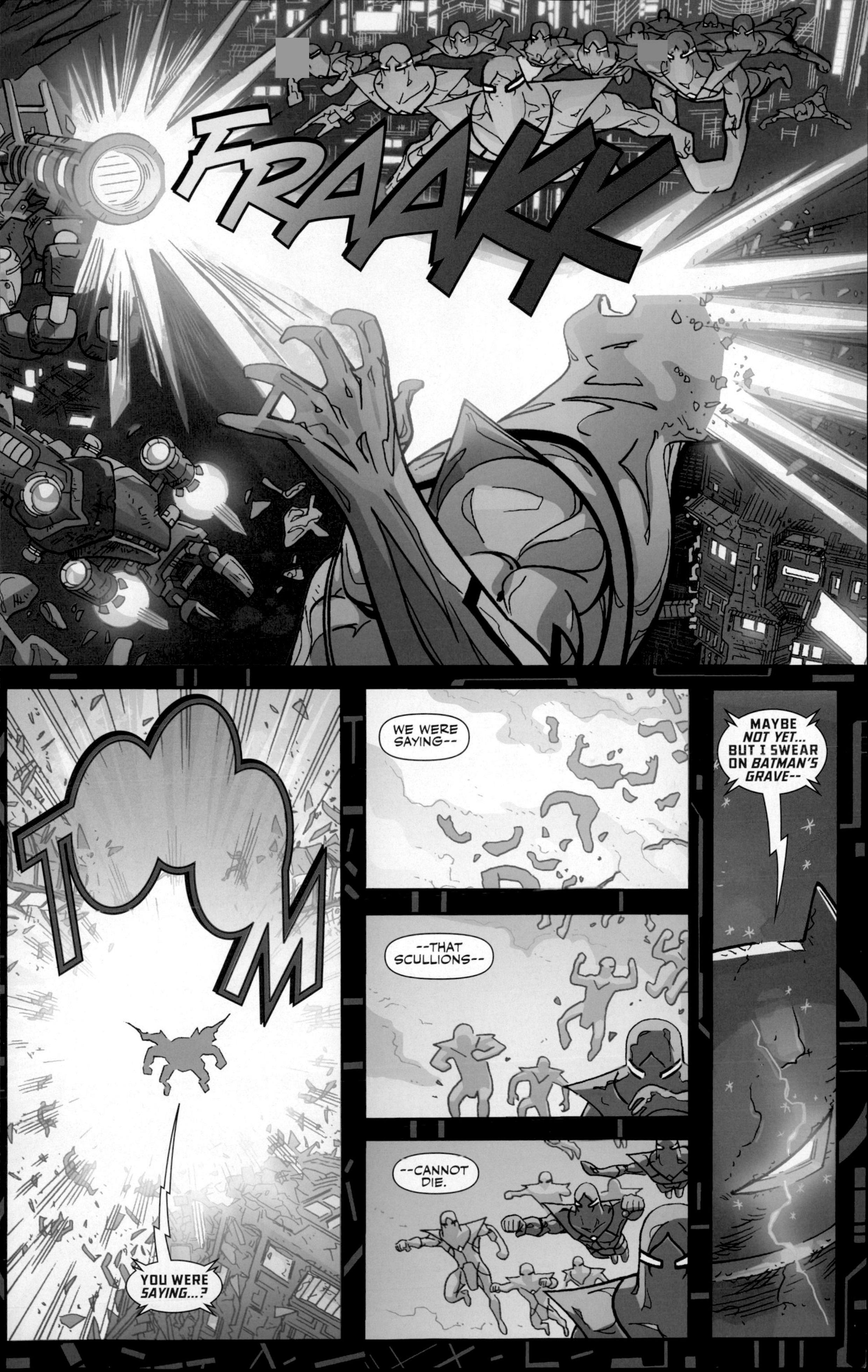
FRAAKK
TOOM
YOU WERE SAYING...?
WE WERE SAYING--
--THAT SCULLIONS--
--CANNOT DIE.
MAYBE NOT YET... BUT I SWEAR ON BATMAN'S GRAVE--

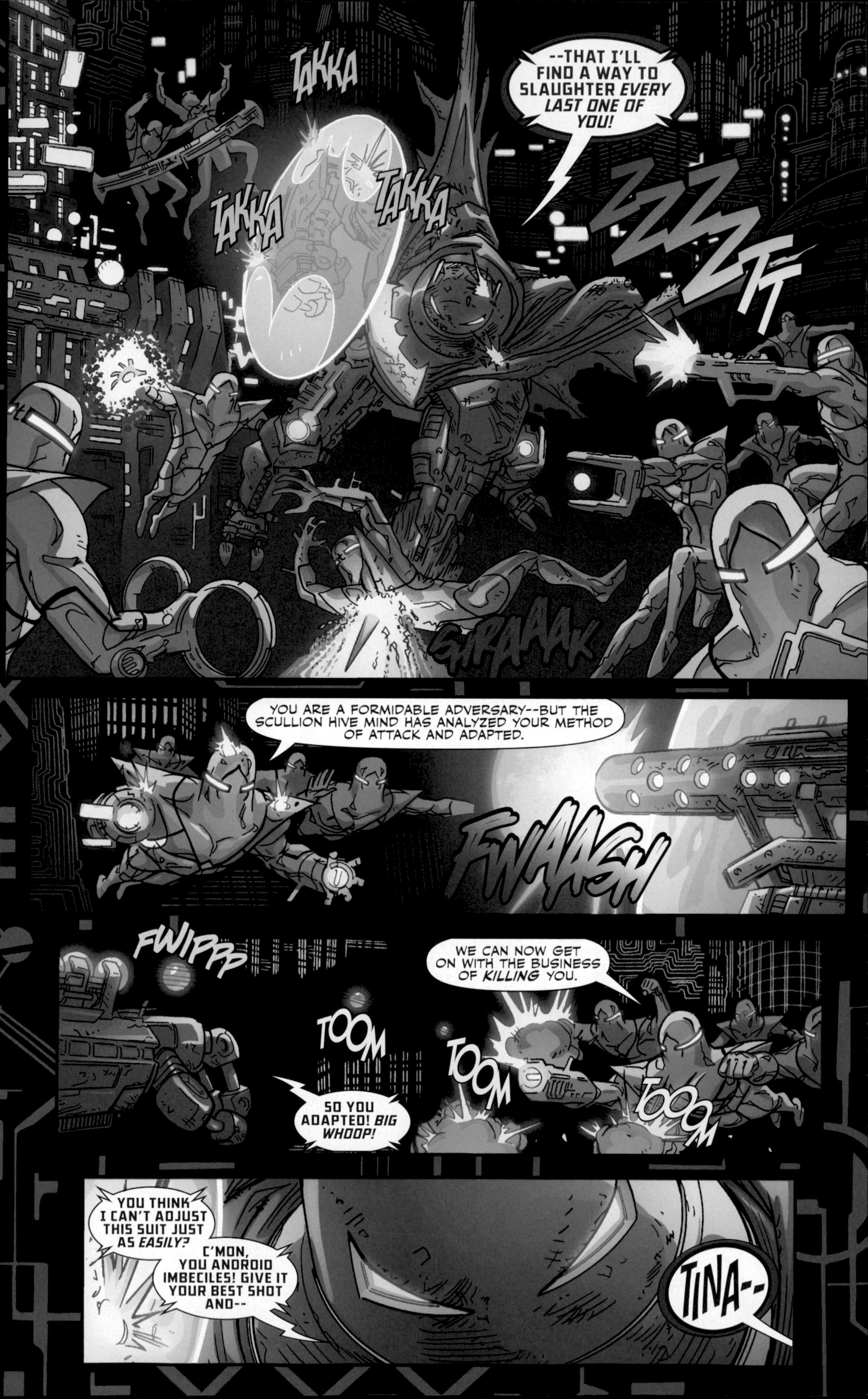
--THAT I'LL FIND A WAY TO SLAUGHTER *EVERY LAST ONE* OF YOU!
TAKKA
TAKKA
TAKKA
ZZZZTT
SHRAAAK
YOU ARE A FORMIDABLE ADVERSARY--BUT THE SCULLION HIVE MIND HAS ANALYZED YOUR METHOD OF ATTACK AND ADAPTED.
FWAASH
FWIPPP
WE CAN NOW GET ON WITH THE BUSINESS OF *KILLING* YOU.
TOOM
TOOM
TOOOM
SO YOU ADAPTED! *BIG WHOOP!*
YOU THINK I CAN'T ADJUST THIS SUIT JUST AS *EASILY?*
C'MON, YOU ANDROID IMBECILES! GIVE IT YOUR BEST SHOT AND--
TINA--

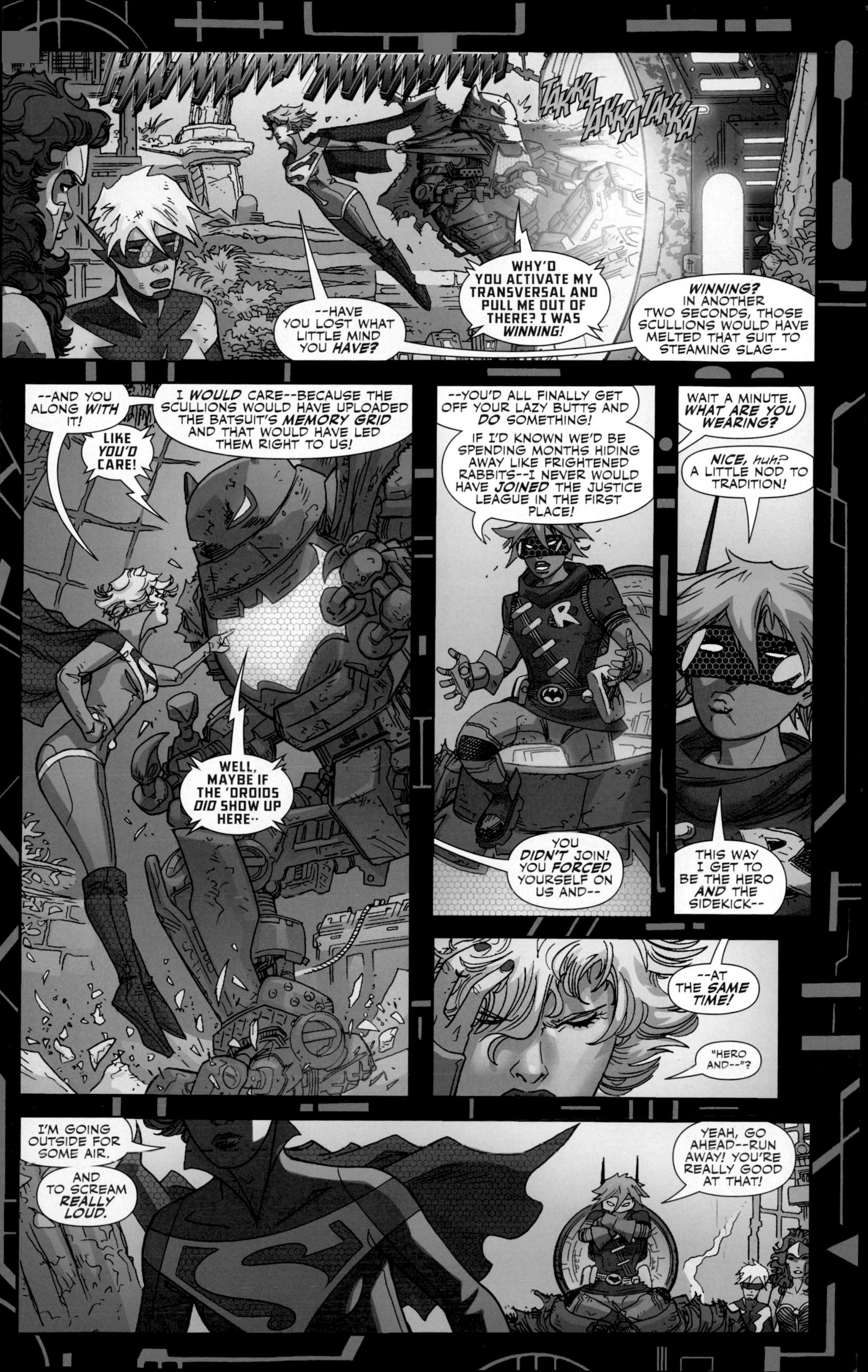
HMMMMMMMMMMMMMM
TAKKA TAKKA TAKKA TAKKA
--HAVE YOU LOST WHAT LITTLE MIND YOU *HAVE?*
WHY'D YOU ACTIVATE MY TRANSVERSAL AND PULL ME OUT OF THERE? I WAS *WINNING!*
WINNING? IN ANOTHER TWO SECONDS, THOSE SCULLIONS WOULD HAVE MELTED THAT SUIT TO STEAMING SLAG--
--AND YOU ALONG *WITH* IT!
LIKE *YOU'D* CARE!
I *WOULD* CARE--BECAUSE THE SCULLIONS WOULD HAVE UPLOADED THE BATSUIT'S *MEMORY GRID* AND THAT WOULD HAVE LED THEM RIGHT TO US!
WELL, MAYBE IF THE 'DROIDS *DID* SHOW UP HERE--
--YOU'D ALL FINALLY GET OFF YOUR LAZY BUTTS AND *DO* SOMETHING!
IF I'D KNOWN WE'D BE SPENDING MONTHS HIDING AWAY LIKE FRIGHTENED RABBITS--I NEVER WOULD HAVE *JOINED* THE JUSTICE LEAGUE IN THE FIRST PLACE!
YOU *DIDN'T* JOIN! YOU *FORCED* YOURSELF ON US AND--
WAIT A MINUTE. *WHAT ARE YOU WEARING?*
NICE, huh? A LITTLE NOD TO TRADITION!
THIS WAY I GET TO BE THE HERO *AND* THE SIDEKICK--
--AT THE *SAME TIME!*
"HERO AND--"?
I'M GOING OUTSIDE FOR SOME AIR.
AND TO SCREAM *REALLY LOUD.*
YEAH, GO AHEAD--RUN AWAY! YOU'RE REALLY GOOD AT THAT!

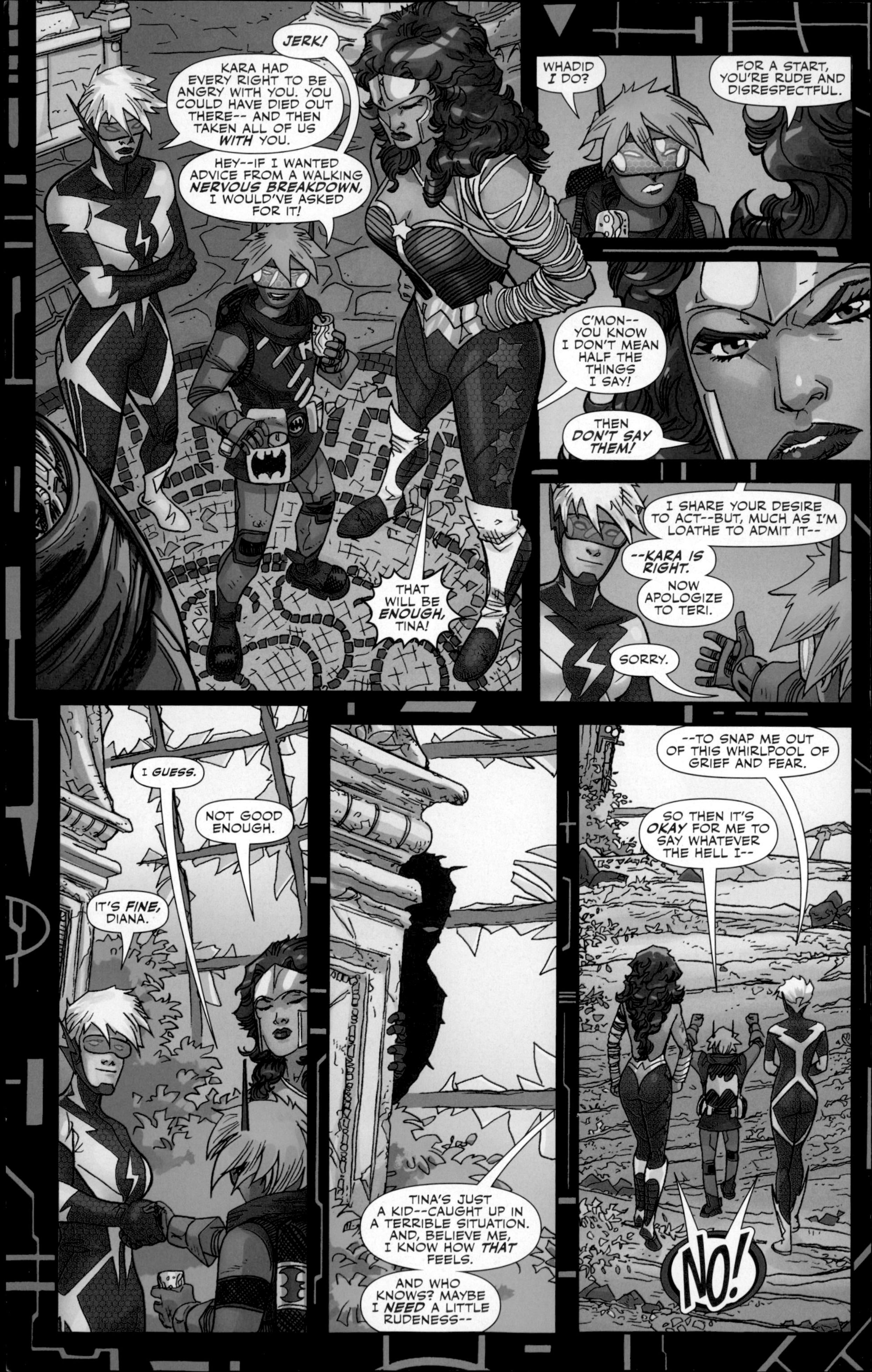
JERK!
KARA HAD EVERY RIGHT TO BE ANGRY WITH YOU. YOU COULD HAVE DIED OUT THERE-- AND THEN TAKEN ALL OF US *WITH* YOU.
HEY--IF I WANTED ADVICE FROM A WALKING *NERVOUS BREAKDOWN,* I WOULD'VE ASKED FOR IT!
THAT WILL BE *ENOUGH,* TINA!
WHADID *I* DO?
FOR A START, YOU'RE RUDE AND DISRESPECTFUL.
C'MON-- YOU KNOW I DON'T MEAN HALF THE THINGS I SAY!
THEN *DON'T SAY THEM!*
I SHARE YOUR DESIRE TO ACT--BUT, MUCH AS I'M LOATHE TO ADMIT IT--
--KARA IS RIGHT.
NOW APOLOGIZE TO TERI.
SORRY.
I *GUESS.*
NOT GOOD ENOUGH.
IT'S *FINE,* DIANA.
TINA'S JUST A KID--CAUGHT UP IN A TERRIBLE SITUATION. AND, BELIEVE ME, I KNOW HOW *THAT* FEELS.
AND WHO KNOWS? MAYBE I *NEED* A LITTLE RUDENESS--
--TO SNAP ME OUT OF THIS WHIRLPOOL OF GRIEF AND FEAR.
SO THEN IT'S *OKAY* FOR ME TO SAY WHATEVER THE HELL I--
NO!

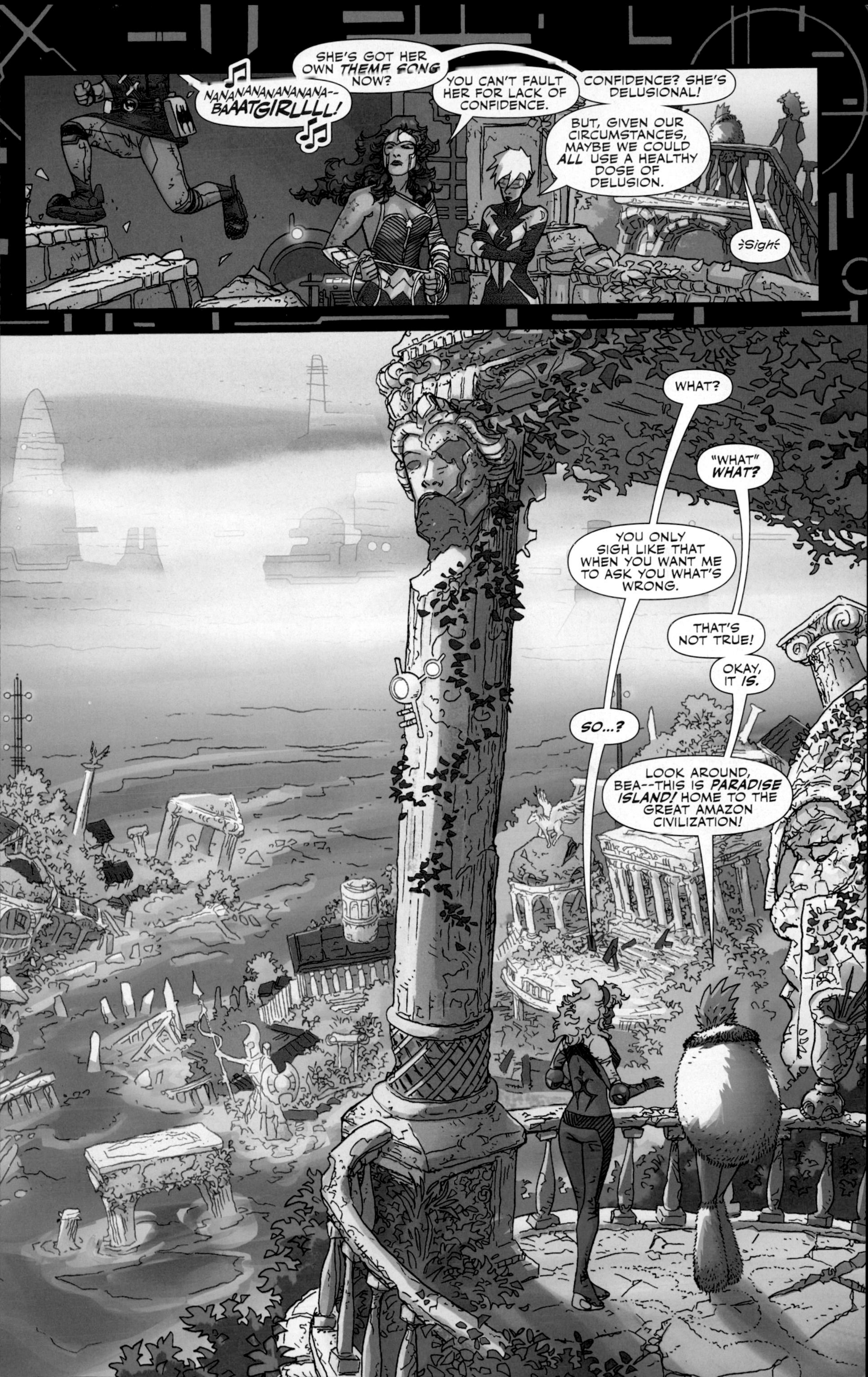

NANANANANANANANA--BAAATGIRLLLLL!
SHE'S GOT HER OWN THEME SONG NOW?
YOU CAN'T FAULT HER FOR LACK OF CONFIDENCE.
CONFIDENCE? SHE'S DELUSIONAL!
BUT, GIVEN OUR CIRCUMSTANCES, MAYBE WE COULD ALL USE A HEALTHY DOSE OF DELUSION.
Sigh
WHAT?
"WHAT" WHAT?
YOU ONLY SIGH LIKE THAT WHEN YOU WANT ME TO ASK YOU WHAT'S WRONG.
THAT'S NOT TRUE!
OKAY, IT IS.
SO...?
LOOK AROUND, BEA--THIS IS PARADISE ISLAND! HOME TO THE GREAT AMAZON CIVILIZATION!

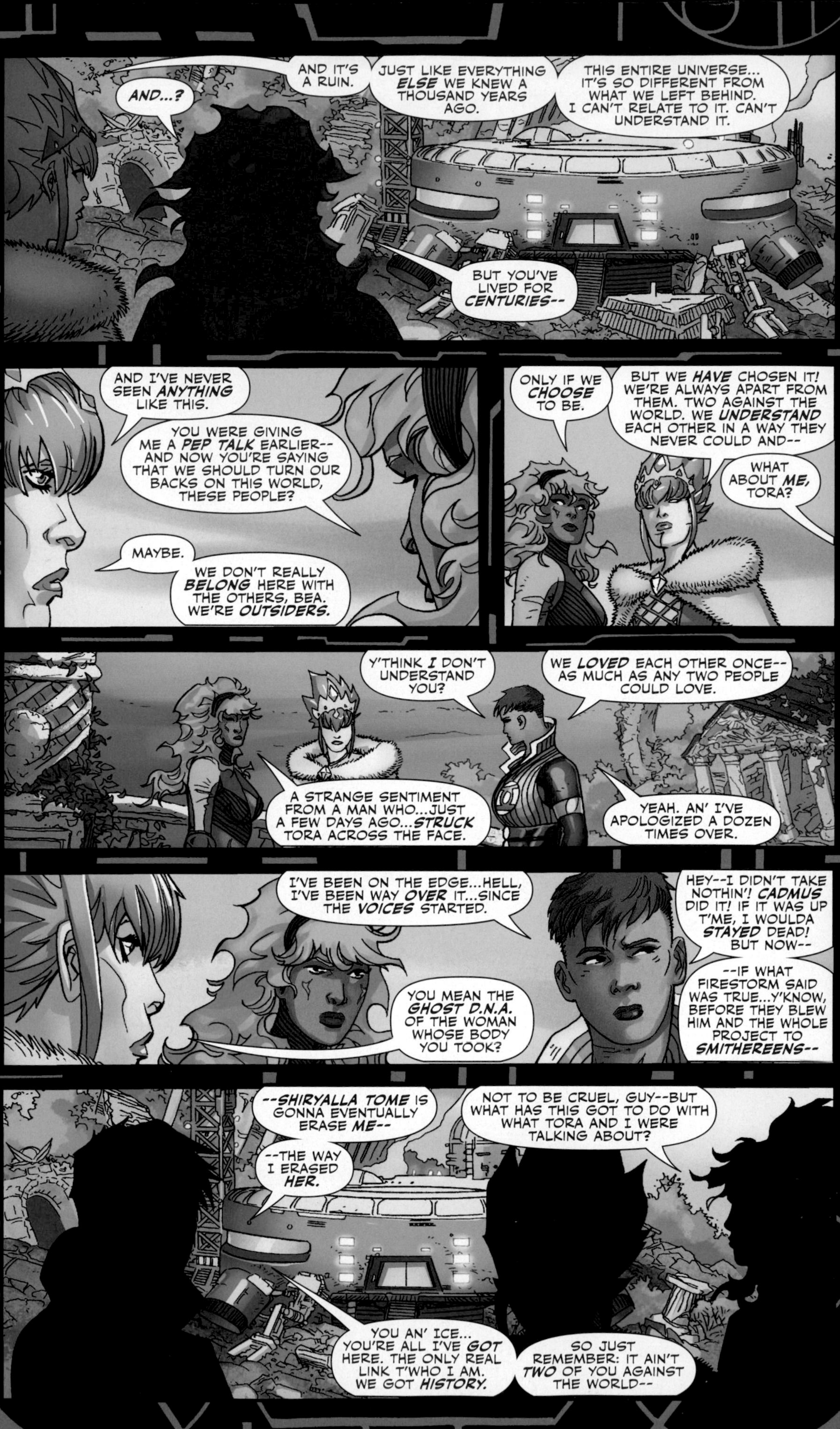
AND...?
AND IT'S A RUIN.
JUST LIKE EVERYTHING ELSE WE KNEW A THOUSAND YEARS AGO.
THIS ENTIRE UNIVERSE... IT'S SO DIFFERENT FROM WHAT WE LEFT BEHIND. I CAN'T RELATE TO IT. CAN'T UNDERSTAND IT.
BUT YOU'VE LIVED FOR CENTURIES--
AND I'VE NEVER SEEN ANYTHING LIKE THIS.
YOU WERE GIVING ME A PEP TALK EARLIER-- AND NOW YOU'RE SAYING THAT WE SHOULD TURN OUR BACKS ON THIS WORLD, THESE PEOPLE?
MAYBE.
WE DON'T REALLY BELONG HERE WITH THE OTHERS, BEA. WE'RE OUTSIDERS.
ONLY IF WE CHOOSE TO BE.
BUT WE HAVE CHOSEN IT! WE'RE ALWAYS APART FROM THEM. TWO AGAINST THE WORLD. WE UNDERSTAND EACH OTHER IN A WAY THEY NEVER COULD AND--
WHAT ABOUT ME, TORA?
Y'THINK I DON'T UNDERSTAND YOU?
WE LOVED EACH OTHER ONCE-- AS MUCH AS ANY TWO PEOPLE COULD LOVE.
A STRANGE SENTIMENT FROM A MAN WHO...JUST A FEW DAYS AGO...STRUCK TORA ACROSS THE FACE.
YEAH. AN' I'VE APOLOGIZED A DOZEN TIMES OVER.
I'VE BEEN ON THE EDGE...HELL, I'VE BEEN WAY OVER IT...SINCE THE VOICES STARTED.
YOU MEAN THE GHOST D.N.A. OF THE WOMAN WHOSE BODY YOU TOOK?
HEY--I DIDN'T TAKE NOTHIN'! CADMUS DID IT! IF IT WAS UP T'ME, I WOULDA STAYED DEAD! BUT NOW--
--IF WHAT FIRESTORM SAID WAS TRUE...Y'KNOW, BEFORE THEY BLEW HIM AND THE WHOLE PROJECT TO SMITHEREENS--
--SHIRYALLA TOME IS GONNA EVENTUALLY ERASE ME--
--THE WAY I ERASED HER.
NOT TO BE CRUEL, GUY--BUT WHAT HAS THIS GOT TO DO WITH WHAT TORA AND I WERE TALKING ABOUT?
YOU AN' ICE... YOU'RE ALL I'VE GOT HERE. THE ONLY REAL LINK T'WHO I AM. WE GOT HISTORY.
SO JUST REMEMBER: IT AIN'T TWO OF YOU AGAINST THE WORLD--

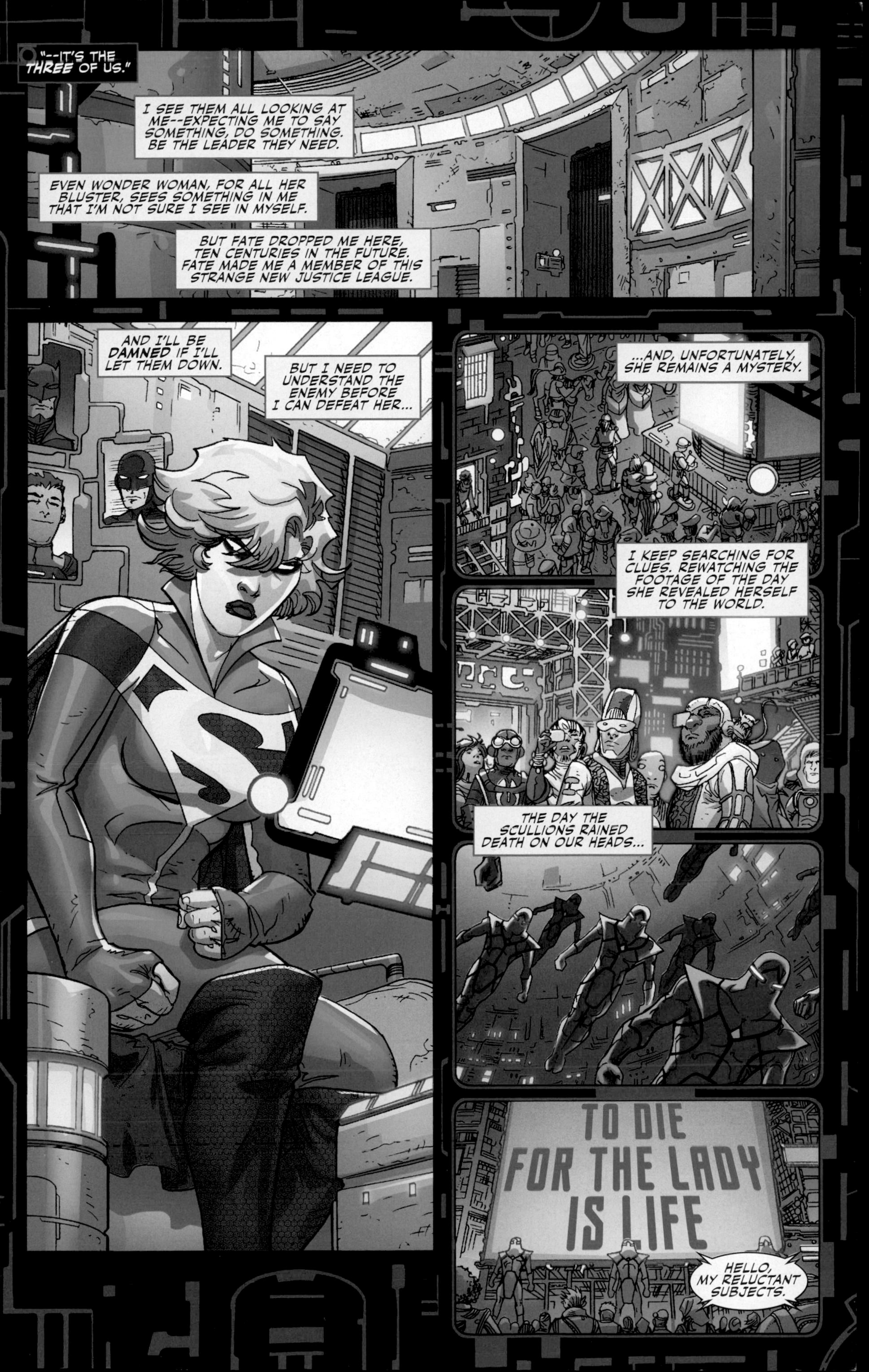
"--IT'S THE THREE OF US."
I SEE THEM ALL LOOKING AT ME--EXPECTING ME TO SAY SOMETHING, DO SOMETHING. BE THE LEADER THEY NEED.
EVEN WONDER WOMAN, FOR ALL HER BLUSTER, SEES SOMETHING IN ME THAT I'M NOT SURE I SEE IN MYSELF.
BUT FATE DROPPED ME HERE, TEN CENTURIES IN THE FUTURE. FATE MADE ME A MEMBER OF THIS STRANGE NEW JUSTICE LEAGUE.
AND I'LL BE DAMNED IF I'LL LET THEM DOWN.
BUT I NEED TO UNDERSTAND THE ENEMY BEFORE I CAN DEFEAT HER...
...AND, UNFORTUNATELY, SHE REMAINS A MYSTERY.
I KEEP SEARCHING FOR CLUES. REWATCHING THE FOOTAGE OF THE DAY SHE REVEALED HERSELF TO THE WORLD.
THE DAY THE SCULLIONS RAINED DEATH ON OUR HEADS...
TO DIE FOR THE LADY IS LIFE
HELLO, MY RELUCTANT SUBJECTS.

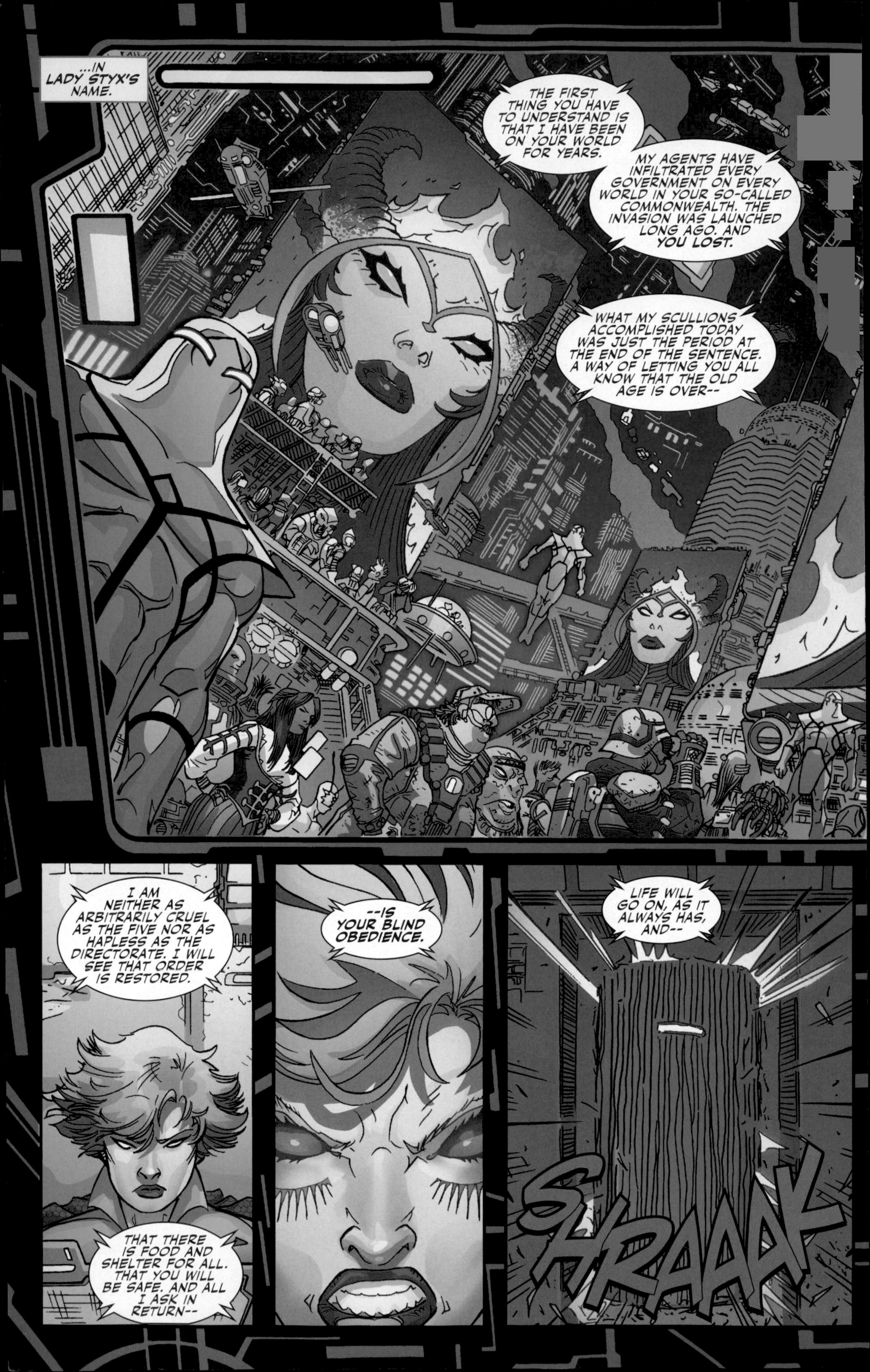
...IN LADY STYX'S NAME.
THE FIRST THING YOU HAVE TO UNDERSTAND IS THAT I HAVE BEEN ON YOUR WORLD FOR YEARS.
MY AGENTS HAVE INFILTRATED EVERY GOVERNMENT ON EVERY WORLD IN YOUR SO-CALLED COMMONWEALTH. THE INVASION WAS LAUNCHED LONG AGO. AND YOU LOST.
WHAT MY SCULLIONS ACCOMPLISHED TODAY WAS JUST THE PERIOD AT THE END OF THE SENTENCE. A WAY OF LETTING YOU ALL KNOW THAT THE OLD AGE IS OVER--
I AM NEITHER AS ARBITRARILY CRUEL AS THE FIVE NOR AS HAPLESS AS THE DIRECTORATE. I WILL SEE THAT ORDER IS RESTORED.
THAT THERE IS FOOD AND SHELTER FOR ALL. THAT YOU WILL BE SAFE. AND ALL I ASK IN RETURN--
--IS YOUR BLIND OBEDIENCE.
LIFE WILL GO ON, AS IT ALWAYS HAS, AND--
SHRAAK

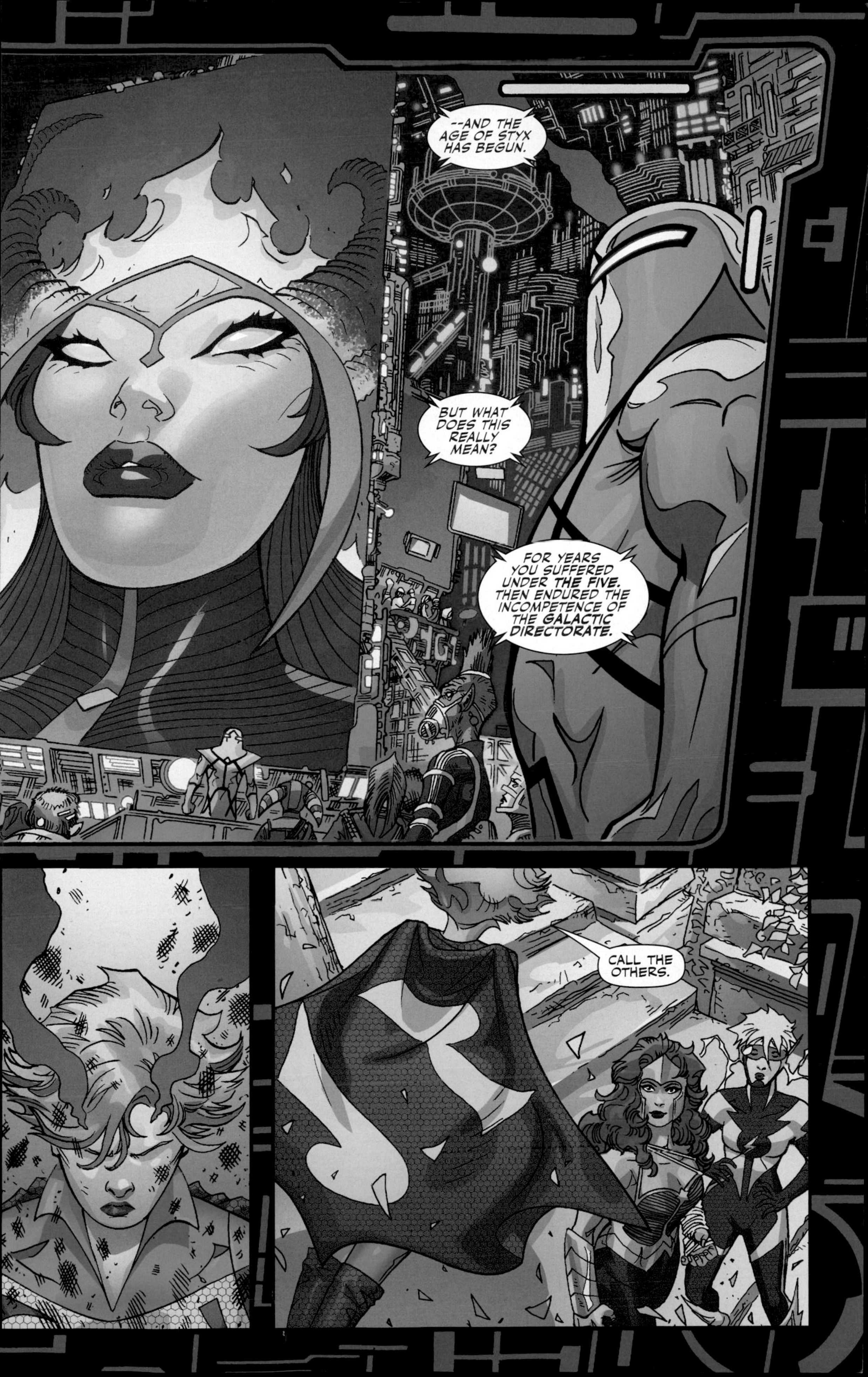
--AND THE AGE OF STYX HAS BEGUN.
BUT WHAT DOES THIS REALLY MEAN?
FOR YEARS YOU SUFFERED UNDER THE FIVE. THEN ENDURED THE INCOMPETENCE OF THE GALACTIC DIRECTORATE.
CALL THE OTHERS.

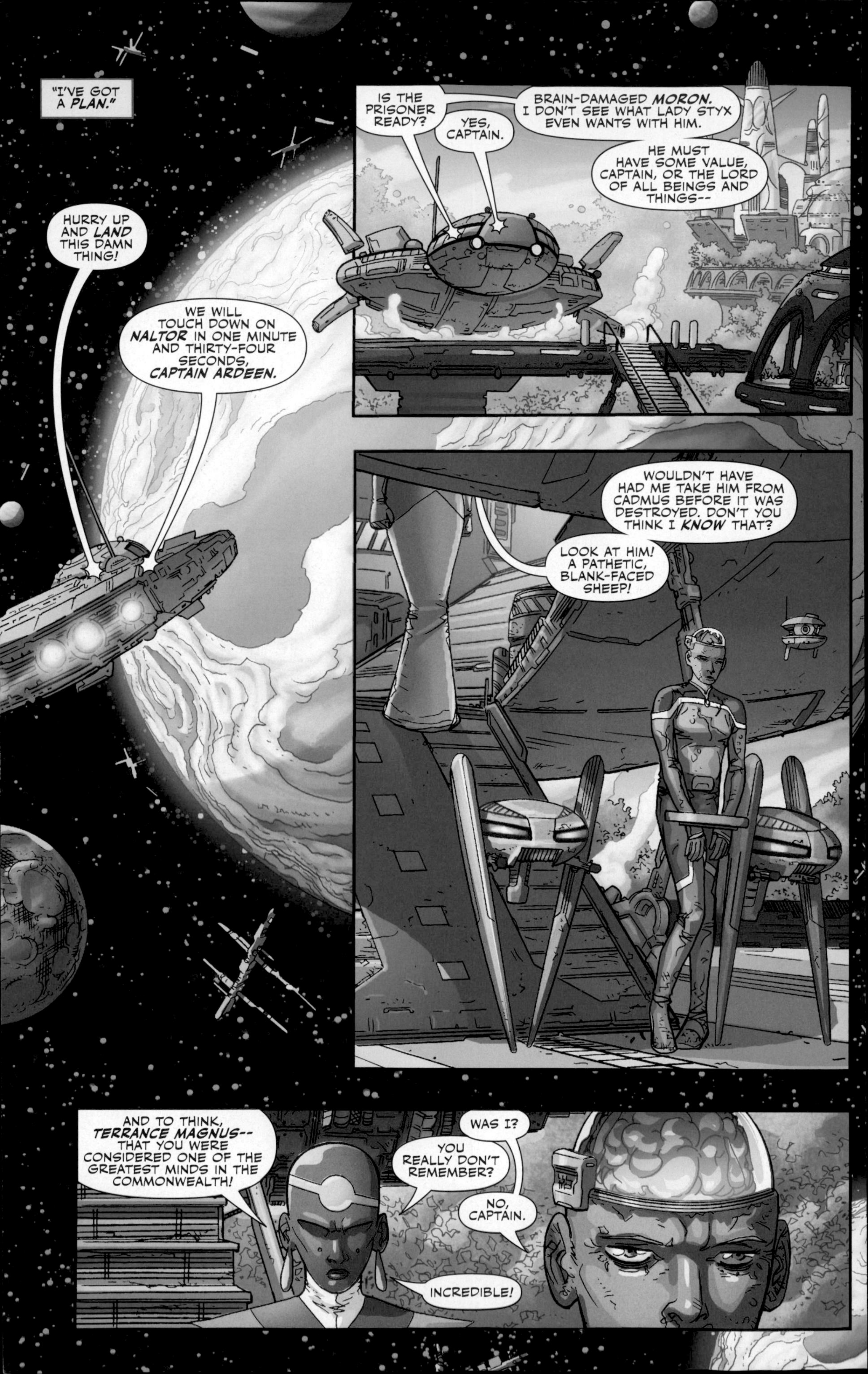
"I'VE GOT A PLAN."
HURRY UP AND LAND THIS DAMN THING!
WE WILL TOUCH DOWN ON NALTOR IN ONE MINUTE AND THIRTY-FOUR SECONDS, CAPTAIN ARDEEN.
IS THE PRISONER READY?
YES, CAPTAIN.
BRAIN-DAMAGED MORON. I DON'T SEE WHAT LADY STYX EVEN WANTS WITH HIM.
HE MUST HAVE SOME VALUE, CAPTAIN, OR THE LORD OF ALL BEINGS AND THINGS--
WOULDN'T HAVE HAD ME TAKE HIM FROM CADMUS BEFORE IT WAS DESTROYED. DON'T YOU THINK I KNOW THAT?
LOOK AT HIM! A PATHETIC, BLANK-FACED SHEEP!
AND TO THINK, TERRANCE MAGNUS-- THAT YOU WERE CONSIDERED ONE OF THE GREATEST MINDS IN THE COMMONWEALTH!
WAS I?
YOU REALLY DON'T REMEMBER?
NO, CAPTAIN.
INCREDIBLE!

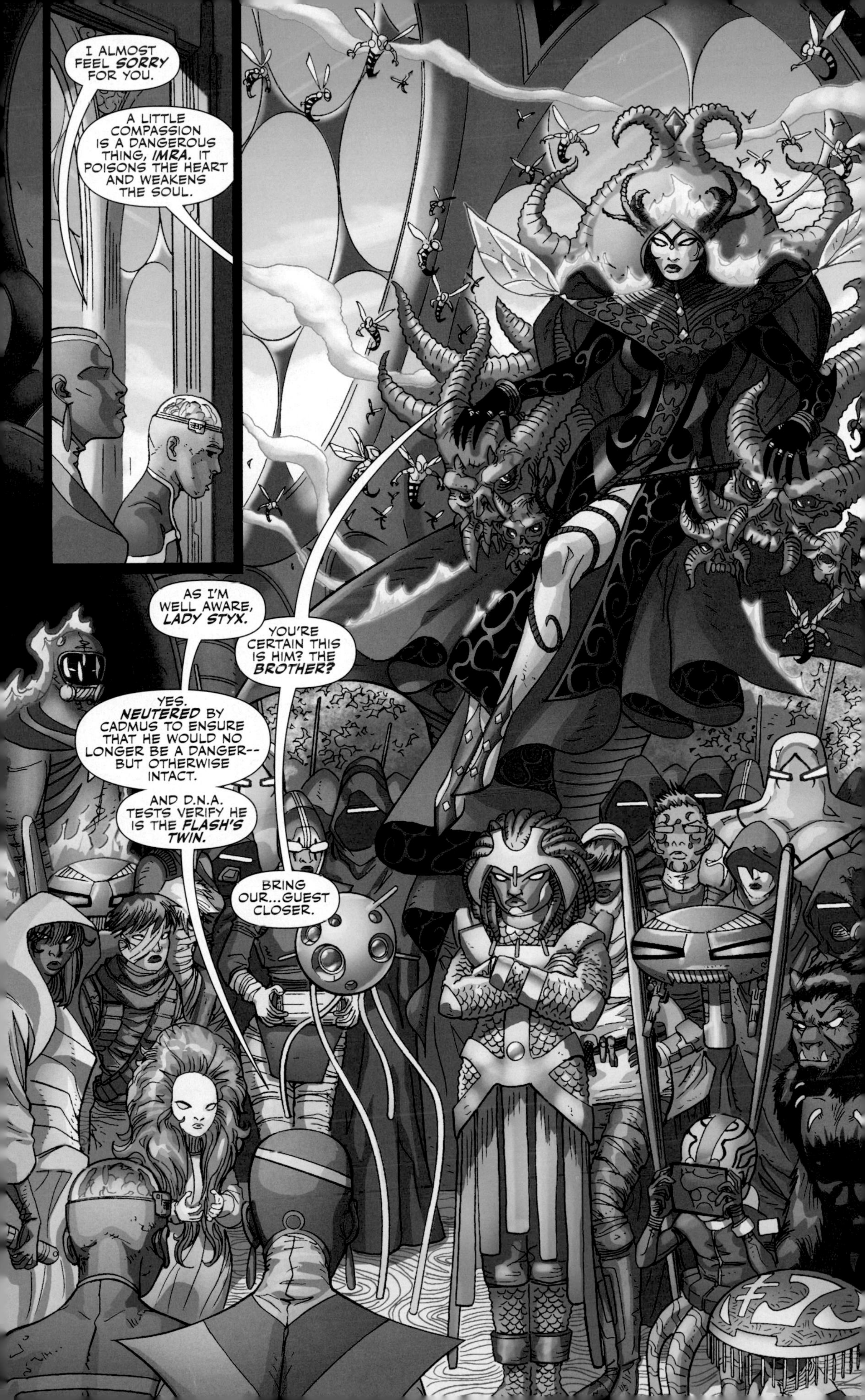
I ALMOST FEEL **SORRY** FOR YOU.
A LITTLE COMPASSION IS A DANGEROUS THING, **IMRA.** IT POISONS THE HEART AND WEAKENS THE SOUL.
AS I'M WELL AWARE, **LADY STYX.**
YOU'RE CERTAIN THIS IS HIM? THE **BROTHER?**
YES. **NEUTERED** BY CADMUS TO ENSURE THAT HE WOULD NO LONGER BE A DANGER-- BUT OTHERWISE INTACT.
AND D.N.A. TESTS VERIFY HE IS THE **FLASH'S TWIN.**
BRING OUR...GUEST CLOSER.

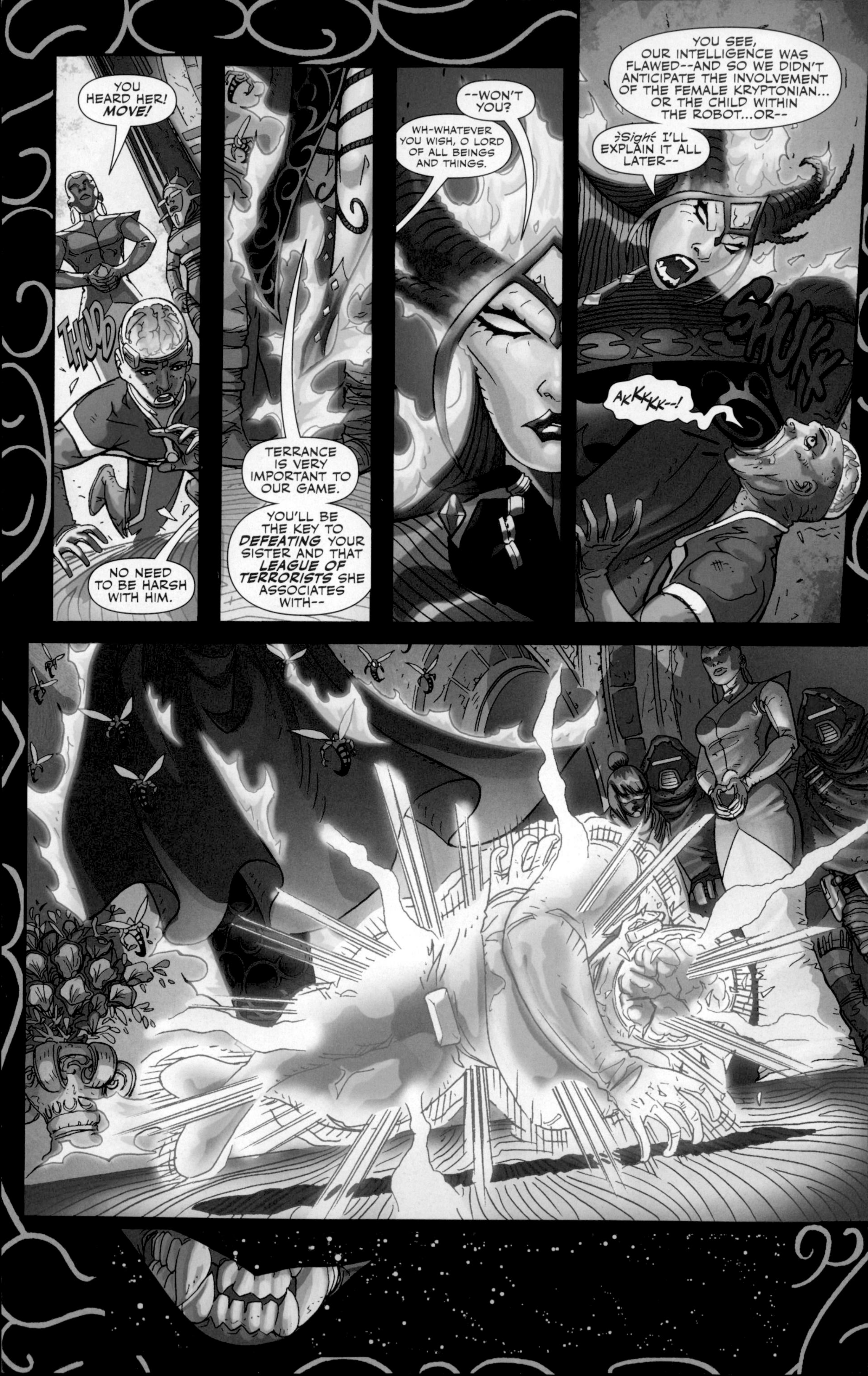
YOU HEARD HER! MOVE!
THUD
NO NEED TO BE HARSH WITH HIM.
TERRANCE IS VERY IMPORTANT TO OUR GAME.
YOU'LL BE THE KEY TO DEFEATING YOUR SISTER AND THAT LEAGUE OF TERRORISTS SHE ASSOCIATES WITH--
--WON'T YOU?
WH-WHATEVER YOU WISH, O LORD OF ALL BEINGS AND THINGS.
YOU SEE, OUR INTELLIGENCE WAS FLAWED--AND SO WE DIDN'T ANTICIPATE THE INVOLVEMENT OF THE FEMALE KRYPTONIAN... OR THE CHILD WITHIN THE ROBOT...OR--
SIGH I'LL EXPLAIN IT ALL LATER--
SHUKK
AKKKKK--!

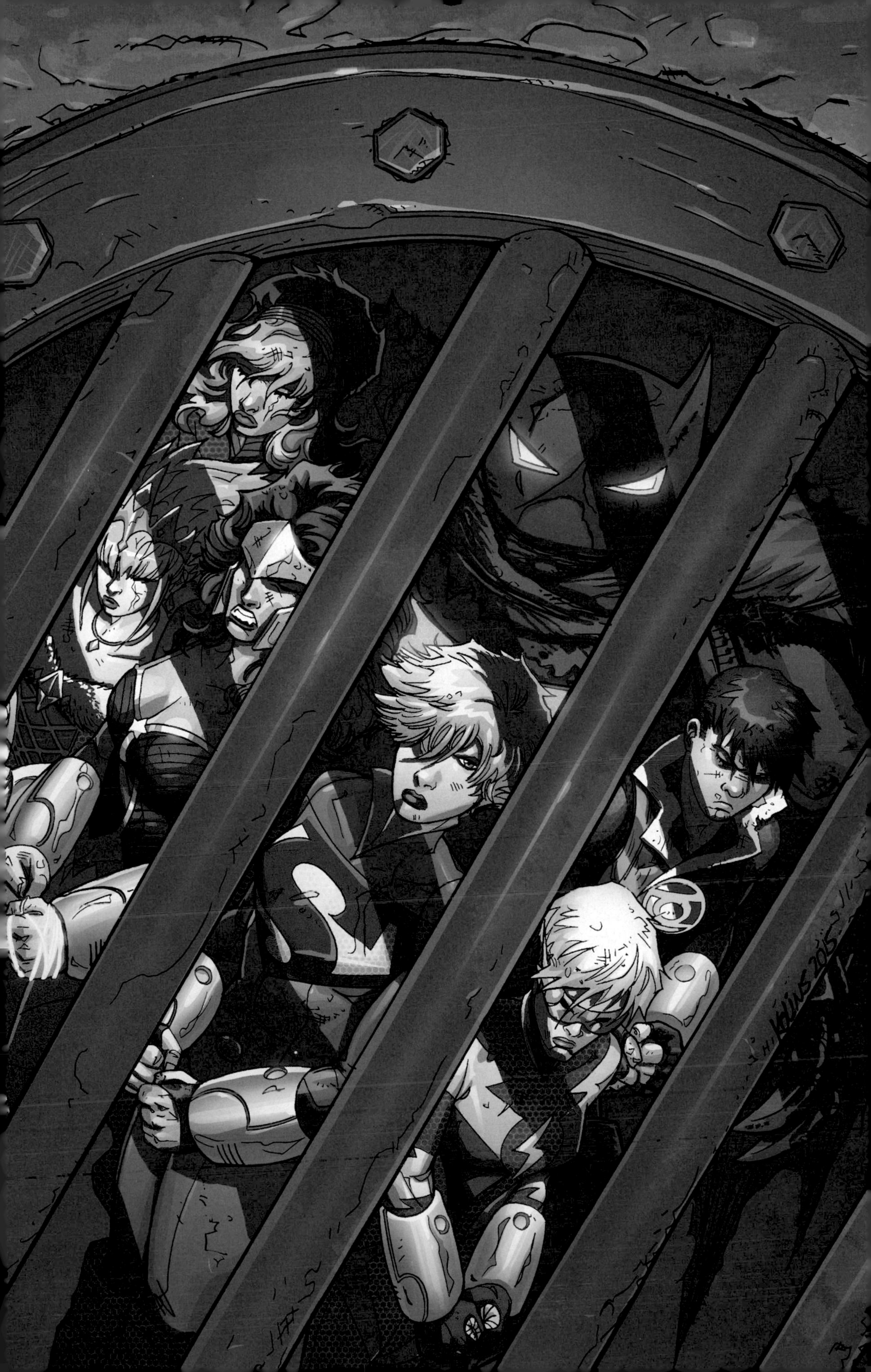

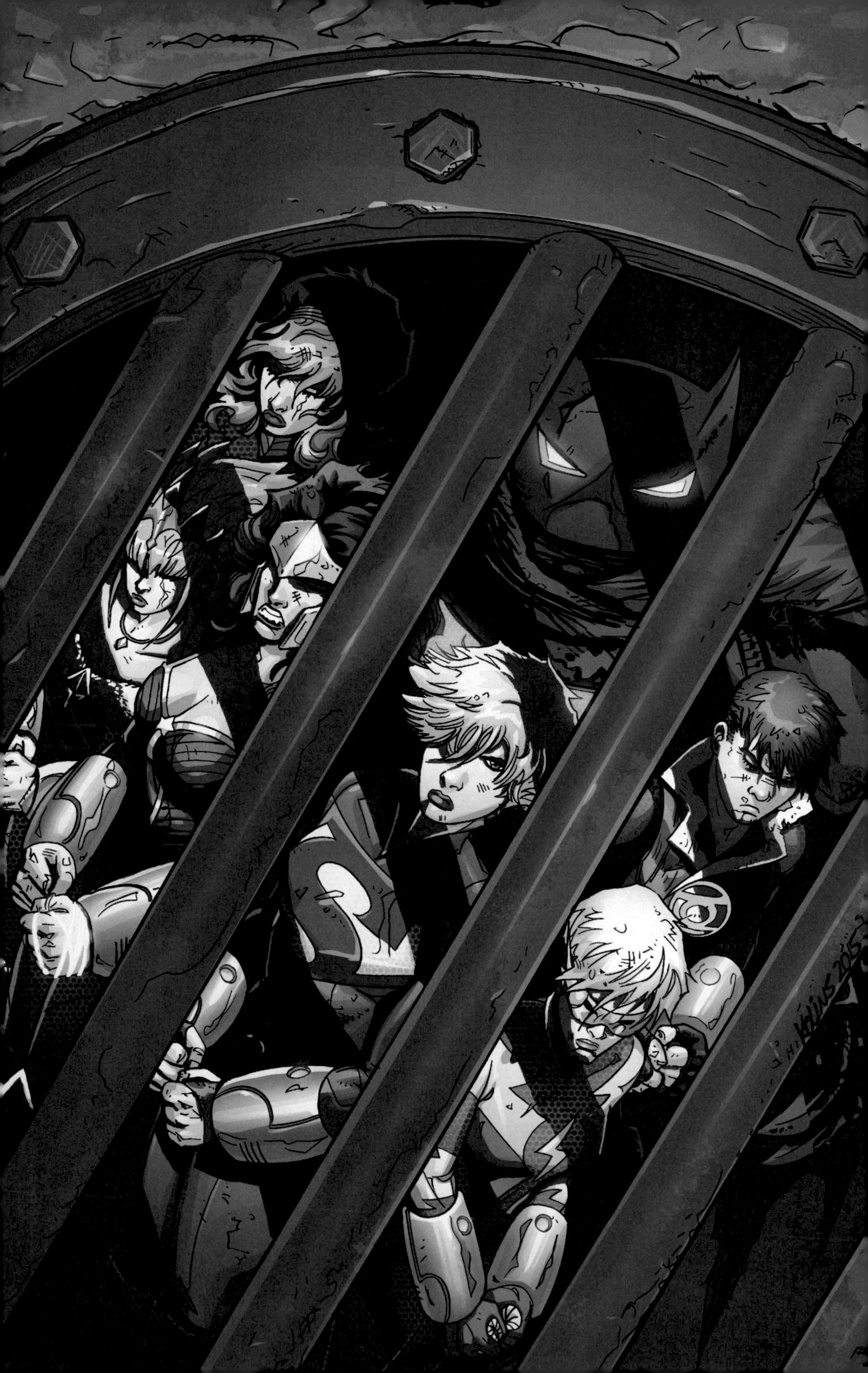
KOLINS 2015

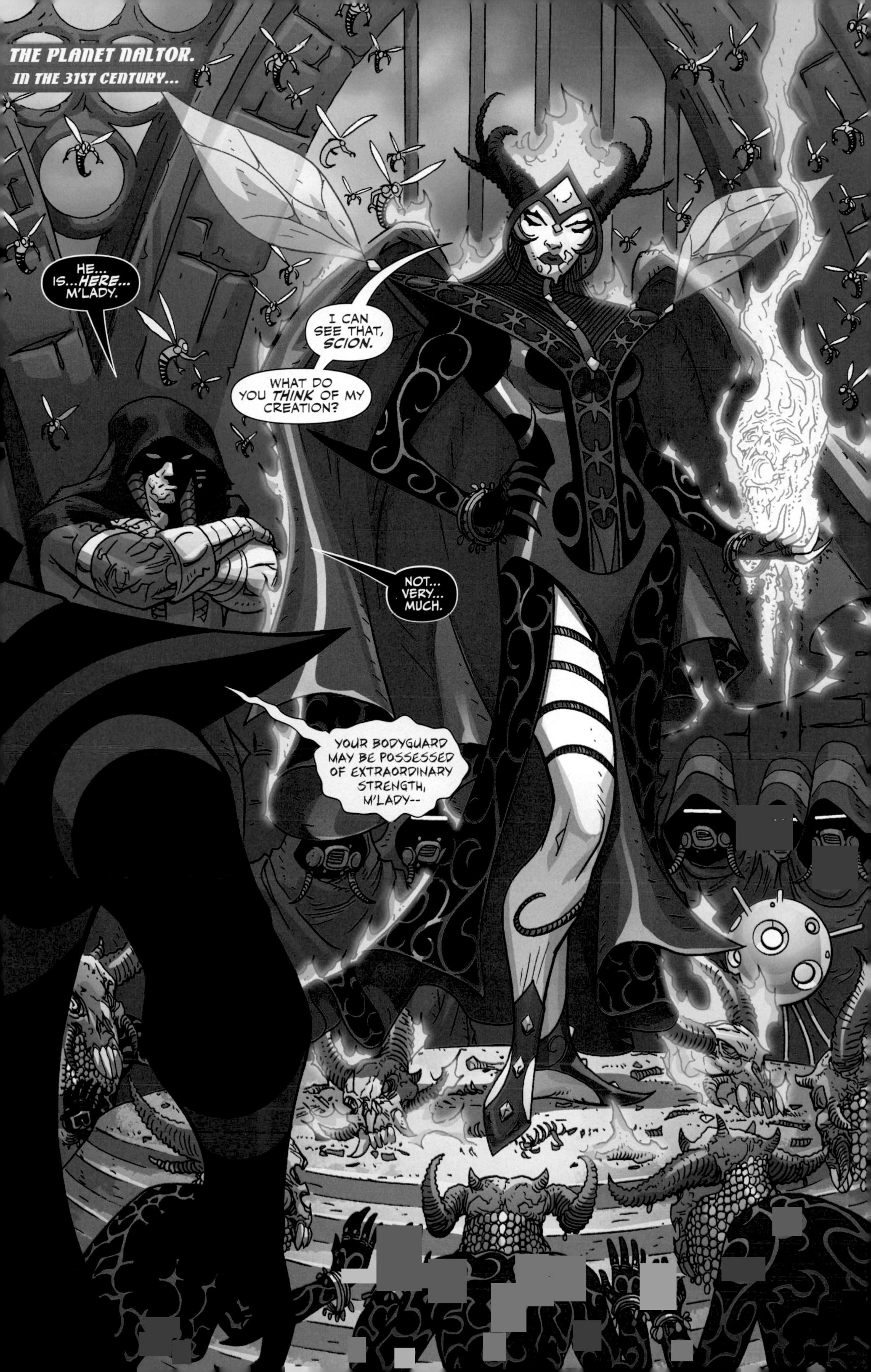
THE PLANET NALTOR.
IN THE 31ST CENTURY...
HE... IS...HERE... M'LADY.
I CAN SEE THAT, SCION.
WHAT DO YOU THINK OF MY CREATION?
NOT... VERY... MUCH.
YOUR BODYGUARD MAY BE POSSESSED OF EXTRAORDINARY STRENGTH, M'LADY--

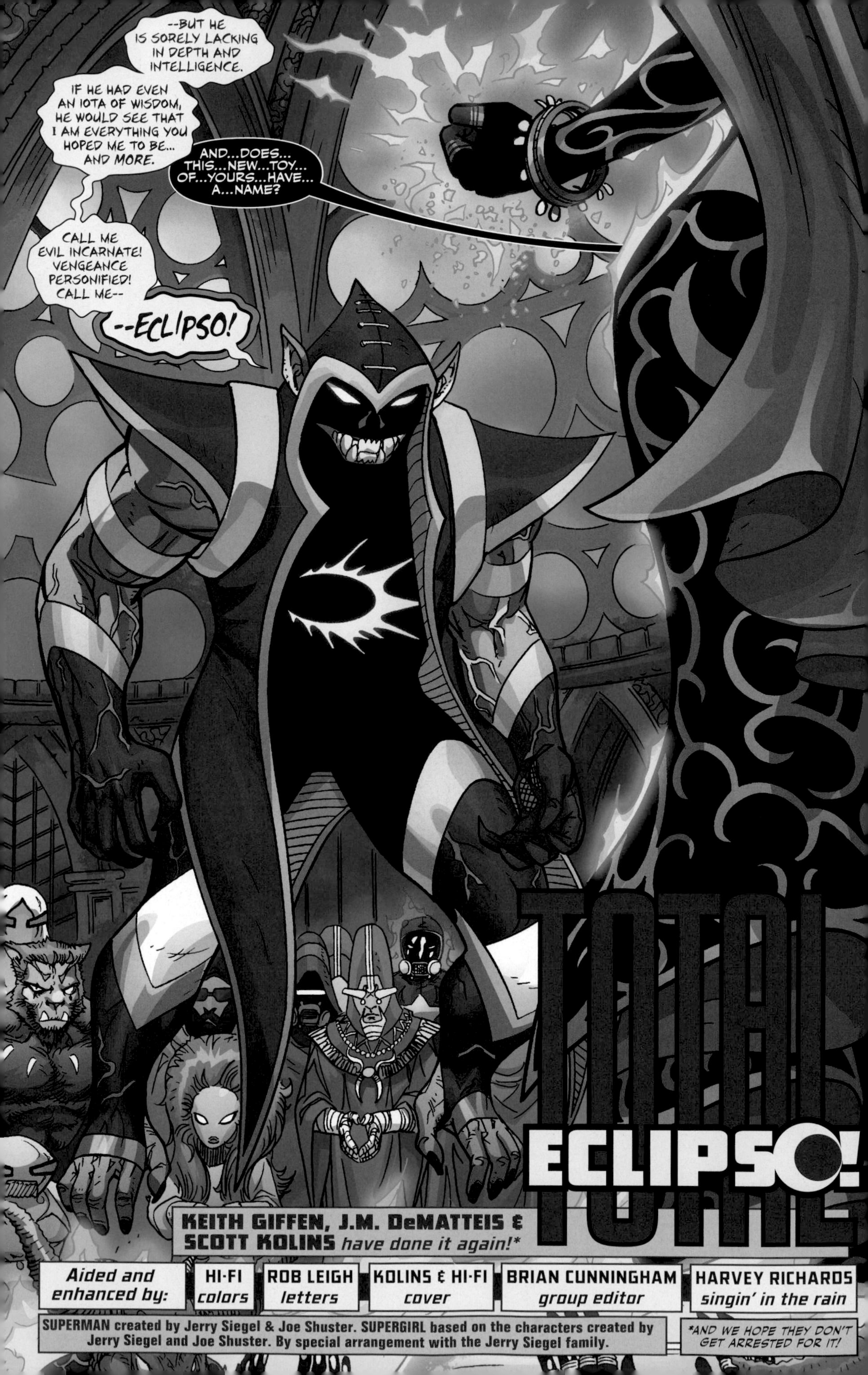
--BUT HE IS SORELY LACKING IN DEPTH AND INTELLIGENCE.
IF HE HAD EVEN AN IOTA OF WISDOM, HE WOULD SEE THAT I AM EVERYTHING YOU HOPED ME TO BE... AND MORE.
AND...DOES... THIS...NEW...TOY... OF...YOURS...HAVE... A...NAME?
CALL ME EVIL INCARNATE! VENGEANCE PERSONIFIED! CALL ME--
--ECLIPSO!
TOTAL ECLIPSO!

KEITH GIFFEN, J.M. DeMATTEIS & SCOTT KOLINS *have done it again!**

Aided and enhanced by: HI-FI *colors* | ROB LEIGH *letters* | KOLINS & HI-FI *cover* | BRIAN CUNNINGHAM *group editor* | HARVEY RICHARDS *singin' in the rain*

*AND WE HOPE THEY DON'T GET ARRESTED FOR IT!

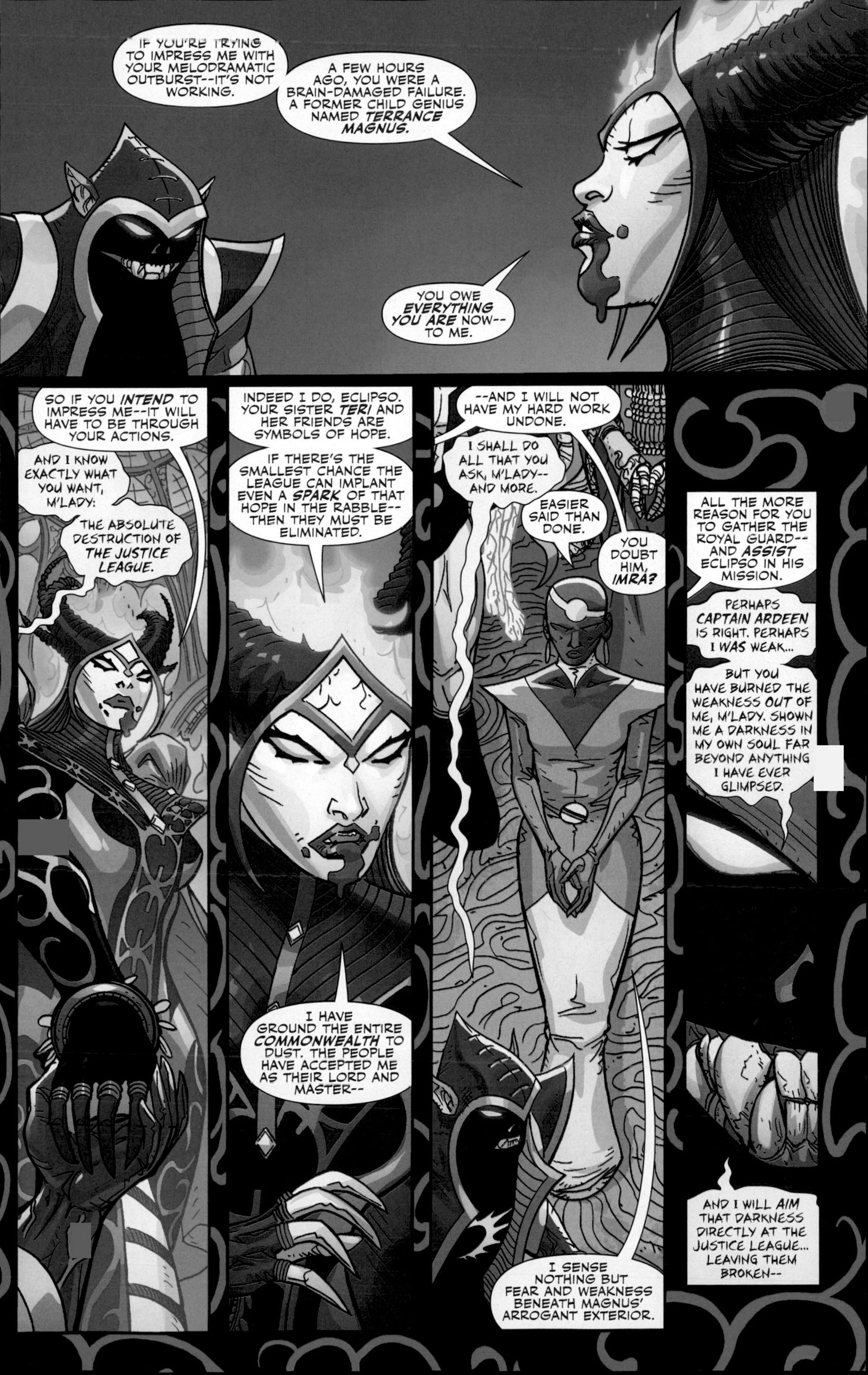
IF YOU'RE TRYING TO IMPRESS ME WITH YOUR MELODRAMATIC OUTBURST--IT'S NOT WORKING.
A FEW HOURS AGO, YOU WERE A BRAIN-DAMAGED FAILURE. A FORMER CHILD GENIUS NAMED TERRANCE MAGNUS.
YOU OWE EVERYTHING YOU ARE NOW--TO ME.
SO IF YOU INTEND TO IMPRESS ME--IT WILL HAVE TO BE THROUGH YOUR ACTIONS.
AND I KNOW EXACTLY WHAT YOU WANT, M'LADY:
THE ABSOLUTE DESTRUCTION OF THE JUSTICE LEAGUE.
INDEED I DO, ECLIPSO. YOUR SISTER TERI AND HER FRIENDS ARE SYMBOLS OF HOPE.
IF THERE'S THE SMALLEST CHANCE THE LEAGUE CAN IMPLANT EVEN A SPARK OF THAT HOPE IN THE RABBLE--THEN THEY MUST BE ELIMINATED.
I HAVE GROUND THE ENTIRE COMMONWEALTH TO DUST. THE PEOPLE HAVE ACCEPTED ME AS THEIR LORD AND MASTER--
--AND I WILL NOT HAVE MY HARD WORK UNDONE.
I SHALL DO ALL THAT YOU ASK, M'LADY--AND MORE.
EASIER SAID THAN DONE.
YOU DOUBT HIM, IMRA?
I SENSE NOTHING BUT FEAR AND WEAKNESS BENEATH MAGNUS' ARROGANT EXTERIOR.
ALL THE MORE REASON FOR YOU TO GATHER THE ROYAL GUARD--AND ASSIST ECLIPSO IN HIS MISSION.
PERHAPS CAPTAIN ARDEEN IS RIGHT. PERHAPS I WAS WEAK...
BUT YOU HAVE BURNED THE WEAKNESS OUT OF ME, M'LADY. SHOWN ME A DARKNESS IN MY OWN SOUL FAR BEYOND ANYTHING I HAVE EVER GLIMPSED.
AND I WILL AIM THAT DARKNESS DIRECTLY AT THE JUSTICE LEAGUE... LEAVING THEM BROKEN--

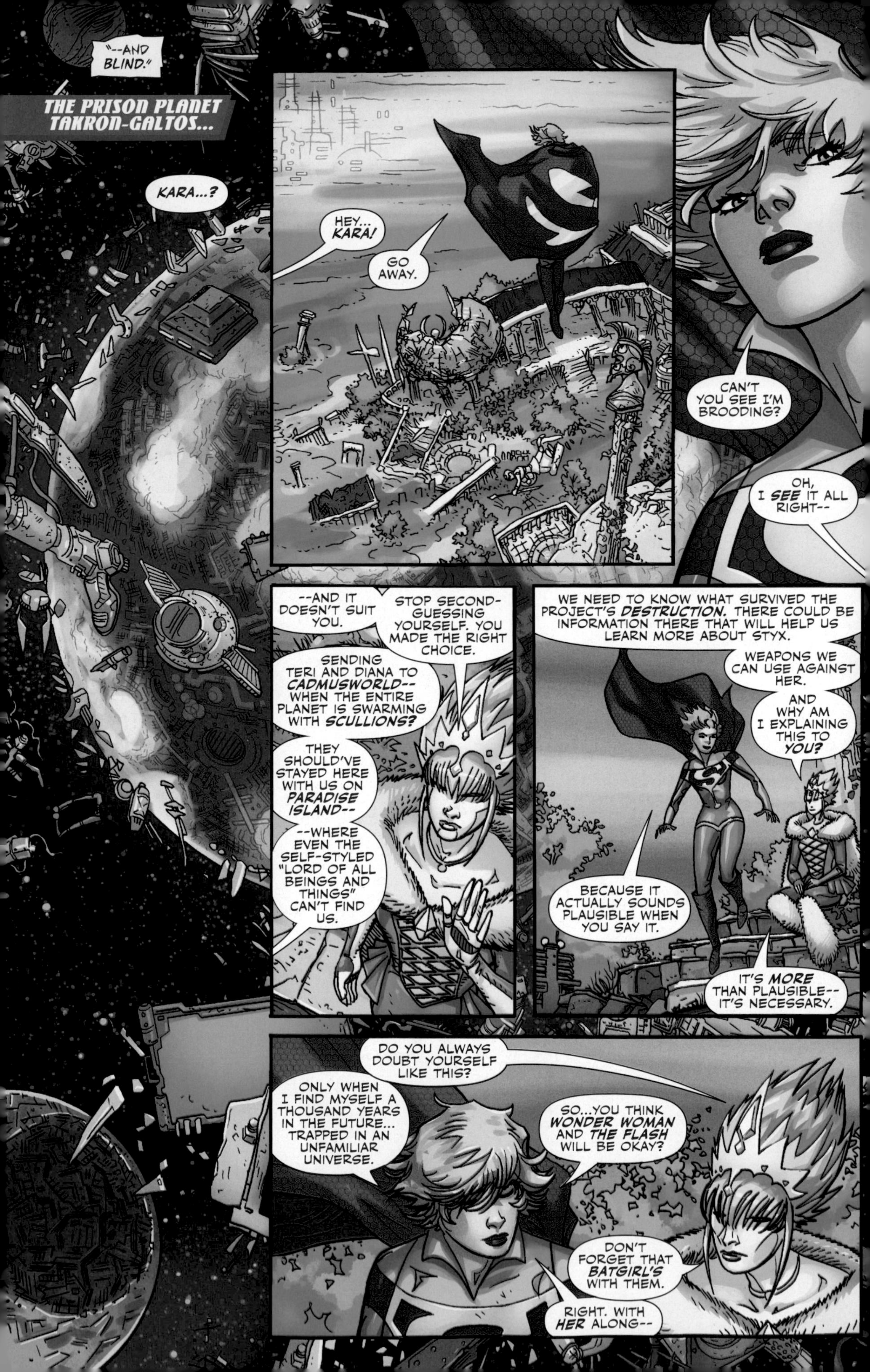
"--AND BLIND."
THE PRISON PLANET TAKRON-GALTOS...
KARA...?
HEY... KARA!
GO AWAY.
CAN'T YOU SEE I'M BROODING?
OH, I SEE IT ALL RIGHT--
--AND IT DOESN'T SUIT YOU.
STOP SECOND-GUESSING YOURSELF. YOU MADE THE RIGHT CHOICE.
SENDING TERI AND DIANA TO CADMUSWORLD-- WHEN THE ENTIRE PLANET IS SWARMING WITH SCULLIONS?
THEY SHOULD'VE STAYED HERE WITH US ON PARADISE ISLAND--
--WHERE EVEN THE SELF-STYLED "LORD OF ALL BEINGS AND THINGS" CAN'T FIND US.
WE NEED TO KNOW WHAT SURVIVED THE PROJECT'S DESTRUCTION. THERE COULD BE INFORMATION THERE THAT WILL HELP US LEARN MORE ABOUT STYX.
WEAPONS WE CAN USE AGAINST HER.
AND WHY AM I EXPLAINING THIS TO YOU?
BECAUSE IT ACTUALLY SOUNDS PLAUSIBLE WHEN YOU SAY IT.
IT'S MORE THAN PLAUSIBLE-- IT'S NECESSARY.
DO YOU ALWAYS DOUBT YOURSELF LIKE THIS?
ONLY WHEN I FIND MYSELF A THOUSAND YEARS IN THE FUTURE... TRAPPED IN AN UNFAMILIAR UNIVERSE.
SO...YOU THINK WONDER WOMAN AND THE FLASH WILL BE OKAY?
DON'T FORGET THAT BATGIRL'S WITH THEM.
RIGHT. WITH HER ALONG--

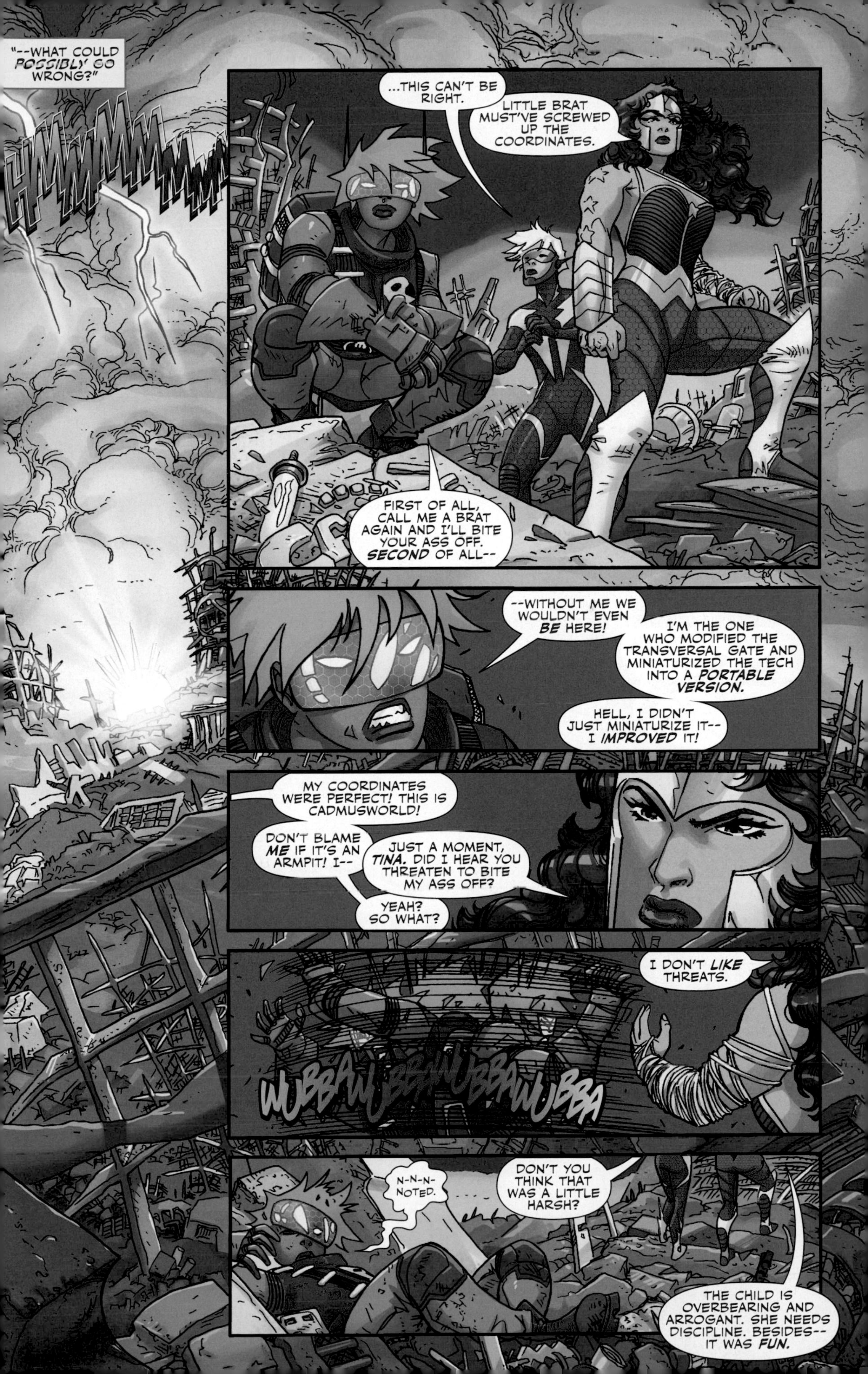
"--WHAT COULD POSSIBLY GO WRONG?"
HMMMMMMMMM
...THIS CAN'T BE RIGHT.
LITTLE BRAT MUST'VE SCREWED UP THE COORDINATES.
FIRST OF ALL, CALL ME A BRAT AGAIN AND I'LL BITE YOUR ASS OFF. SECOND OF ALL--
--WITHOUT ME WE WOULDN'T EVEN BE HERE!
I'M THE ONE WHO MODIFIED THE TRANSVERSAL GATE AND MINIATURIZED THE TECH INTO A PORTABLE VERSION.
HELL, I DIDN'T JUST MINIATURIZE IT-- I IMPROVED IT!
MY COORDINATES WERE PERFECT! THIS IS CADMUSWORLD!
DON'T BLAME ME IF IT'S AN ARMPIT! I--
JUST A MOMENT, TINA. DID I HEAR YOU THREATEN TO BITE MY ASS OFF?
YEAH? SO WHAT?
I DON'T LIKE THREATS.
WUBBAWUBBAWUBBAWUBBA
N-N-N-NOTED.
DON'T YOU THINK THAT WAS A LITTLE HARSH?
THE CHILD IS OVERBEARING AND ARROGANT. SHE NEEDS DISCIPLINE. BESIDES-- IT WAS FUN.

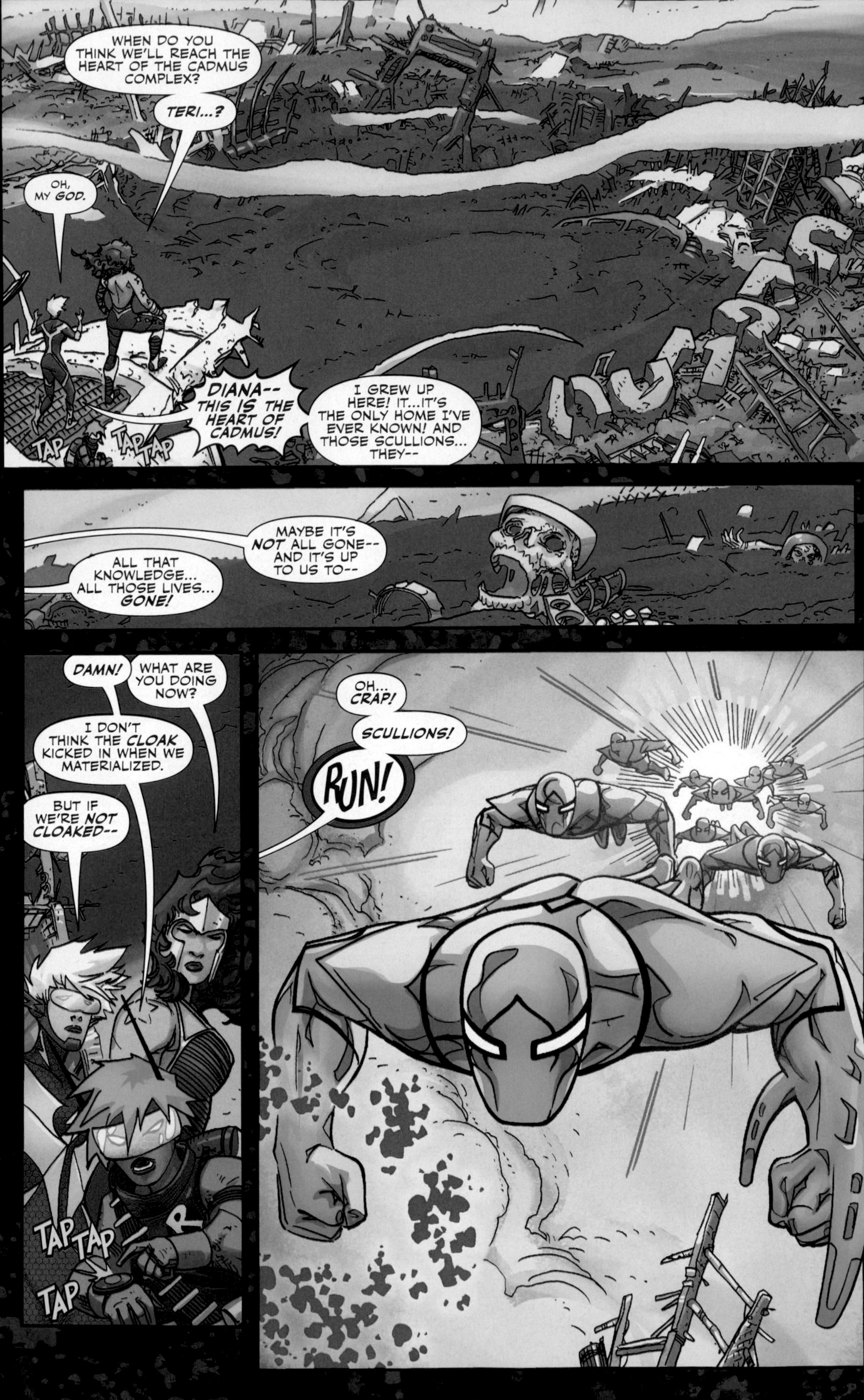

WHEN DO YOU THINK WE'LL REACH THE HEART OF THE CADMUS COMPLEX?
TERI...?
OH, MY GOD.
DIANA-- THIS IS THE HEART OF CADMUS!
I GREW UP HERE! IT...IT'S THE ONLY HOME I'VE EVER KNOWN! AND THOSE SCULLIONS... THEY--
TAP
TAP TAP
ALL THAT KNOWLEDGE... ALL THOSE LIVES... GONE!
MAYBE IT'S NOT ALL GONE-- AND IT'S UP TO US TO--
DAMN!
WHAT ARE YOU DOING NOW?
I DON'T THINK THE CLOAK KICKED IN WHEN WE MATERIALIZED.
BUT IF WE'RE NOT CLOAKED--
TAP TAP
TAP
OH... CRAP!
SCULLIONS!
RUN!

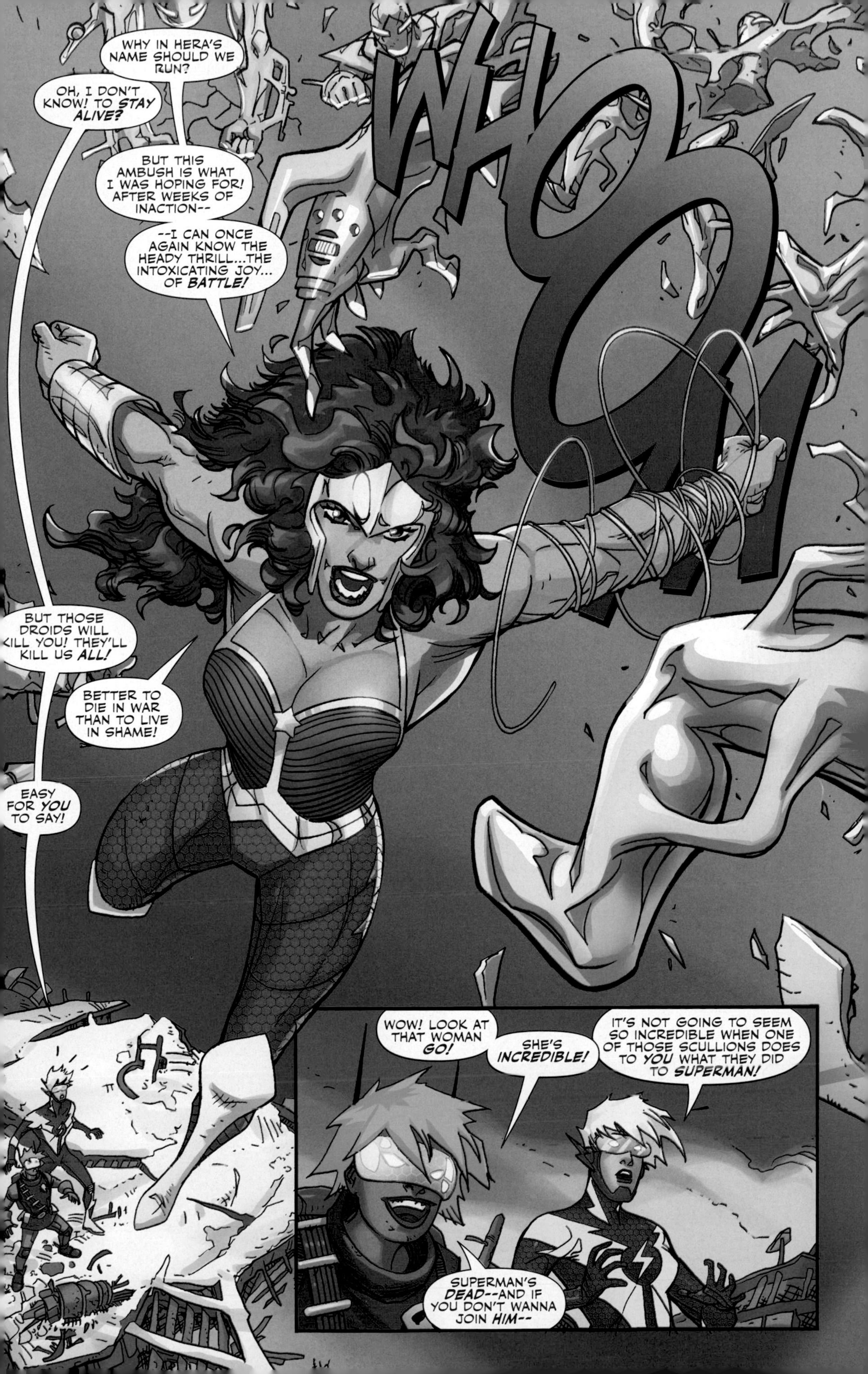
WHY IN HERA'S NAME SHOULD WE RUN?
OH, I DON'T KNOW! TO STAY ALIVE?
BUT THIS AMBUSH IS WHAT I WAS HOPING FOR! AFTER WEEKS OF INACTION--
--I CAN ONCE AGAIN KNOW THE HEADY THRILL...THE INTOXICATING JOY... OF BATTLE!
WHOOM
BUT THOSE DROIDS WILL KILL YOU! THEY'LL KILL US ALL!
BETTER TO DIE IN WAR THAN TO LIVE IN SHAME!
EASY FOR YOU TO SAY!
WOW! LOOK AT THAT WOMAN GO!
SHE'S INCREDIBLE!
IT'S NOT GOING TO SEEM SO INCREDIBLE WHEN ONE OF THOSE SCULLIONS DOES TO YOU WHAT THEY DID TO SUPERMAN!
SUPERMAN'S DEAD--AND IF YOU DON'T WANNA JOIN HIM--

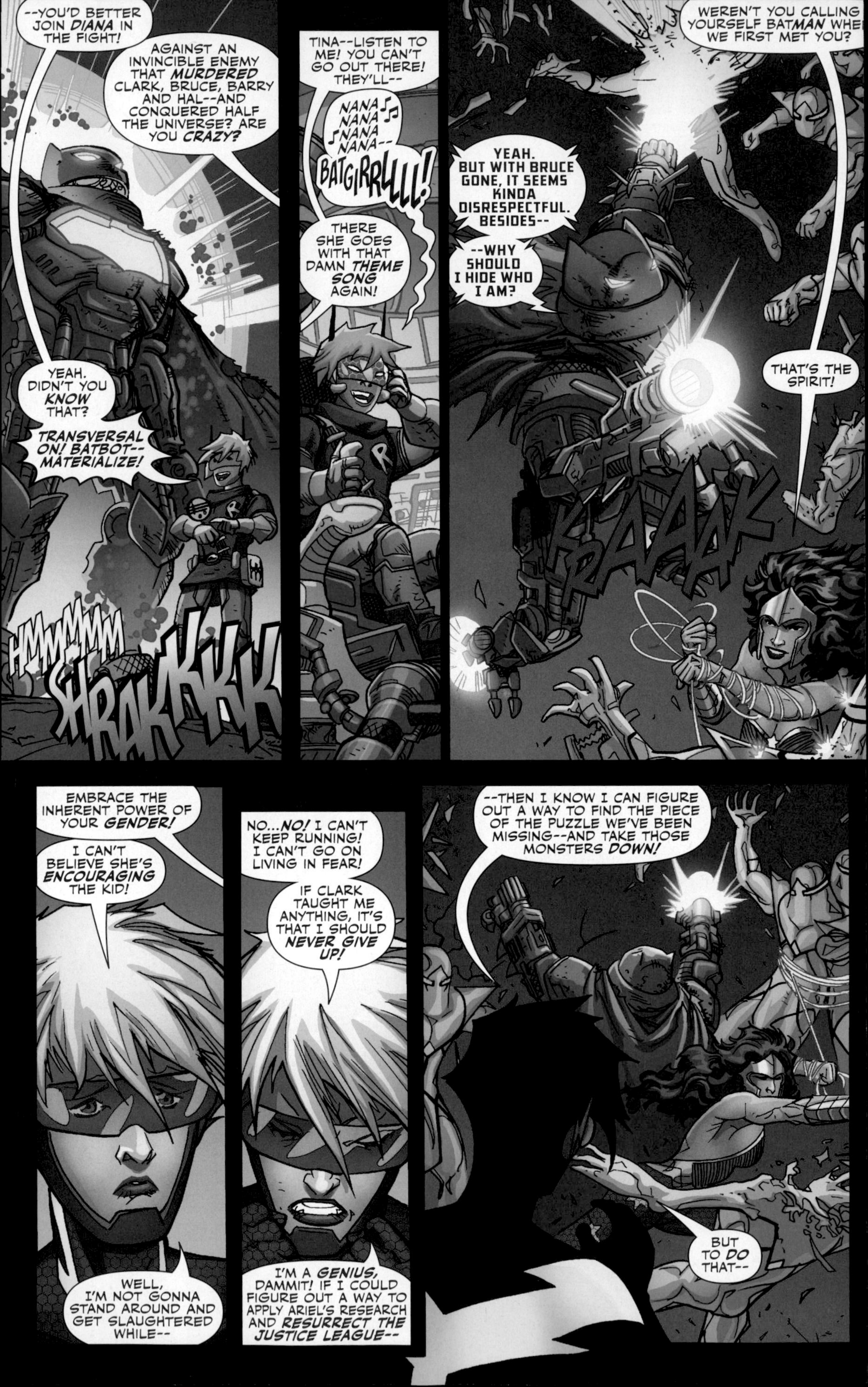
--YOU'D BETTER JOIN DIANA IN THE FIGHT!
AGAINST AN INVINCIBLE ENEMY THAT MURDERED CLARK, BRUCE, BARRY AND HAL--AND CONQUERED HALF THE UNIVERSE? ARE YOU CRAZY?
YEAH. DIDN'T YOU KNOW THAT?
TRANSVERSAL ON! BATBOT--MATERIALIZE!
HMMMMM
SHRAKKKK
TINA--LISTEN TO ME! YOU CAN'T GO OUT THERE! THEY'LL--
NANA NANA NANA NANA--
BATGIRRLLLL!
THERE SHE GOES WITH THAT DAMN THEME SONG AGAIN!
WEREN'T YOU CALLING YOURSELF BATMAN WHEN WE FIRST MET YOU?
YEAH. BUT WITH BRUCE GONE, IT SEEMS KINDA DISRESPECTFUL. BESIDES--
--WHY SHOULD I HIDE WHO I AM?
THAT'S THE SPIRIT!
KRAAAK
EMBRACE THE INHERENT POWER OF YOUR GENDER!
I CAN'T BELIEVE SHE'S ENCOURAGING THE KID!
WELL, I'M NOT GONNA STAND AROUND AND GET SLAUGHTERED WHILE--
NO...NO! I CAN'T KEEP RUNNING! I CAN'T GO ON LIVING IN FEAR!
IF CLARK TAUGHT ME ANYTHING, IT'S THAT I SHOULD NEVER GIVE UP!
I'M A GENIUS, DAMMIT! IF I COULD FIGURE OUT A WAY TO APPLY ARIEL'S RESEARCH AND RESURRECT THE JUSTICE LEAGUE--
--THEN I KNOW I CAN FIGURE OUT A WAY TO FIND THE PIECE OF THE PUZZLE WE'VE BEEN MISSING--AND TAKE THOSE MONSTERS DOWN!
BUT TO DO THAT--

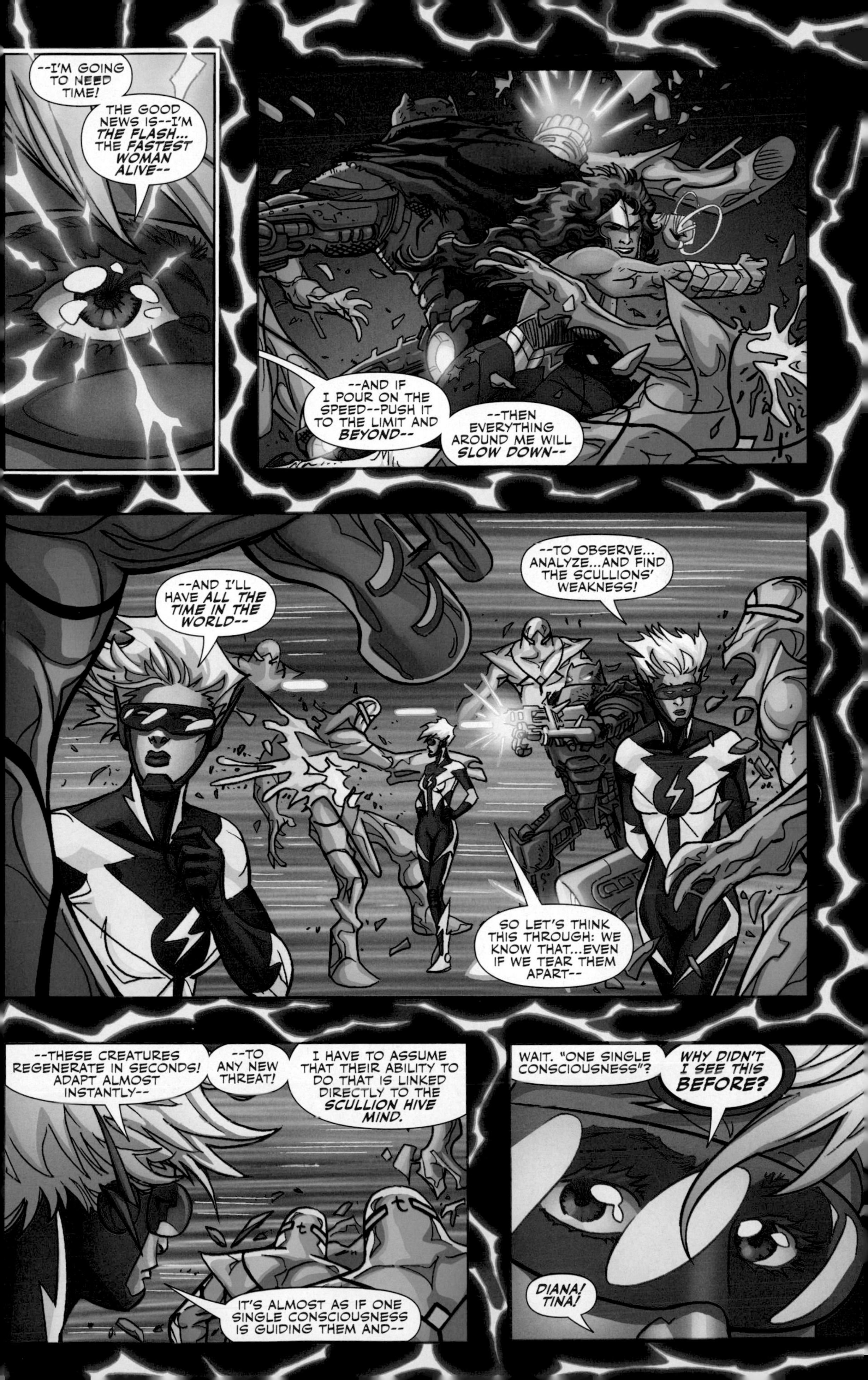
--I'M GOING TO NEED TIME!
THE GOOD NEWS IS--I'M THE FLASH... THE FASTEST WOMAN ALIVE--
--AND IF I POUR ON THE SPEED--PUSH IT TO THE LIMIT AND BEYOND--
--THEN EVERYTHING AROUND ME WILL SLOW DOWN--
--AND I'LL HAVE ALL THE TIME IN THE WORLD--
--TO OBSERVE... ANALYZE...AND FIND THE SCULLIONS' WEAKNESS!
SO LET'S THINK THIS THROUGH: WE KNOW THAT...EVEN IF WE TEAR THEM APART--
--THESE CREATURES REGENERATE IN SECONDS! ADAPT ALMOST INSTANTLY--
--TO ANY NEW THREAT!
I HAVE TO ASSUME THAT THEIR ABILITY TO DO THAT IS LINKED DIRECTLY TO THE SCULLION HIVE MIND.
IT'S ALMOST AS IF ONE SINGLE CONSCIOUSNESS IS GUIDING THEM AND--
WAIT. "ONE SINGLE CONSCIOUSNESS"?
WHY DIDN'T I SEE THIS BEFORE?
DIANA! TINA!

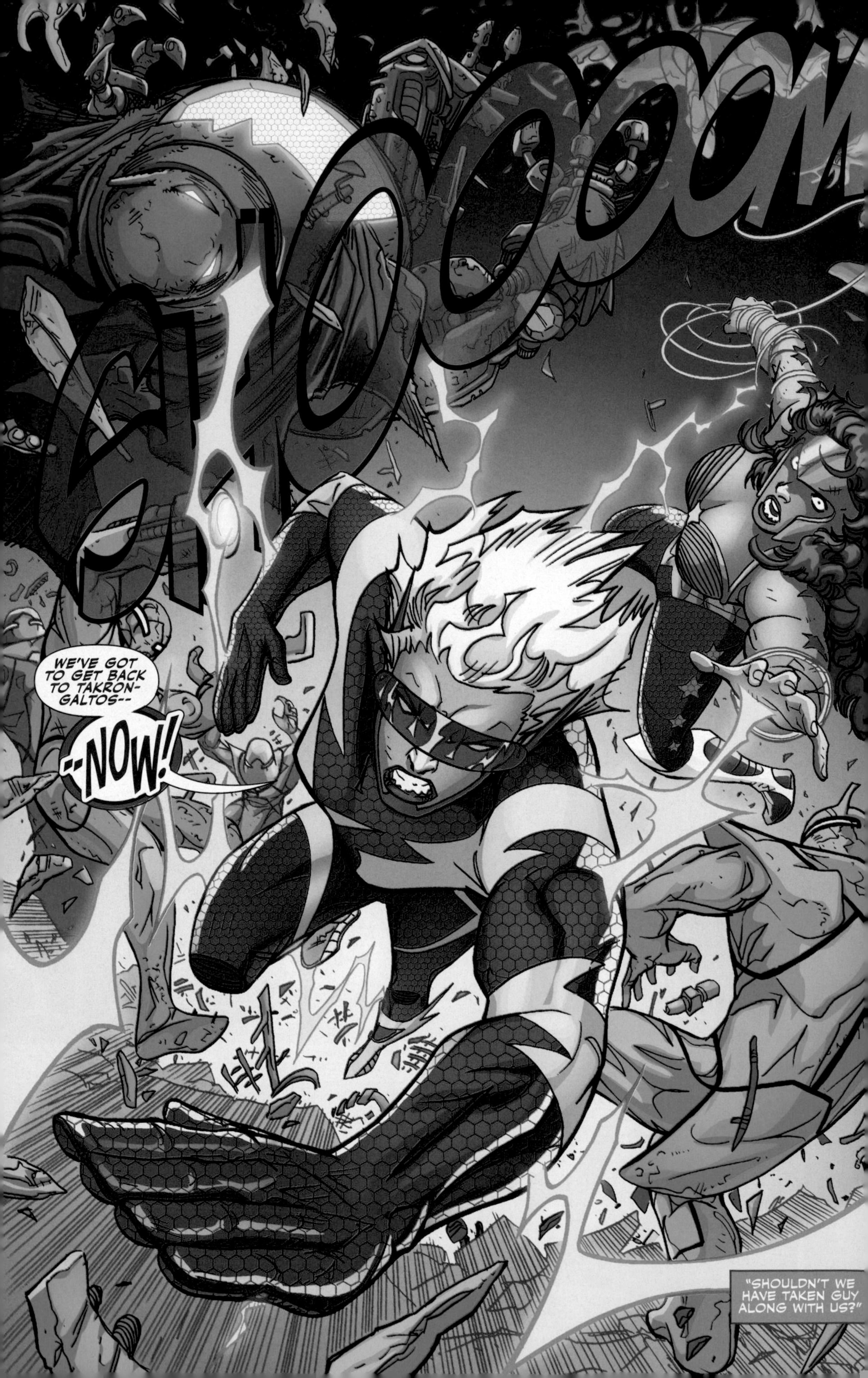
WE'VE GOT TO GET BACK TO TAKRON-GALTOS--
--NOW!
"SHOULDN'T WE HAVE TAKEN GUY ALONG WITH US?"

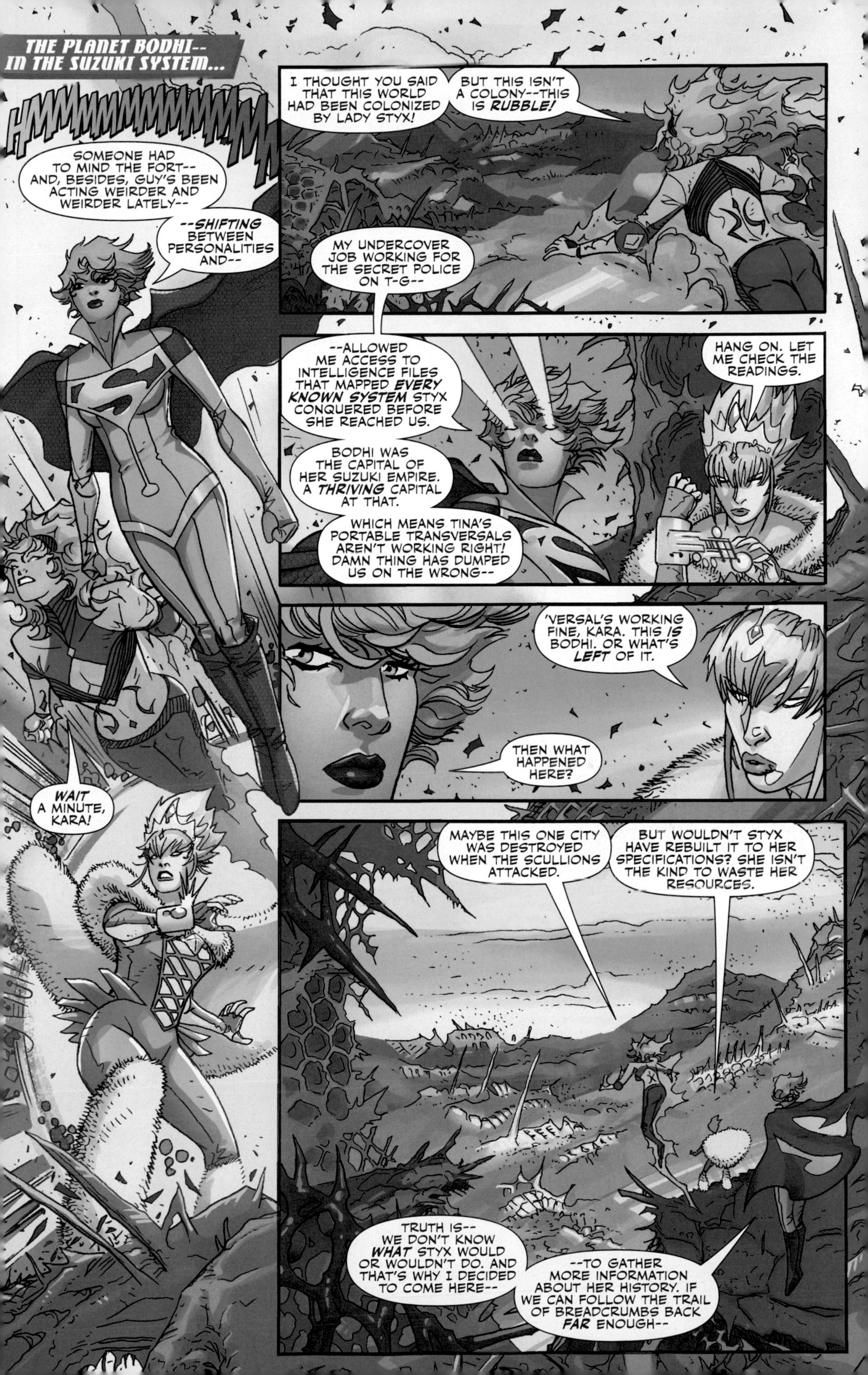
THE PLANET BODHI--
IN THE SUZUKI SYSTEM...
HMMMMMMMMMMM
SOMEONE HAD TO MIND THE FORT-- AND, BESIDES, GUY'S BEEN ACTING WEIRDER AND WEIRDER LATELY--
--SHIFTING BETWEEN PERSONALITIES AND--
WAIT A MINUTE, KARA!
I THOUGHT YOU SAID THAT THIS WORLD HAD BEEN COLONIZED BY LADY STYX!
BUT THIS ISN'T A COLONY--THIS IS RUBBLE!
MY UNDERCOVER JOB WORKING FOR THE SECRET POLICE ON T-G--
--ALLOWED ME ACCESS TO INTELLIGENCE FILES THAT MAPPED EVERY KNOWN SYSTEM STYX CONQUERED BEFORE SHE REACHED US.
BODHI WAS THE CAPITAL OF HER SUZUKI EMPIRE. A THRIVING CAPITAL AT THAT.
WHICH MEANS TINA'S PORTABLE TRANSVERSALS AREN'T WORKING RIGHT! DAMN THING HAS DUMPED US ON THE WRONG--
HANG ON. LET ME CHECK THE READINGS.
'VERSAL'S WORKING FINE, KARA. THIS IS BODHI. OR WHAT'S LEFT OF IT.
THEN WHAT HAPPENED HERE?
MAYBE THIS ONE CITY WAS DESTROYED WHEN THE SCULLIONS ATTACKED.
BUT WOULDN'T STYX HAVE REBUILT IT TO HER SPECIFICATIONS? SHE ISN'T THE KIND TO WASTE HER RESOURCES.
TRUTH IS-- WE DON'T KNOW WHAT STYX WOULD OR WOULDN'T DO. AND THAT'S WHY I DECIDED TO COME HERE--
--TO GATHER MORE INFORMATION ABOUT HER HISTORY. IF WE CAN FOLLOW THE TRAIL OF BREADCRUMBS BACK FAR ENOUGH--

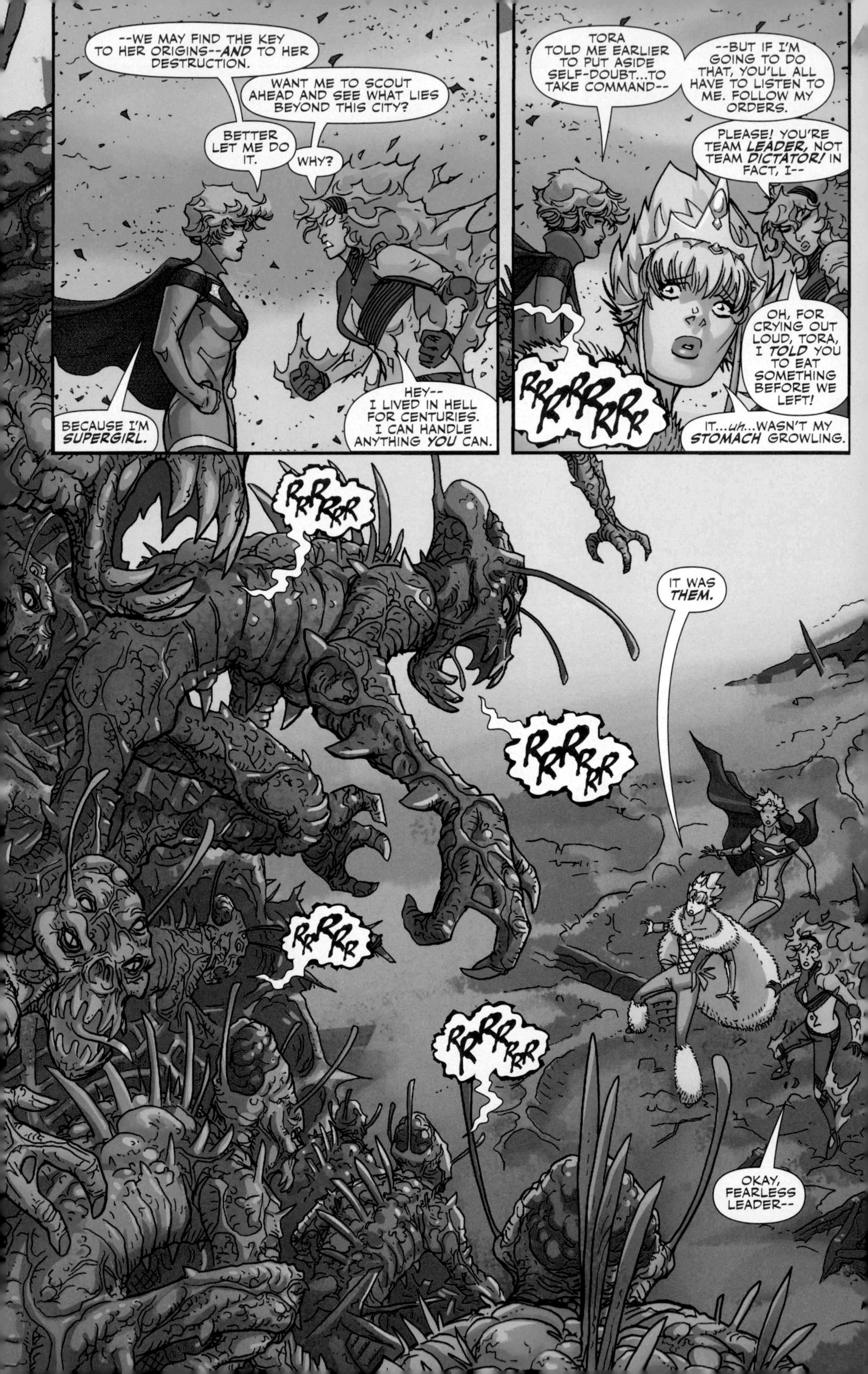
--WE MAY FIND THE KEY TO HER ORIGINS--AND TO HER DESTRUCTION.
WANT ME TO SCOUT AHEAD AND SEE WHAT LIES BEYOND THIS CITY?
BETTER LET ME DO IT.
WHY?
BECAUSE I'M SUPERGIRL.
HEY-- I LIVED IN HELL FOR CENTURIES. I CAN HANDLE ANYTHING YOU CAN.
TORA TOLD ME EARLIER TO PUT ASIDE SELF-DOUBT...TO TAKE COMMAND--
--BUT IF I'M GOING TO DO THAT, YOU'LL ALL HAVE TO LISTEN TO ME. FOLLOW MY ORDERS.
PLEASE! YOU'RE TEAM LEADER, NOT TEAM DICTATOR! IN FACT, I--
RRRRRRRR
OH, FOR CRYING OUT LOUD, TORA, I TOLD YOU TO EAT SOMETHING BEFORE WE LEFT!
IT...uh...WASN'T MY STOMACH GROWLING.
RRRRRR
IT WAS THEM.
RRRRRR
RRRRR
RRRRRR
OKAY, FEARLESS LEADER--

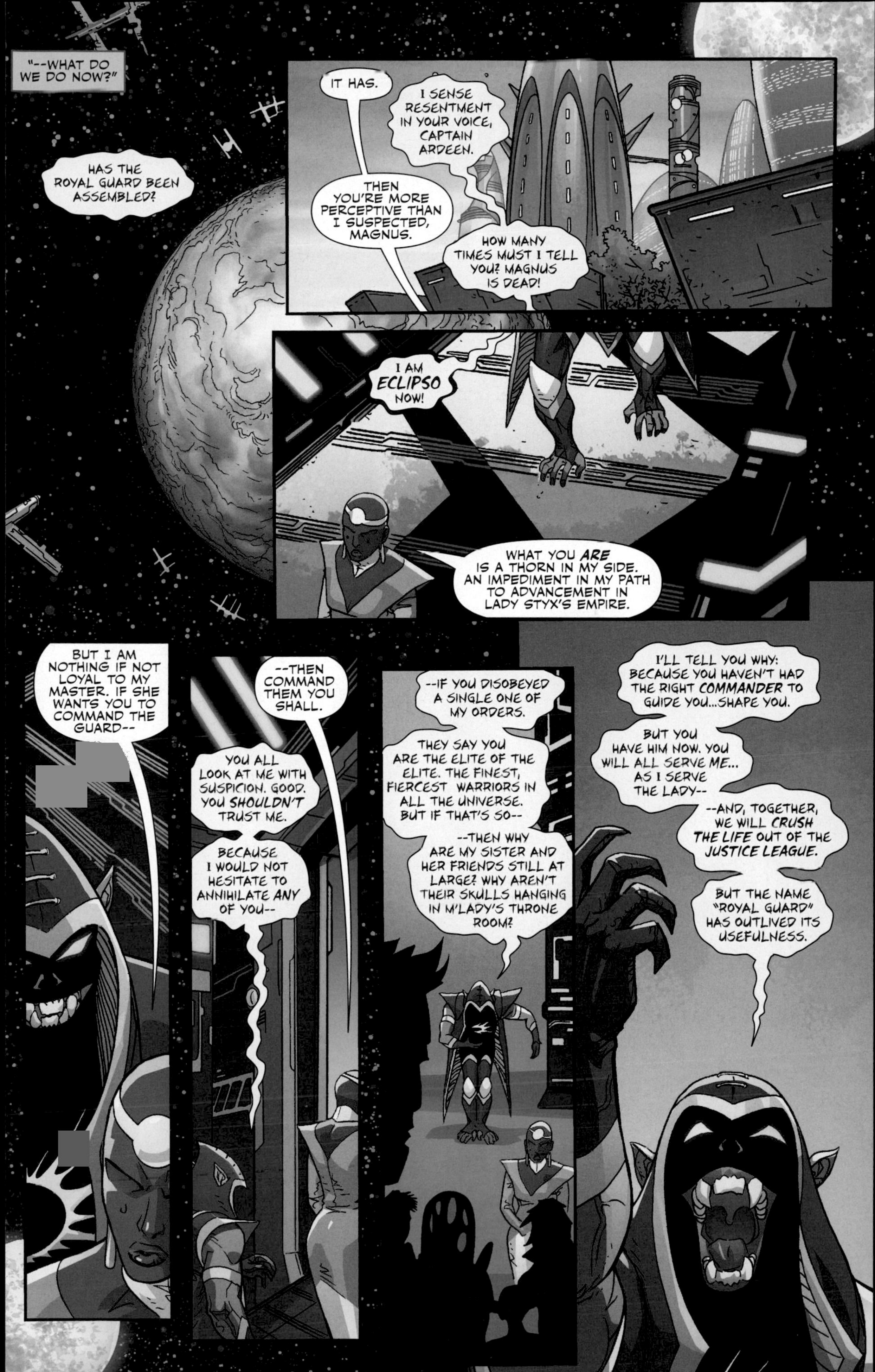
"--WHAT DO WE DO NOW?"
HAS THE ROYAL GUARD BEEN ASSEMBLED?
IT HAS.
I SENSE RESENTMENT IN YOUR VOICE, CAPTAIN ARDEEN.
THEN YOU'RE MORE PERCEPTIVE THAN I SUSPECTED, MAGNUS.
HOW MANY TIMES MUST I TELL YOU? MAGNUS IS DEAD!
I AM *ECLIPSO* NOW!
WHAT YOU *ARE* IS A THORN IN MY SIDE. AN IMPEDIMENT IN MY PATH TO ADVANCEMENT IN LADY STYX'S EMPIRE.
BUT I AM NOTHING IF NOT LOYAL TO MY MASTER. IF SHE WANTS YOU TO COMMAND THE GUARD--
--THEN COMMAND THEM YOU SHALL.
YOU ALL LOOK AT ME WITH SUSPICION. GOOD. YOU *SHOULDN'T* TRUST ME.
BECAUSE I WOULD NOT HESITATE TO ANNIHILATE *ANY* OF YOU--
--IF YOU DISOBEYED A SINGLE ONE OF MY ORDERS.
THEY SAY YOU ARE THE ELITE OF THE ELITE. THE FINEST, FIERCEST WARRIORS IN ALL THE UNIVERSE. BUT IF THAT'S SO--
--THEN WHY ARE MY SISTER AND HER FRIENDS STILL AT LARGE? WHY AREN'T THEIR SKULLS HANGING IN M'LADY'S THRONE ROOM?
I'LL TELL YOU WHY: BECAUSE YOU HAVEN'T HAD THE RIGHT *COMMANDER* TO GUIDE YOU...SHAPE YOU.
BUT YOU HAVE HIM NOW. YOU WILL ALL SERVE *ME*... AS I SERVE THE LADY--
--AND, TOGETHER, WE WILL *CRUSH THE LIFE* OUT OF THE *JUSTICE LEAGUE*.
BUT THE NAME "ROYAL GUARD" HAS OUTLIVED ITS USEFULNESS.

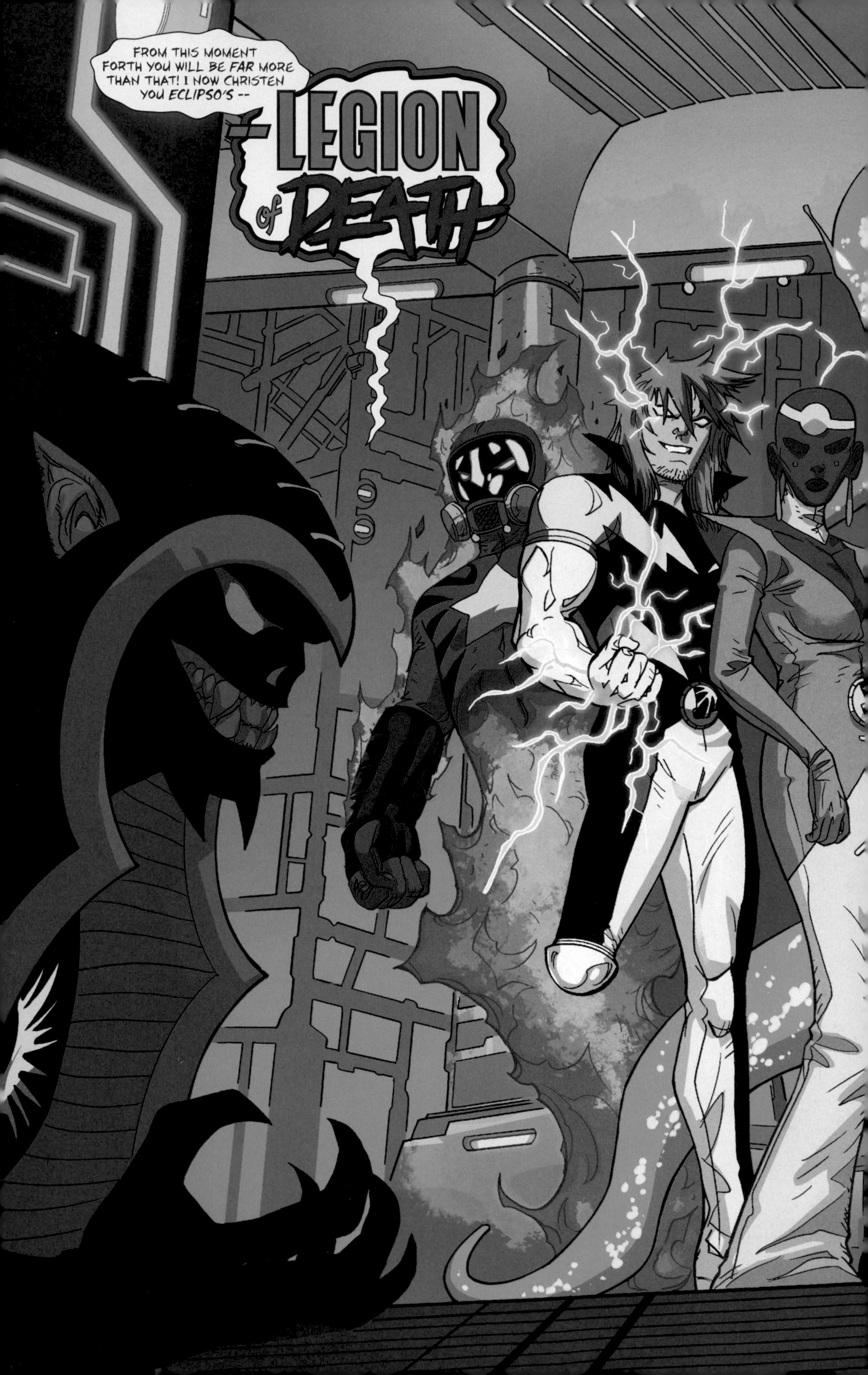
FROM THIS MOMENT FORTH YOU WILL BE FAR MORE THAN THAT! I NOW CHRISTEN YOU ECLIPSO'S --
LEGION of DEATH

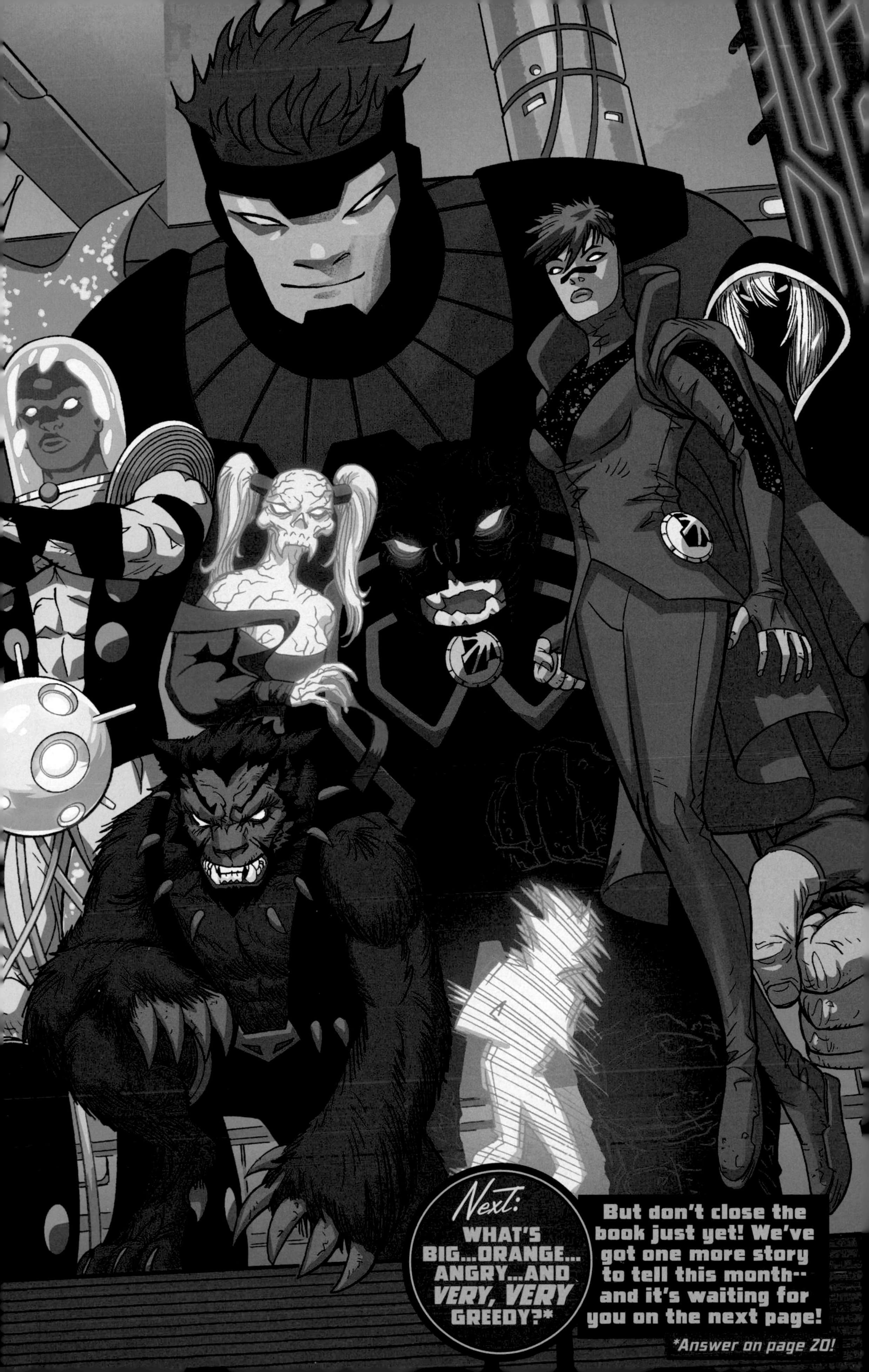
Next:
WHAT'S BIG...ORANGE... ANGRY...AND VERY, VERY GREEDY?*
But don't close the book just yet! We've got one more story to tell this month-- and it's waiting for you on the next page!
*Answer on page 20!

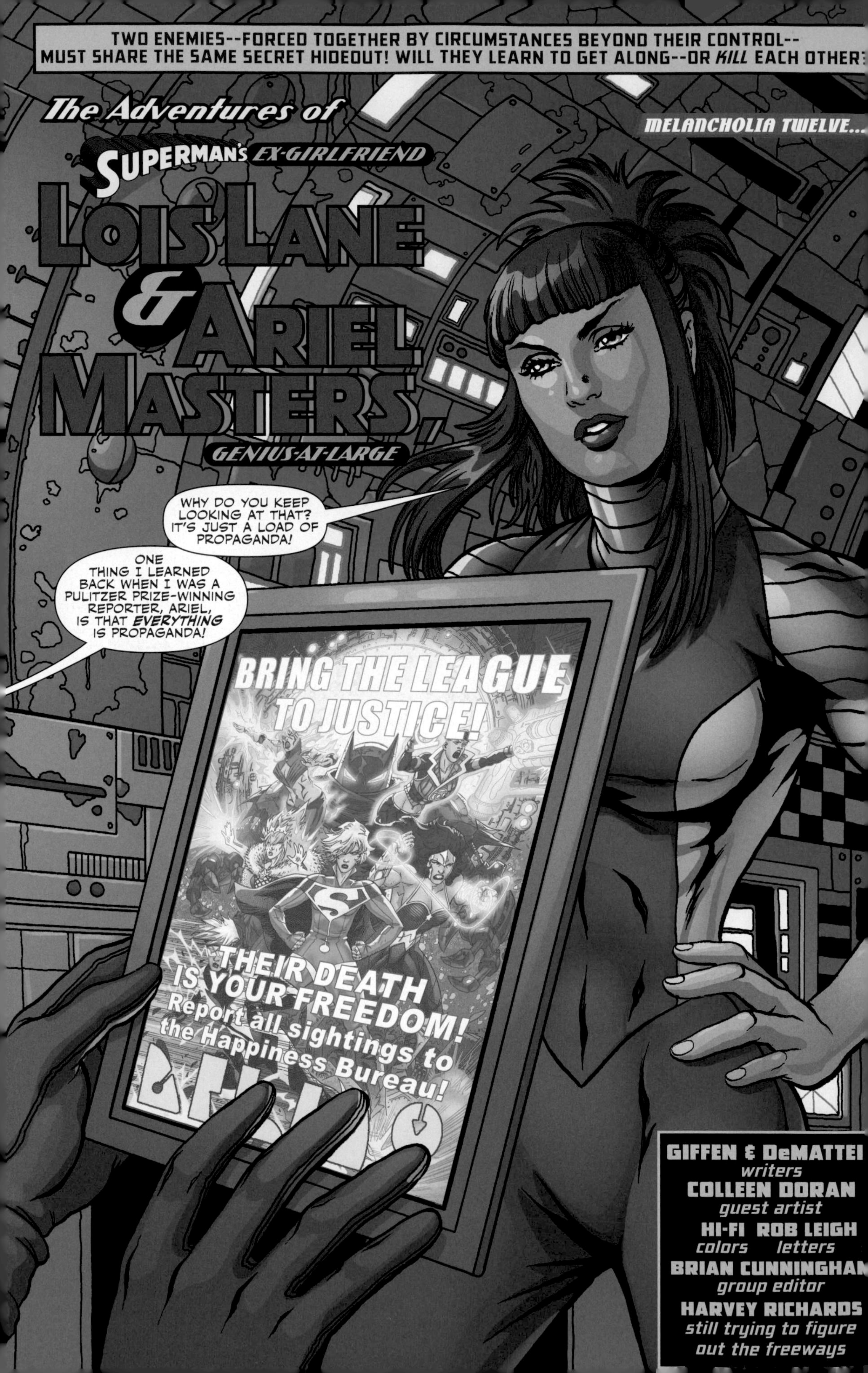
TWO ENEMIES--FORCED TOGETHER BY CIRCUMSTANCES BEYOND THEIR CONTROL--
MUST SHARE THE SAME SECRET HIDEOUT! WILL THEY LEARN TO GET ALONG--OR KILL EACH OTHER?
The Adventures of
SUPERMAN's EX-GIRLFRIEND
LOIS LANE & ARIEL MASTERS,
GENIUS-AT-LARGE
MELANCHOLIA TWELVE...
WHY DO YOU KEEP LOOKING AT THAT? IT'S JUST A LOAD OF PROPAGANDA!
ONE THING I LEARNED BACK WHEN I WAS A PULITZER PRIZE-WINNING REPORTER, ARIEL, IS THAT EVERYTHING IS PROPAGANDA!
BRING THE LEAGUE TO JUSTICE!
THEIR DEATH IS YOUR FREEDOM!
Report all sightings to the Happiness Bureau!
GIFFEN & DeMATTEIS writers
COLLEEN DORAN guest artist
HI-FI colors
ROB LEIGH letters
BRIAN CUNNINGHAM group editor
HARVEY RICHARDS still trying to figure out the freeways

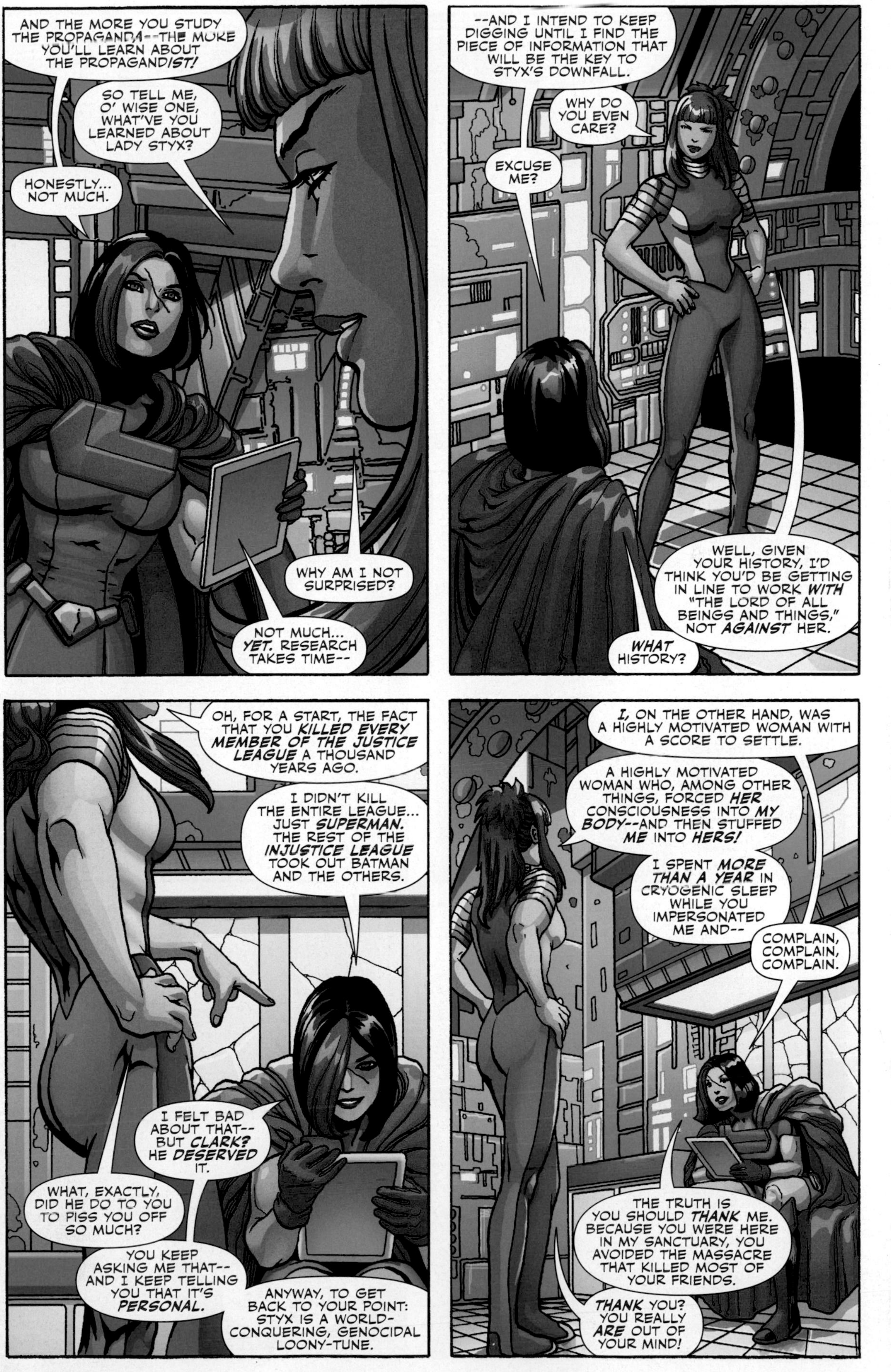
AND THE MORE YOU STUDY THE PROPAGANDA--THE MORE YOU'LL LEARN ABOUT THE PROPAGANDIST!
SO TELL ME, O' WISE ONE, WHAT'VE YOU LEARNED ABOUT LADY STYX?
HONESTLY... NOT MUCH.
WHY AM I NOT SURPRISED?
NOT MUCH... YET. RESEARCH TAKES TIME--
--AND I INTEND TO KEEP DIGGING UNTIL I FIND THE PIECE OF INFORMATION THAT WILL BE THE KEY TO STYX'S DOWNFALL.
WHY DO YOU EVEN CARE?
EXCUSE ME?
WELL, GIVEN YOUR HISTORY, I'D THINK YOU'D BE GETTING IN LINE TO WORK WITH "THE LORD OF ALL BEINGS AND THINGS," NOT AGAINST HER.
WHAT HISTORY?
OH, FOR A START, THE FACT THAT YOU KILLED EVERY MEMBER OF THE JUSTICE LEAGUE A THOUSAND YEARS AGO.
I DIDN'T KILL THE ENTIRE LEAGUE... JUST SUPERMAN. THE REST OF THE INJUSTICE LEAGUE TOOK OUT BATMAN AND THE OTHERS.
I FELT BAD ABOUT THAT--BUT CLARK? HE DESERVED IT.
WHAT, EXACTLY, DID HE DO TO YOU TO PISS YOU OFF SO MUCH?
YOU KEEP ASKING ME THAT--AND I KEEP TELLING YOU THAT IT'S PERSONAL.
ANYWAY, TO GET BACK TO YOUR POINT: STYX IS A WORLD-CONQUERING, GENOCIDAL LOONY-TUNE.
I, ON THE OTHER HAND, WAS A HIGHLY MOTIVATED WOMAN WITH A SCORE TO SETTLE.
A HIGHLY MOTIVATED WOMAN WHO, AMONG OTHER THINGS, FORCED HER CONSCIOUSNESS INTO MY BODY--AND THEN STUFFED ME INTO HERS!
I SPENT MORE THAN A YEAR IN CRYOGENIC SLEEP WHILE YOU IMPERSONATED ME AND--
COMPLAIN, COMPLAIN, COMPLAIN.
THE TRUTH IS YOU SHOULD THANK ME. BECAUSE YOU WERE HERE IN MY SANCTUARY, YOU AVOIDED THE MASSACRE THAT KILLED MOST OF YOUR FRIENDS.
THANK YOU? YOU REALLY ARE OUT OF YOUR MIND!

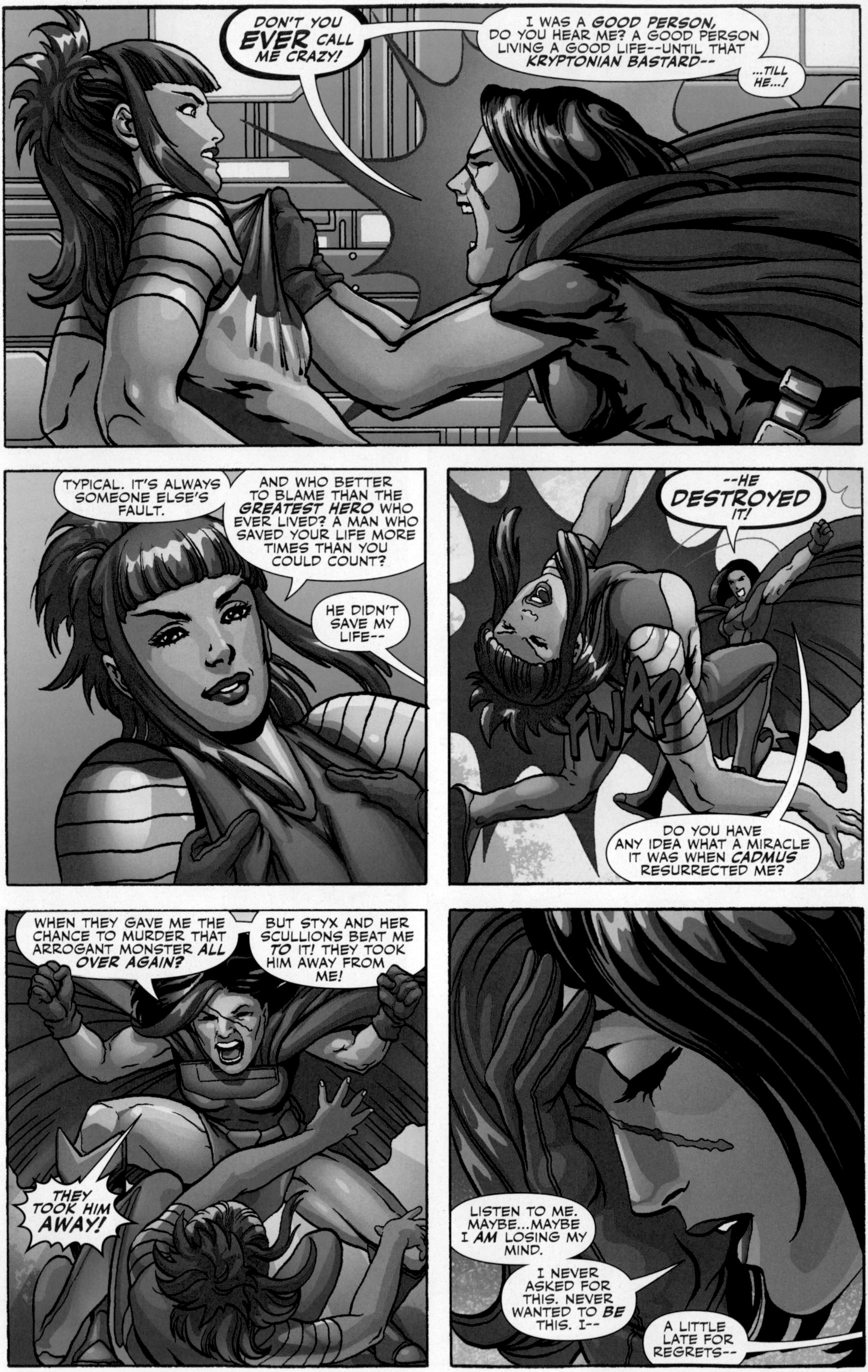
DON'T YOU EVER CALL ME CRAZY!
I WAS A GOOD PERSON, DO YOU HEAR ME? A GOOD PERSON LIVING A GOOD LIFE--UNTIL THAT KRYPTONIAN BASTARD--
...TILL HE...!
TYPICAL. IT'S ALWAYS SOMEONE ELSE'S FAULT.
AND WHO BETTER TO BLAME THAN THE GREATEST HERO WHO EVER LIVED? A MAN WHO SAVED YOUR LIFE MORE TIMES THAN YOU COULD COUNT?
HE DIDN'T SAVE MY LIFE--
--HE DESTROYED IT!
FWAP
DO YOU HAVE ANY IDEA WHAT A MIRACLE IT WAS WHEN CADMUS RESURRECTED ME?
WHEN THEY GAVE ME THE CHANCE TO MURDER THAT ARROGANT MONSTER ALL OVER AGAIN?
BUT STYX AND HER SCULLIONS BEAT ME TO IT! THEY TOOK HIM AWAY FROM ME!
THEY TOOK HIM AWAY!
LISTEN TO ME. MAYBE...MAYBE I AM LOSING MY MIND.
I NEVER ASKED FOR THIS. NEVER WANTED TO BE THIS. I--
A LITTLE LATE FOR REGRETS--

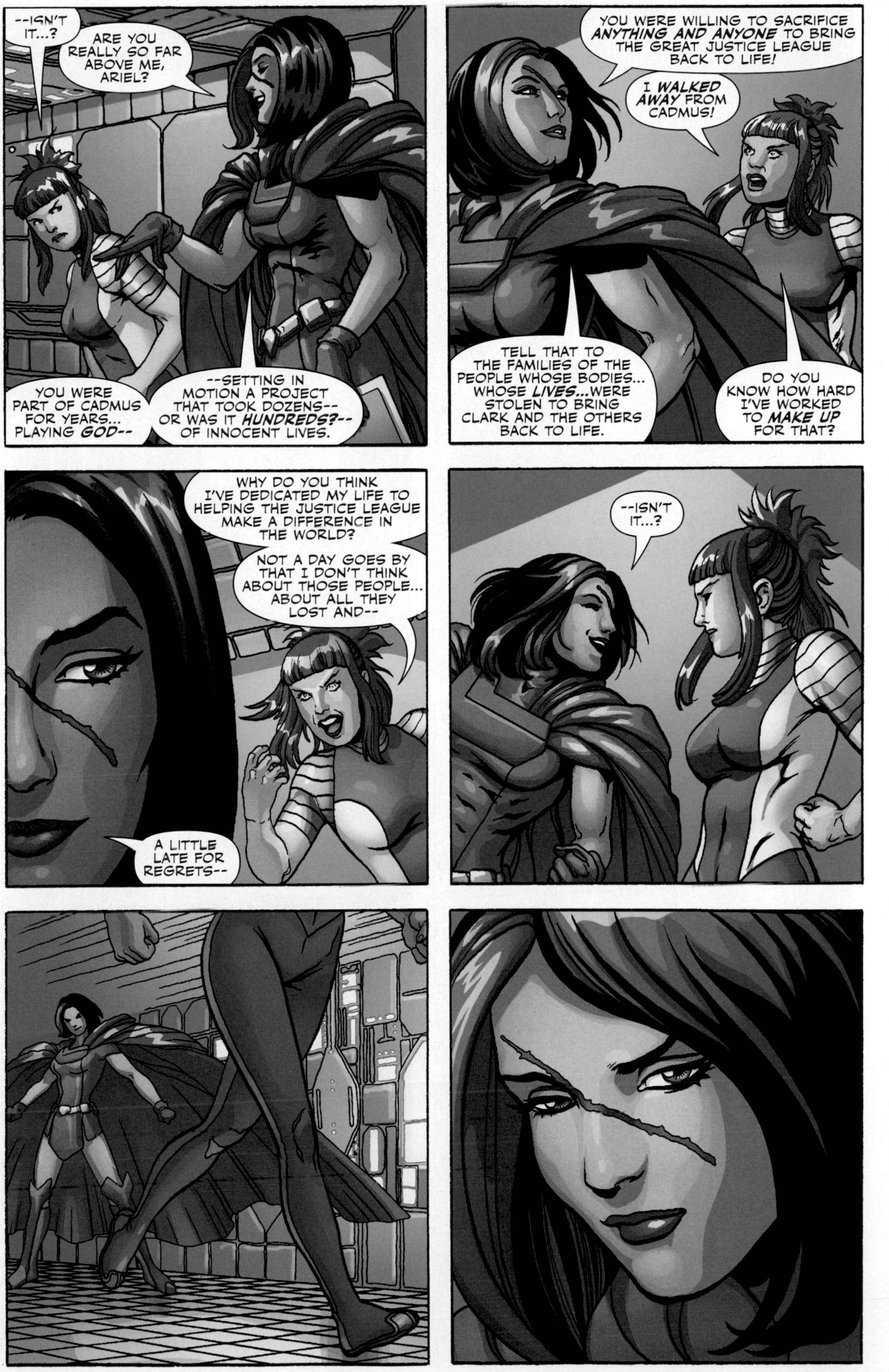
--ISN'T IT...?
ARE YOU REALLY SO FAR ABOVE ME, ARIEL?
YOU WERE PART OF CADMUS FOR YEARS... PLAYING GOD--
--SETTING IN MOTION A PROJECT THAT TOOK DOZENS-- OR WAS IT HUNDREDS?-- OF INNOCENT LIVES.
YOU WERE WILLING TO SACRIFICE ANYTHING AND ANYONE TO BRING THE GREAT JUSTICE LEAGUE BACK TO LIFE!
I WALKED AWAY FROM CADMUS!
TELL THAT TO THE FAMILIES OF THE PEOPLE WHOSE BODIES... WHOSE LIVES...WERE STOLEN TO BRING CLARK AND THE OTHERS BACK TO LIFE.
DO YOU KNOW HOW HARD I'VE WORKED TO MAKE UP FOR THAT?
WHY DO YOU THINK I'VE DEDICATED MY LIFE TO HELPING THE JUSTICE LEAGUE MAKE A DIFFERENCE IN THE WORLD?
NOT A DAY GOES BY THAT I DON'T THINK ABOUT THOSE PEOPLE... ABOUT ALL THEY LOST AND--
A LITTLE LATE FOR REGRETS--
--ISN'T IT...?

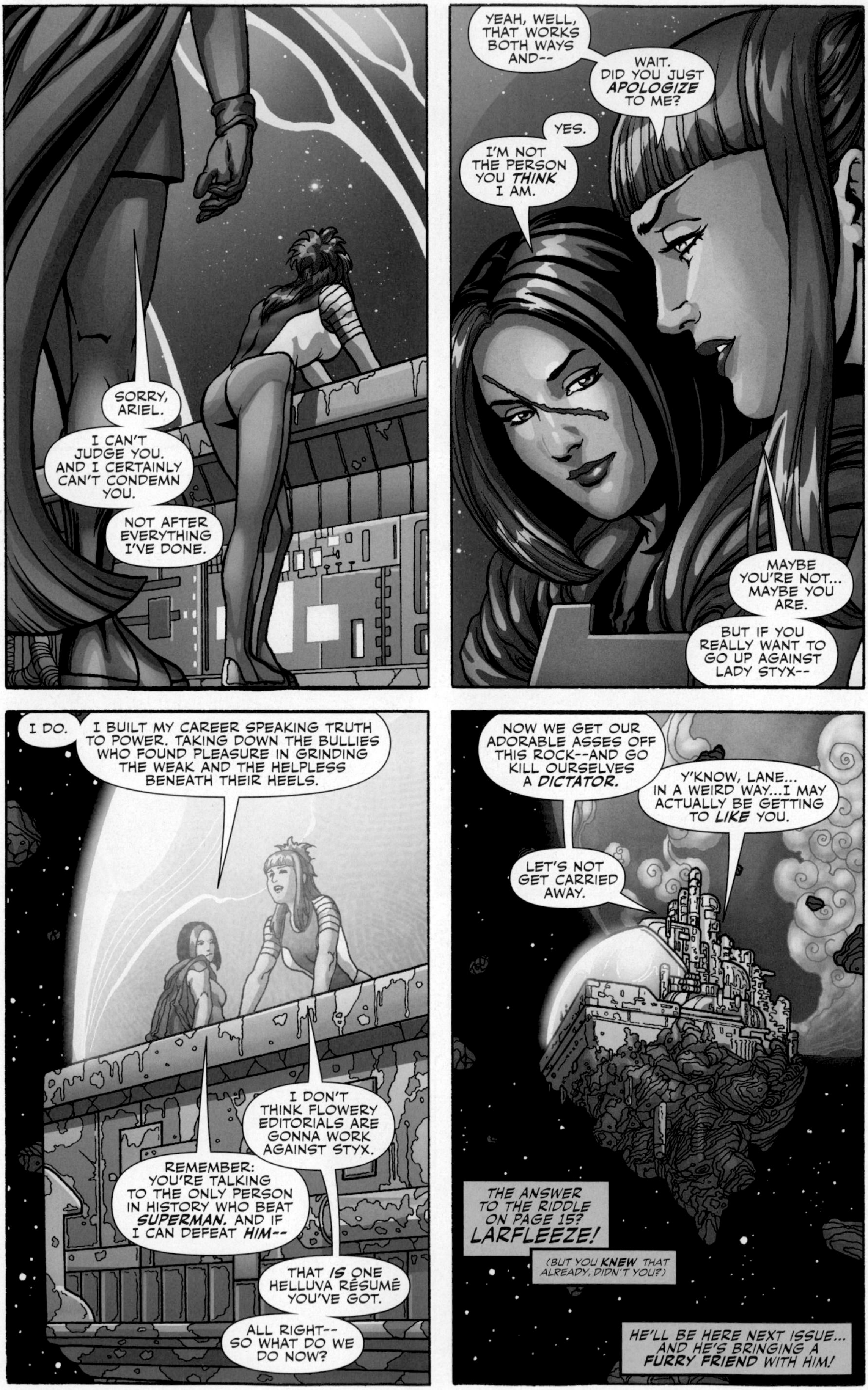
SORRY, ARIEL.
I CAN'T JUDGE YOU. AND I CERTAINLY CAN'T CONDEMN YOU.
NOT AFTER EVERYTHING I'VE DONE.
YEAH, WELL, THAT WORKS BOTH WAYS AND--
WAIT. DID YOU JUST APOLOGIZE TO ME?
YES.
I'M NOT THE PERSON YOU THINK I AM.
MAYBE YOU'RE NOT... MAYBE YOU ARE.
BUT IF YOU REALLY WANT TO GO UP AGAINST LADY STYX--
I DO.
I BUILT MY CAREER SPEAKING TRUTH TO POWER. TAKING DOWN THE BULLIES WHO FOUND PLEASURE IN GRINDING THE WEAK AND THE HELPLESS BENEATH THEIR HEELS.
I DON'T THINK FLOWERY EDITORIALS ARE GONNA WORK AGAINST STYX.
REMEMBER: YOU'RE TALKING TO THE ONLY PERSON IN HISTORY WHO BEAT SUPERMAN. AND IF I CAN DEFEAT HIM--
THAT IS ONE HELLUVA RÉSUMÉ YOU'VE GOT.
ALL RIGHT-- SO WHAT DO WE DO NOW?
NOW WE GET OUR ADORABLE ASSES OFF THIS ROCK--AND GO KILL OURSELVES A DICTATOR.
Y'KNOW, LANE... IN A WEIRD WAY...I MAY ACTUALLY BE GETTING TO LIKE YOU.
LET'S NOT GET CARRIED AWAY.
THE ANSWER TO THE RIDDLE ON PAGE 15? LARFLEEZE!
(BUT YOU KNEW THAT ALREADY, DIDN'T YOU?)
HE'LL BE HERE NEXT ISSUE... AND HE'S BRINGING A FURRY FRIEND WITH HIM!

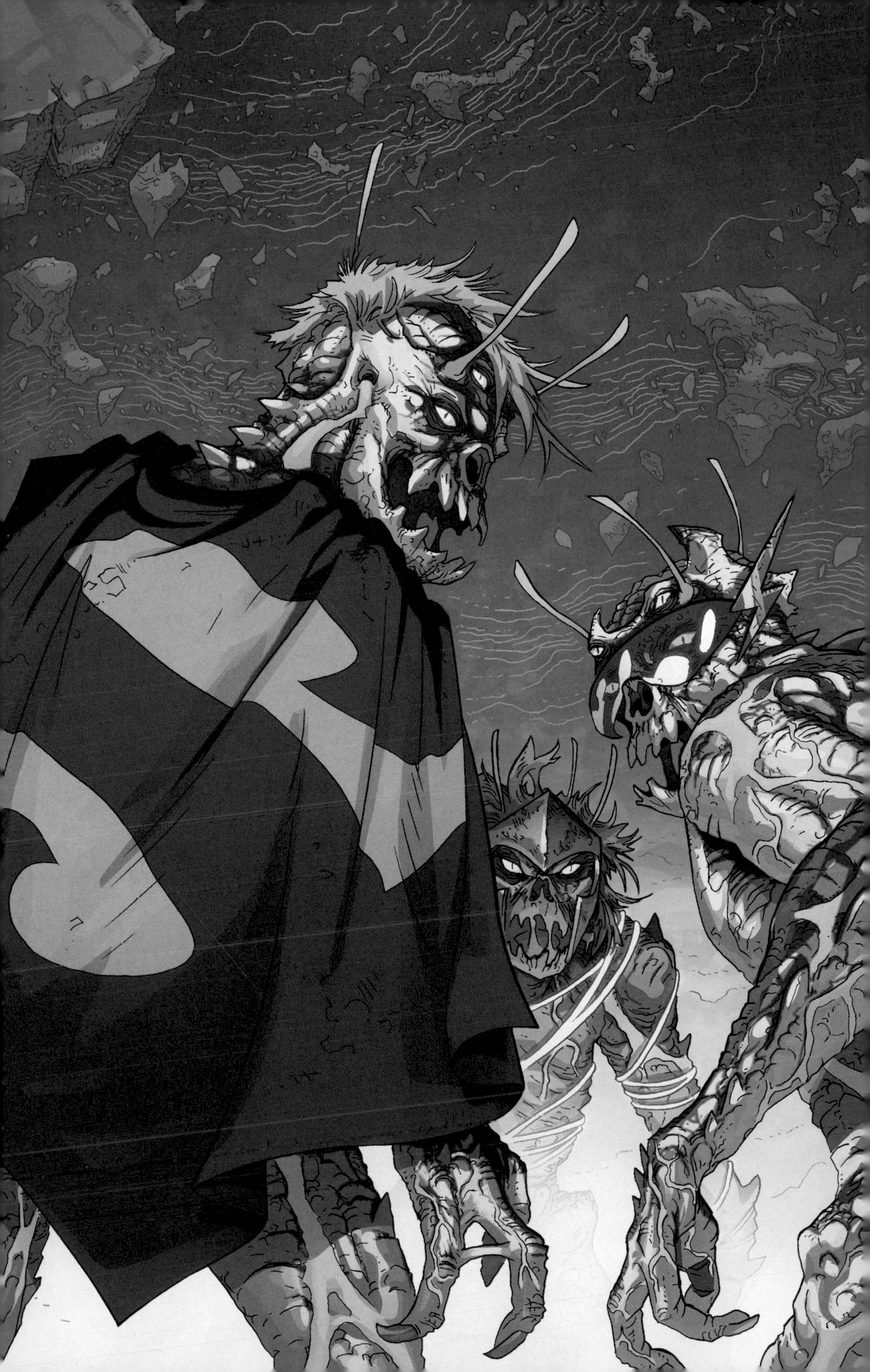

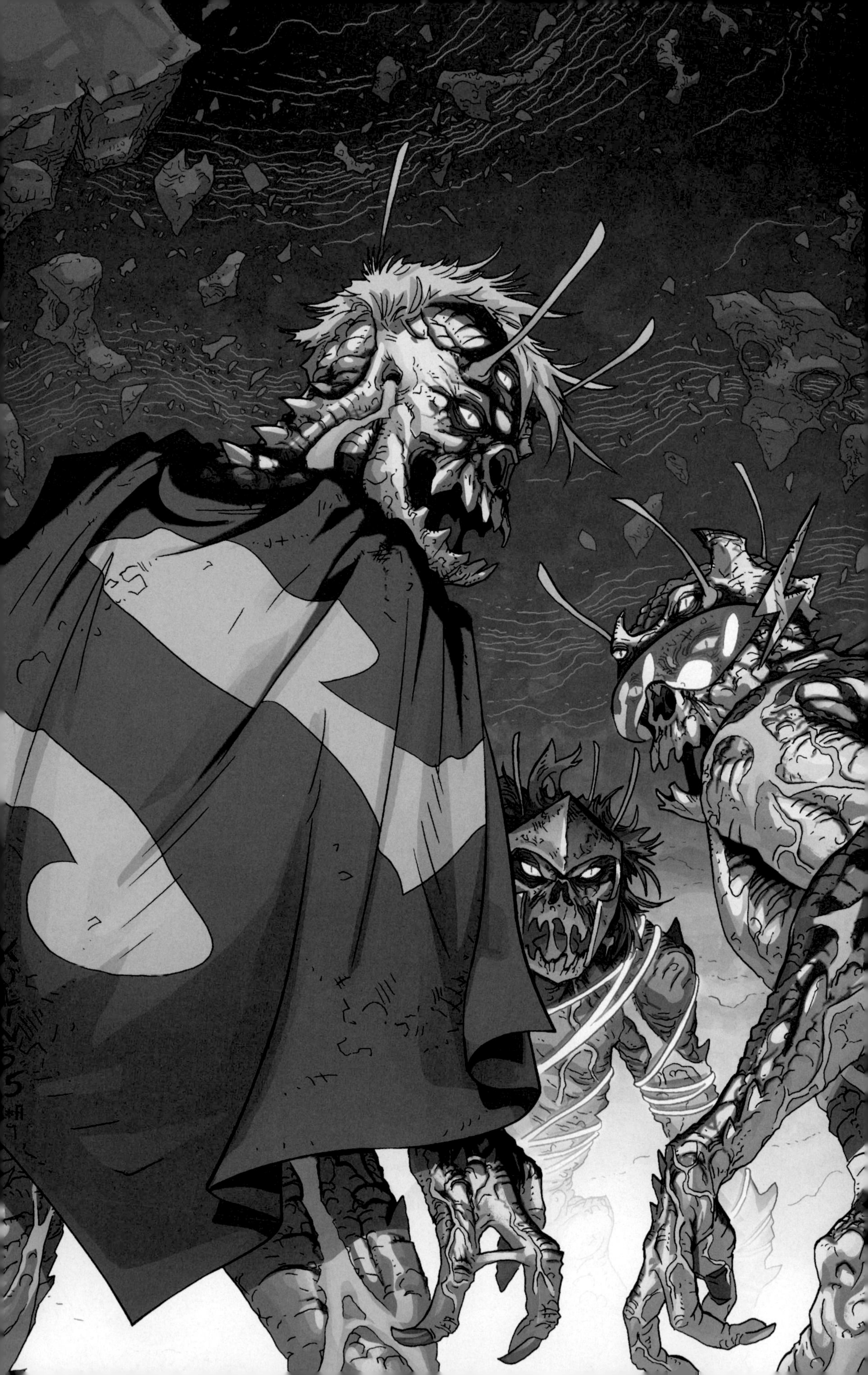

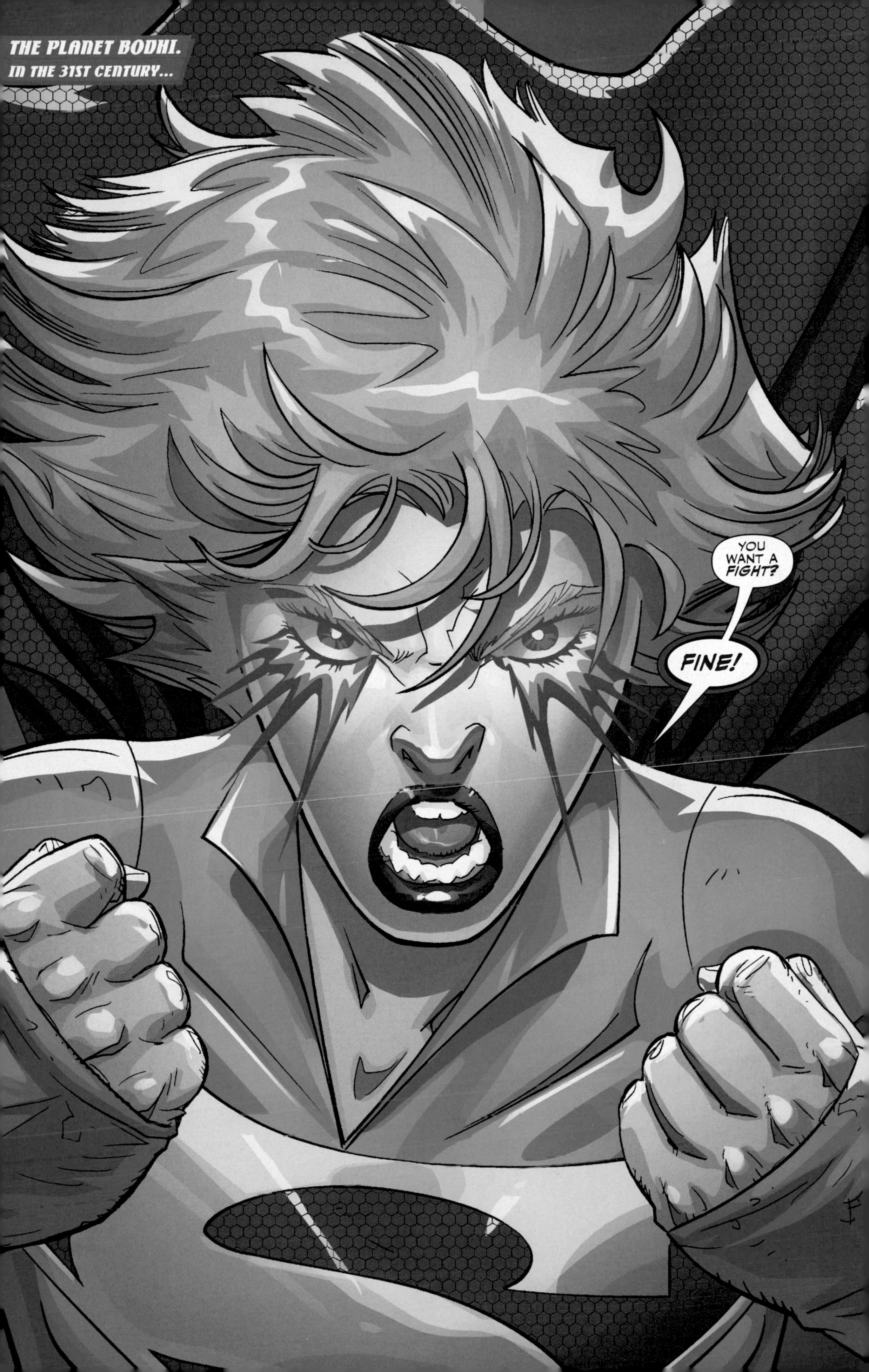
THE PLANET BODHI.
IN THE 31ST CENTURY...
YOU WANT A FIGHT?
FINE!

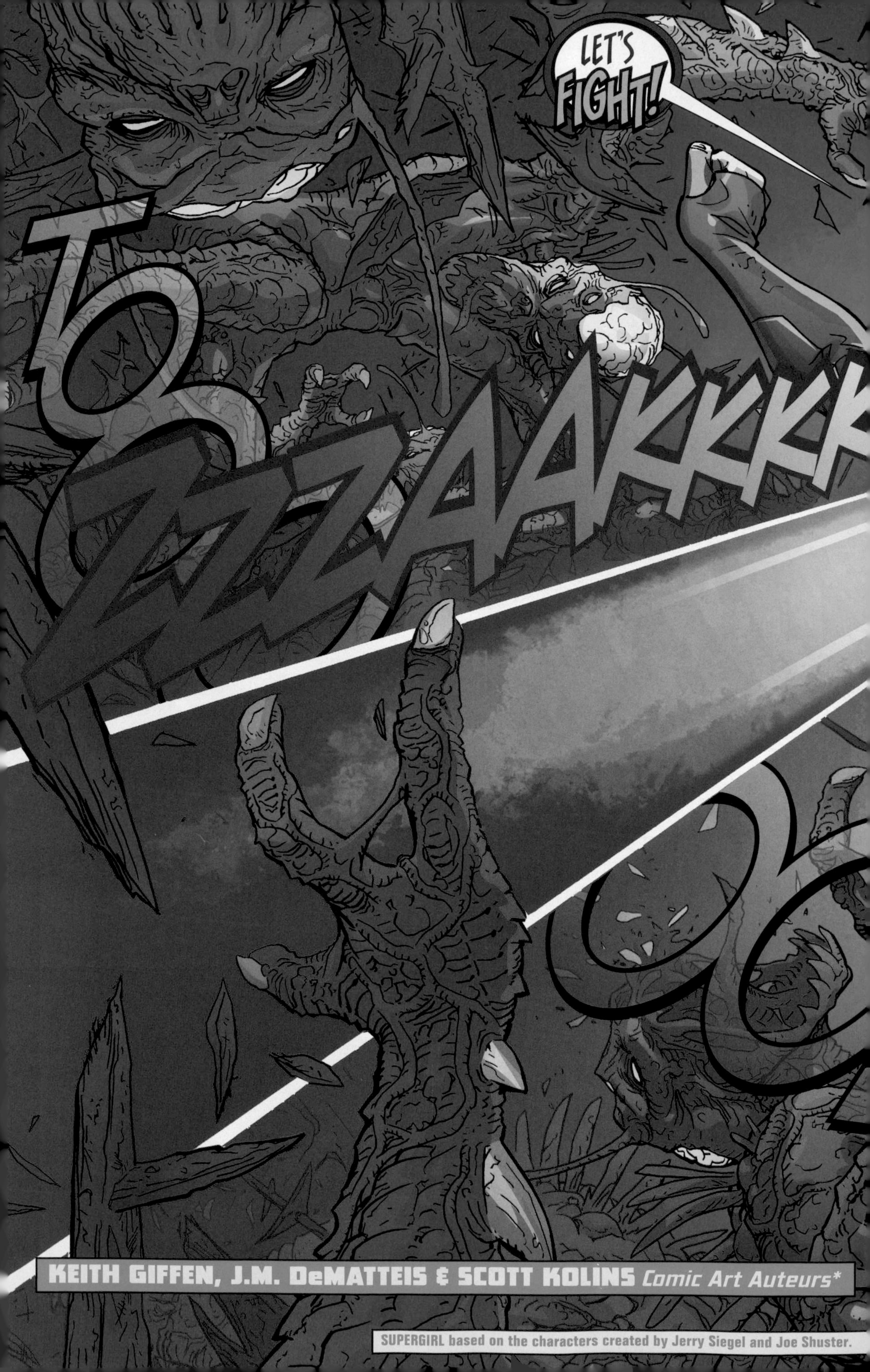
LET'S FIGHT!
TZZZAAKKKK
KEITH GIFFEN, J.M. DeMATTEIS & SCOTT KOLINS Comic Art Auteurs*
SUPERGIRL based on the characters created by Jerry Siegel and Joe Shuster.

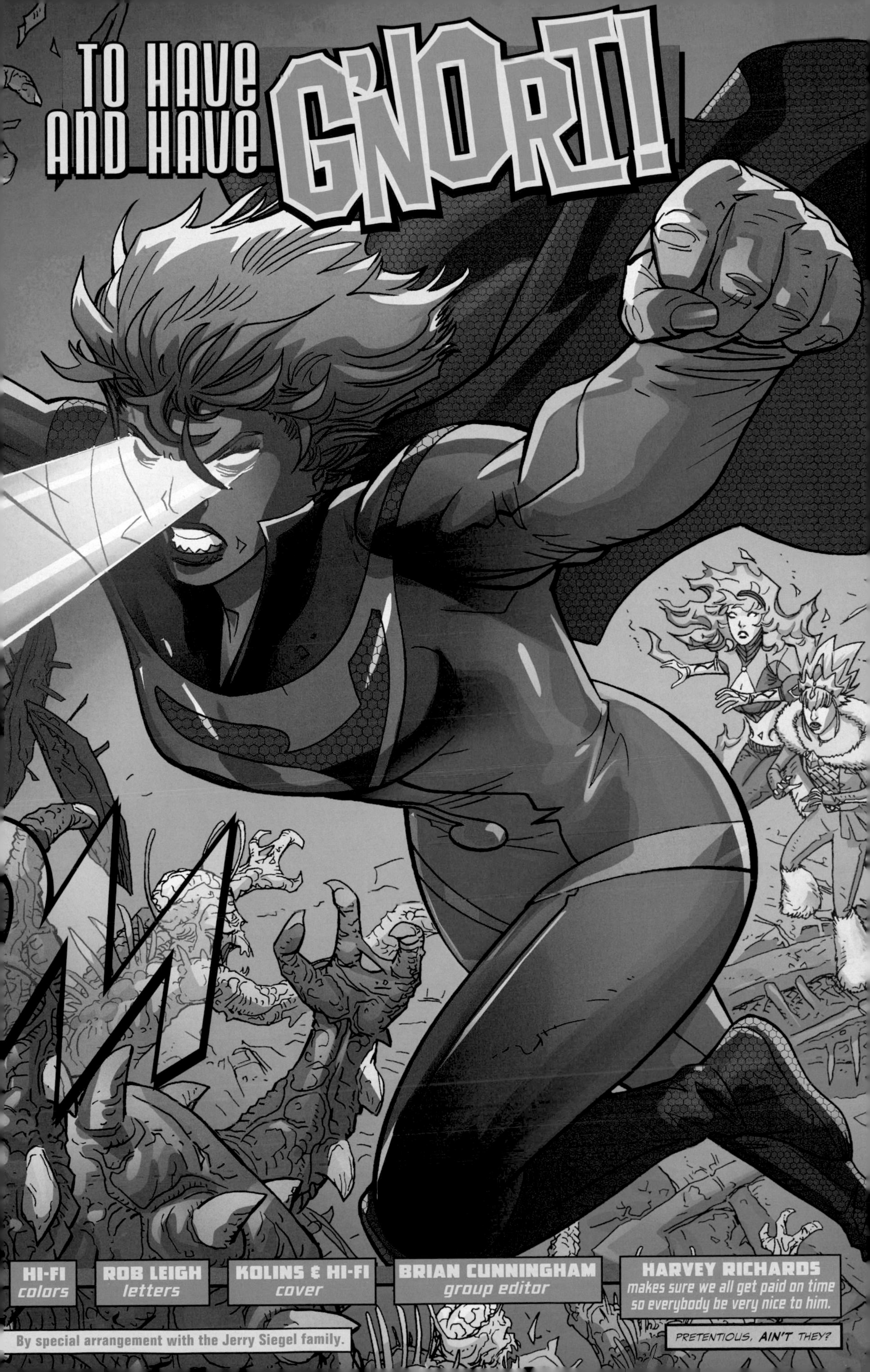

TO HAVE AND HAVE G'NORT!
HI-FI colors
ROB LEIGH letters
KOLINS & HI-FI cover
BRIAN CUNNINGHAM group editor
HARVEY RICHARDS makes sure we all get paid on time so everybody be very nice to him.
By special arrangement with the Jerry Siegel family.
PRETENTIOUS, AIN'T THEY?

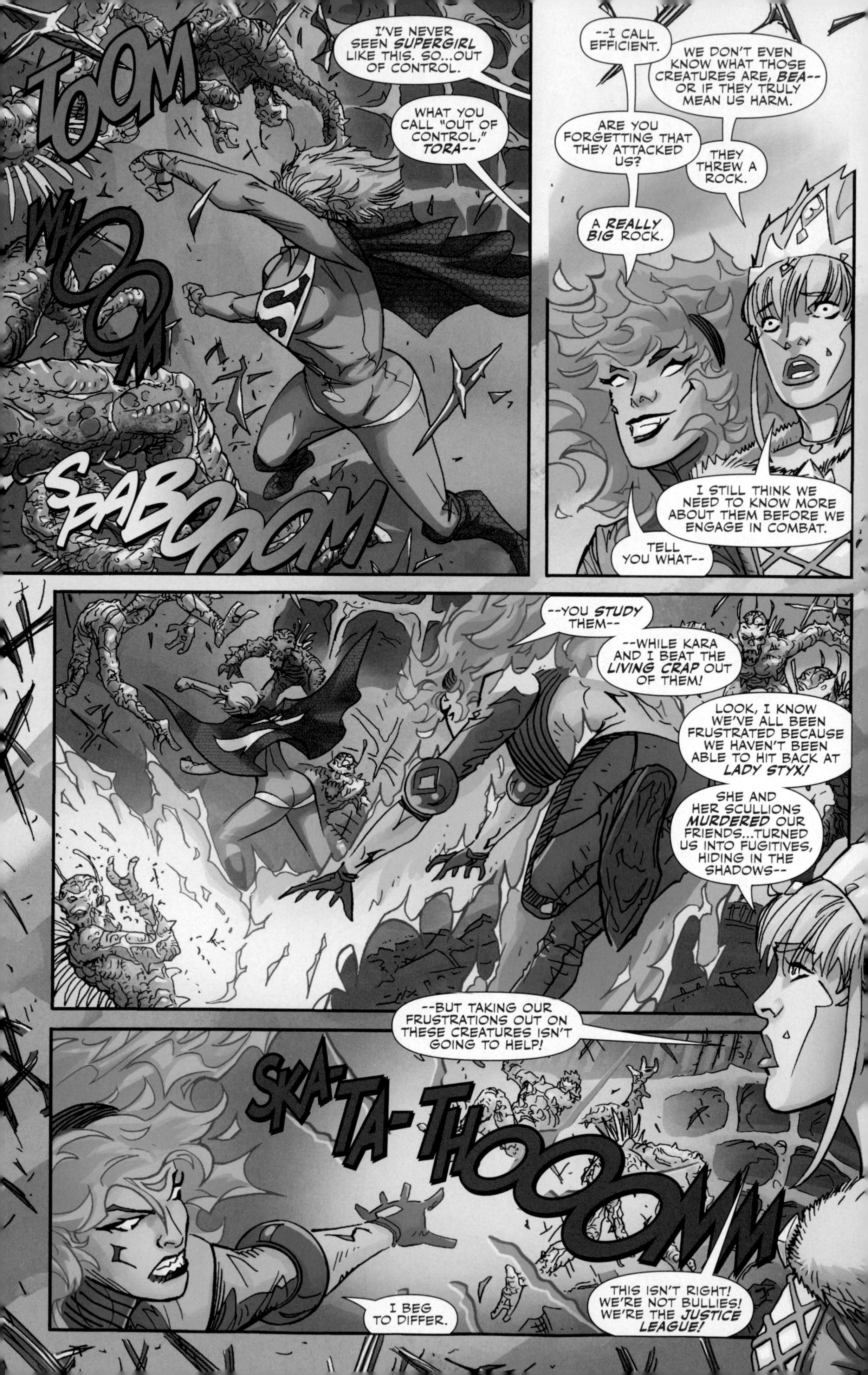
TOOM
I'VE NEVER SEEN SUPERGIRL LIKE THIS. SO...OUT OF CONTROL.
WHAT YOU CALL "OUT OF CONTROL," TORA--
WHOOOM
SPABOOOM
--I CALL EFFICIENT.
WE DON'T EVEN KNOW WHAT THOSE CREATURES ARE, BEA-- OR IF THEY TRULY MEAN US HARM.
ARE YOU FORGETTING THAT THEY ATTACKED US?
THEY THREW A ROCK.
A REALLY BIG ROCK.
I STILL THINK WE NEED TO KNOW MORE ABOUT THEM BEFORE WE ENGAGE IN COMBAT.
TELL YOU WHAT--
--YOU STUDY THEM--
--WHILE KARA AND I BEAT THE LIVING CRAP OUT OF THEM!
LOOK, I KNOW WE'VE ALL BEEN FRUSTRATED BECAUSE WE HAVEN'T BEEN ABLE TO HIT BACK AT LADY STYX!
SHE AND HER SCULLIONS MURDERED OUR FRIENDS...TURNED US INTO FUGITIVES, HIDING IN THE SHADOWS--
--BUT TAKING OUR FRUSTRATIONS OUT ON THESE CREATURES ISN'T GOING TO HELP!
SKA-TA-THOOOMM
I BEG TO DIFFER.
THIS ISN'T RIGHT! WE'RE NOT BULLIES! WE'RE THE JUSTICE LEAGUE!

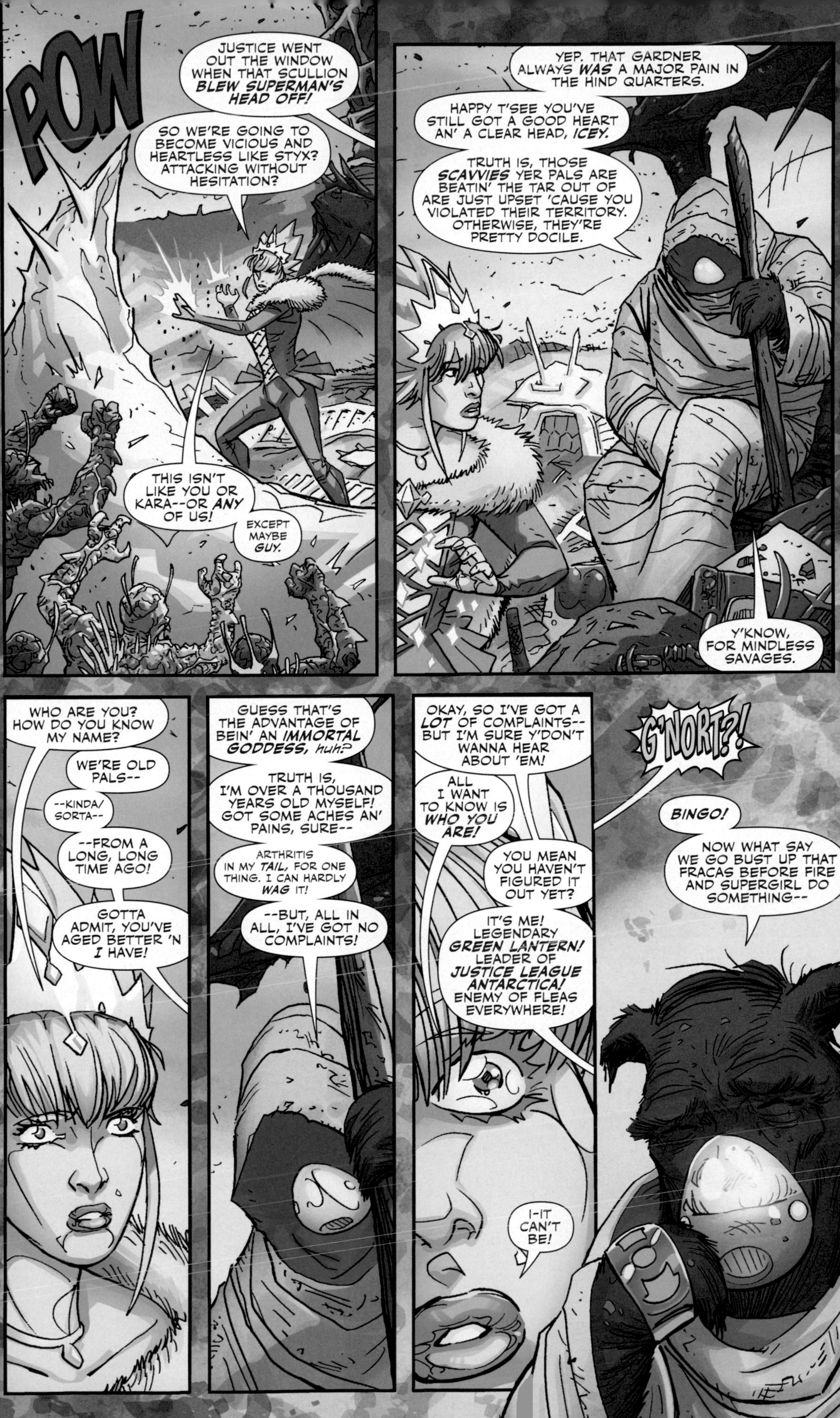
POW
JUSTICE WENT OUT THE WINDOW WHEN THAT SCULLION BLEW SUPERMAN'S HEAD OFF!
SO WE'RE GOING TO BECOME VICIOUS AND HEARTLESS LIKE STYX? ATTACKING WITHOUT HESITATION?
THIS ISN'T LIKE YOU OR KARA--OR ANY OF US!
EXCEPT MAYBE GUY.
YEP. THAT GARDNER ALWAYS WAS A MAJOR PAIN IN THE HIND QUARTERS.
HAPPY T'SEE YOU'VE STILL GOT A GOOD HEART AN' A CLEAR HEAD, ICEY.
TRUTH IS, THOSE SCAVVIES YER PALS ARE BEATIN' THE TAR OUT OF ARE JUST UPSET 'CAUSE YOU VIOLATED THEIR TERRITORY. OTHERWISE, THEY'RE PRETTY DOCILE.
Y'KNOW, FOR MINDLESS SAVAGES.
WHO ARE YOU? HOW DO YOU KNOW MY NAME?
WE'RE OLD PALS--
--KINDA/ SORTA--
--FROM A LONG, LONG TIME AGO!
GOTTA ADMIT, YOU'VE AGED BETTER 'N I HAVE!
GUESS THAT'S THE ADVANTAGE OF BEIN' AN IMMORTAL GODDESS, huh?
TRUTH IS, I'M OVER A THOUSAND YEARS OLD MYSELF! GOT SOME ACHES AN' PAINS, SURE--
ARTHRITIS IN MY TAIL, FOR ONE THING. I CAN HARDLY WAG IT!
--BUT, ALL IN ALL, I'VE GOT NO COMPLAINTS!
OKAY, SO I'VE GOT A LOT OF COMPLAINTS--BUT I'M SURE Y'DON'T WANNA HEAR ABOUT 'EM!
ALL I WANT TO KNOW IS WHO YOU ARE!
YOU MEAN YOU HAVEN'T FIGURED IT OUT YET?
IT'S ME! LEGENDARY GREEN LANTERN! LEADER OF JUSTICE LEAGUE ANTARCTICA! ENEMY OF FLEAS EVERYWHERE!
I-IT CAN'T BE!
G'NORT?!
BINGO!
NOW WHAT SAY WE GO BUST UP THAT FRACAS BEFORE FIRE AND SUPERGIRL DO SOMETHING--

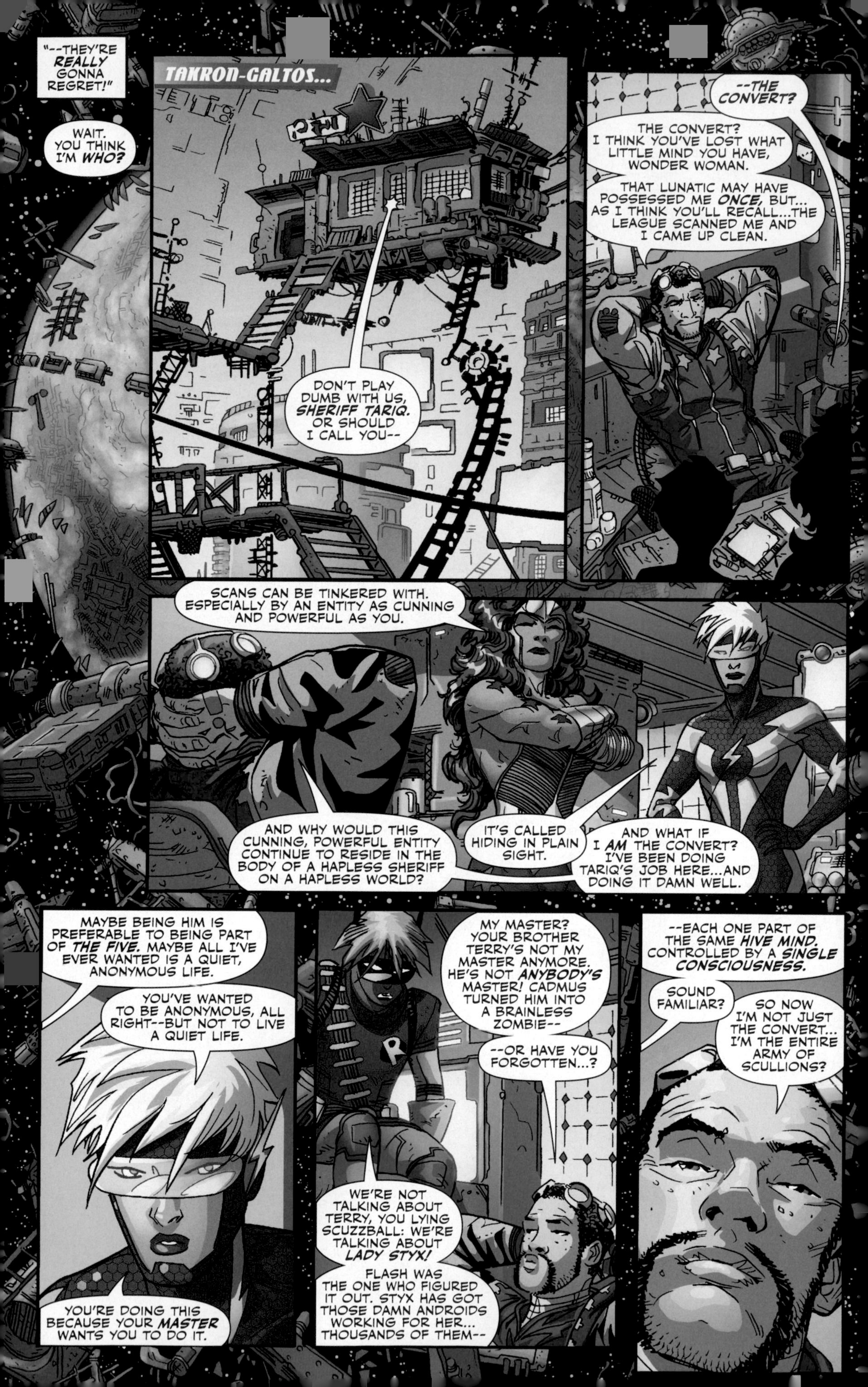
"--THEY'RE REALLY GONNA REGRET!"
WAIT. YOU THINK I'M WHO?
TAKRON-GALTOS...
DON'T PLAY DUMB WITH US, SHERIFF TARIQ. OR SHOULD I CALL YOU--
--THE CONVERT?
THE CONVERT? I THINK YOU'VE LOST WHAT LITTLE MIND YOU HAVE, WONDER WOMAN.
THAT LUNATIC MAY HAVE POSSESSED ME ONCE, BUT... AS I THINK YOU'LL RECALL...THE LEAGUE SCANNED ME AND I CAME UP CLEAN.
SCANS CAN BE TINKERED WITH. ESPECIALLY BY AN ENTITY AS CUNNING AND POWERFUL AS YOU.
AND WHY WOULD THIS CUNNING, POWERFUL ENTITY CONTINUE TO RESIDE IN THE BODY OF A HAPLESS SHERIFF ON A HAPLESS WORLD?
IT'S CALLED HIDING IN PLAIN SIGHT.
AND WHAT IF I AM THE CONVERT? I'VE BEEN DOING TARIQ'S JOB HERE...AND DOING IT DAMN WELL.
MAYBE BEING HIM IS PREFERABLE TO BEING PART OF THE FIVE. MAYBE ALL I'VE EVER WANTED IS A QUIET, ANONYMOUS LIFE.
YOU'VE WANTED TO BE ANONYMOUS, ALL RIGHT--BUT NOT TO LIVE A QUIET LIFE.
YOU'RE DOING THIS BECAUSE YOUR MASTER WANTS YOU TO DO IT.
MY MASTER? YOUR BROTHER TERRY'S NOT MY MASTER ANYMORE. HE'S NOT ANYBODY'S MASTER! CADMUS TURNED HIM INTO A BRAINLESS ZOMBIE--
--OR HAVE YOU FORGOTTEN...?
WE'RE NOT TALKING ABOUT TERRY, YOU LYING SCUZZBALL: WE'RE TALKING ABOUT LADY STYX!
FLASH WAS THE ONE WHO FIGURED IT OUT. STYX HAS GOT THOSE DAMN ANDROIDS WORKING FOR HER... THOUSANDS OF THEM--
--EACH ONE PART OF THE SAME HIVE MIND. CONTROLLED BY A SINGLE CONSCIOUSNESS.
SOUND FAMILIAR?
SO NOW I'M NOT JUST THE CONVERT... I'M THE ENTIRE ARMY OF SCULLIONS?

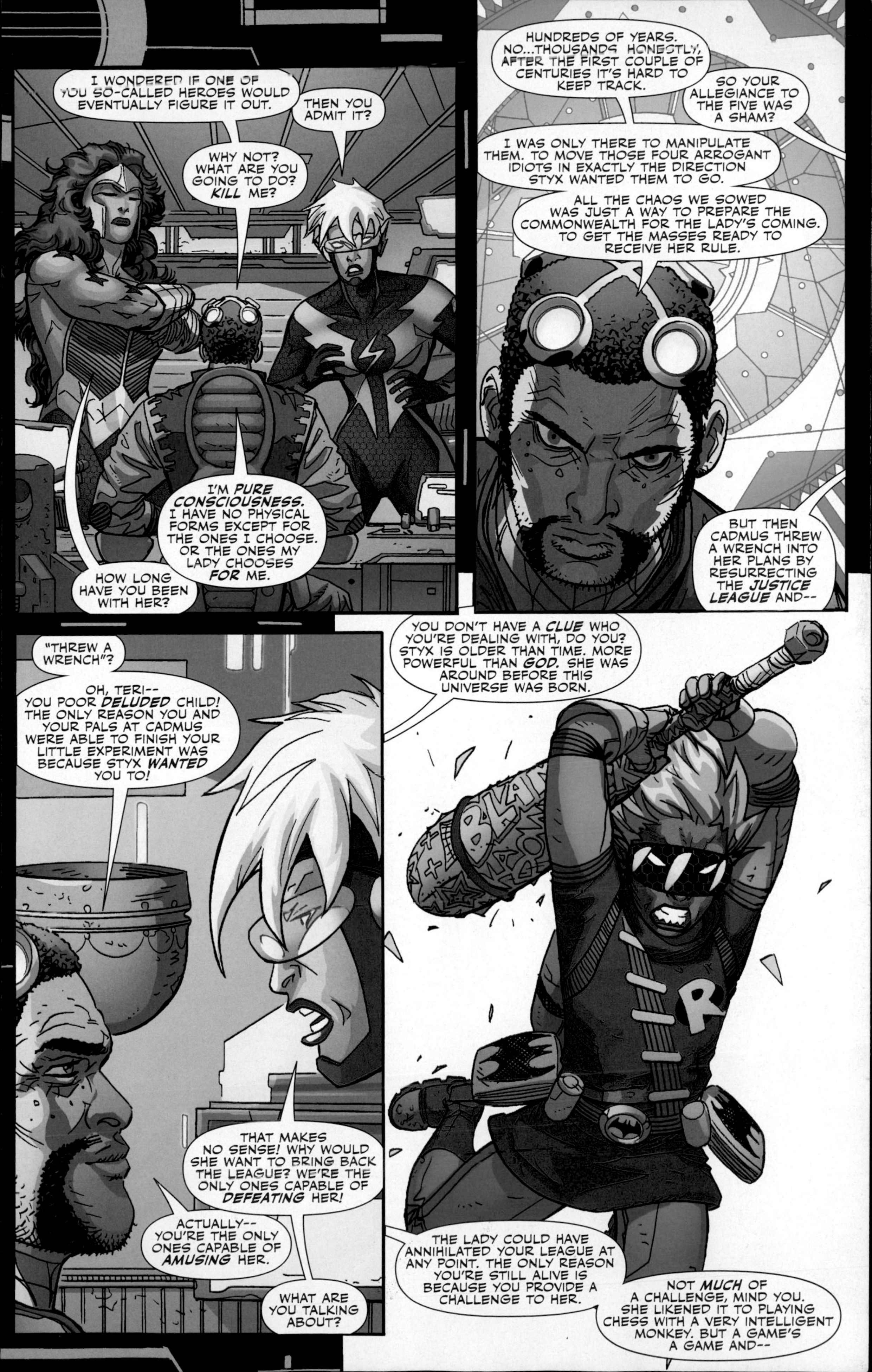
I WONDERED IF ONE OF YOU SO-CALLED HEROES WOULD EVENTUALLY FIGURE IT OUT.
THEN YOU ADMIT IT?
WHY NOT? WHAT ARE YOU GOING TO DO? KILL ME?
I'M PURE CONSCIOUSNESS. I HAVE NO PHYSICAL FORMS EXCEPT FOR THE ONES I CHOOSE. OR THE ONES MY LADY CHOOSES FOR ME.
HOW LONG HAVE YOU BEEN WITH HER?
HUNDREDS OF YEARS. NO...THOUSANDS HONESTLY, AFTER THE FIRST COUPLE OF CENTURIES IT'S HARD TO KEEP TRACK.
SO YOUR ALLEGIANCE TO THE FIVE WAS A SHAM?
I WAS ONLY THERE TO MANIPULATE THEM. TO MOVE THOSE FOUR ARROGANT IDIOTS IN EXACTLY THE DIRECTION STYX WANTED THEM TO GO.
ALL THE CHAOS WE SOWED WAS JUST A WAY TO PREPARE THE COMMONWEALTH FOR THE LADY'S COMING. TO GET THE MASSES READY TO RECEIVE HER RULE.
BUT THEN CADMUS THREW A WRENCH INTO HER PLANS BY RESURRECTING THE JUSTICE LEAGUE AND--
"THREW A WRENCH"?
OH, TERI-- YOU POOR DELUDED CHILD! THE ONLY REASON YOU AND YOUR PALS AT CADMUS WERE ABLE TO FINISH YOUR LITTLE EXPERIMENT WAS BECAUSE STYX WANTED YOU TO!
THAT MAKES NO SENSE! WHY WOULD SHE WANT TO BRING BACK THE LEAGUE? WE'RE THE ONLY ONES CAPABLE OF DEFEATING HER!
ACTUALLY-- YOU'RE THE ONLY ONES CAPABLE OF AMUSING HER.
WHAT ARE YOU TALKING ABOUT?
YOU DON'T HAVE A CLUE WHO YOU'RE DEALING WITH, DO YOU? STYX IS OLDER THAN TIME. MORE POWERFUL THAN GOD. SHE WAS AROUND BEFORE THIS UNIVERSE WAS BORN.
THE LADY COULD HAVE ANNIHILATED YOUR LEAGUE AT ANY POINT. THE ONLY REASON YOU'RE STILL ALIVE IS BECAUSE YOU PROVIDE A CHALLENGE TO HER.
NOT MUCH OF A CHALLENGE, MIND YOU. SHE LIKENED IT TO PLAYING CHESS WITH A VERY INTELLIGENT MONKEY. BUT A GAME'S A GAME AND--

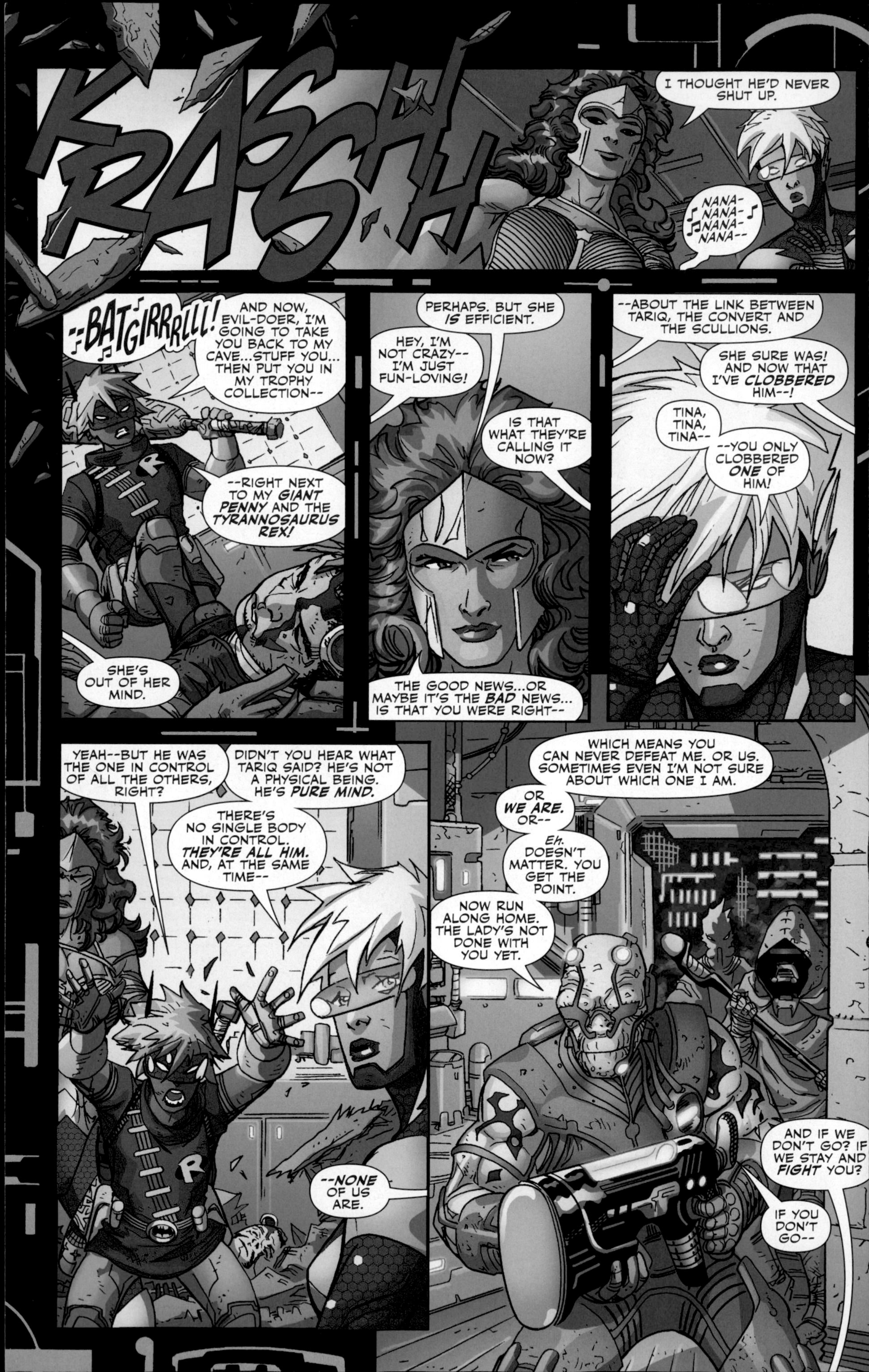

KRASH
KRASH
I THOUGHT HE'D NEVER SHUT UP.
NANA-NANA-NANA-NANA--
BATGIRRRLLL!
AND NOW, EVIL-DOER, I'M GOING TO TAKE YOU BACK TO MY CAVE...STUFF YOU... THEN PUT YOU IN MY TROPHY COLLECTION--
--RIGHT NEXT TO MY GIANT PENNY AND THE TYRANNOSAURUS REX!
SHE'S OUT OF HER MIND.
PERHAPS. BUT SHE IS EFFICIENT.
HEY, I'M NOT CRAZY-- I'M JUST FUN-LOVING!
IS THAT WHAT THEY'RE CALLING IT NOW?
THE GOOD NEWS...OR MAYBE IT'S THE BAD NEWS... IS THAT YOU WERE RIGHT--
--ABOUT THE LINK BETWEEN TARIQ, THE CONVERT AND THE SCULLIONS.
SHE SURE WAS! AND NOW THAT I'VE CLOBBERED HIM--!
TINA, TINA, TINA--
--YOU ONLY CLOBBERED ONE OF HIM!
YEAH--BUT HE WAS THE ONE IN CONTROL OF ALL THE OTHERS, RIGHT?
DIDN'T YOU HEAR WHAT TARIQ SAID? HE'S NOT A PHYSICAL BEING. HE'S PURE MIND.
THERE'S NO SINGLE BODY IN CONTROL. THEY'RE ALL HIM. AND, AT THE SAME TIME--
--NONE OF US ARE.
WHICH MEANS YOU CAN NEVER DEFEAT ME. OR US. SOMETIMES EVEN I'M NOT SURE ABOUT WHICH ONE I AM.
OR WE ARE. OR--
Eh. DOESN'T MATTER. YOU GET THE POINT.
NOW RUN ALONG HOME. THE LADY'S NOT DONE WITH YOU YET.
AND IF WE DON'T GO? IF WE STAY AND FIGHT YOU?
IF YOU DON'T GO--

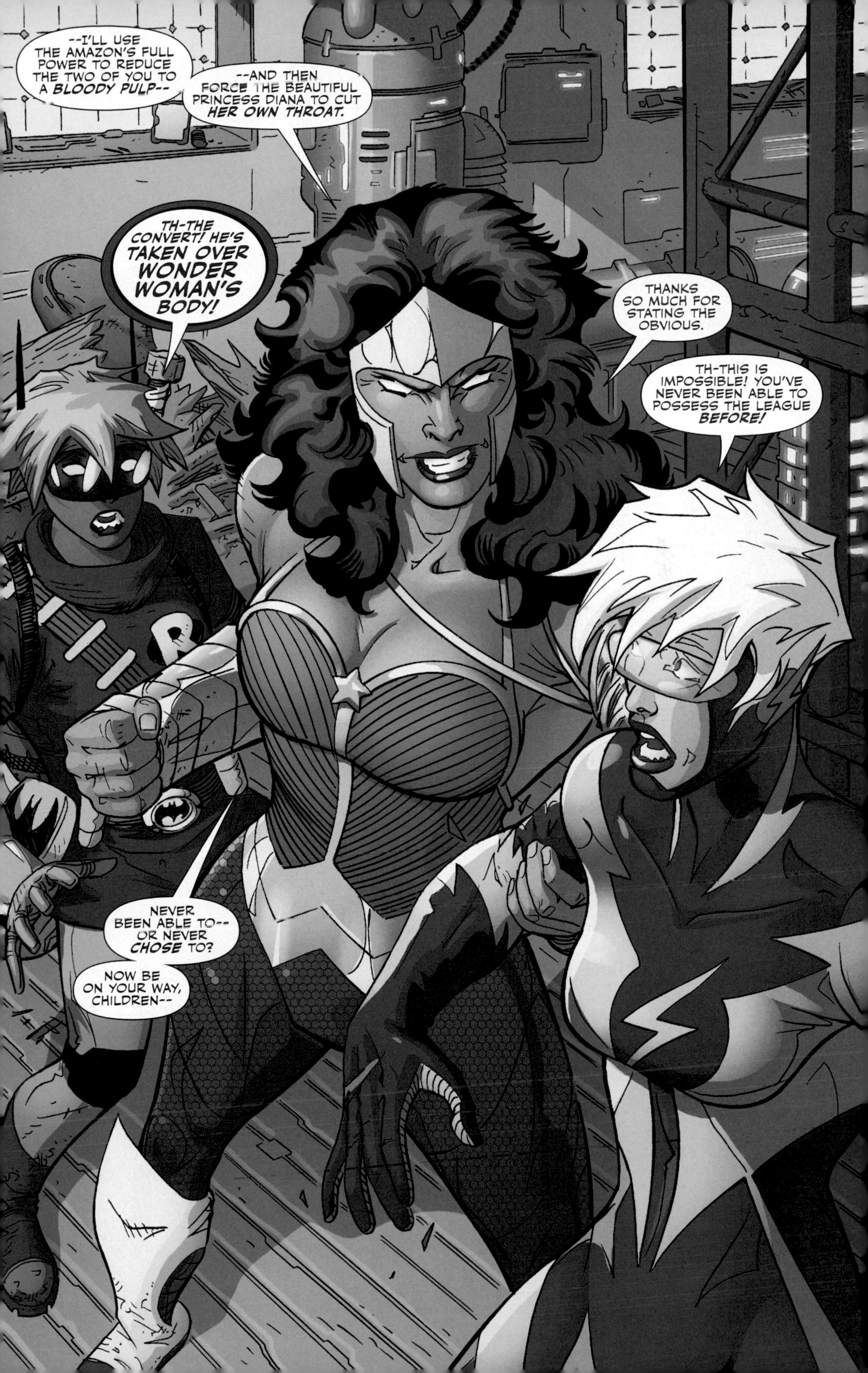
--I'LL USE THE AMAZON'S FULL POWER TO REDUCE THE TWO OF YOU TO A BLOODY PULP--
--AND THEN FORCE THE BEAUTIFUL PRINCESS DIANA TO CUT HER OWN THROAT.
TH-THE CONVERT! HE'S TAKEN OVER WONDER WOMAN'S BODY!
THANKS SO MUCH FOR STATING THE OBVIOUS.
TH-THIS IS IMPOSSIBLE! YOU'VE NEVER BEEN ABLE TO POSSESS THE LEAGUE BEFORE!
NEVER BEEN ABLE TO-- OR NEVER CHOSE TO?
NOW BE ON YOUR WAY, CHILDREN--

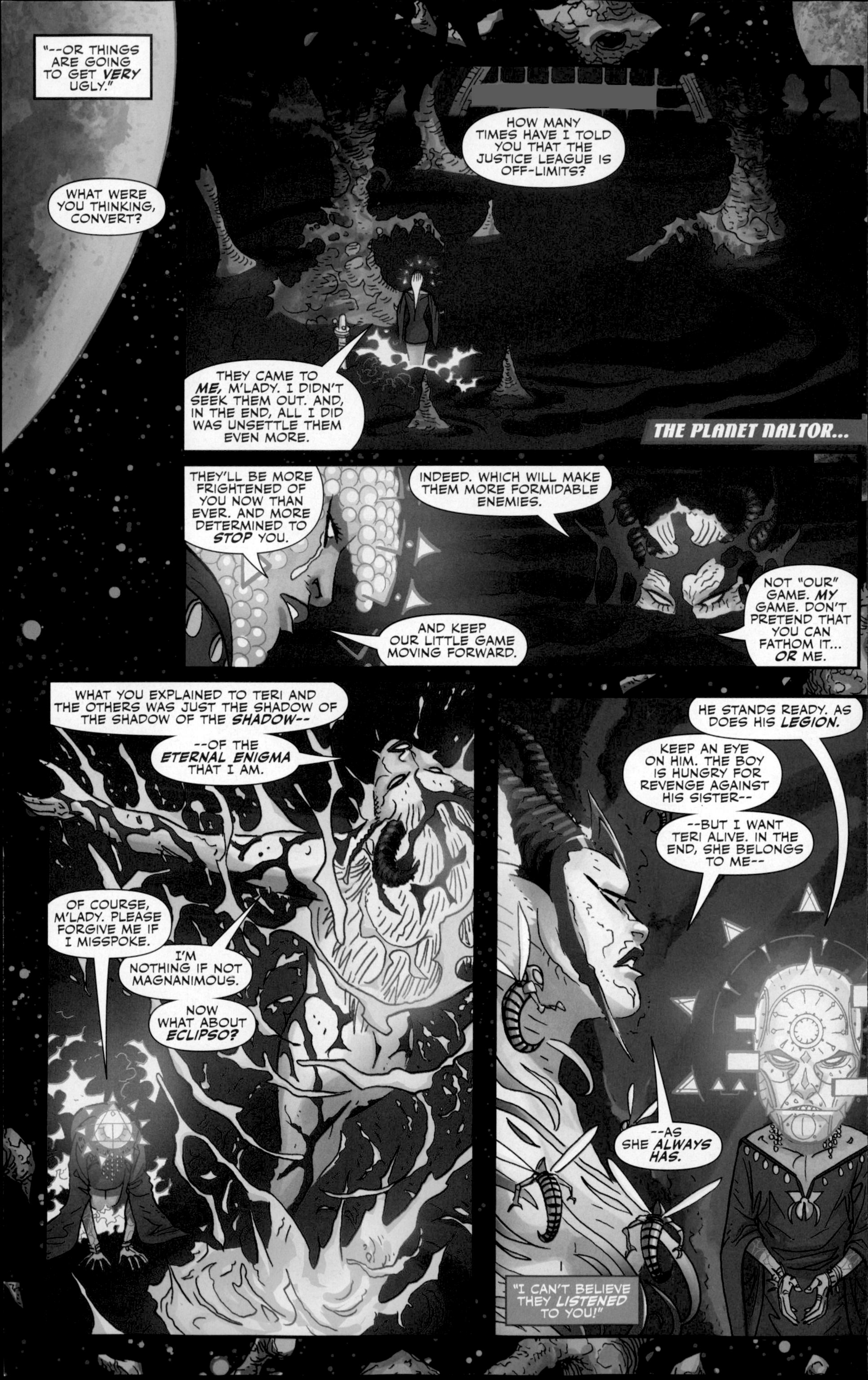
"--OR THINGS ARE GOING TO GET VERY UGLY."
HOW MANY TIMES HAVE I TOLD YOU THAT THE JUSTICE LEAGUE IS OFF-LIMITS?
WHAT WERE YOU THINKING, CONVERT?
THEY CAME TO ME, M'LADY. I DIDN'T SEEK THEM OUT. AND, IN THE END, ALL I DID WAS UNSETTLE THEM EVEN MORE.
THE PLANET NALTOR...
THEY'LL BE MORE FRIGHTENED OF YOU NOW THAN EVER. AND MORE DETERMINED TO STOP YOU.
INDEED. WHICH WILL MAKE THEM MORE FORMIDABLE ENEMIES.
AND KEEP OUR LITTLE GAME MOVING FORWARD.
NOT "OUR" GAME. MY GAME. DON'T PRETEND THAT YOU CAN FATHOM IT... OR ME.
WHAT YOU EXPLAINED TO TERI AND THE OTHERS WAS JUST THE SHADOW OF THE SHADOW OF THE SHADOW--
--OF THE ETERNAL ENIGMA THAT I AM.
OF COURSE, M'LADY. PLEASE FORGIVE ME IF I MISSPOKE.
I'M NOTHING IF NOT MAGNANIMOUS.
NOW WHAT ABOUT ECLIPSO?
HE STANDS READY. AS DOES HIS LEGION.
KEEP AN EYE ON HIM. THE BOY IS HUNGRY FOR REVENGE AGAINST HIS SISTER--
--BUT I WANT TERI ALIVE. IN THE END, SHE BELONGS TO ME--
--AS SHE ALWAYS HAS.
"I CAN'T BELIEVE THEY LISTENED TO YOU!"

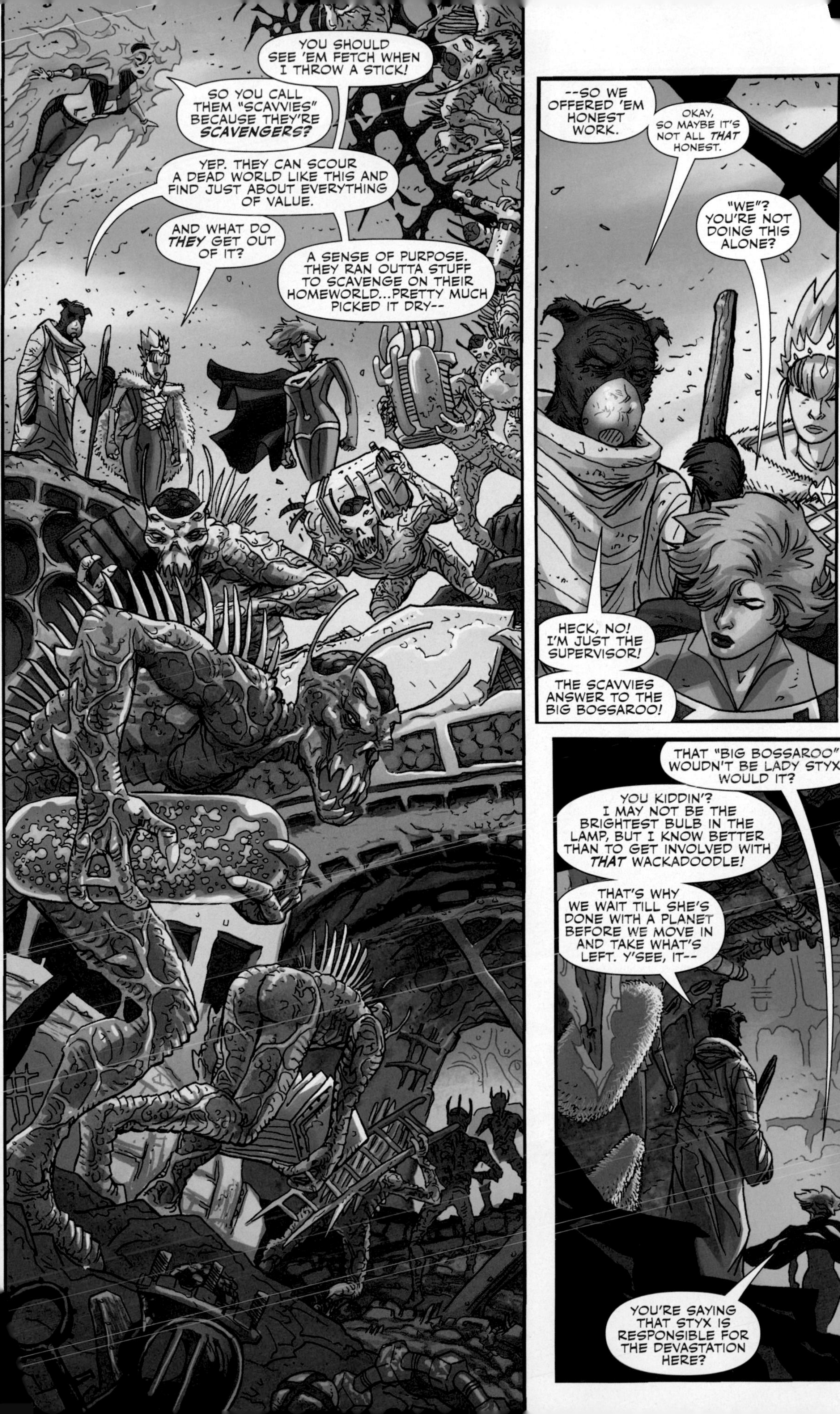

SO YOU CALL THEM "SCAVVIES" BECAUSE THEY'RE *SCAVENGERS?*
YOU SHOULD SEE 'EM FETCH WHEN I THROW A STICK!
YEP. THEY CAN SCOUR A DEAD WORLD LIKE THIS AND FIND JUST ABOUT EVERYTHING OF VALUE.
AND WHAT DO *THEY* GET OUT OF IT?
A SENSE OF PURPOSE. THEY RAN OUTTA STUFF TO SCAVENGE ON THEIR HOMEWORLD...PRETTY MUCH PICKED IT DRY--
--SO WE OFFERED 'EM HONEST WORK.
OKAY, SO MAYBE IT'S NOT ALL *THAT* HONEST.
"WE"? YOU'RE NOT DOING THIS ALONE?
HECK, NO! I'M JUST THE SUPERVISOR!
THE SCAVVIES ANSWER TO THE BIG BOSSAROO!
THAT "BIG BOSSAROO" WOUDN'T BE LADY STYX, WOULD IT?
YOU KIDDIN'? I MAY NOT BE THE BRIGHTEST BULB IN THE LAMP, BUT I KNOW BETTER THAN TO GET INVOLVED WITH *THAT* WACKADOODLE!
THAT'S WHY WE WAIT TILL SHE'S DONE WITH A PLANET BEFORE WE MOVE IN AND TAKE WHAT'S LEFT. Y'SEE, IT--
YOU'RE SAYING THAT STYX IS RESPONSIBLE FOR THE DEVASTATION HERE?

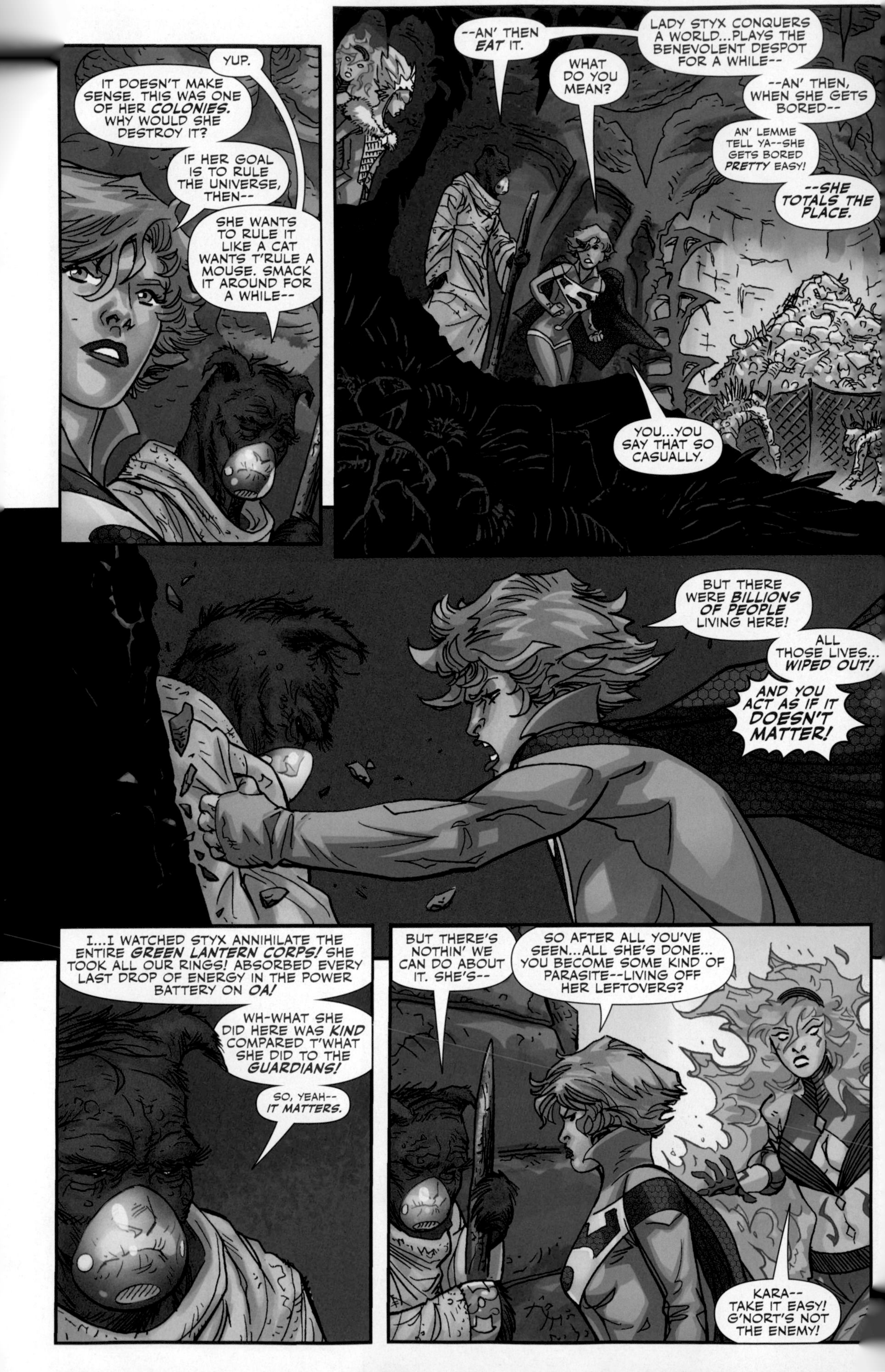
YUP.
IT DOESN'T MAKE SENSE. THIS WAS ONE OF HER COLONIES. WHY WOULD SHE DESTROY IT?
IF HER GOAL IS TO RULE THE UNIVERSE, THEN--
SHE WANTS TO RULE IT LIKE A CAT WANTS T'RULE A MOUSE. SMACK IT AROUND FOR A WHILE--
--AN' THEN EAT IT.
WHAT DO YOU MEAN?
LADY STYX CONQUERS A WORLD...PLAYS THE BENEVOLENT DESPOT FOR A WHILE--
--AN' THEN, WHEN SHE GETS BORED--
AN' LEMME TELL YA--SHE GETS BORED PRETTY EASY!
--SHE TOTALS THE PLACE.
YOU...YOU SAY THAT SO CASUALLY.
BUT THERE WERE BILLIONS OF PEOPLE LIVING HERE!
ALL THOSE LIVES... WIPED OUT!
AND YOU ACT AS IF IT DOESN'T MATTER!
I...I WATCHED STYX ANNIHILATE THE ENTIRE GREEN LANTERN CORPS! SHE TOOK ALL OUR RINGS! ABSORBED EVERY LAST DROP OF ENERGY IN THE POWER BATTERY ON OA!
WH-WHAT SHE DID HERE WAS KIND COMPARED T'WHAT SHE DID TO THE GUARDIANS!
SO, YEAH-- IT MATTERS.
BUT THERE'S NOTHIN' WE CAN DO ABOUT IT. SHE'S--
SO AFTER ALL YOU'VE SEEN...ALL SHE'S DONE... YOU BECOME SOME KIND OF PARASITE--LIVING OFF HER LEFTOVERS?
KARA-- TAKE IT EASY! G'NORT'S NOT THE ENEMY!

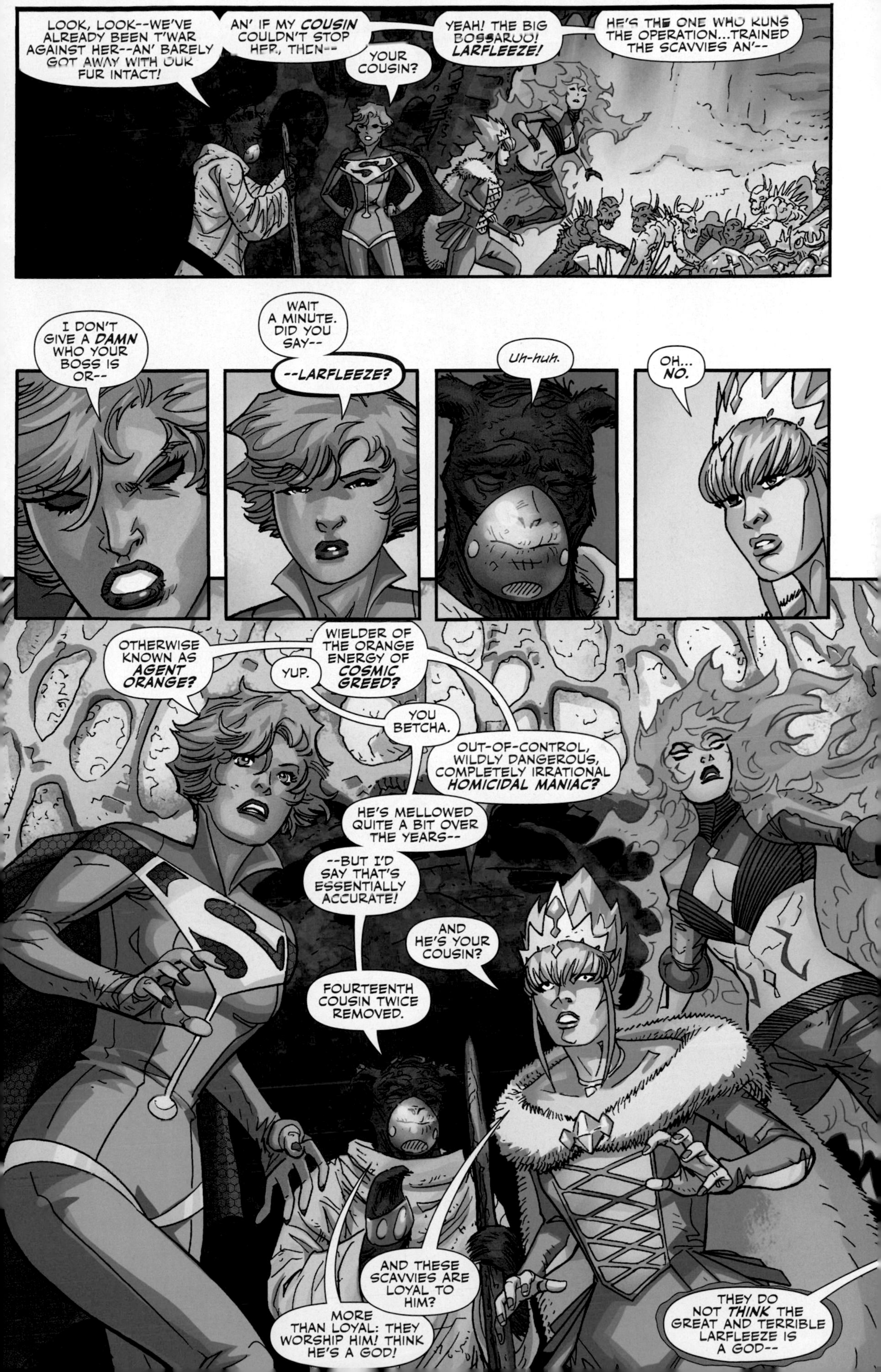

LOOK, LOOK--WE'VE ALREADY BEEN T'WAR AGAINST HER--AN' BARELY GOT AWAY WITH OUR FUR INTACT!
AN' IF MY *COUSIN* COULDN'T STOP HER, THEN--
YOUR COUSIN?
YEAH! THE BIG BOSSAROO! *LARFLEEZE!*
HE'S THE ONE WHO RUNS THE OPERATION...TRAINED THE SCAVVIES AN'--
I DON'T GIVE A *DAMN* WHO YOUR BOSS IS OR--
WAIT A MINUTE. DID YOU SAY--
--LARFLEEZE?
Uh-huh.
OH... *NO.*
OTHERWISE KNOWN AS *AGENT ORANGE?*
YUP.
WIELDER OF THE ORANGE ENERGY OF *COSMIC GREED?*
YOU BETCHA.
OUT-OF-CONTROL, WILDLY DANGEROUS, COMPLETELY IRRATIONAL *HOMICIDAL MANIAC?*
HE'S MELLOWED QUITE A BIT OVER THE YEARS--
--BUT I'D SAY THAT'S ESSENTIALLY ACCURATE!
AND HE'S YOUR COUSIN?
FOURTEENTH COUSIN TWICE REMOVED.
AND THESE SCAVVIES ARE LOYAL TO HIM?
MORE THAN LOYAL: THEY WORSHIP HIM! THINK HE'S A GOD!
THEY DO NOT *THINK* THE GREAT AND TERRIBLE LARFLEEZE IS A GOD--

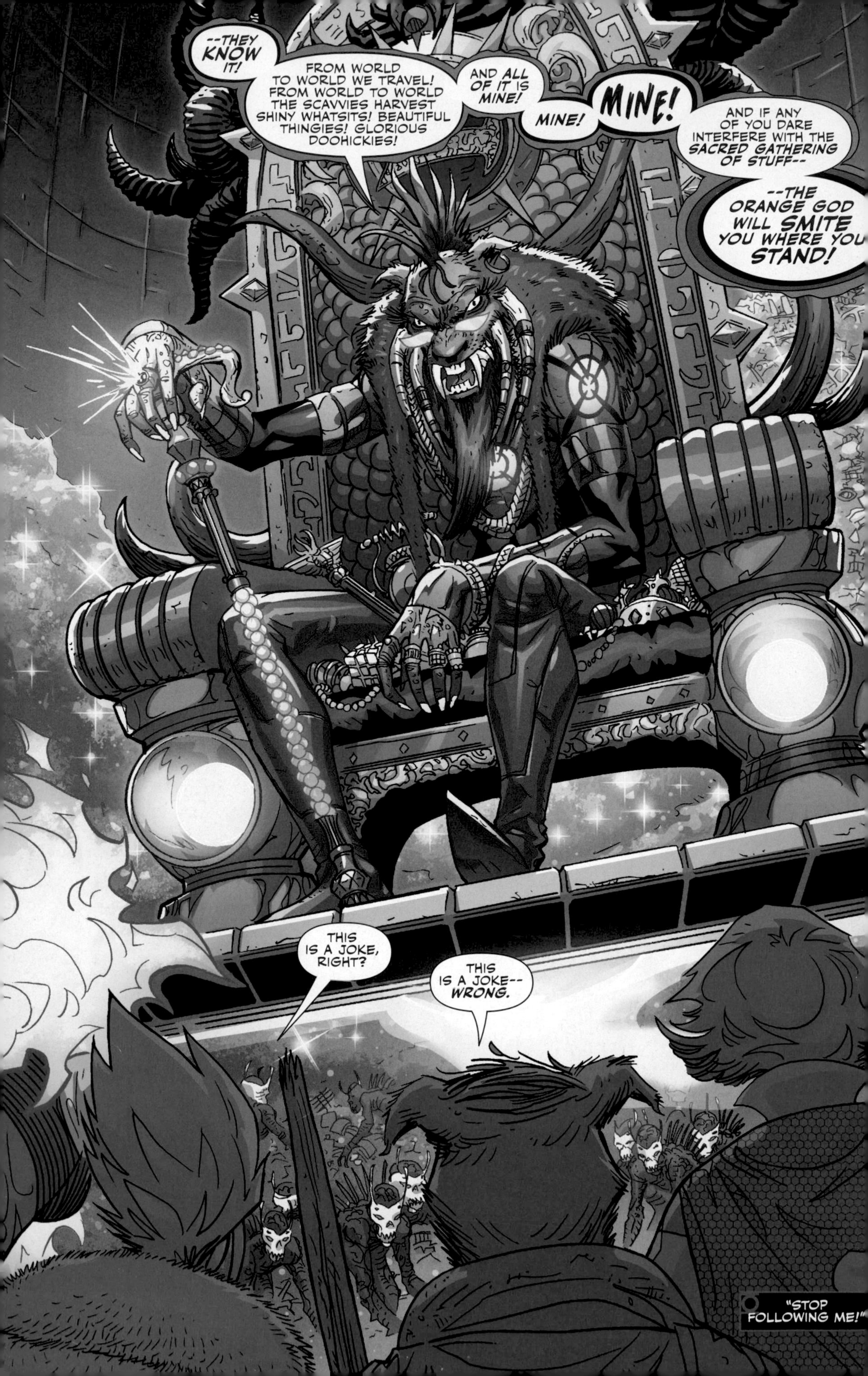
--THEY KNOW IT!
FROM WORLD TO WORLD WE TRAVEL! FROM WORLD TO WORLD THE SCAVVIES HARVEST SHINY WHATSITS! BEAUTIFUL THINGIES! GLORIOUS DOOHICKIES!
AND ALL OF IT IS MINE!
MINE!
MINE!
AND IF ANY OF YOU DARE INTERFERE WITH THE SACRED GATHERING OF STUFF--
--THE ORANGE GOD WILL SMITE YOU WHERE YOU STAND!
THIS IS A JOKE, RIGHT?
THIS IS A JOKE-- WRONG.
"STOP FOLLOWING ME!"

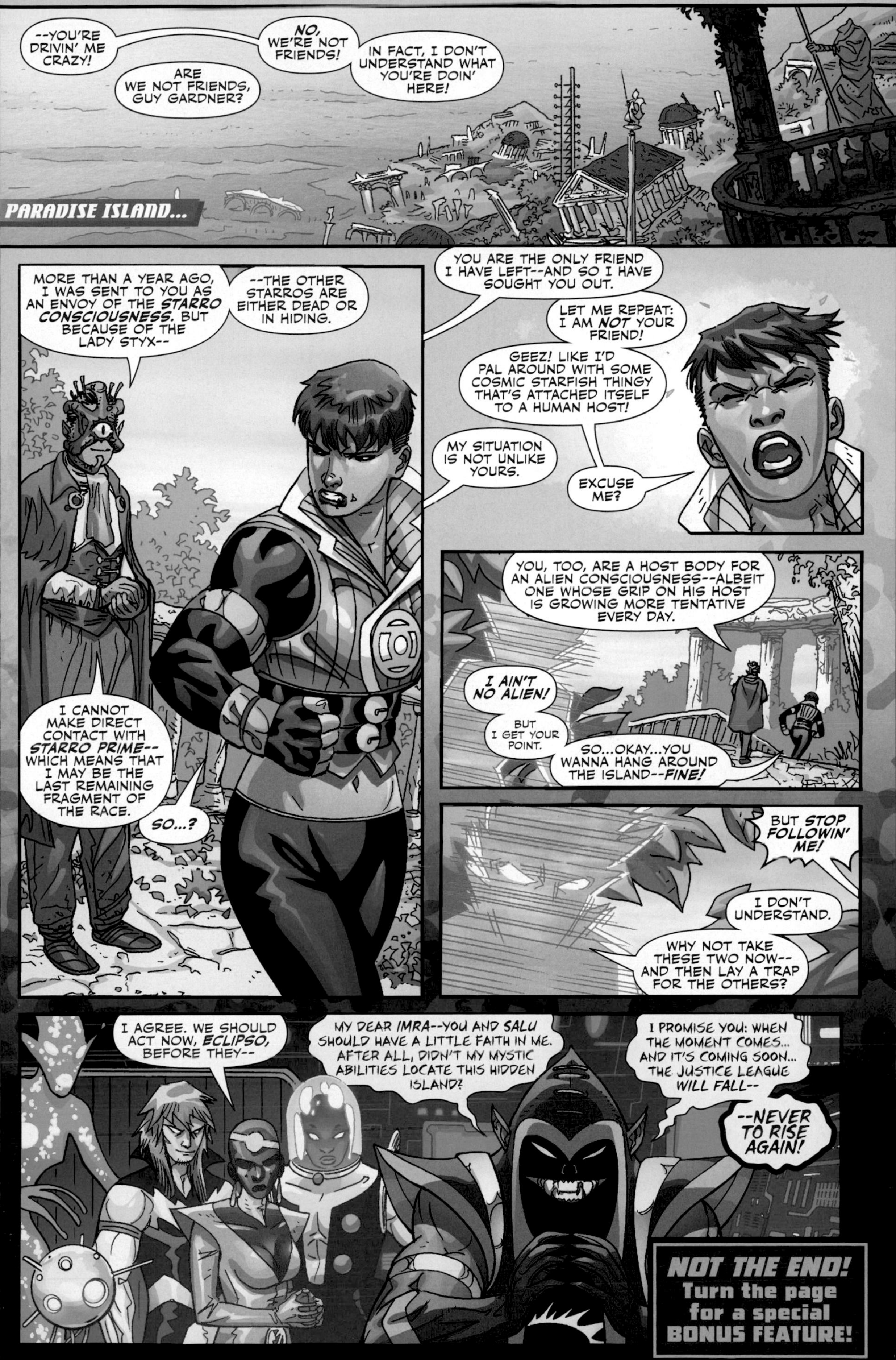
--YOU'RE DRIVIN' ME CRAZY!
ARE WE NOT FRIENDS, GUY GARDNER?
NO, WE'RE NOT FRIENDS!
IN FACT, I DON'T UNDERSTAND WHAT YOU'RE DOIN' HERE!
PARADISE ISLAND...
MORE THAN A YEAR AGO, I WAS SENT TO YOU AS AN ENVOY OF THE STARRO CONSCIOUSNESS. BUT BECAUSE OF THE LADY STYX--
--THE OTHER STARROS ARE EITHER DEAD OR IN HIDING.
YOU ARE THE ONLY FRIEND I HAVE LEFT--AND SO I HAVE SOUGHT YOU OUT.
LET ME REPEAT: I AM NOT YOUR FRIEND!
GEEZ! LIKE I'D PAL AROUND WITH SOME COSMIC STARFISH THINGY THAT'S ATTACHED ITSELF TO A HUMAN HOST!
MY SITUATION IS NOT UNLIKE YOURS.
EXCUSE ME?
I CANNOT MAKE DIRECT CONTACT WITH STARRO PRIME--WHICH MEANS THAT I MAY BE THE LAST REMAINING FRAGMENT OF THE RACE.
SO...?
YOU, TOO, ARE A HOST BODY FOR AN ALIEN CONSCIOUSNESS--ALBEIT ONE WHOSE GRIP ON HIS HOST IS GROWING MORE TENTATIVE EVERY DAY.
I AIN'T NO ALIEN!
BUT I GET YOUR POINT.
SO...OKAY...YOU WANNA HANG AROUND THE ISLAND--FINE!
BUT STOP FOLLOWIN' ME!
I DON'T UNDERSTAND.
WHY NOT TAKE THESE TWO NOW--AND THEN LAY A TRAP FOR THE OTHERS?
I AGREE. WE SHOULD ACT NOW, ECLIPSO, BEFORE THEY--
MY DEAR IMRA--YOU AND SALU SHOULD HAVE A LITTLE FAITH IN ME. AFTER ALL, DIDN'T MY MYSTIC ABILITIES LOCATE THIS HIDDEN ISLAND?
I PROMISE YOU: WHEN THE MOMENT COMES... AND IT'S COMING SOON... THE JUSTICE LEAGUE WILL FALL--
--NEVER TO RISE AGAIN!
NOT THE END! Turn the page for a special BONUS FEATURE!

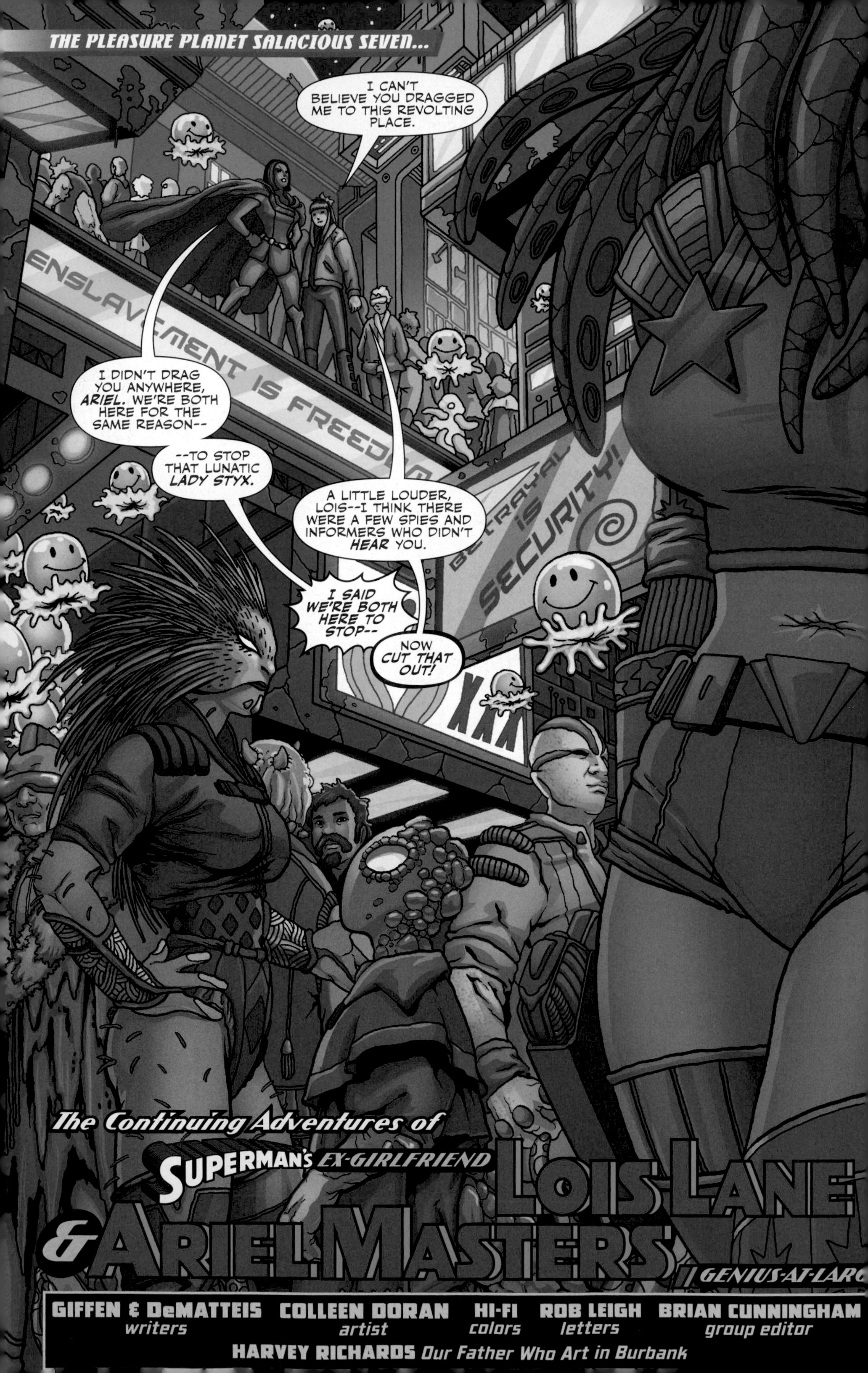

THE PLEASURE PLANET SALACIOUS SEVEN...
I CAN'T BELIEVE YOU DRAGGED ME TO THIS REVOLTING PLACE.
I DIDN'T DRAG YOU ANYWHERE, ARIEL. WE'RE BOTH HERE FOR THE SAME REASON--
--TO STOP THAT LUNATIC LADY STYX.
A LITTLE LOUDER, LOIS--I THINK THERE WERE A FEW SPIES AND INFORMERS WHO DIDN'T HEAR YOU.
I SAID WE'RE BOTH HERE TO STOP--
NOW CUT THAT OUT!
ENSLAVEMENT IS FREEDOM
BETRAYAL IS SECURITY!
XXX
The Continuing Adventures of
SUPERMAN'S EX-GIRLFRIEND LOIS LANE & ARIEL MASTERS, GENIUS-AT-LARG
GIFFEN & DeMATTEIS writers
COLLEEN DORAN artist
HI-FI colors
ROB LEIGH letters
BRIAN CUNNINGHAM group editor
HARVEY RICHARDS Our Father Who Art in Burbank

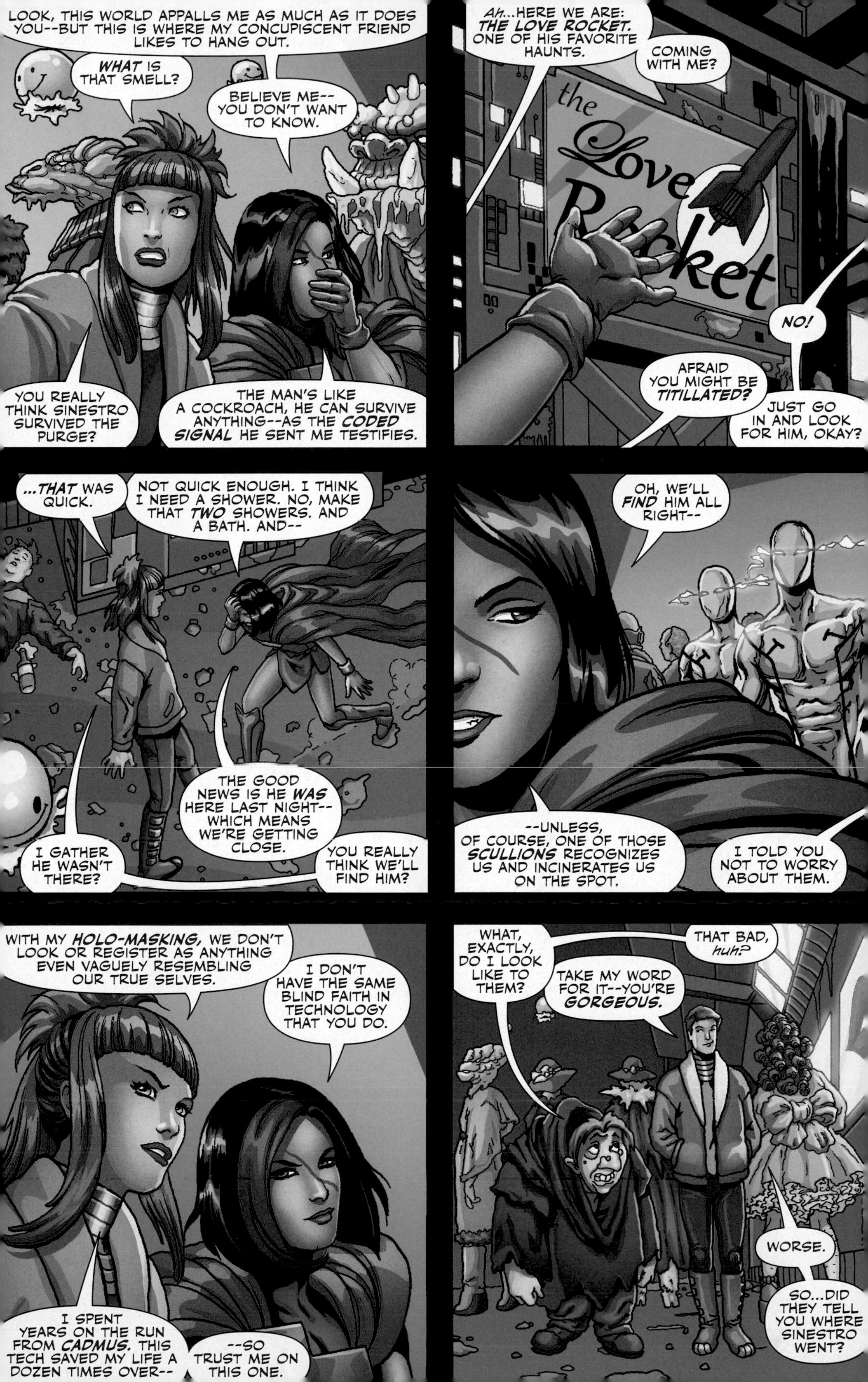
LOOK, THIS WORLD APPALLS ME AS MUCH AS IT DOES YOU--BUT THIS IS WHERE MY CONCUPISCENT FRIEND LIKES TO HANG OUT.
WHAT IS THAT SMELL?
BELIEVE ME-- YOU DON'T WANT TO KNOW.
YOU REALLY THINK SINESTRO SURVIVED THE PURGE?
THE MAN'S LIKE A COCKROACH, HE CAN SURVIVE ANYTHING--AS THE CODED SIGNAL HE SENT ME TESTIFIES.
Ah...HERE WE ARE: THE LOVE ROCKET. ONE OF HIS FAVORITE HAUNTS.
COMING WITH ME?
the Love Rocket
NO!
AFRAID YOU MIGHT BE TITILLATED?
JUST GO IN AND LOOK FOR HIM, OKAY?
...THAT WAS QUICK.
NOT QUICK ENOUGH. I THINK I NEED A SHOWER. NO, MAKE THAT TWO SHOWERS. AND A BATH. AND--
I GATHER HE WASN'T THERE?
THE GOOD NEWS IS HE WAS HERE LAST NIGHT-- WHICH MEANS WE'RE GETTING CLOSE.
YOU REALLY THINK WE'LL FIND HIM?
OH, WE'LL FIND HIM ALL RIGHT--
--UNLESS, OF COURSE, ONE OF THOSE SCULLIONS RECOGNIZES US AND INCINERATES US ON THE SPOT.
I TOLD YOU NOT TO WORRY ABOUT THEM.
WITH MY HOLO-MASKING, WE DON'T LOOK OR REGISTER AS ANYTHING EVEN VAGUELY RESEMBLING OUR TRUE SELVES.
I DON'T HAVE THE SAME BLIND FAITH IN TECHNOLOGY THAT YOU DO.
I SPENT YEARS ON THE RUN FROM CADMUS. THIS TECH SAVED MY LIFE A DOZEN TIMES OVER--
--SO TRUST ME ON THIS ONE.
WHAT, EXACTLY, DO I LOOK LIKE TO THEM?
THAT BAD, huh?
TAKE MY WORD FOR IT--YOU'RE GORGEOUS.
WORSE.
SO...DID THEY TELL YOU WHERE SINESTRO WENT?

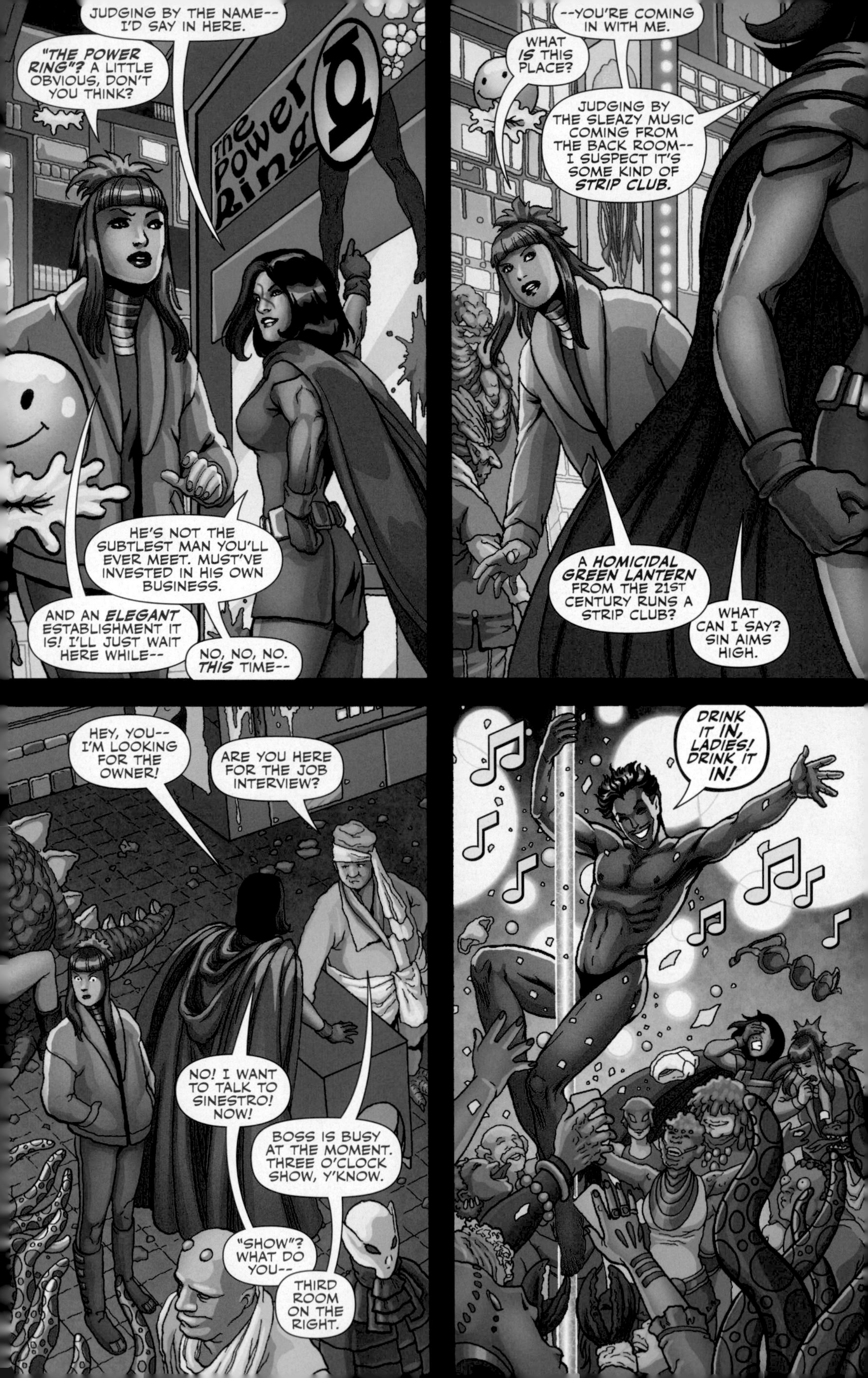
JUDGING BY THE NAME-- I'D SAY IN HERE.
"THE POWER RING"? A LITTLE OBVIOUS, DON'T YOU THINK?
The Power Ring
HE'S NOT THE SUBTLEST MAN YOU'LL EVER MEET. MUST'VE INVESTED IN HIS OWN BUSINESS.
AND AN ELEGANT ESTABLISHMENT IT IS! I'LL JUST WAIT HERE WHILE--
NO, NO, NO. THIS TIME--
--YOU'RE COMING IN WITH ME.
WHAT IS THIS PLACE?
JUDGING BY THE SLEAZY MUSIC COMING FROM THE BACK ROOM-- I SUSPECT IT'S SOME KIND OF STRIP CLUB.
A HOMICIDAL GREEN LANTERN FROM THE 21ST CENTURY RUNS A STRIP CLUB?
WHAT CAN I SAY? SIN AIMS HIGH.
HEY, YOU-- I'M LOOKING FOR THE OWNER!
ARE YOU HERE FOR THE JOB INTERVIEW?
NO! I WANT TO TALK TO SINESTRO! NOW!
BOSS IS BUSY AT THE MOMENT. THREE O'CLOCK SHOW, Y'KNOW.
"SHOW"? WHAT DO YOU--
THIRD ROOM ON THE RIGHT.
DRINK IT IN, LADIES! DRINK IT IN!

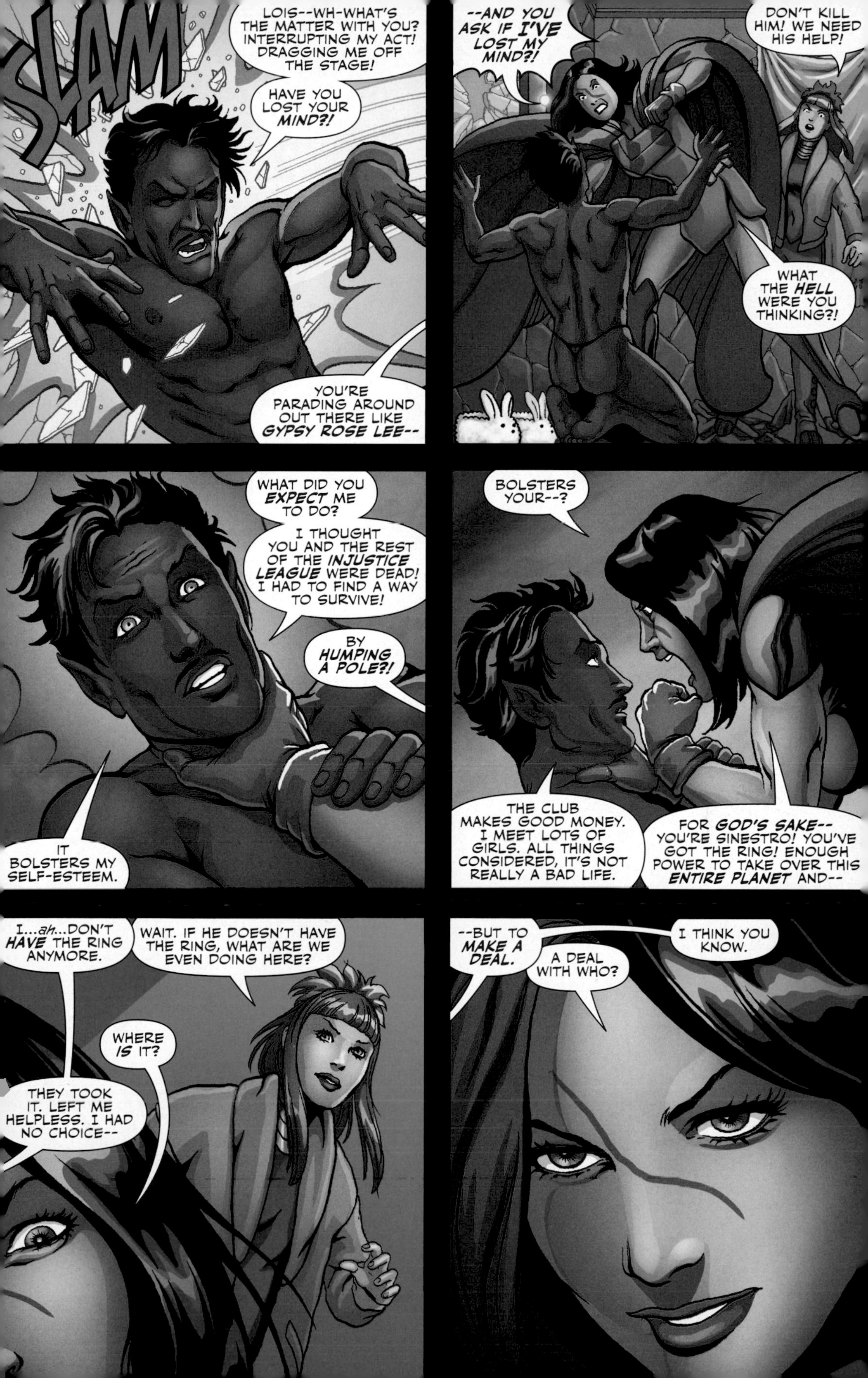
SLAM
LOIS--WH-WHAT'S THE MATTER WITH YOU? INTERRUPTING MY ACT! DRAGGING ME OFF THE STAGE!
HAVE YOU LOST YOUR MIND?!
YOU'RE PARADING AROUND OUT THERE LIKE GYPSY ROSE LEE--
--AND YOU ASK IF I'VE LOST MY MIND?!
DON'T KILL HIM! WE NEED HIS HELP!
WHAT THE HELL WERE YOU THINKING?!
WHAT DID YOU EXPECT ME TO DO?
I THOUGHT YOU AND THE REST OF THE INJUSTICE LEAGUE WERE DEAD! I HAD TO FIND A WAY TO SURVIVE!
BY HUMPING A POLE?!
IT BOLSTERS MY SELF-ESTEEM.
BOLSTERS YOUR--?
THE CLUB MAKES GOOD MONEY. I MEET LOTS OF GIRLS. ALL THINGS CONSIDERED, IT'S NOT REALLY A BAD LIFE.
FOR GOD'S SAKE-- YOU'RE SINESTRO! YOU'VE GOT THE RING! ENOUGH POWER TO TAKE OVER THIS ENTIRE PLANET AND--
I...ah...DON'T HAVE THE RING ANYMORE.
WAIT. IF HE DOESN'T HAVE THE RING, WHAT ARE WE EVEN DOING HERE?
WHERE IS IT?
THEY TOOK IT. LEFT ME HELPLESS. I HAD NO CHOICE--
--BUT TO MAKE A DEAL.
A DEAL WITH WHO?
I THINK YOU KNOW.

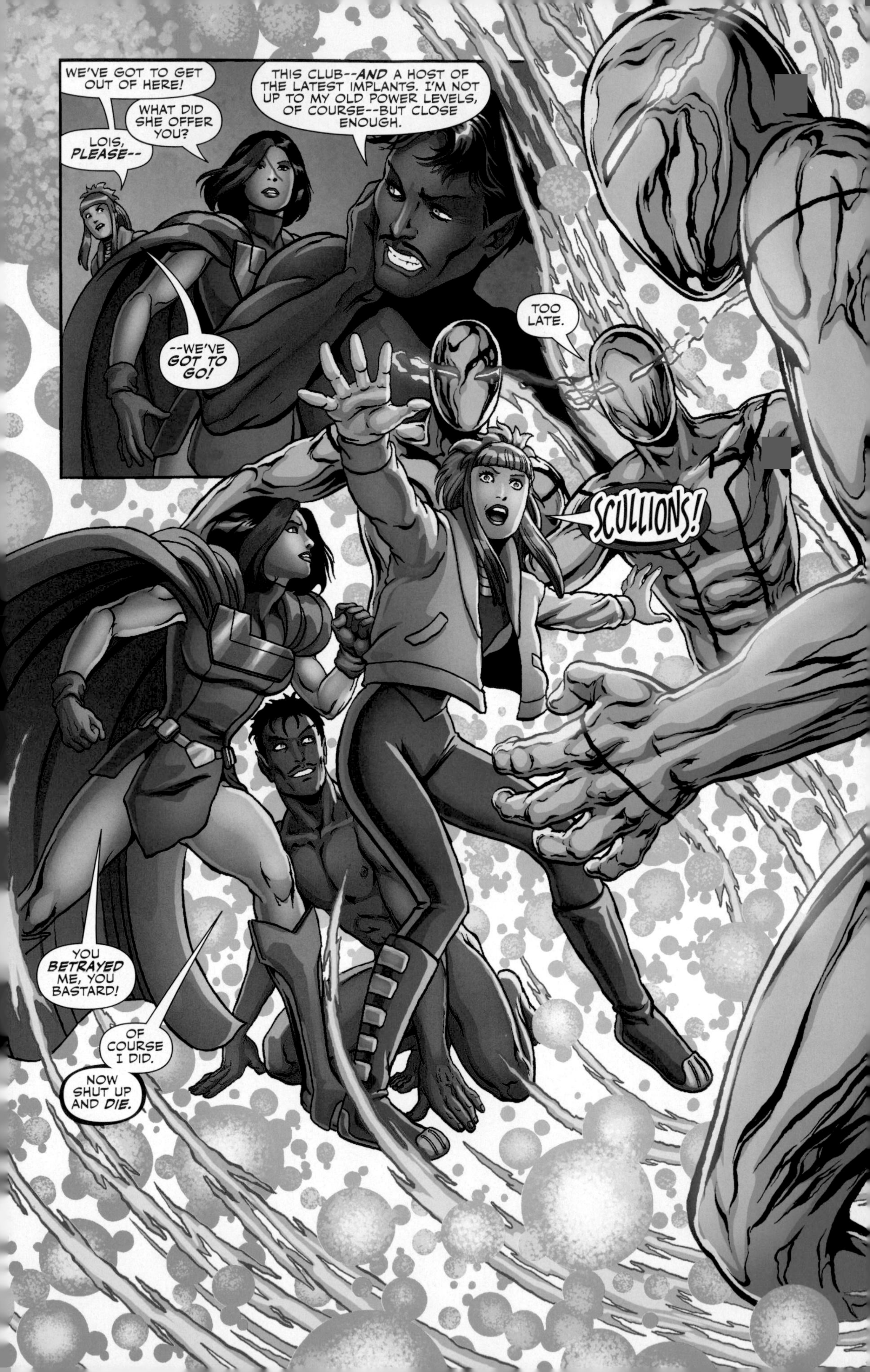
WE'VE GOT TO GET OUT OF HERE!
THIS CLUB--AND A HOST OF THE LATEST IMPLANTS. I'M NOT UP TO MY OLD POWER LEVELS, OF COURSE--BUT CLOSE ENOUGH.
WHAT DID SHE OFFER YOU?
LOIS, PLEASE--
--WE'VE GOT TO GO!
TOO LATE.
SCULLIONS!
YOU BETRAYED ME, YOU BASTARD!
OF COURSE I DID.
NOW SHUT UP AND DIE.

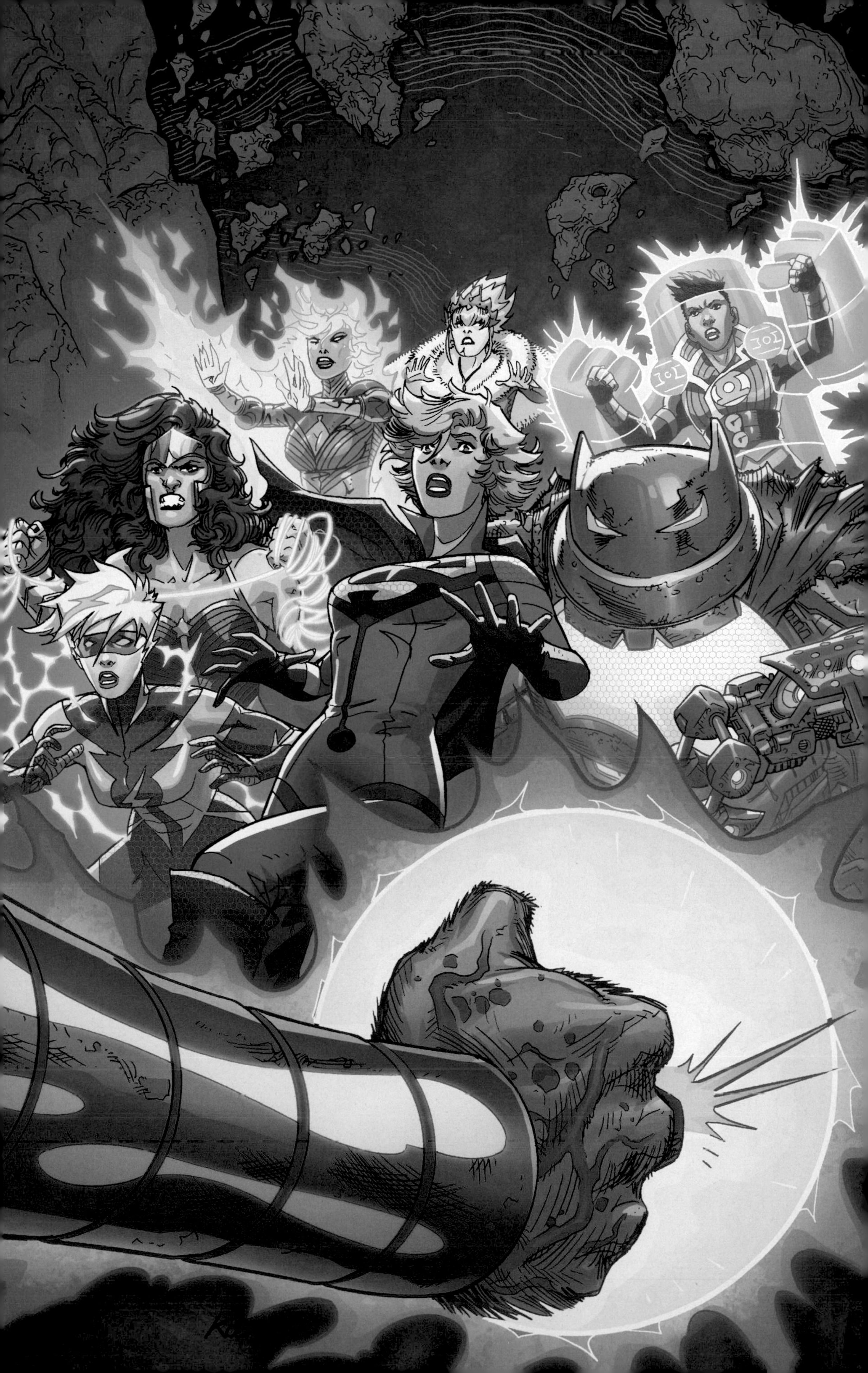

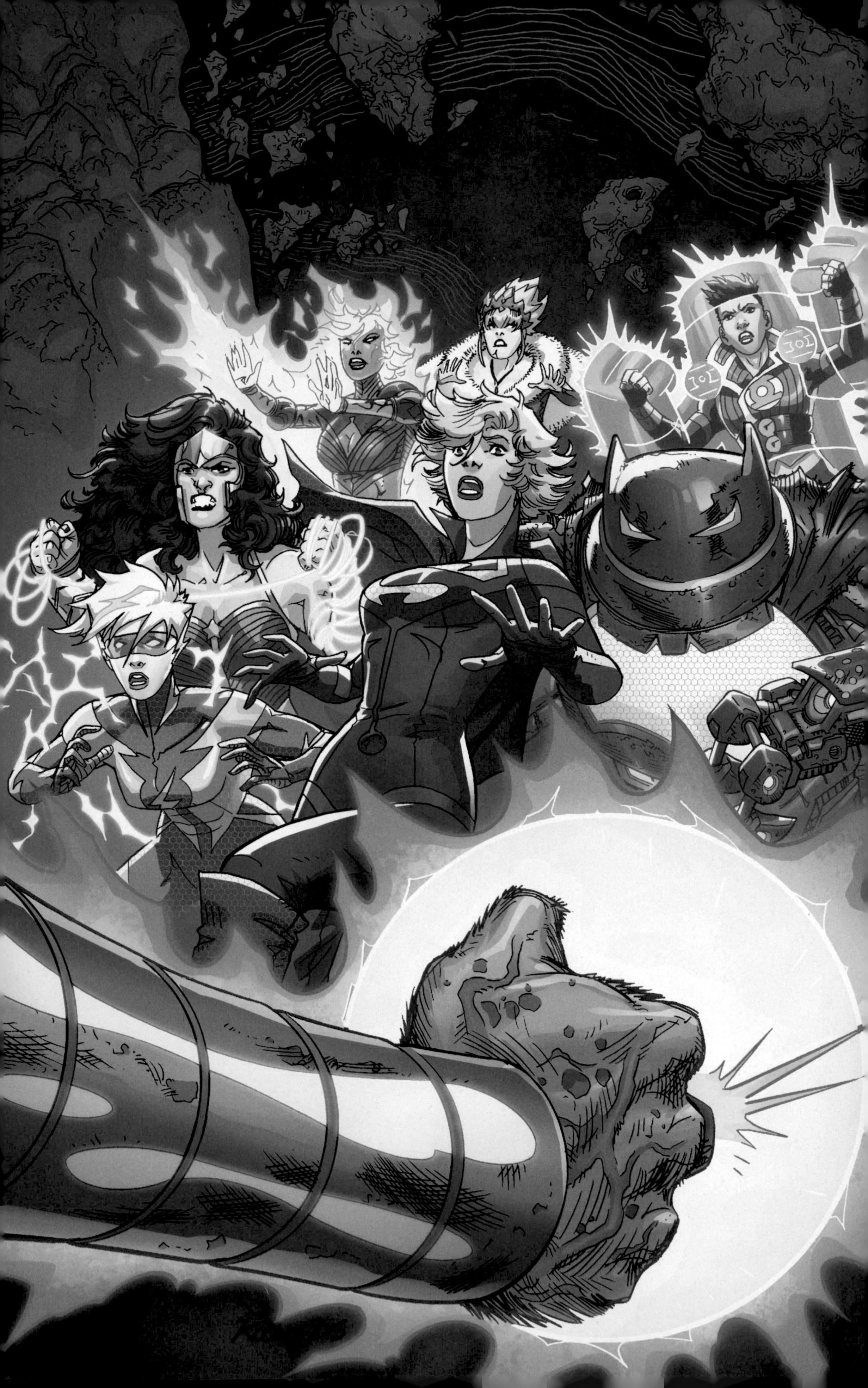

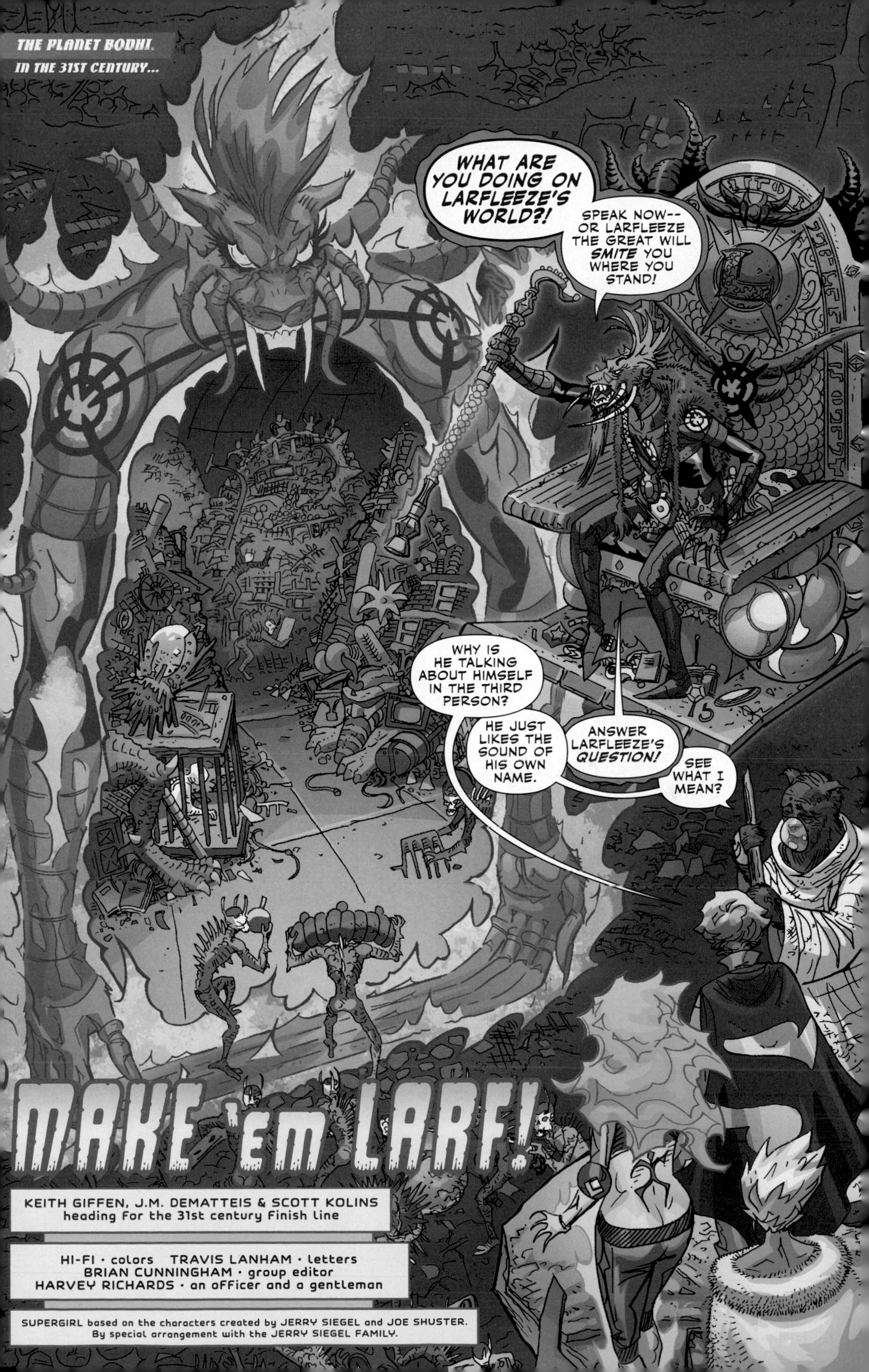
THE PLANET BODHI.
IN THE 31ST CENTURY...
WHAT ARE YOU DOING ON LARFLEEZE'S WORLD?!
SPEAK NOW-- OR LARFLEEZE THE GREAT WILL SMITE YOU WHERE YOU STAND!
WHY IS HE TALKING ABOUT HIMSELF IN THE THIRD PERSON?
HE JUST LIKES THE SOUND OF HIS OWN NAME.
ANSWER LARFLEEZE'S QUESTION!
SEE WHAT I MEAN?
MAKE 'EM LARF!
KEITH GIFFEN, J.M. DEMATTEIS & SCOTT KOLINS heading for the 31st century finish line
HI-FI · colors TRAVIS LANHAM · letters
BRIAN CUNNINGHAM · group editor
HARVEY RICHARDS · an officer and a gentleman
SUPERGIRL based on the characters created by JERRY SIEGEL and JOE SHUSTER. By special arrangement with the JERRY SIEGEL FAMILY.

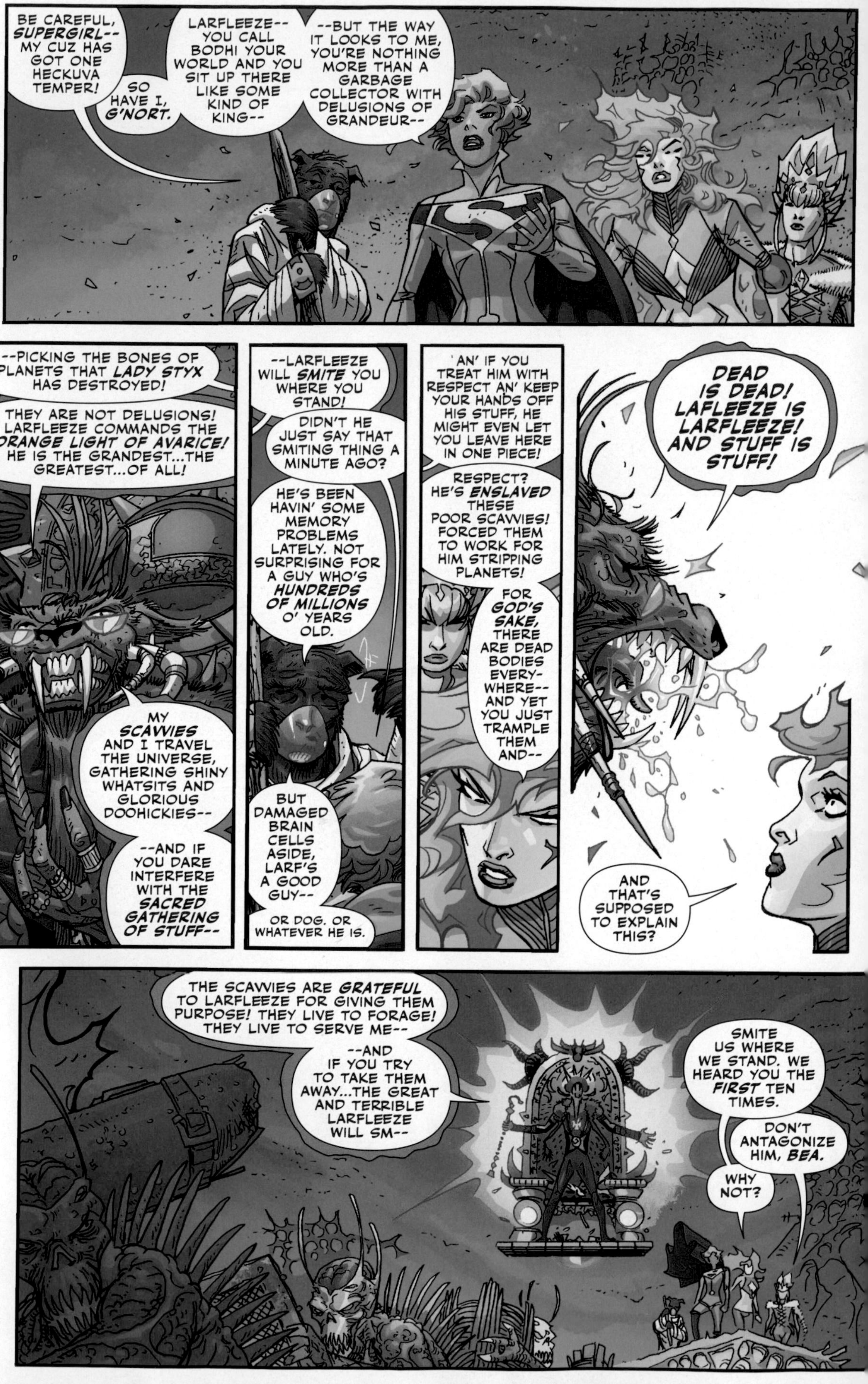
BE CAREFUL, SUPERGIRL-- MY CUZ HAS GOT ONE HECKUVA TEMPER!
SO HAVE I, G'NORT.
LARFLEEZE-- YOU CALL BODHI YOUR WORLD AND YOU SIT UP THERE LIKE SOME KIND OF KING--
--BUT THE WAY IT LOOKS TO ME, YOU'RE NOTHING MORE THAN A GARBAGE COLLECTOR WITH DELUSIONS OF GRANDEUR--
--PICKING THE BONES OF PLANETS THAT LADY STYX HAS DESTROYED!
THEY ARE NOT DELUSIONS! LARFLEEZE COMMANDS THE ORANGE LIGHT OF AVARICE! HE IS THE GRANDEST...THE GREATEST...OF ALL!
MY SCAVVIES AND I TRAVEL THE UNIVERSE, GATHERING SHINY WHATSITS AND GLORIOUS DOOHICKIES--
--AND IF YOU DARE INTERFERE WITH THE SACRED GATHERING OF STUFF--
--LARFLEEZE WILL SMITE YOU WHERE YOU STAND!
DIDN'T HE JUST SAY THAT SMITING THING A MINUTE AGO?
HE'S BEEN HAVIN' SOME MEMORY PROBLEMS LATELY. NOT SURPRISING FOR A GUY WHO'S HUNDREDS OF MILLIONS O' YEARS OLD.
BUT DAMAGED BRAIN CELLS ASIDE, LARF'S A GOOD GUY--
OR DOG. OR WHATEVER HE IS.
'AN' IF YOU TREAT HIM WITH RESPECT AN' KEEP YOUR HANDS OFF HIS STUFF, HE MIGHT EVEN LET YOU LEAVE HERE IN ONE PIECE!
RESPECT? HE'S ENSLAVED THESE POOR SCAVVIES! FORCED THEM TO WORK FOR HIM STRIPPING PLANETS!
FOR GOD'S SAKE, THERE ARE DEAD BODIES EVERY-WHERE-- AND YET YOU JUST TRAMPLE THEM AND--
DEAD IS DEAD! LAFLEEZE IS LARFLEEZE! AND STUFF IS STUFF!
AND THAT'S SUPPOSED TO EXPLAIN THIS?
THE SCAVVIES ARE GRATEFUL TO LARFLEEZE FOR GIVING THEM PURPOSE! THEY LIVE TO FORAGE! THEY LIVE TO SERVE ME--
--AND IF YOU TRY TO TAKE THEM AWAY...THE GREAT AND TERRIBLE LARFLEEZE WILL SM--
SMITE US WHERE WE STAND. WE HEARD YOU THE FIRST TEN TIMES.
DON'T ANTAGONIZE HIM, BEA.
WHY NOT?

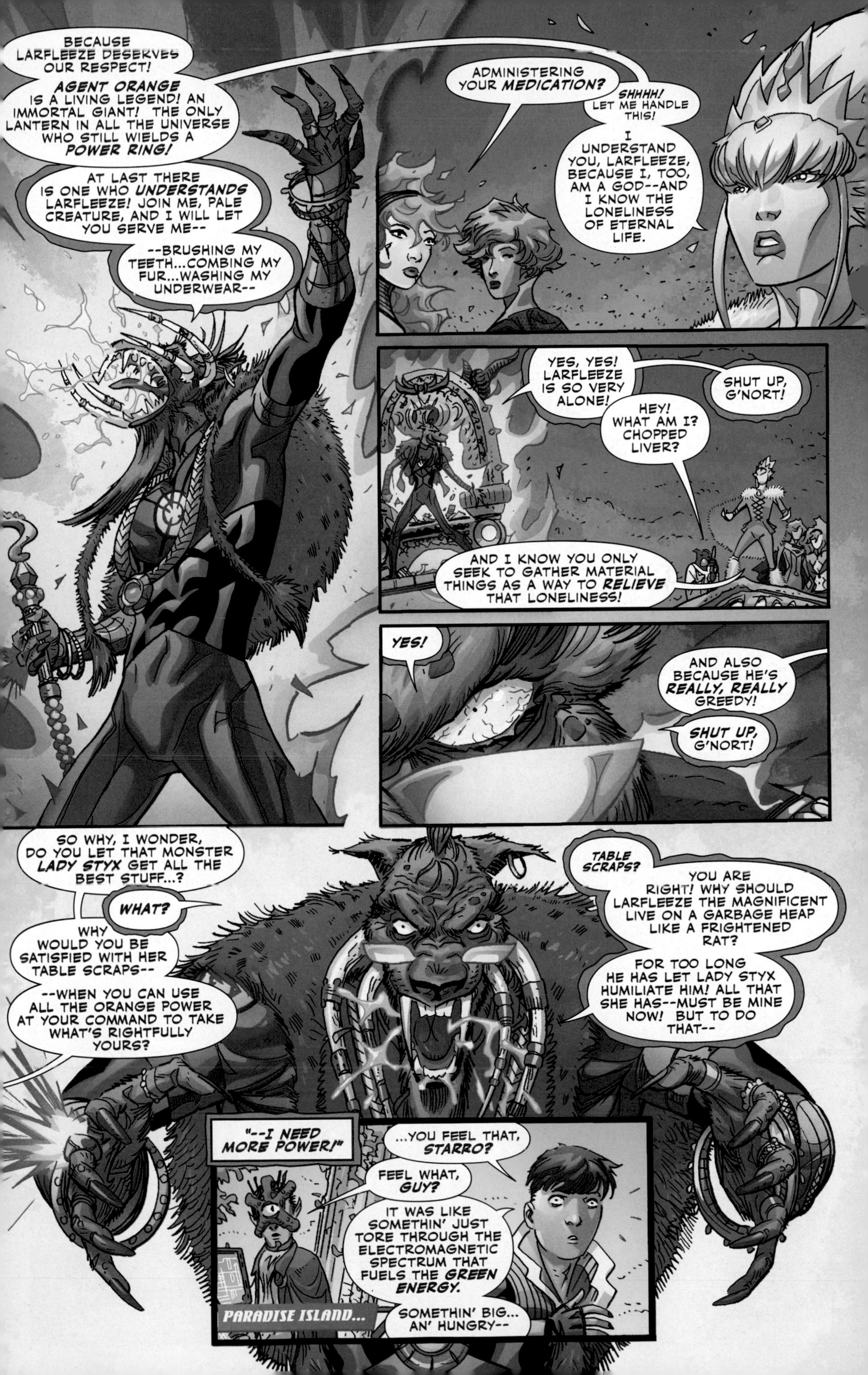

BECAUSE LARFLEEZE DESERVES OUR RESPECT!
AGENT ORANGE IS A LIVING LEGEND! AN IMMORTAL GIANT! THE ONLY LANTERN IN ALL THE UNIVERSE WHO STILL WIELDS A POWER RING!
AT LAST THERE IS ONE WHO UNDERSTANDS LARFLEEZE! JOIN ME, PALE CREATURE, AND I WILL LET YOU SERVE ME--
--BRUSHING MY TEETH...COMBING MY FUR...WASHING MY UNDERWEAR--
ADMINISTERING YOUR MEDICATION?
SHHHH! LET ME HANDLE THIS!
I UNDERSTAND YOU, LARFLEEZE, BECAUSE I, TOO, AM A GOD--AND I KNOW THE LONELINESS OF ETERNAL LIFE.
YES, YES! LARFLEEZE IS SO VERY ALONE!
SHUT UP, G'NORT!
HEY! WHAT AM I? CHOPPED LIVER?
AND I KNOW YOU ONLY SEEK TO GATHER MATERIAL THINGS AS A WAY TO RELIEVE THAT LONELINESS!
YES!
AND ALSO BECAUSE HE'S REALLY, REALLY GREEDY!
SHUT UP, G'NORT!
SO WHY, I WONDER, DO YOU LET THAT MONSTER LADY STYX GET ALL THE BEST STUFF...?
WHAT?
WHY WOULD YOU BE SATISFIED WITH HER TABLE SCRAPS--
--WHEN YOU CAN USE ALL THE ORANGE POWER AT YOUR COMMAND TO TAKE WHAT'S RIGHTFULLY YOURS?
TABLE SCRAPS?
YOU ARE RIGHT! WHY SHOULD LARFLEEZE THE MAGNIFICENT LIVE ON A GARBAGE HEAP LIKE A FRIGHTENED RAT?
FOR TOO LONG HE HAS LET LADY STYX HUMILIATE HIM! ALL THAT SHE HAS--MUST BE MINE NOW! BUT TO DO THAT--
"--I NEED MORE POWER!"
PARADISE ISLAND...
...YOU FEEL THAT, STARRO?
FEEL WHAT, GUY?
IT WAS LIKE SOMETHIN' JUST TORE THROUGH THE ELECTROMAGNETIC SPECTRUM THAT FUELS THE GREEN ENERGY.
SOMETHIN' BIG... AN' HUNGRY--

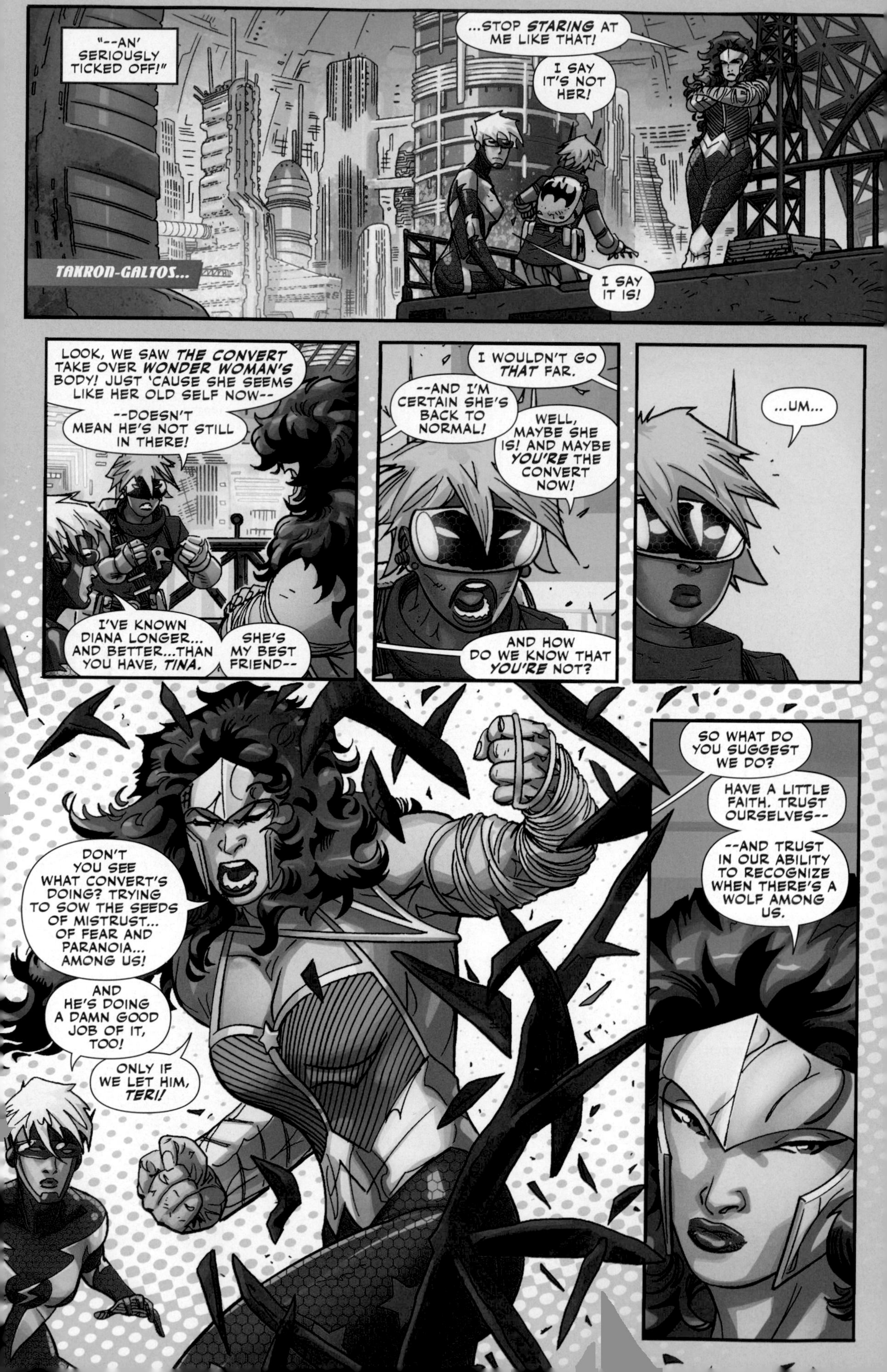
"--AN' SERIOUSLY TICKED OFF!"
TAKRON-GALTOS...
...STOP STARING AT ME LIKE THAT!
I SAY IT'S NOT HER!
I SAY IT IS!
LOOK, WE SAW THE CONVERT TAKE OVER WONDER WOMAN'S BODY! JUST 'CAUSE SHE SEEMS LIKE HER OLD SELF NOW--
--DOESN'T MEAN HE'S NOT STILL IN THERE!
I'VE KNOWN DIANA LONGER... AND BETTER...THAN YOU HAVE, TINA.
SHE'S MY BEST FRIEND--
I WOULDN'T GO THAT FAR.
--AND I'M CERTAIN SHE'S BACK TO NORMAL!
WELL, MAYBE SHE IS! AND MAYBE YOU'RE THE CONVERT NOW!
AND HOW DO WE KNOW THAT YOU'RE NOT?
...UM...
DON'T YOU SEE WHAT CONVERT'S DOING? TRYING TO SOW THE SEEDS OF MISTRUST... OF FEAR AND PARANOIA... AMONG US!
AND HE'S DOING A DAMN GOOD JOB OF IT, TOO!
ONLY IF WE LET HIM, TERI!
SO WHAT DO YOU SUGGEST WE DO?
HAVE A LITTLE FAITH. TRUST OURSELVES--
--AND TRUST IN OUR ABILITY TO RECOGNIZE WHEN THERE'S A WOLF AMONG US.

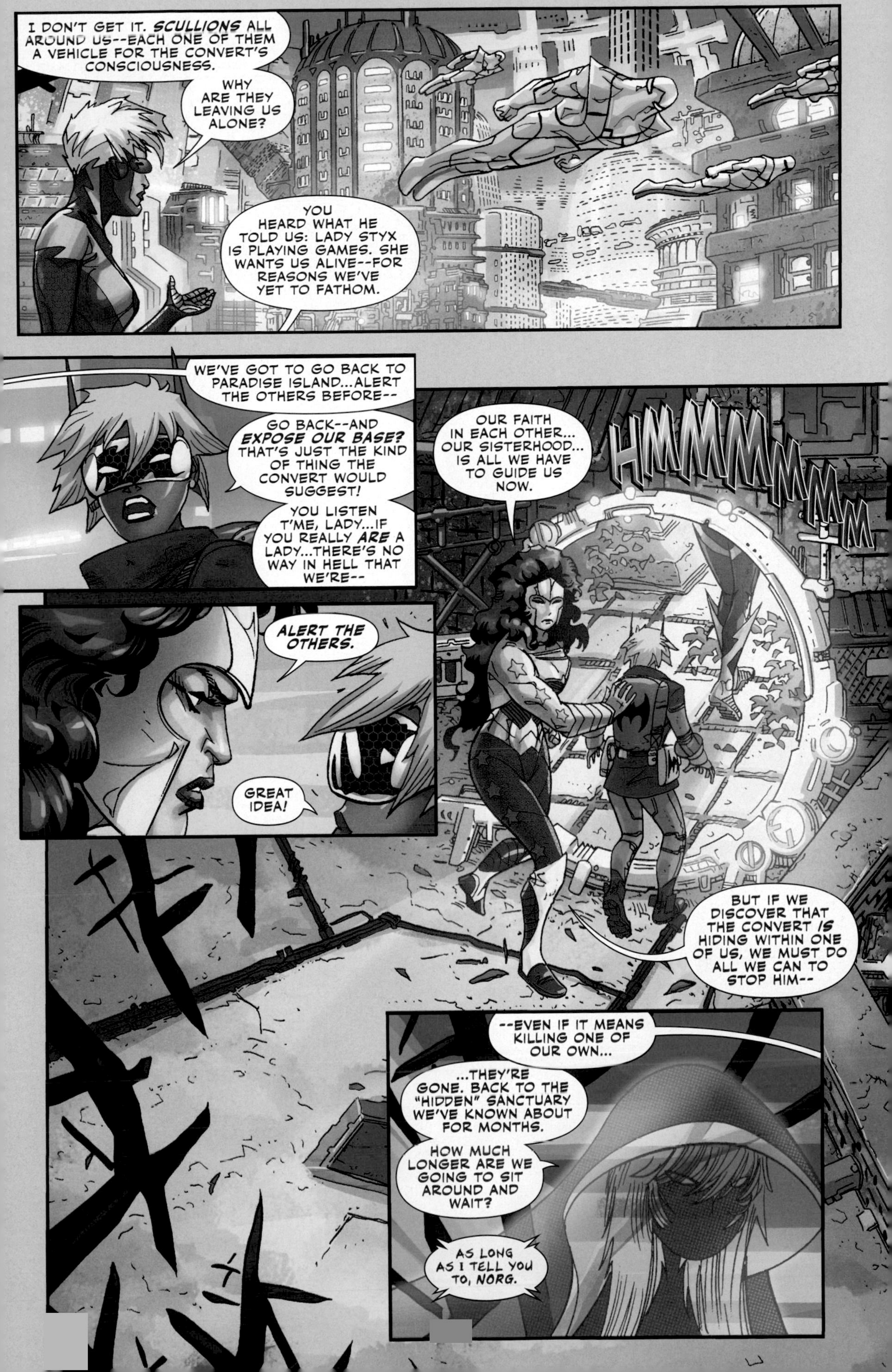

I DON'T GET IT. SCULLIONS ALL AROUND US--EACH ONE OF THEM A VEHICLE FOR THE CONVERT'S CONSCIOUSNESS.
WHY ARE THEY LEAVING US ALONE?
YOU HEARD WHAT HE TOLD US: LADY STYX IS PLAYING GAMES. SHE WANTS US ALIVE--FOR REASONS WE'VE YET TO FATHOM.
WE'VE GOT TO GO BACK TO PARADISE ISLAND...ALERT THE OTHERS BEFORE--
GO BACK--AND EXPOSE OUR BASE? THAT'S JUST THE KIND OF THING THE CONVERT WOULD SUGGEST!
YOU LISTEN T'ME, LADY...IF YOU REALLY ARE A LADY...THERE'S NO WAY IN HELL THAT WE'RE--
ALERT THE OTHERS.
GREAT IDEA!
OUR FAITH IN EACH OTHER... OUR SISTERHOOD... IS ALL WE HAVE TO GUIDE US NOW.
HMMMMMMMM
BUT IF WE DISCOVER THAT THE CONVERT IS HIDING WITHIN ONE OF US, WE MUST DO ALL WE CAN TO STOP HIM--
--EVEN IF IT MEANS KILLING ONE OF OUR OWN...
...THEY'RE GONE. BACK TO THE "HIDDEN" SANCTUARY WE'VE KNOWN ABOUT FOR MONTHS.
HOW MUCH LONGER ARE WE GOING TO SIT AROUND AND WAIT?
AS LONG AS I TELL YOU TO, NORG.

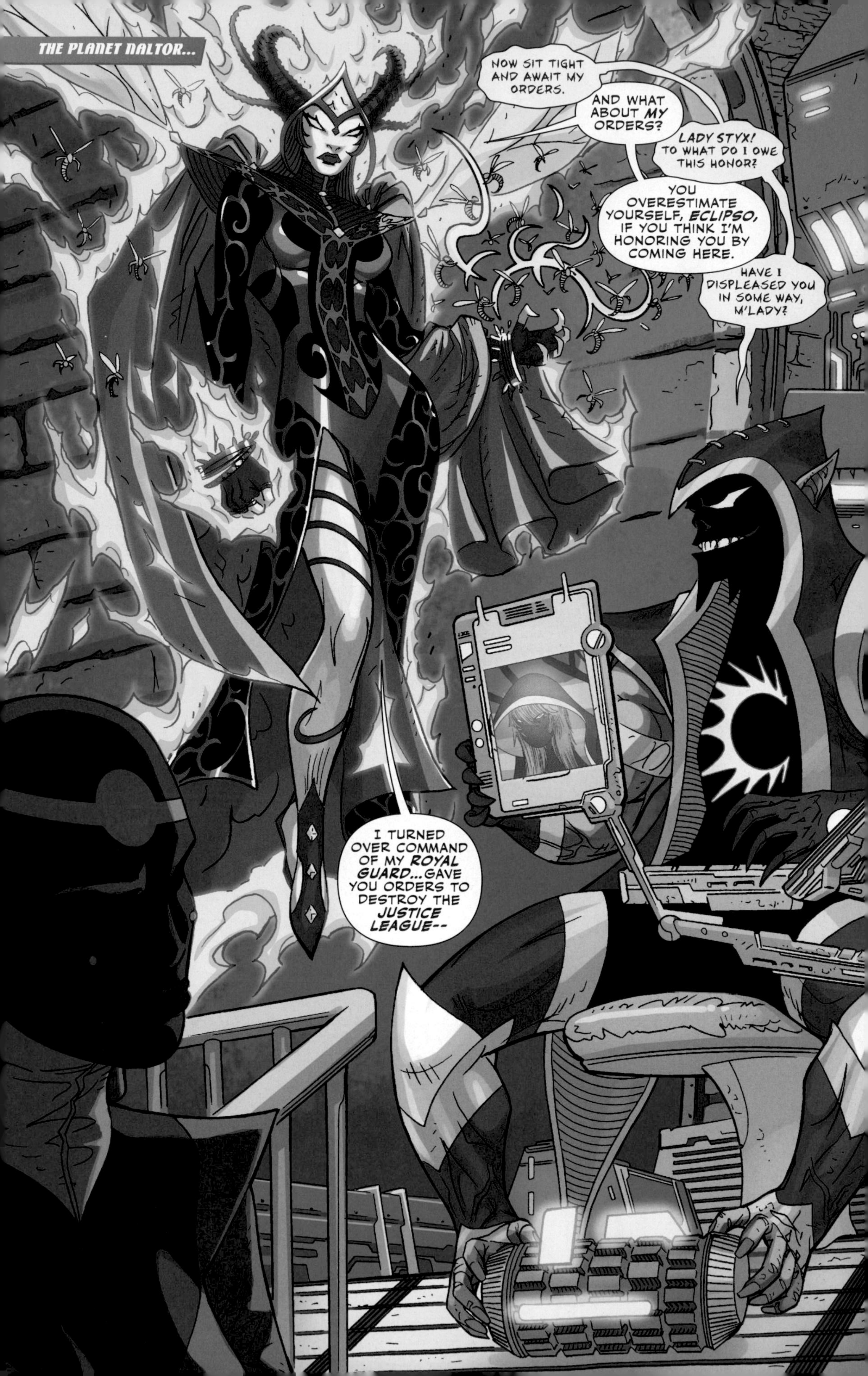
THE PLANET NALTOR...
NOW SIT TIGHT AND AWAIT MY ORDERS.
AND WHAT ABOUT MY ORDERS?
LADY STYX! TO WHAT DO I OWE THIS HONOR?
YOU OVERESTIMATE YOURSELF, ECLIPSO, IF YOU THINK I'M HONORING YOU BY COMING HERE.
HAVE I DISPLEASED YOU IN SOME WAY, M'LADY?
I TURNED OVER COMMAND OF MY ROYAL GUARD...GAVE YOU ORDERS TO DESTROY THE JUSTICE LEAGUE--

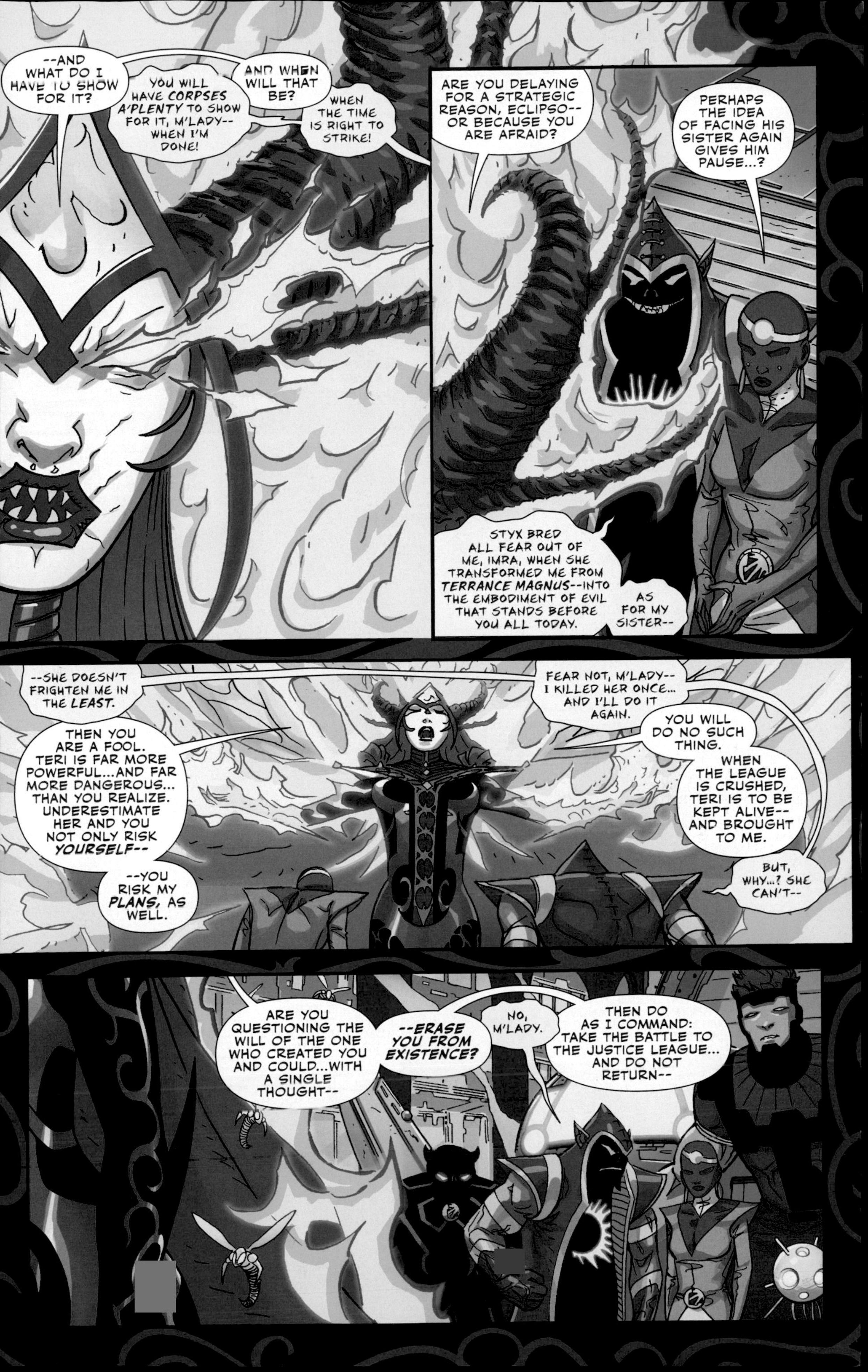
--AND WHAT DO I HAVE TO SHOW FOR IT?
YOU WILL HAVE CORPSES A'PLENTY TO SHOW FOR IT, M'LADY-- WHEN I'M DONE!
AND WHEN WILL THAT BE?
WHEN THE TIME IS RIGHT TO STRIKE!
ARE YOU DELAYING FOR A STRATEGIC REASON, ECLIPSO-- OR BECAUSE YOU ARE AFRAID?
PERHAPS THE IDEA OF FACING HIS SISTER AGAIN GIVES HIM PAUSE...?
STYX BRED ALL FEAR OUT OF ME, IMRA, WHEN SHE TRANSFORMED ME FROM TERRANCE MAGNUS--INTO THE EMBODIMENT OF EVIL THAT STANDS BEFORE YOU ALL TODAY.
AS FOR MY SISTER--
--SHE DOESN'T FRIGHTEN ME IN THE LEAST.
FEAR NOT, M'LADY-- I KILLED HER ONCE... AND I'LL DO IT AGAIN.
THEN YOU ARE A FOOL. TERI IS FAR MORE POWERFUL...AND FAR MORE DANGEROUS... THAN YOU REALIZE. UNDERESTIMATE HER AND YOU NOT ONLY RISK YOURSELF--
--YOU RISK MY PLANS, AS WELL.
YOU WILL DO NO SUCH THING.
WHEN THE LEAGUE IS CRUSHED, TERI IS TO BE KEPT ALIVE-- AND BROUGHT TO ME.
BUT, WHY...? SHE CAN'T--
ARE YOU QUESTIONING THE WILL OF THE ONE WHO CREATED YOU AND COULD...WITH A SINGLE THOUGHT--
--ERASE YOU FROM EXISTENCE?
NO, M'LADY.
THEN DO AS I COMMAND: TAKE THE BATTLE TO THE JUSTICE LEAGUE... AND DO NOT RETURN--

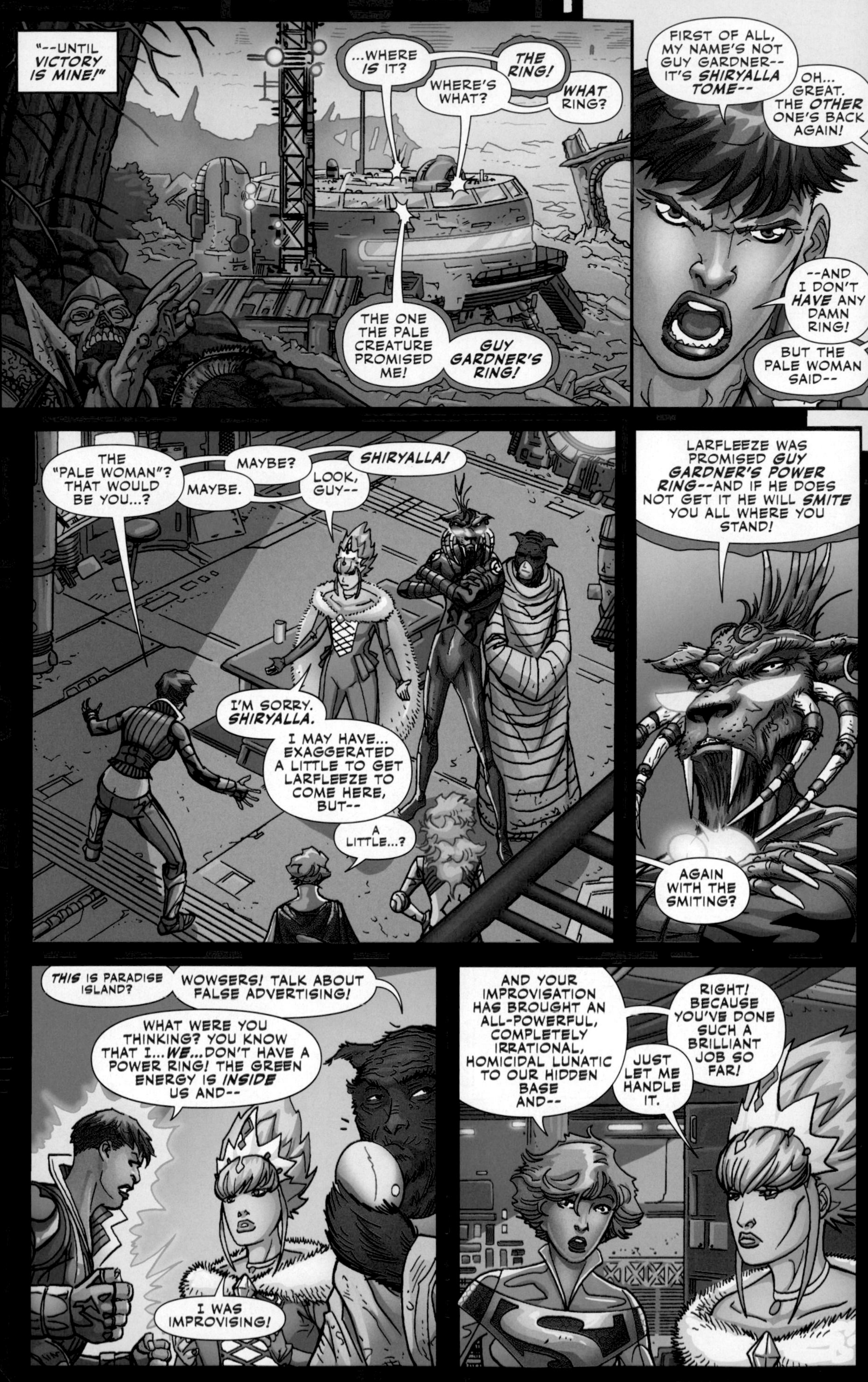
"--UNTIL VICTORY IS MINE!"
...WHERE IS IT?
WHERE'S WHAT?
THE RING!
WHAT RING?
THE ONE THE PALE CREATURE PROMISED ME!
GUY GARDNER'S RING!
FIRST OF ALL, MY NAME'S NOT GUY GARDNER-- IT'S SHIRYALLA TOME--
OH... GREAT. THE OTHER ONE'S BACK AGAIN!
--AND I DON'T HAVE ANY DAMN RING!
BUT THE PALE WOMAN SAID--
THE "PALE WOMAN"? THAT WOULD BE YOU...?
MAYBE?
MAYBE.
SHIRYALLA!
LOOK, GUY--
I'M SORRY. SHIRYALLA.
I MAY HAVE... EXAGGERATED A LITTLE TO GET LARFLEEZE TO COME HERE, BUT--
A LITTLE...?
LARFLEEZE WAS PROMISED GUY GARDNER'S POWER RING--AND IF HE DOES NOT GET IT HE WILL SMITE YOU ALL WHERE YOU STAND!
AGAIN WITH THE SMITING?
THIS IS PARADISE ISLAND?
WOWSERS! TALK ABOUT FALSE ADVERTISING!
WHAT WERE YOU THINKING? YOU KNOW THAT I...WE...DON'T HAVE A POWER RING! THE GREEN ENERGY IS INSIDE US AND--
I WAS IMPROVISING!
AND YOUR IMPROVISATION HAS BROUGHT AN ALL-POWERFUL, COMPLETELY IRRATIONAL, HOMICIDAL LUNATIC TO OUR HIDDEN BASE AND--
JUST LET ME HANDLE IT.
RIGHT! BECAUSE YOU'VE DONE SUCH A BRILLIANT JOB SO FAR!

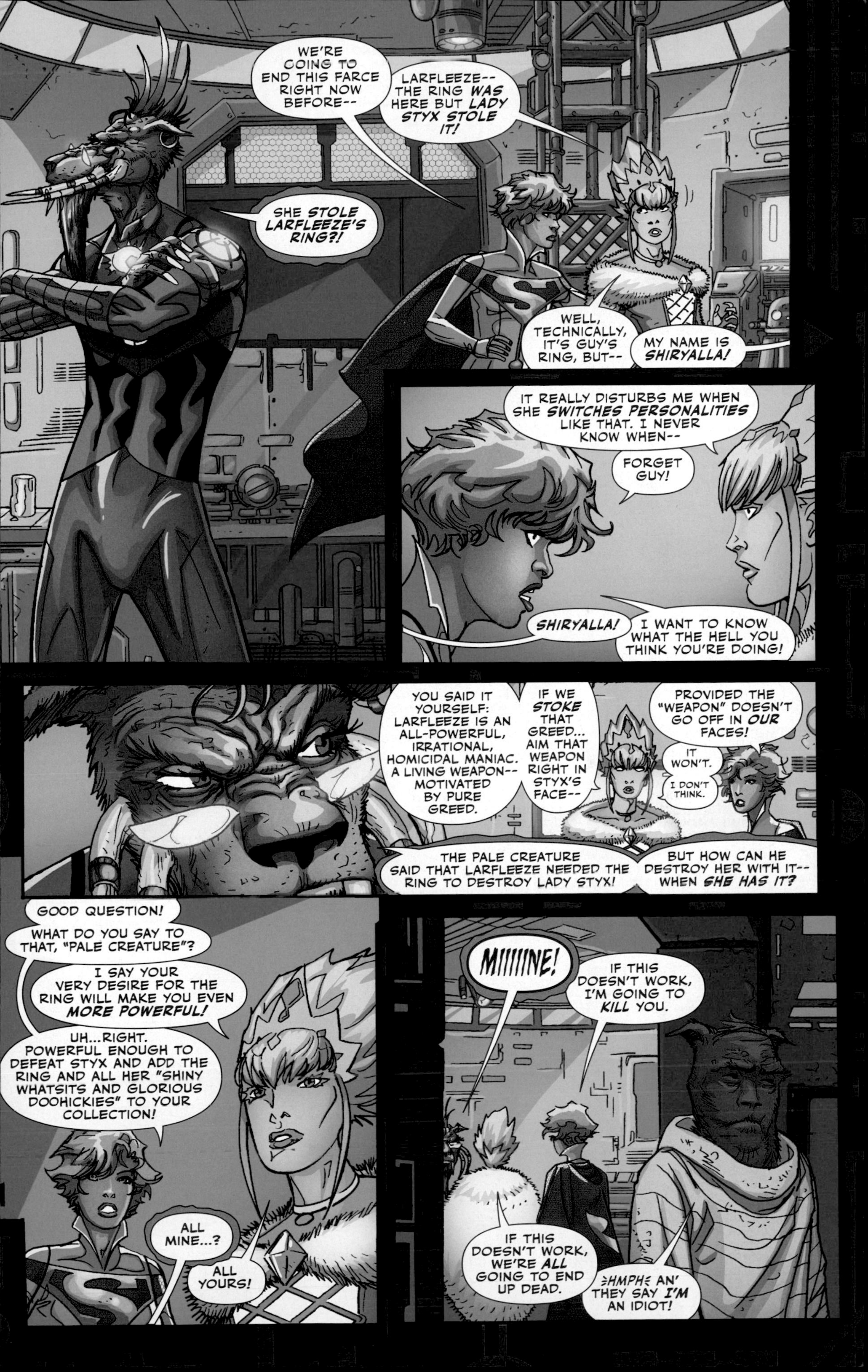
WE'RE COMING TO END THIS FARCE RIGHT NOW BEFORE--
LARFLEEZE-- THE RING WAS HERE BUT LADY STYX STOLE IT!
SHE STOLE LARFLEEZE'S RING?!
WELL, TECHNICALLY, IT'S GUY'S RING, BUT--
MY NAME IS SHIRYALLA!
IT REALLY DISTURBS ME WHEN SHE SWITCHES PERSONALITIES LIKE THAT. I NEVER KNOW WHEN--
FORGET GUY!
SHIRYALLA!
I WANT TO KNOW WHAT THE HELL YOU THINK YOU'RE DOING!
YOU SAID IT YOURSELF: LARFLEEZE IS AN ALL-POWERFUL, IRRATIONAL, HOMICIDAL MANIAC. A LIVING WEAPON-- MOTIVATED BY PURE GREED.
IF WE STOKE THAT GREED... AIM THAT WEAPON RIGHT IN STYX'S FACE--
PROVIDED THE "WEAPON" DOESN'T GO OFF IN OUR FACES!
IT WON'T.
I DON'T THINK.
THE PALE CREATURE SAID THAT LARFLEEZE NEEDED THE RING TO DESTROY LADY STYX!
BUT HOW CAN HE DESTROY HER WITH IT-- WHEN SHE HAS IT?
GOOD QUESTION!
WHAT DO YOU SAY TO THAT, "PALE CREATURE"?
I SAY YOUR VERY DESIRE FOR THE RING WILL MAKE YOU EVEN MORE POWERFUL!
UH...RIGHT. POWERFUL ENOUGH TO DEFEAT STYX AND ADD THE RING AND ALL HER "SHINY WHATSITS AND GLORIOUS DOOHICKIES" TO YOUR COLLECTION!
ALL MINE...?
ALL YOURS!
MIIIIINE!
IF THIS DOESN'T WORK, I'M GOING TO KILL YOU.
IF THIS DOESN'T WORK, WE'RE ALL GOING TO END UP DEAD.
HMPH AN' THEY SAY I'M AN IDIOT!

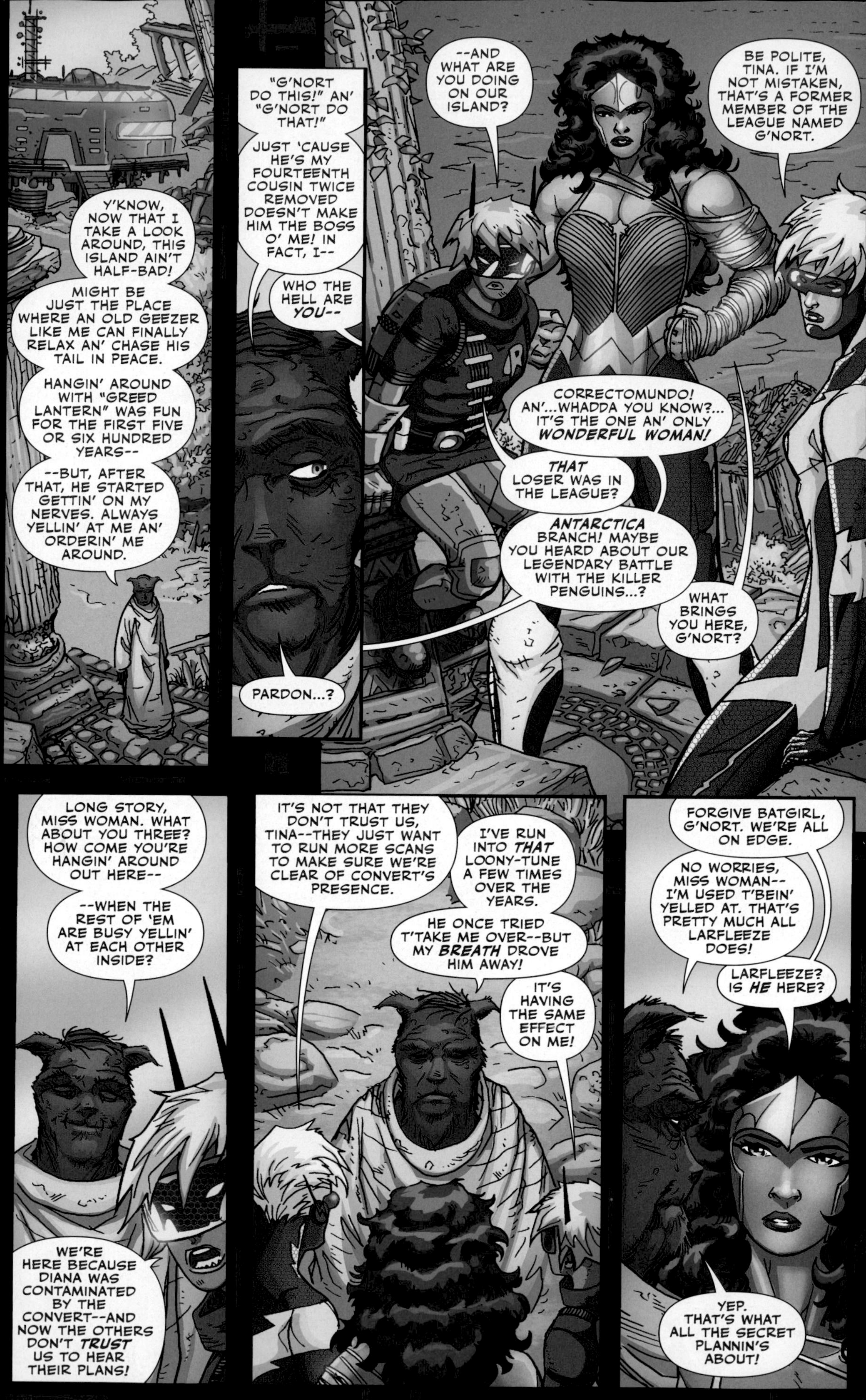
Y'KNOW, NOW THAT I TAKE A LOOK AROUND, THIS ISLAND AIN'T HALF-BAD!
MIGHT BE JUST THE PLACE WHERE AN OLD GEEZER LIKE ME CAN FINALLY RELAX AN' CHASE HIS TAIL IN PEACE.
HANGIN' AROUND WITH "GREED LANTERN" WAS FUN FOR THE FIRST FIVE OR SIX HUNDRED YEARS--
--BUT, AFTER THAT, HE STARTED GETTIN' ON MY NERVES. ALWAYS YELLIN' AT ME AN' ORDERIN' ME AROUND.
"G'NORT DO THIS!" AN' "G'NORT DO THAT!"
JUST 'CAUSE HE'S MY FOURTEENTH COUSIN TWICE REMOVED DOESN'T MAKE HIM THE BOSS O' ME! IN FACT, I--
WHO THE HELL ARE YOU--
PARDON...?
--AND WHAT ARE YOU DOING ON OUR ISLAND?
BE POLITE, TINA. IF I'M NOT MISTAKEN, THAT'S A FORMER MEMBER OF THE LEAGUE NAMED G'NORT.
CORRECTOMUNDO! AN'...WHADDA YOU KNOW?... IT'S THE ONE AN' ONLY WONDERFUL WOMAN!
THAT LOSER WAS IN THE LEAGUE?
ANTARCTICA BRANCH! MAYBE YOU HEARD ABOUT OUR LEGENDARY BATTLE WITH THE KILLER PENGUINS...?
WHAT BRINGS YOU HERE, G'NORT?
LONG STORY, MISS WOMAN. WHAT ABOUT YOU THREE? HOW COME YOU'RE HANGIN' AROUND OUT HERE--
--WHEN THE REST OF 'EM ARE BUSY YELLIN' AT EACH OTHER INSIDE?
WE'RE HERE BECAUSE DIANA WAS CONTAMINATED BY THE CONVERT--AND NOW THE OTHERS DON'T TRUST US TO HEAR THEIR PLANS!
IT'S NOT THAT THEY DON'T TRUST US, TINA--THEY JUST WANT TO RUN MORE SCANS TO MAKE SURE WE'RE CLEAR OF CONVERT'S PRESENCE.
I'VE RUN INTO THAT LOONY-TUNE A FEW TIMES OVER THE YEARS.
HE ONCE TRIED T'TAKE ME OVER--BUT MY BREATH DROVE HIM AWAY!
IT'S HAVING THE SAME EFFECT ON ME!
FORGIVE BATGIRL, G'NORT. WE'RE ALL ON EDGE.
NO WORRIES, MISS WOMAN-- I'M USED T'BEIN' YELLED AT. THAT'S PRETTY MUCH ALL LARFLEEZE DOES!
LARFLEEZE? IS HE HERE?
YEP. THAT'S WHAT ALL THE SECRET PLANNIN'S ABOUT!

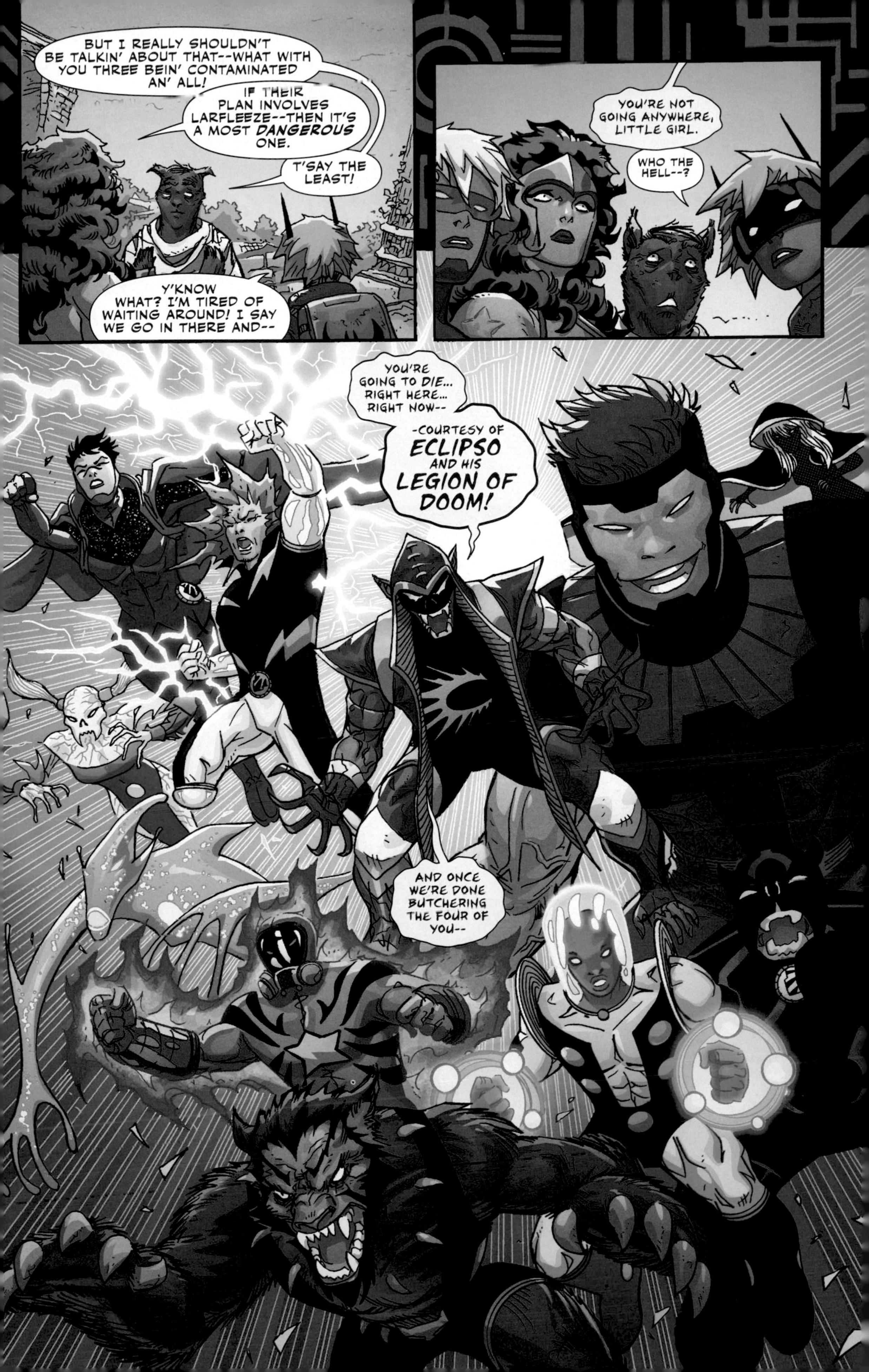
BUT I REALLY SHOULDN'T BE TALKIN' ABOUT THAT--WHAT WITH YOU THREE BEIN' CONTAMINATED AN' ALL!
IF THEIR PLAN INVOLVES LARFLEEZE--THEN IT'S A MOST DANGEROUS ONE.
T'SAY THE LEAST!
Y'KNOW WHAT? I'M TIRED OF WAITING AROUND! I SAY WE GO IN THERE AND--
YOU'RE NOT GOING ANYWHERE, LITTLE GIRL.
WHO THE HELL--?
YOU'RE GOING TO DIE... RIGHT HERE... RIGHT NOW--
-COURTESY OF ECLIPSO AND HIS LEGION OF DOOM!
AND ONCE WE'RE DONE BUTCHERING THE FOUR OF YOU--

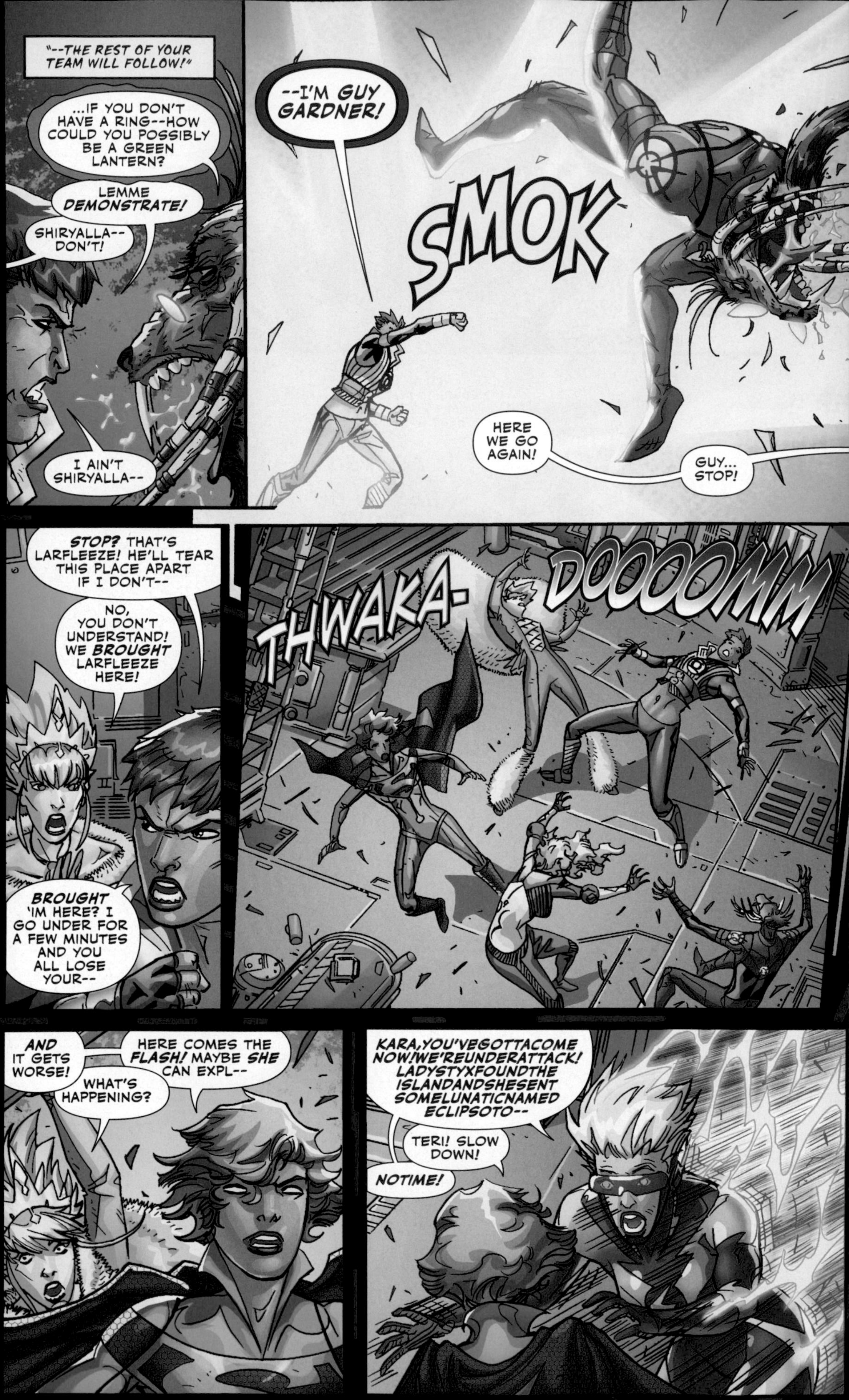
"--THE REST OF YOUR TEAM WILL FOLLOW!"
...IF YOU DON'T HAVE A RING--HOW COULD YOU POSSIBLY BE A GREEN LANTERN?
LEMME DEMONSTRATE!
SHIRYALLA-- DON'T!
I AIN'T SHIRYALLA--
--I'M GUY GARDNER!
SMOK
HERE WE GO AGAIN!
GUY... STOP!
STOP? THAT'S LARFLEEZE! HE'LL TEAR THIS PLACE APART IF I DON'T--
NO, YOU DON'T UNDERSTAND! WE BROUGHT LARFLEEZE HERE!
BROUGHT 'IM HERE? I GO UNDER FOR A FEW MINUTES AND YOU ALL LOSE YOUR--
THWAKA-
DOOOOMM
AND IT GETS WORSE!
HERE COMES THE FLASH! MAYBE SHE CAN EXPL--
WHAT'S HAPPENING?
KARA,YOU'VEGOTTACOME NOW!WE'REUNDERATTACK! LADYSTYXFOUNDTHE ISLANDANDSHESENT SOMELUNATICNAMED ECLIPSOTO--
TERI! SLOW DOWN!
NOTIME!

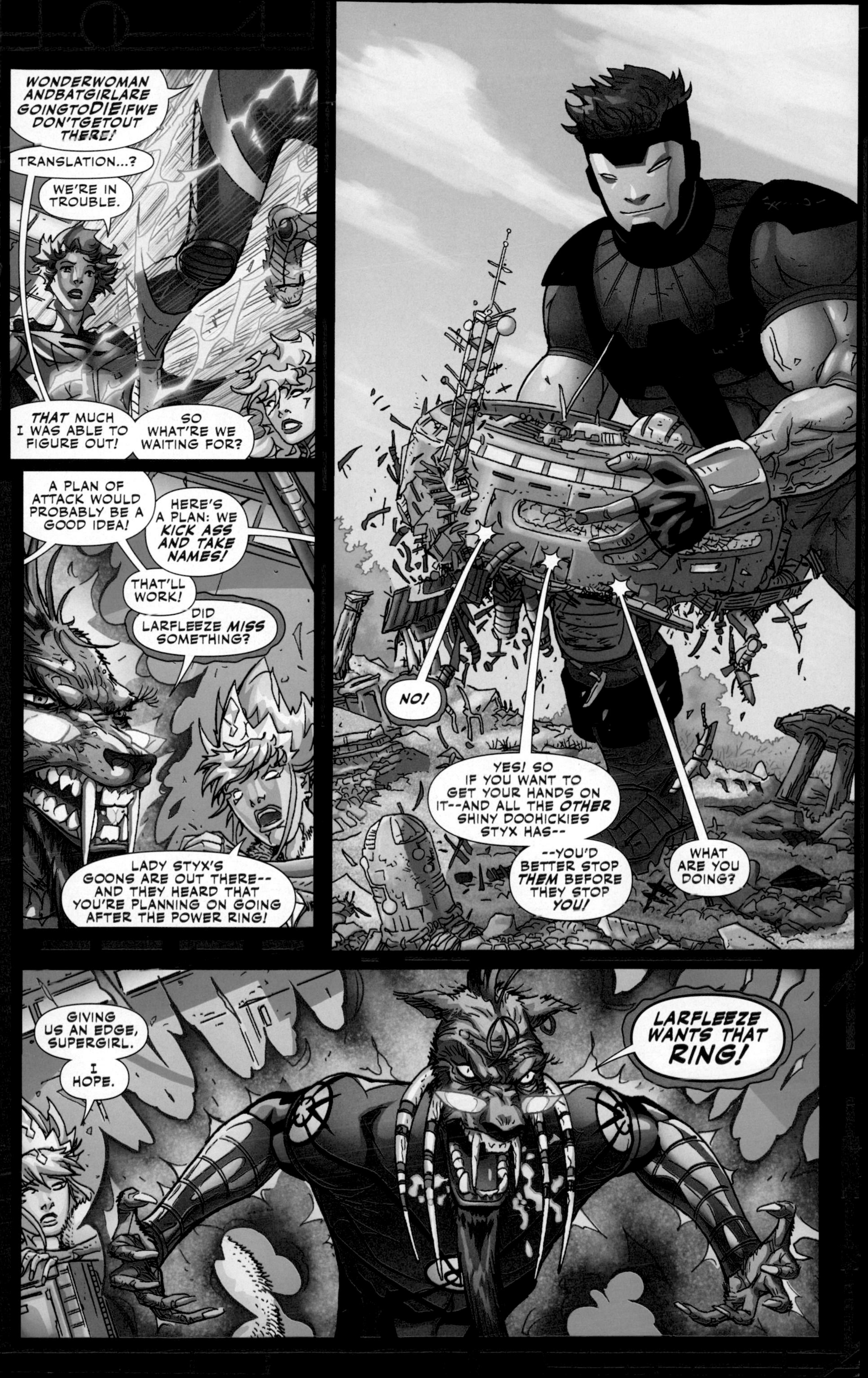

WONDERWOMAN ANDBATGIRLARE GOINGTODIEIFWE DON'TGETOUT THERE!
TRANSLATION...?
WE'RE IN TROUBLE.
THAT MUCH I WAS ABLE TO FIGURE OUT!
SO WHAT'RE WE WAITING FOR?
A PLAN OF ATTACK WOULD PROBABLY BE A GOOD IDEA!
HERE'S A PLAN: WE KICK ASS AND TAKE NAMES!
THAT'LL WORK!
DID LARFLEEZE MISS SOMETHING?
LADY STYX'S GOONS ARE OUT THERE-- AND THEY HEARD THAT YOU'RE PLANNING ON GOING AFTER THE POWER RING!
NO!
YES! SO IF YOU WANT TO GET YOUR HANDS ON IT--AND ALL THE OTHER SHINY DOOHICKIES STYX HAS--
--YOU'D BETTER STOP THEM BEFORE THEY STOP YOU!
WHAT ARE YOU DOING?
GIVING US AN EDGE, SUPERGIRL.
I HOPE.
LARFLEEZE WANTS THAT RING!

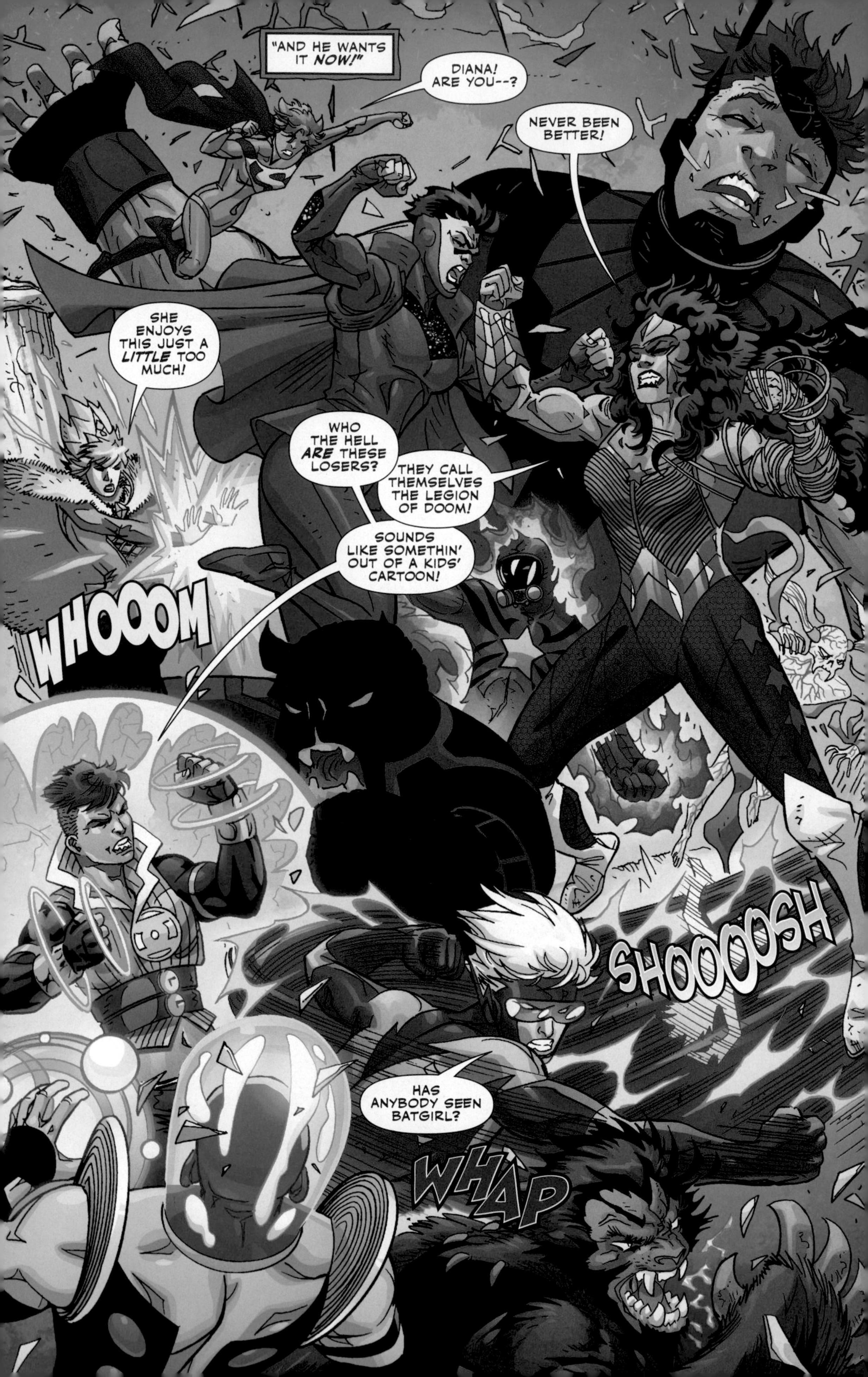

"AND HE WANTS IT NOW!"
DIANA! ARE YOU--?
NEVER BEEN BETTER!
SHE ENJOYS THIS JUST A LITTLE TOO MUCH!
WHO THE HELL ARE THESE LOSERS?
THEY CALL THEMSELVES THE LEGION OF DOOM!
SOUNDS LIKE SOMETHIN' OUT OF A KIDS' CARTOON!
WHOOOM
SHOOOOSH
HAS ANYBODY SEEN BATGIRL?
WHAP

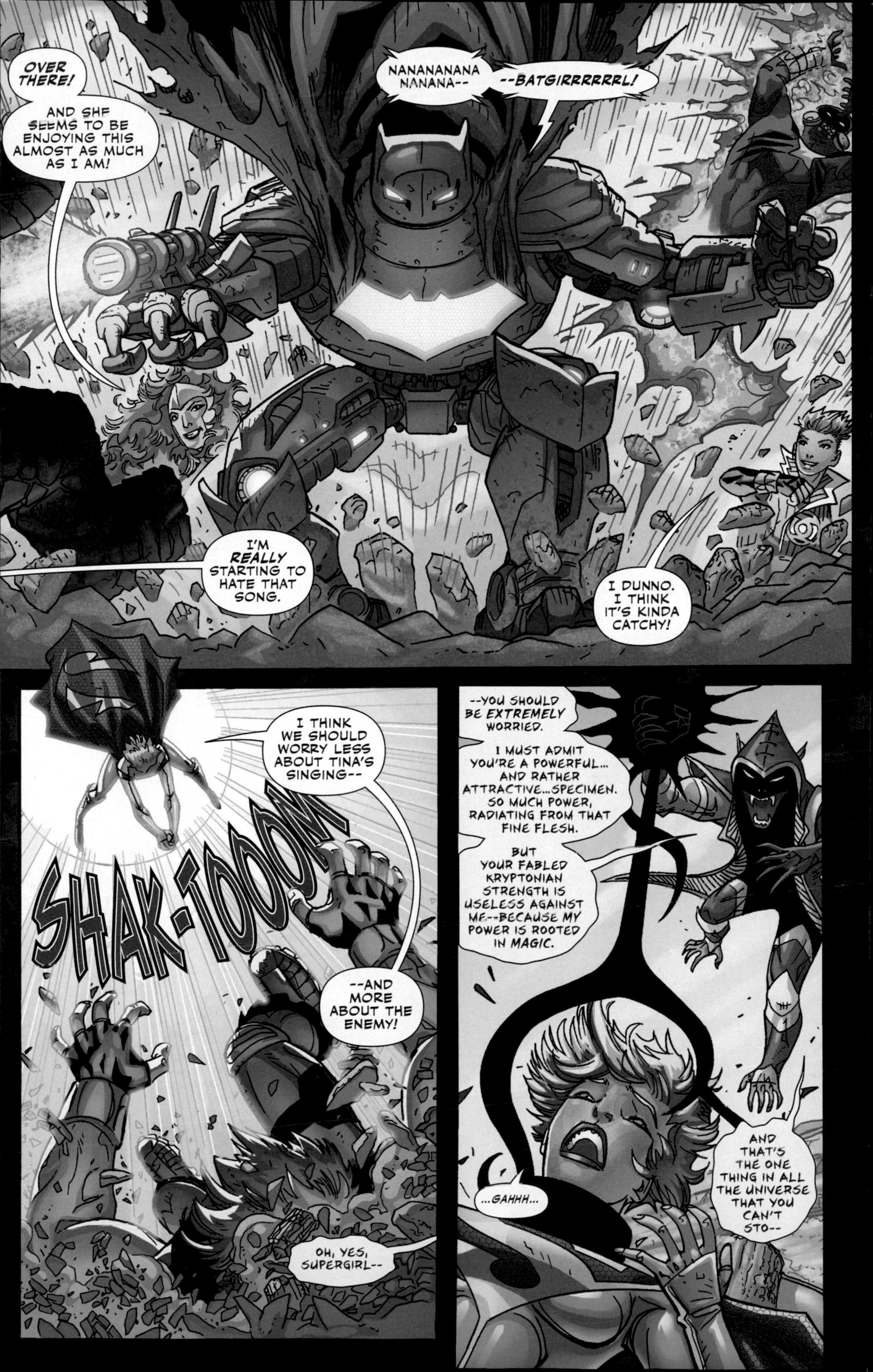
OVER THERE!
AND SHE SEEMS TO BE ENJOYING THIS ALMOST AS MUCH AS I AM!
NANANANANA NANANA--
--BATGIRRRRRRL!
I'M REALLY STARTING TO HATE THAT SONG.
I DUNNO. I THINK IT'S KINDA CATCHY!
I THINK WE SHOULD WORRY LESS ABOUT TINA'S SINGING--
SHAK-TOOOM
--AND MORE ABOUT THE ENEMY!
OH, YES, SUPERGIRL--
--YOU SHOULD BE EXTREMELY WORRIED.
I MUST ADMIT YOU'RE A POWERFUL... AND RATHER ATTRACTIVE...SPECIMEN. SO MUCH POWER, RADIATING FROM THAT FINE FLESH.
BUT YOUR FABLED KRYPTONIAN STRENGTH IS USELESS AGAINST ME--BECAUSE MY POWER IS ROOTED IN MAGIC.
...GAHHH...
AND THAT'S THE ONE THING IN ALL THE UNIVERSE THAT YOU CAN'T STO--

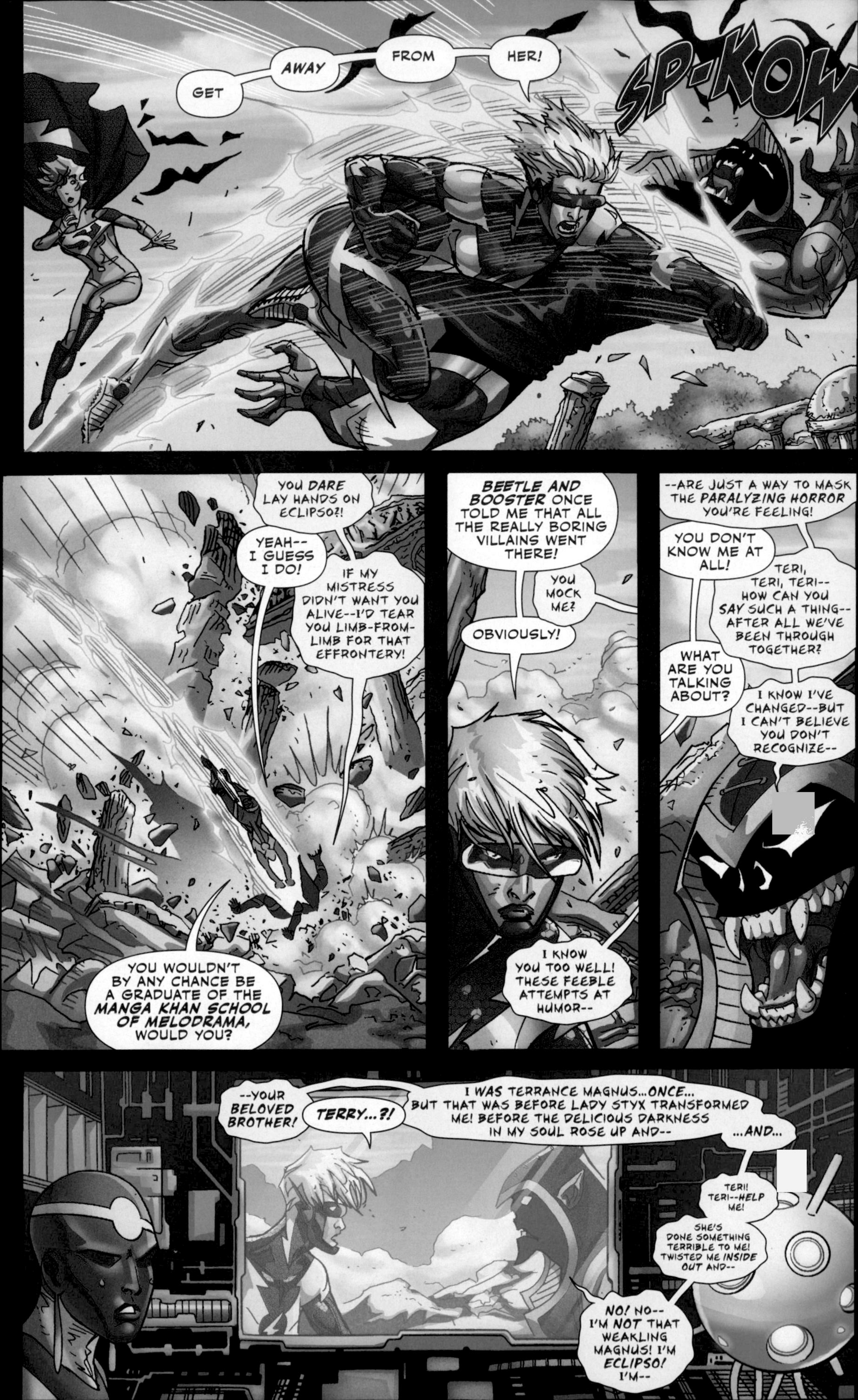
GET AWAY FROM HER!
SP-KOW
YOU DARE LAY HANDS ON ECLIPSO?!
YEAH-- I GUESS I DO!
IF MY MISTRESS DIDN'T WANT YOU ALIVE--I'D TEAR YOU LIMB-FROM-LIMB FOR THAT EFFRONTERY!
YOU WOULDN'T BY ANY CHANCE BE A GRADUATE OF THE MANGA KHAN SCHOOL OF MELODRAMA, WOULD YOU?
BEETLE AND BOOSTER ONCE TOLD ME THAT ALL THE REALLY BORING VILLAINS WENT THERE!
YOU MOCK ME?
OBVIOUSLY!
I KNOW YOU TOO WELL! THESE FEEBLE ATTEMPTS AT HUMOR--
--ARE JUST A WAY TO MASK THE PARALYZING HORROR YOU'RE FEELING!
YOU DON'T KNOW ME AT ALL!
TERI, TERI, TERI-- HOW CAN YOU SAY SUCH A THING-- AFTER ALL WE'VE BEEN THROUGH TOGETHER?
WHAT ARE YOU TALKING ABOUT?
I KNOW I'VE CHANGED--BUT I CAN'T BELIEVE YOU DON'T RECOGNIZE--
--YOUR BELOVED BROTHER!
TERRY...?!
I WAS TERRANCE MAGNUS...ONCE... BUT THAT WAS BEFORE LADY STYX TRANSFORMED ME! BEFORE THE DELICIOUS DARKNESS IN MY SOUL ROSE UP AND--
...AND...
TERI! TERI--HELP ME!
SHE'S DONE SOMETHING TERRIBLE TO ME! TWISTED ME INSIDE OUT AND--
NO! NO-- I'M NOT THAT WEAKLING MAGNUS! I'M ECLIPSO! I'M--

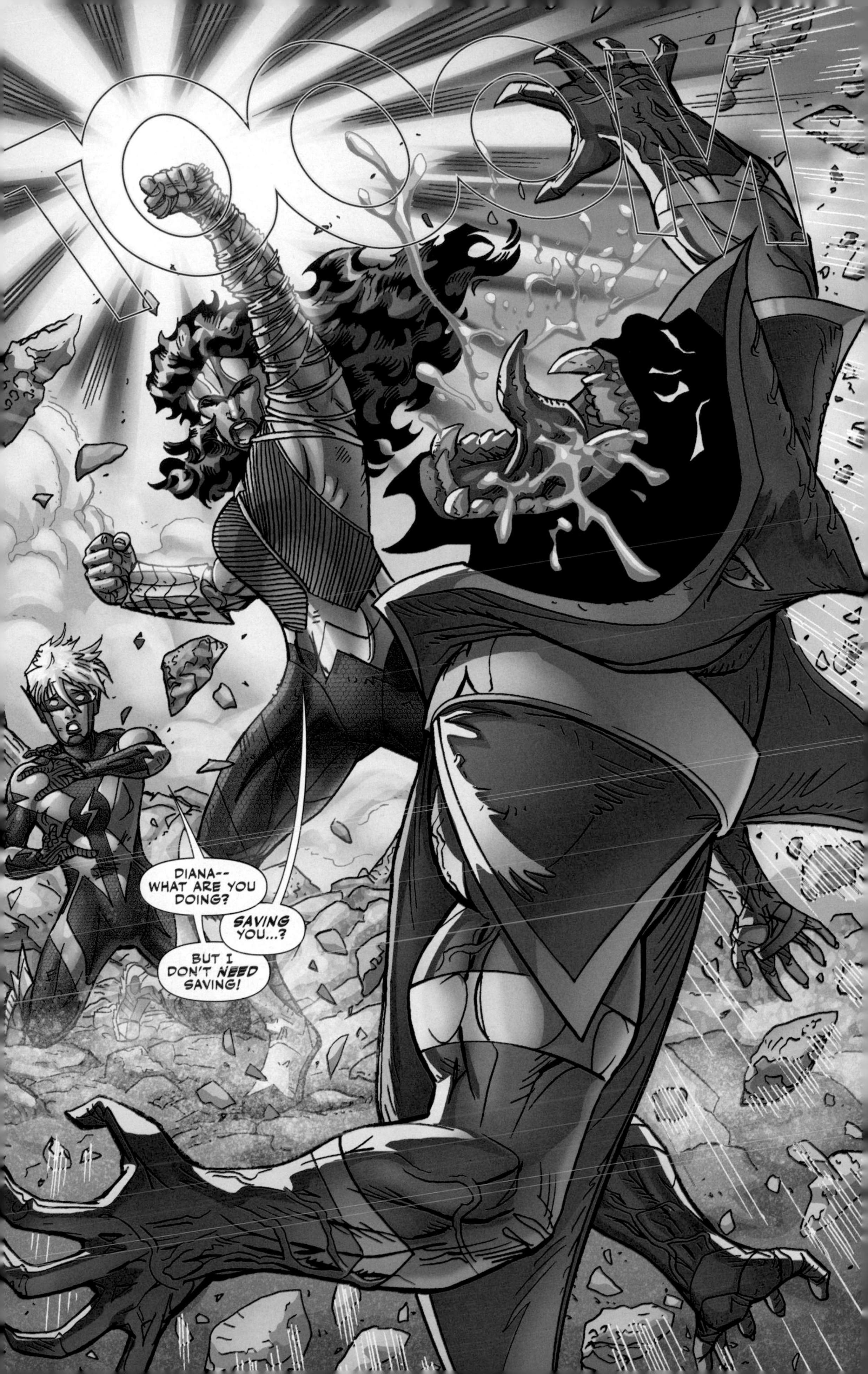

TOOOOM
DIANA--
WHAT ARE YOU
DOING?
SAVING
YOU...?
BUT I
DON'T NEED
SAVING!

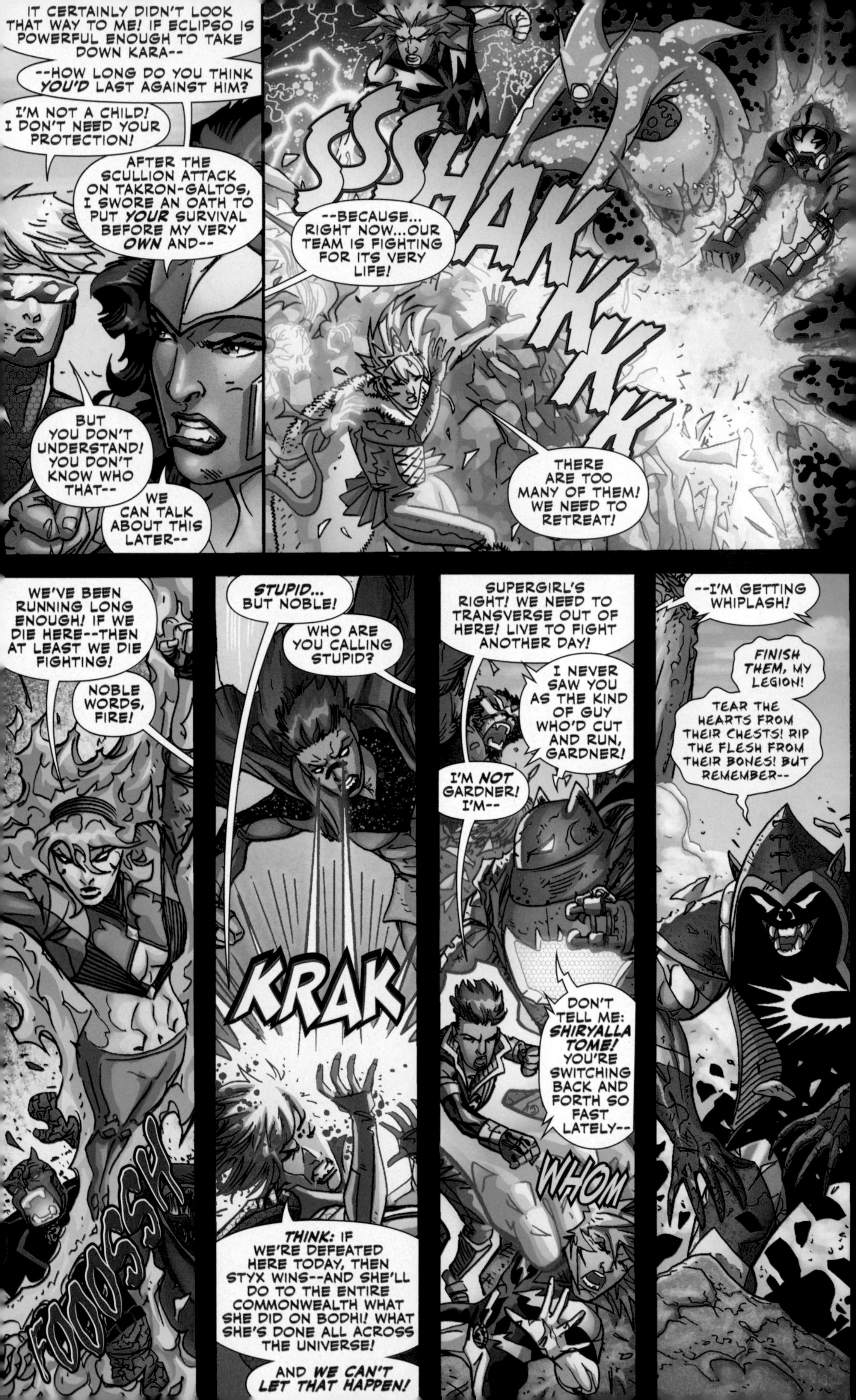

IT CERTAINLY DIDN'T LOOK THAT WAY TO ME! IF ECLIPSO IS POWERFUL ENOUGH TO TAKE DOWN KARA--
--HOW LONG DO YOU THINK YOU'D LAST AGAINST HIM?
I'M NOT A CHILD! I DON'T NEED YOUR PROTECTION!
AFTER THE SCULLION ATTACK ON TAKRON-GALTOS, I SWORE AN OATH TO PUT YOUR SURVIVAL BEFORE MY VERY OWN AND--
BUT YOU DON'T UNDERSTAND! YOU DON'T KNOW WHO THAT--
WE CAN TALK ABOUT THIS LATER--
--BECAUSE... RIGHT NOW...OUR TEAM IS FIGHTING FOR ITS VERY LIFE!
SSSHAKKKK
THERE ARE TOO MANY OF THEM! WE NEED TO RETREAT!
WE'VE BEEN RUNNING LONG ENOUGH! IF WE DIE HERE--THEN AT LEAST WE DIE FIGHTING!
NOBLE WORDS, FIRE!
FOOOSSH
STUPID... BUT NOBLE!
WHO ARE YOU CALLING STUPID?
KRAK
THINK: IF WE'RE DEFEATED HERE TODAY, THEN STYX WINS--AND SHE'LL DO TO THE ENTIRE COMMONWEALTH WHAT SHE DID ON BODHI! WHAT SHE'S DONE ALL ACROSS THE UNIVERSE!
AND WE CAN'T LET THAT HAPPEN!
SUPERGIRL'S RIGHT! WE NEED TO TRANSVERSE OUT OF HERE! LIVE TO FIGHT ANOTHER DAY!
I NEVER SAW YOU AS THE KIND OF GUY WHO'D CUT AND RUN, GARDNER!
I'M NOT GARDNER! I'M--
DON'T TELL ME: SHIRYALLA TOME! YOU'RE SWITCHING BACK AND FORTH SO FAST LATELY--
WHOM
--I'M GETTING WHIPLASH!
FINISH THEM, MY LEGION!
TEAR THE HEARTS FROM THEIR CHESTS! RIP THE FLESH FROM THEIR BONES! BUT REMEMBER--

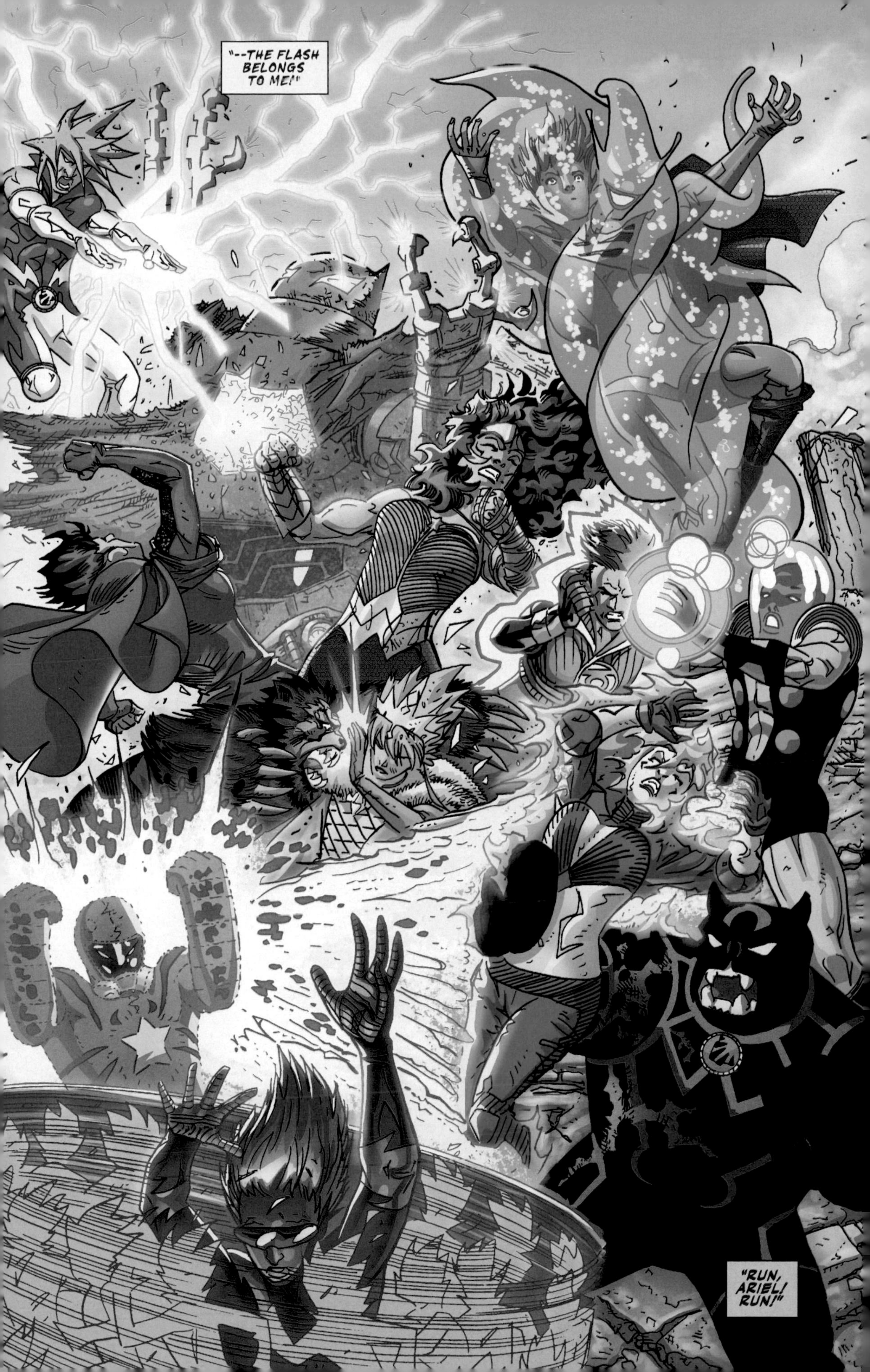
"--THE FLASH BELONGS TO ME!"
"RUN, ARIEL! RUN!"

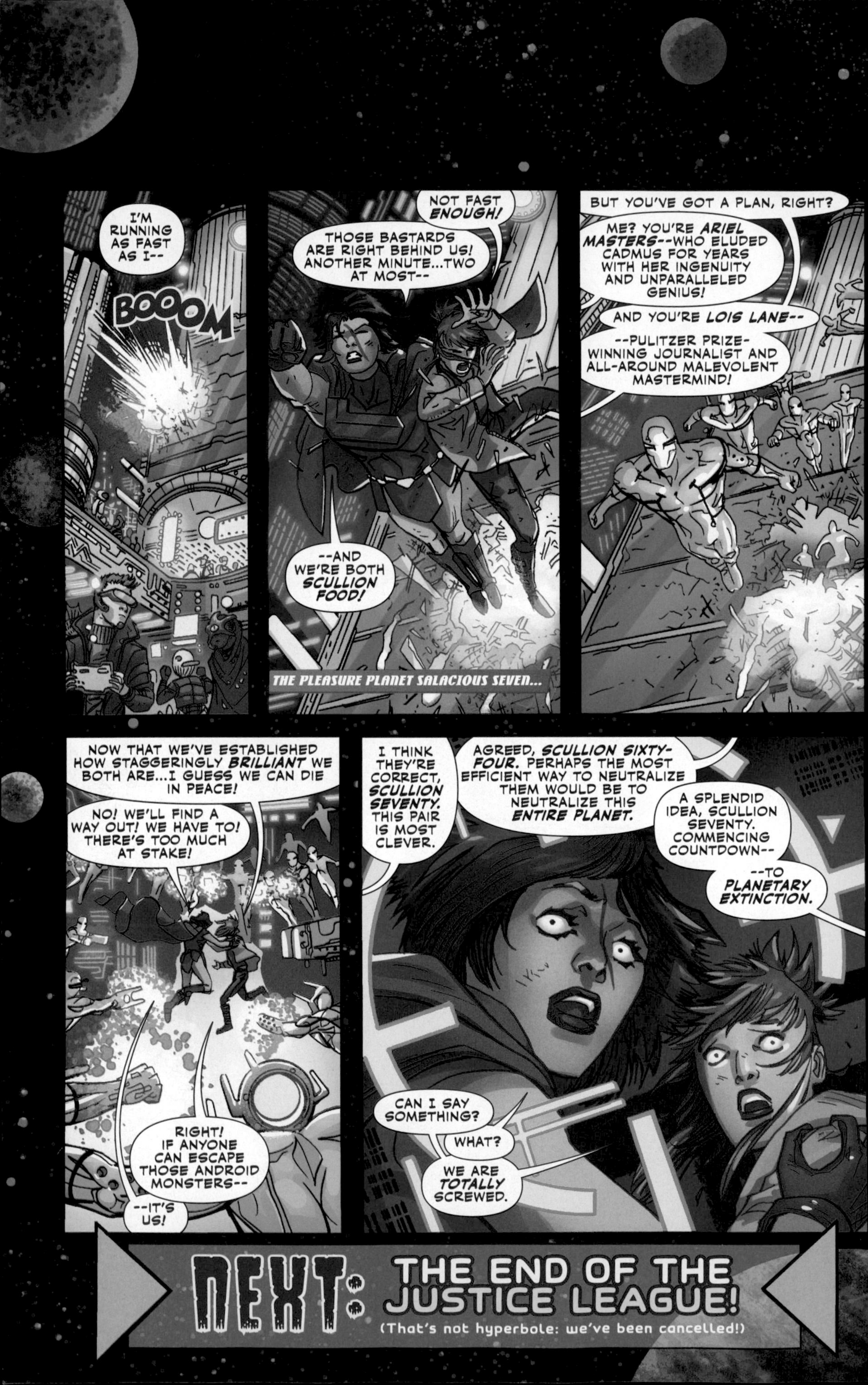
I'M RUNNING AS FAST AS I--
BOOOM
NOT FAST ENOUGH!
THOSE BASTARDS ARE RIGHT BEHIND US! ANOTHER MINUTE...TWO AT MOST--
--AND WE'RE BOTH SCULLION FOOD!
THE PLEASURE PLANET SALACIOUS SEVEN...
BUT YOU'VE GOT A PLAN, RIGHT?
ME? YOU'RE ARIEL MASTERS--WHO ELUDED CADMUS FOR YEARS WITH HER INGENUITY AND UNPARALLELED GENIUS!
AND YOU'RE LOIS LANE--
--PULITZER PRIZE-WINNING JOURNALIST AND ALL-AROUND MALEVOLENT MASTERMIND!
NOW THAT WE'VE ESTABLISHED HOW STAGGERINGLY BRILLIANT WE BOTH ARE...I GUESS WE CAN DIE IN PEACE!
NO! WE'LL FIND A WAY OUT! WE HAVE TO! THERE'S TOO MUCH AT STAKE!
RIGHT! IF ANYONE CAN ESCAPE THOSE ANDROID MONSTERS--
--IT'S US!
I THINK THEY'RE CORRECT, SCULLION SEVENTY. THIS PAIR IS MOST CLEVER.
AGREED, SCULLION SIXTY-FOUR. PERHAPS THE MOST EFFICIENT WAY TO NEUTRALIZE THEM WOULD BE TO NEUTRALIZE THIS ENTIRE PLANET.
A SPLENDID IDEA, SCULLION SEVENTY. COMMENCING COUNTDOWN--
--TO PLANETARY EXTINCTION.
CAN I SAY SOMETHING?
WHAT?
WE ARE TOTALLY SCREWED.
NEXT: THE END OF THE JUSTICE LEAGUE!
(That's not hyperbole: we've been cancelled!)

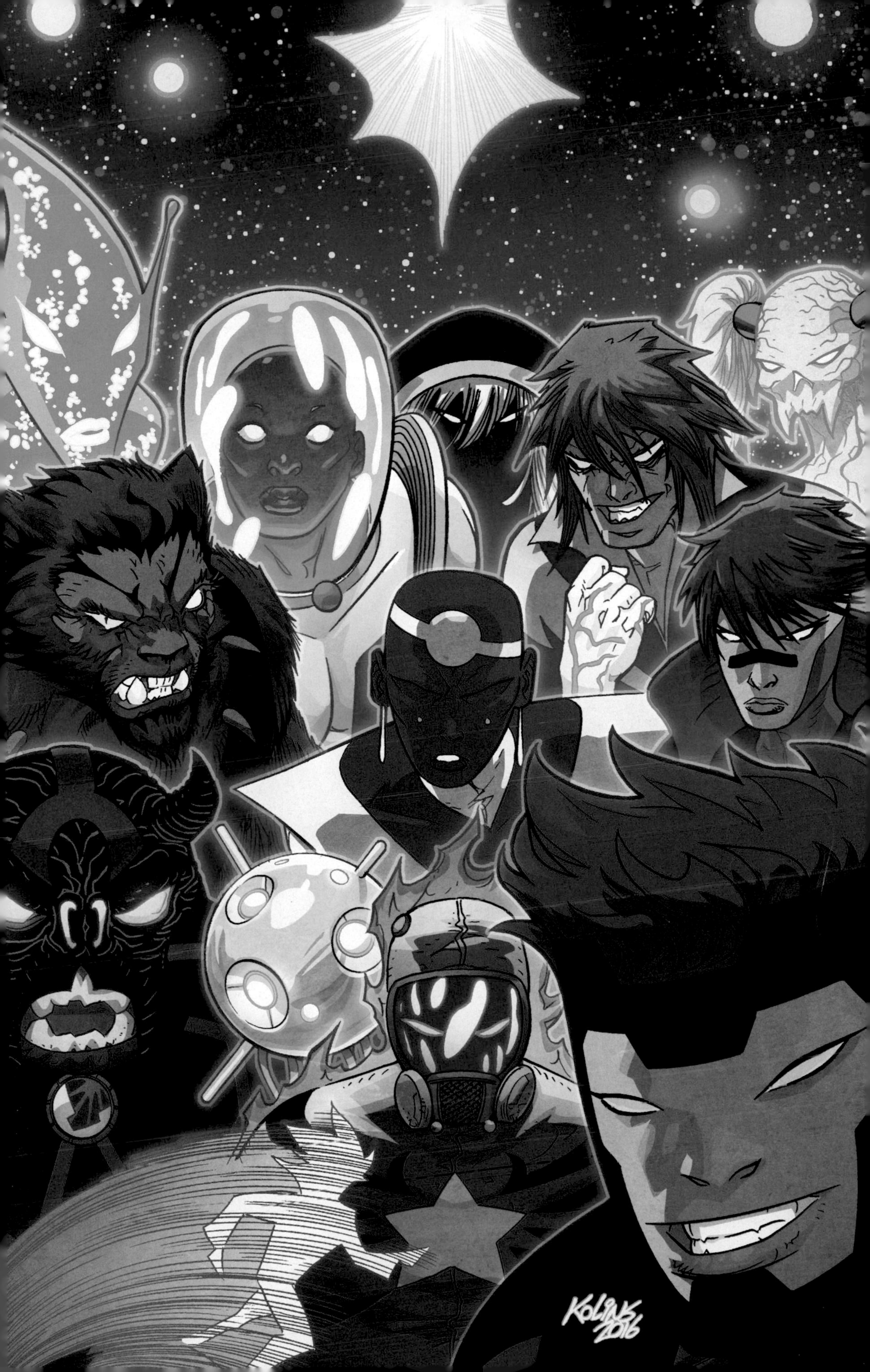
KOLINS
2016

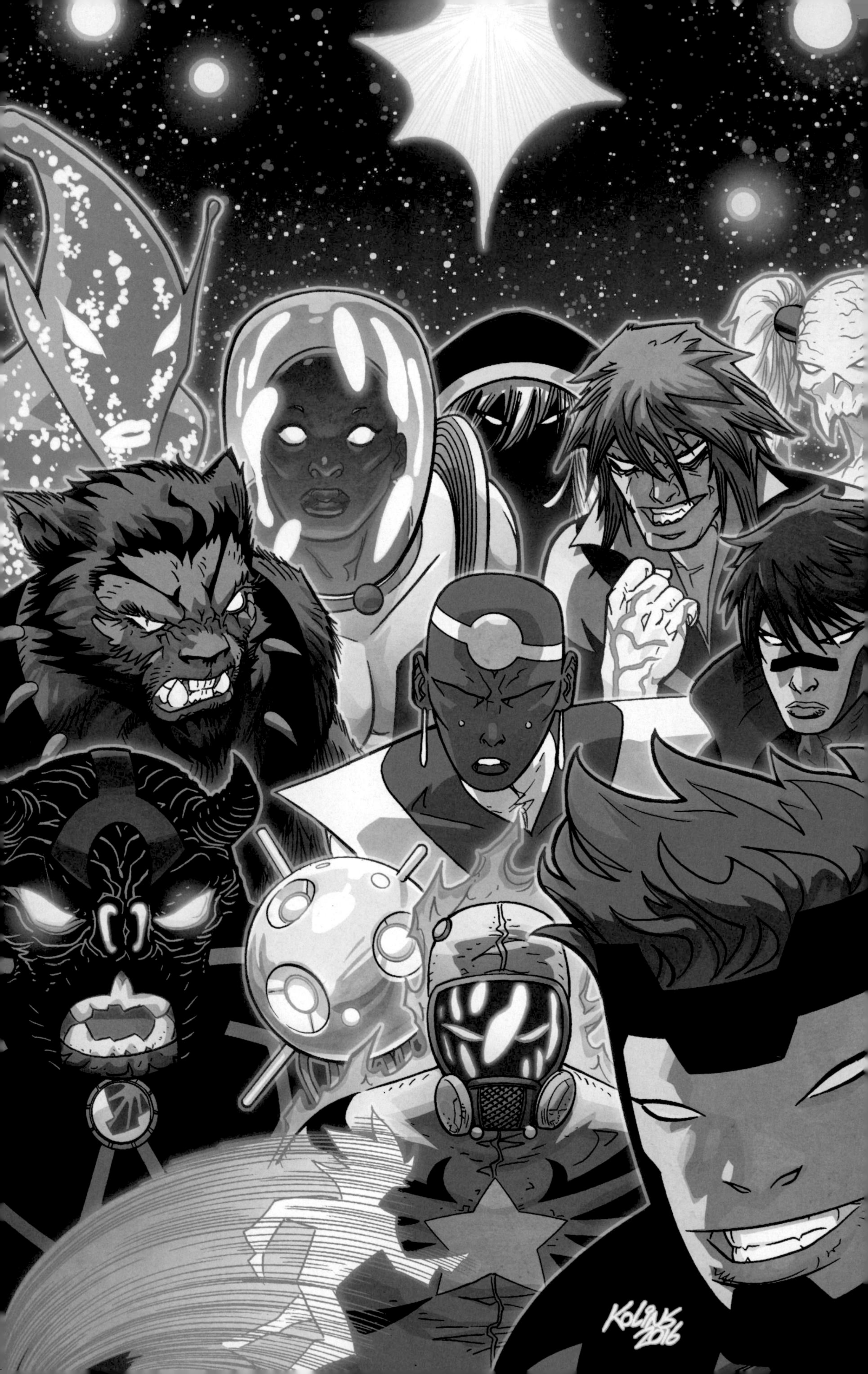
KOLINS
2016

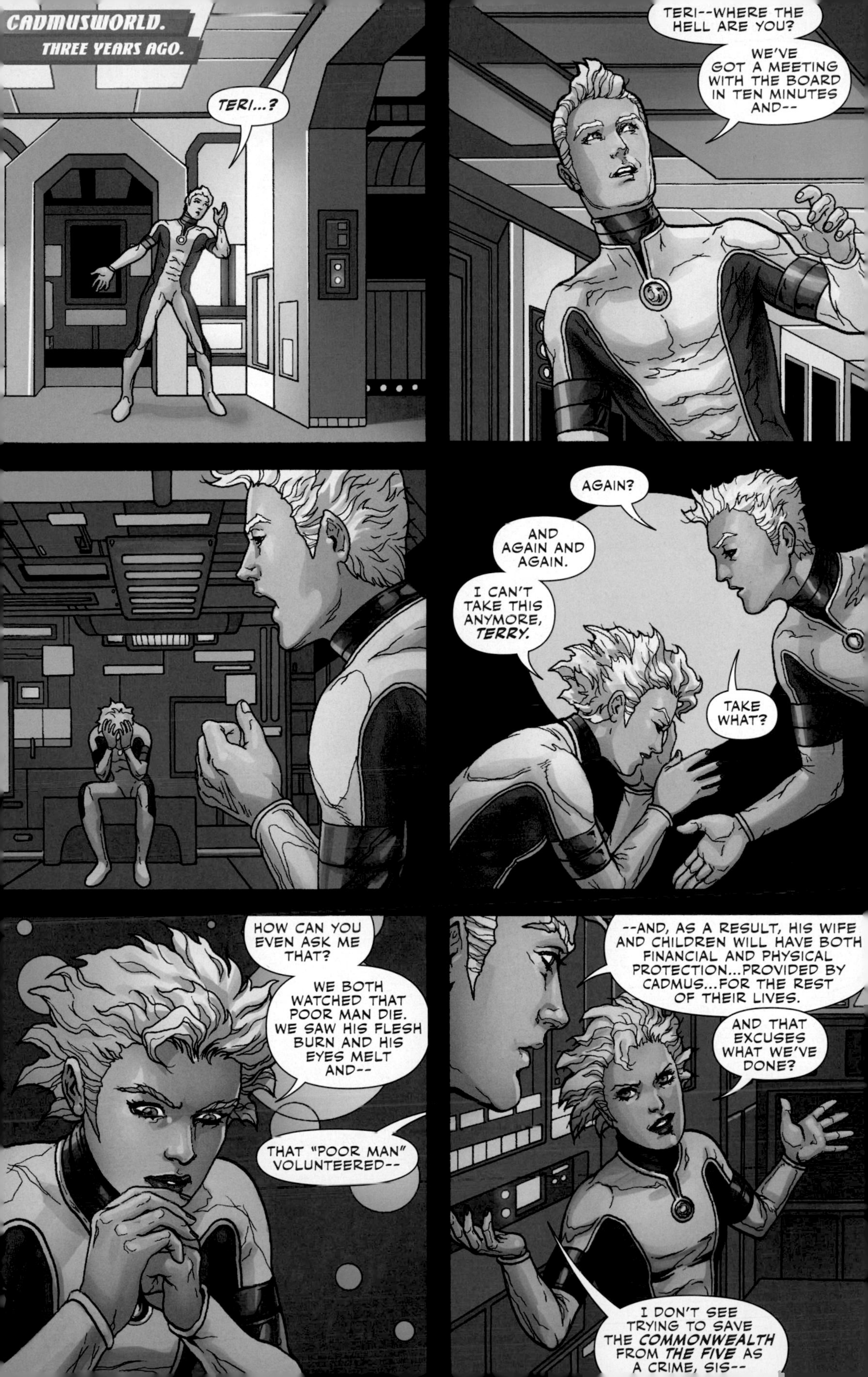
CADMUSWORLD.
THREE YEARS AGO.
TERI...?
TERI--WHERE THE HELL ARE YOU?
WE'VE GOT A MEETING WITH THE BOARD IN TEN MINUTES AND--
AGAIN?
AND AGAIN AND AGAIN.
I CAN'T TAKE THIS ANYMORE, TERRY.
TAKE WHAT?
HOW CAN YOU EVEN ASK ME THAT?
WE BOTH WATCHED THAT POOR MAN DIE. WE SAW HIS FLESH BURN AND HIS EYES MELT AND--
THAT "POOR MAN" VOLUNTEERED--
--AND, AS A RESULT, HIS WIFE AND CHILDREN WILL HAVE BOTH FINANCIAL AND PHYSICAL PROTECTION...PROVIDED BY CADMUS...FOR THE REST OF THEIR LIVES.
AND THAT EXCUSES WHAT WE'VE DONE?
I DON'T SEE TRYING TO SAVE THE COMMONWEALTH FROM THE FIVE AS A CRIME, SIS--

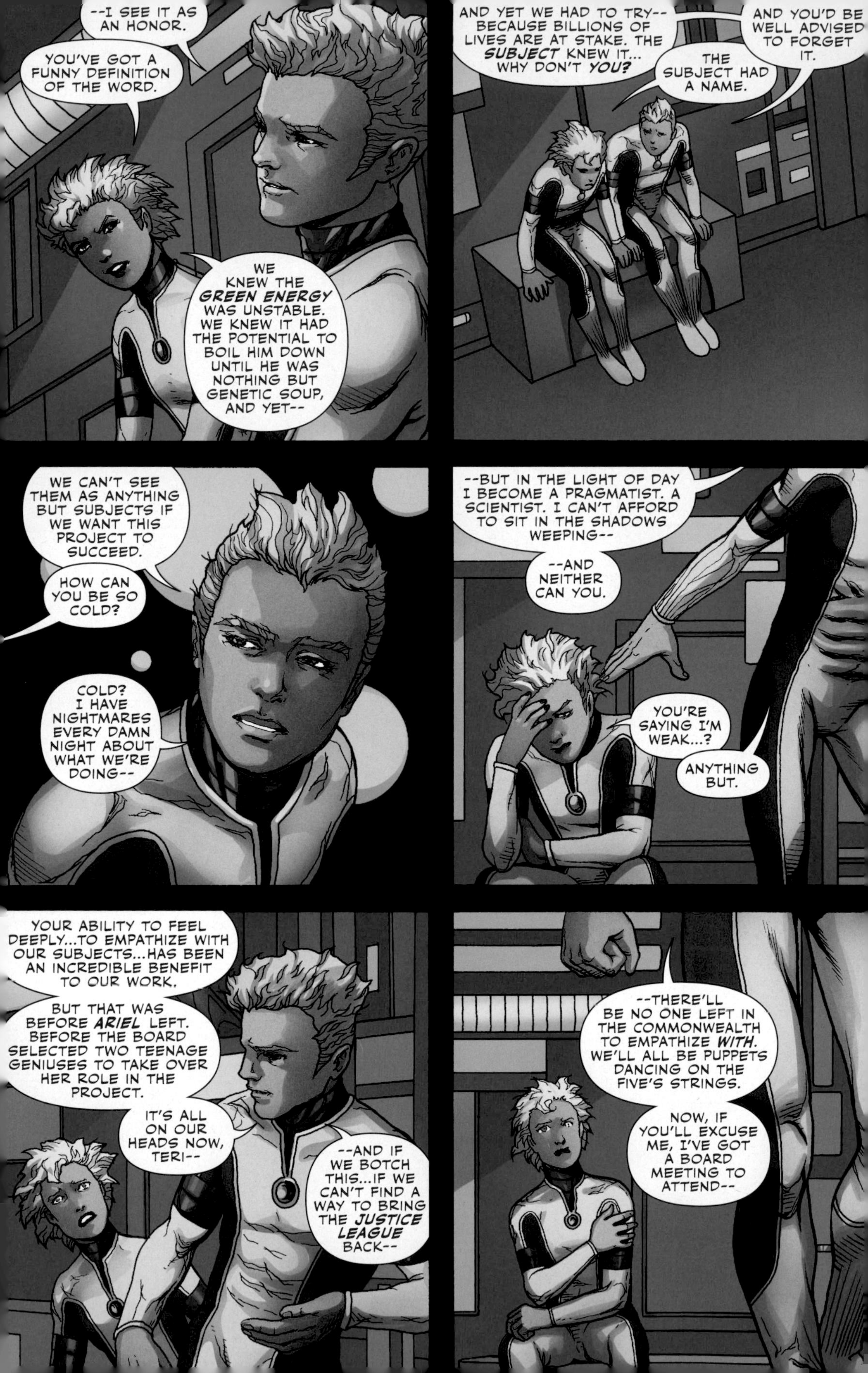
--I SEE IT AS AN HONOR.
YOU'VE GOT A FUNNY DEFINITION OF THE WORD.
WE KNEW THE GREEN ENERGY WAS UNSTABLE. WE KNEW IT HAD THE POTENTIAL TO BOIL HIM DOWN UNTIL HE WAS NOTHING BUT GENETIC SOUP, AND YET--
AND YET WE HAD TO TRY--BECAUSE BILLIONS OF LIVES ARE AT STAKE. THE SUBJECT KNEW IT... WHY DON'T YOU?
THE SUBJECT HAD A NAME.
AND YOU'D BE WELL ADVISED TO FORGET IT.
WE CAN'T SEE THEM AS ANYTHING BUT SUBJECTS IF WE WANT THIS PROJECT TO SUCCEED.
HOW CAN YOU BE SO COLD?
COLD? I HAVE NIGHTMARES EVERY DAMN NIGHT ABOUT WHAT WE'RE DOING--
--BUT IN THE LIGHT OF DAY I BECOME A PRAGMATIST. A SCIENTIST. I CAN'T AFFORD TO SIT IN THE SHADOWS WEEPING--
--AND NEITHER CAN YOU.
YOU'RE SAYING I'M WEAK...?
ANYTHING BUT.
YOUR ABILITY TO FEEL DEEPLY...TO EMPATHIZE WITH OUR SUBJECTS...HAS BEEN AN INCREDIBLE BENEFIT TO OUR WORK.
BUT THAT WAS BEFORE ARIEL LEFT. BEFORE THE BOARD SELECTED TWO TEENAGE GENIUSES TO TAKE OVER HER ROLE IN THE PROJECT.
IT'S ALL ON OUR HEADS NOW, TERI--
--AND IF WE BOTCH THIS...IF WE CAN'T FIND A WAY TO BRING THE JUSTICE LEAGUE BACK--
--THERE'LL BE NO ONE LEFT IN THE COMMONWEALTH TO EMPATHIZE WITH. WE'LL ALL BE PUPPETS DANCING ON THE FIVE'S STRINGS.
NOW, IF YOU'LL EXCUSE ME, I'VE GOT A BOARD MEETING TO ATTEND--

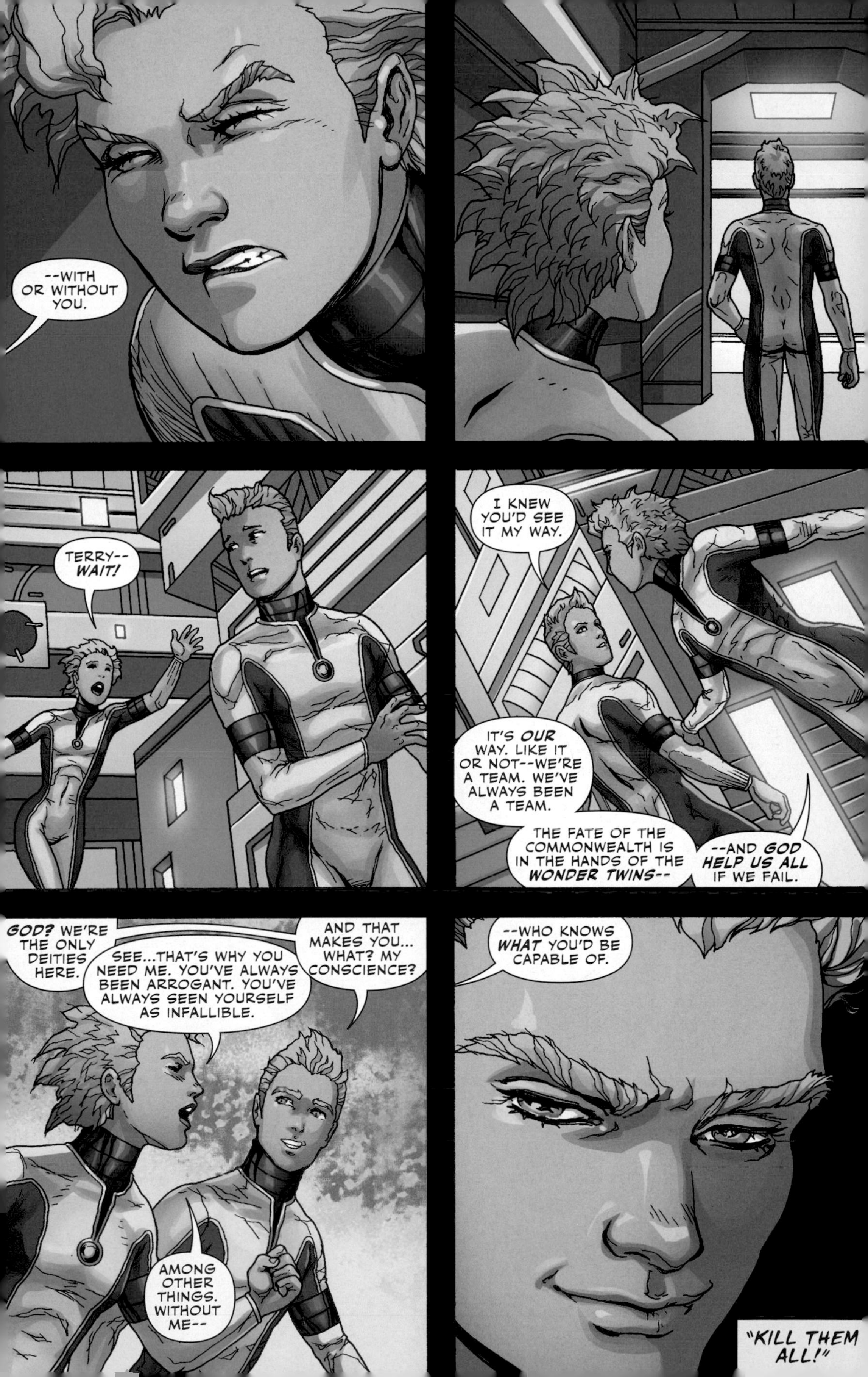
--WITH OR WITHOUT YOU.
TERRY-- *WAIT!*
I KNEW YOU'D SEE IT MY WAY.
IT'S *OUR* WAY. LIKE IT OR NOT--WE'RE A TEAM. WE'VE ALWAYS BEEN A TEAM.
THE FATE OF THE COMMONWEALTH IS IN THE HANDS OF THE *WONDER TWINS*--
--AND *GOD HELP US ALL* IF WE FAIL.
GOD? WE'RE THE ONLY DEITIES HERE.
SEE...THAT'S WHY YOU NEED ME. YOU'VE ALWAYS BEEN ARROGANT. YOU'VE ALWAYS SEEN YOURSELF AS INFALLIBLE.
AND THAT MAKES YOU... WHAT? MY CONSCIENCE?
AMONG OTHER THINGS. WITHOUT ME--
--WHO KNOWS *WHAT* YOU'D BE CAPABLE OF.
"KILL THEM ALL!"

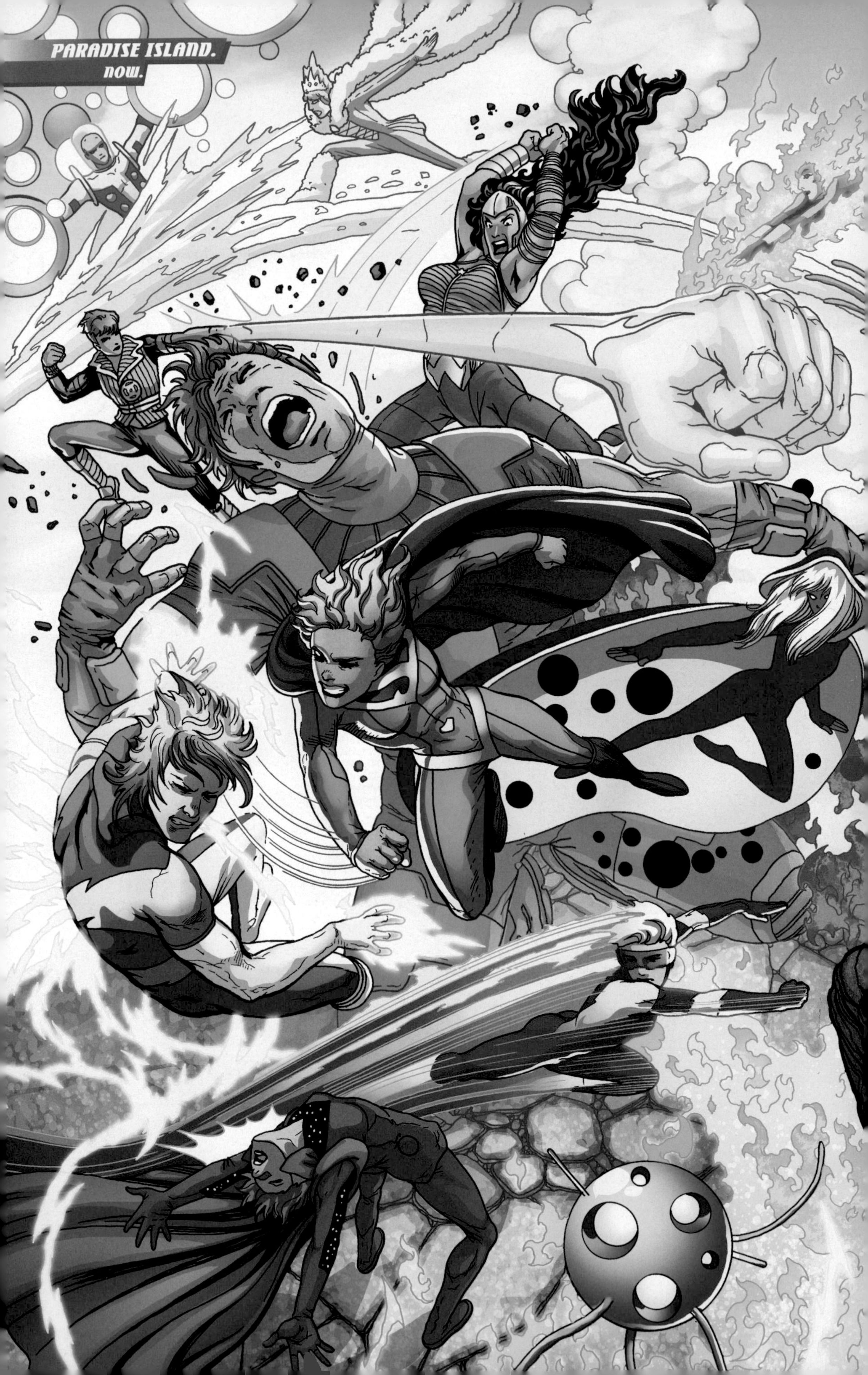
PARADISE ISLAND.
now.

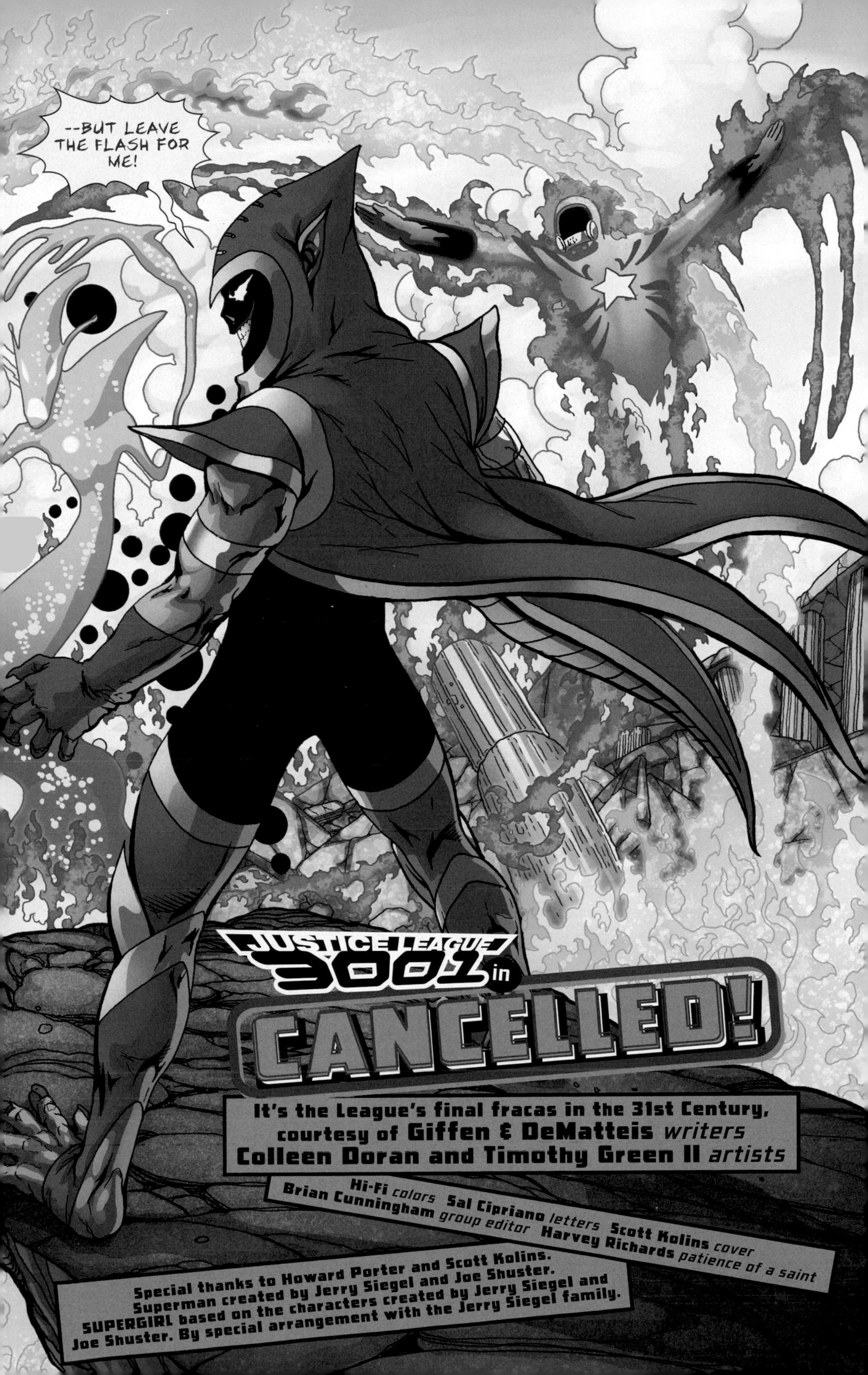
--BUT LEAVE THE FLASH FOR ME!
JUSTICE LEAGUE 3001 in
CANCELLED!
It's the League's final fracas in the 31st Century, courtesy of Giffen & DeMatteis writers Colleen Doran and Timothy Green II artists
Hi-Fi colors Sal Cipriano letters Scott Kolins cover Brian Cunningham group editor Harvey Richards patience of a saint
Special thanks to Howard Porter and Scott Kolins. Superman created by Jerry Siegel and Joe Shuster. SUPERGIRL based on the characters created by Jerry Siegel and Joe Shuster. By special arrangement with the Jerry Siegel family.

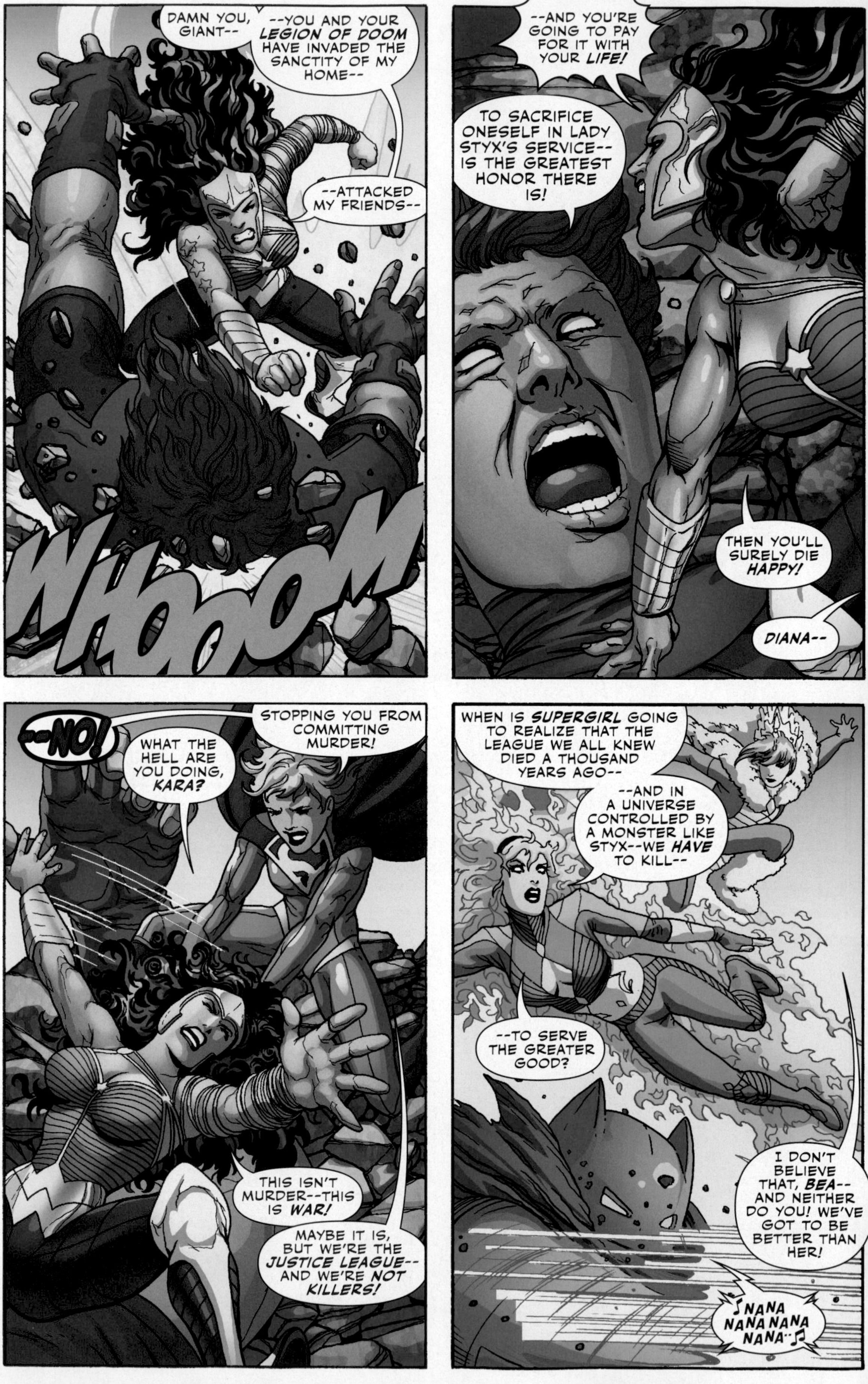
DAMN YOU, GIANT--
--YOU AND YOUR LEGION OF DOOM HAVE INVADED THE SANCTITY OF MY HOME--
--ATTACKED MY FRIENDS--
WHOOOM
--AND YOU'RE GOING TO PAY FOR IT WITH YOUR LIFE!
TO SACRIFICE ONESELF IN LADY STYX'S SERVICE--IS THE GREATEST HONOR THERE IS!
THEN YOU'LL SURELY DIE HAPPY!
DIANA--
--NO!
WHAT THE HELL ARE YOU DOING, KARA?
STOPPING YOU FROM COMMITTING MURDER!
THIS ISN'T MURDER--THIS IS WAR!
MAYBE IT IS, BUT WE'RE THE JUSTICE LEAGUE--AND WE'RE NOT KILLERS!
WHEN IS SUPERGIRL GOING TO REALIZE THAT THE LEAGUE WE ALL KNEW DIED A THOUSAND YEARS AGO--
--AND IN A UNIVERSE CONTROLLED BY A MONSTER LIKE STYX--WE HAVE TO KILL--
--TO SERVE THE GREATER GOOD?
I DON'T BELIEVE THAT, BEA--AND NEITHER DO YOU! WE'VE GOT TO BE BETTER THAN HER!
NANA NANA NANA NANA...

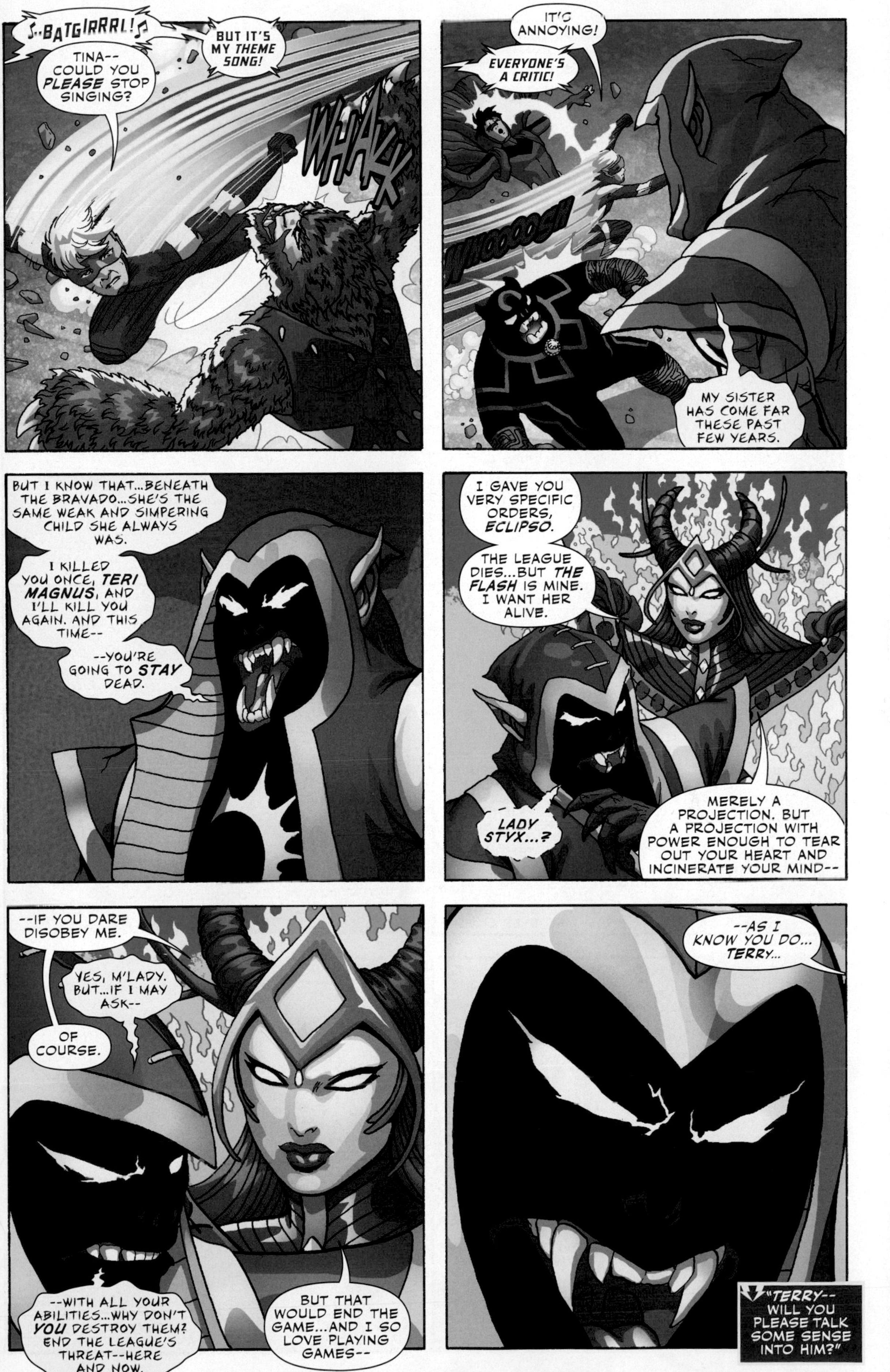

♪..BATGIRRRL!♪
TINA-- COULD YOU PLEASE STOP SINGING?
BUT IT'S MY THEME SONG!
WHAKK
IT'S ANNOYING!
EVERYONE'S A CRITIC!
WHOOOOSH
MY SISTER HAS COME FAR THESE PAST FEW YEARS.
BUT I KNOW THAT...BENEATH THE BRAVADO...SHE'S THE SAME WEAK AND SIMPERING CHILD SHE ALWAYS WAS.
I KILLED YOU ONCE, TERI MAGNUS, AND I'LL KILL YOU AGAIN. AND THIS TIME--
--YOU'RE GOING TO STAY DEAD.
I GAVE YOU VERY SPECIFIC ORDERS, ECLIPSO.
THE LEAGUE DIES...BUT THE FLASH IS MINE. I WANT HER ALIVE.
LADY STYX...?
MERELY A PROJECTION. BUT A PROJECTION WITH POWER ENOUGH TO TEAR OUT YOUR HEART AND INCINERATE YOUR MIND--
--IF YOU DARE DISOBEY ME.
YES, M'LADY. BUT...IF I MAY ASK--
OF COURSE.
--WITH ALL YOUR ABILITIES...WHY DON'T YOU DESTROY THEM? END THE LEAGUE'S THREAT--HERE AND NOW.
BUT THAT WOULD END THE GAME...AND I SO LOVE PLAYING GAMES--
--AS I KNOW YOU DO... TERRY...
"TERRY-- WILL YOU PLEASE TALK SOME SENSE INTO HIM?"

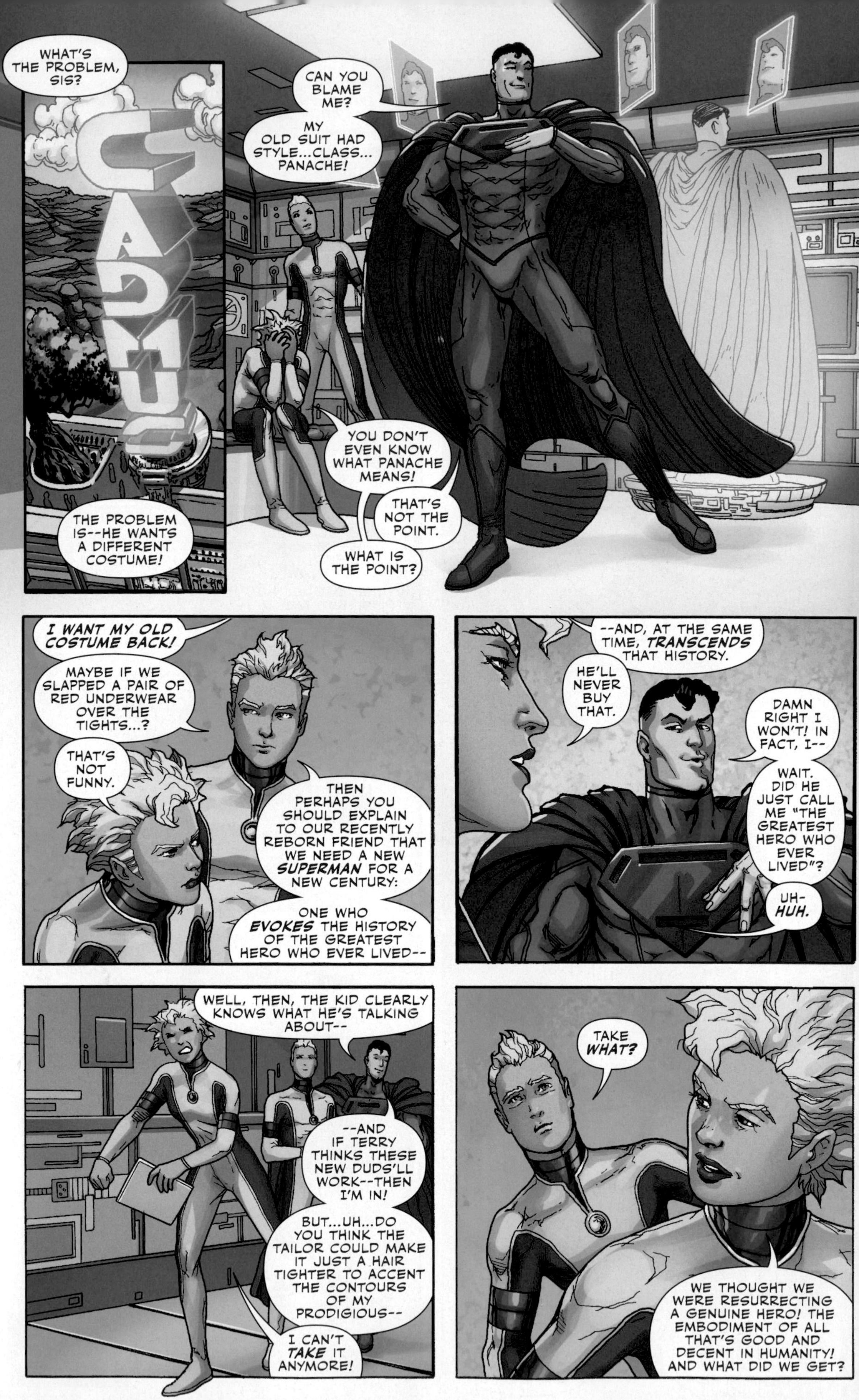
WHAT'S THE PROBLEM, SIS?
CADMUS
THE PROBLEM IS--HE WANTS A DIFFERENT COSTUME!
CAN YOU BLAME ME?
MY OLD SUIT HAD STYLE...CLASS... PANACHE!
YOU DON'T EVEN KNOW WHAT PANACHE MEANS!
THAT'S NOT THE POINT.
WHAT IS THE POINT?
I WANT MY OLD COSTUME BACK!
MAYBE IF WE SLAPPED A PAIR OF RED UNDERWEAR OVER THE TIGHTS...?
THAT'S NOT FUNNY.
THEN PERHAPS YOU SHOULD EXPLAIN TO OUR RECENTLY REBORN FRIEND THAT WE NEED A NEW SUPERMAN FOR A NEW CENTURY:
ONE WHO EVOKES THE HISTORY OF THE GREATEST HERO WHO EVER LIVED--
--AND, AT THE SAME TIME, TRANSCENDS THAT HISTORY.
HE'LL NEVER BUY THAT.
DAMN RIGHT I WON'T! IN FACT, I--
WAIT. DID HE JUST CALL ME "THE GREATEST HERO WHO EVER LIVED"?
UH-HUH.
WELL, THEN, THE KID CLEARLY KNOWS WHAT HE'S TALKING ABOUT--
--AND IF TERRY THINKS THESE NEW DUDS'LL WORK--THEN I'M IN!
BUT...UH...DO YOU THINK THE TAILOR COULD MAKE IT JUST A HAIR TIGHTER TO ACCENT THE CONTOURS OF MY PRODIGIOUS--
I CAN'T TAKE IT ANYMORE!
TAKE WHAT?
WE THOUGHT WE WERE RESURRECTING A GENUINE HERO! THE EMBODIMENT OF ALL THAT'S GOOD AND DECENT IN HUMANITY! AND WHAT DID WE GET?

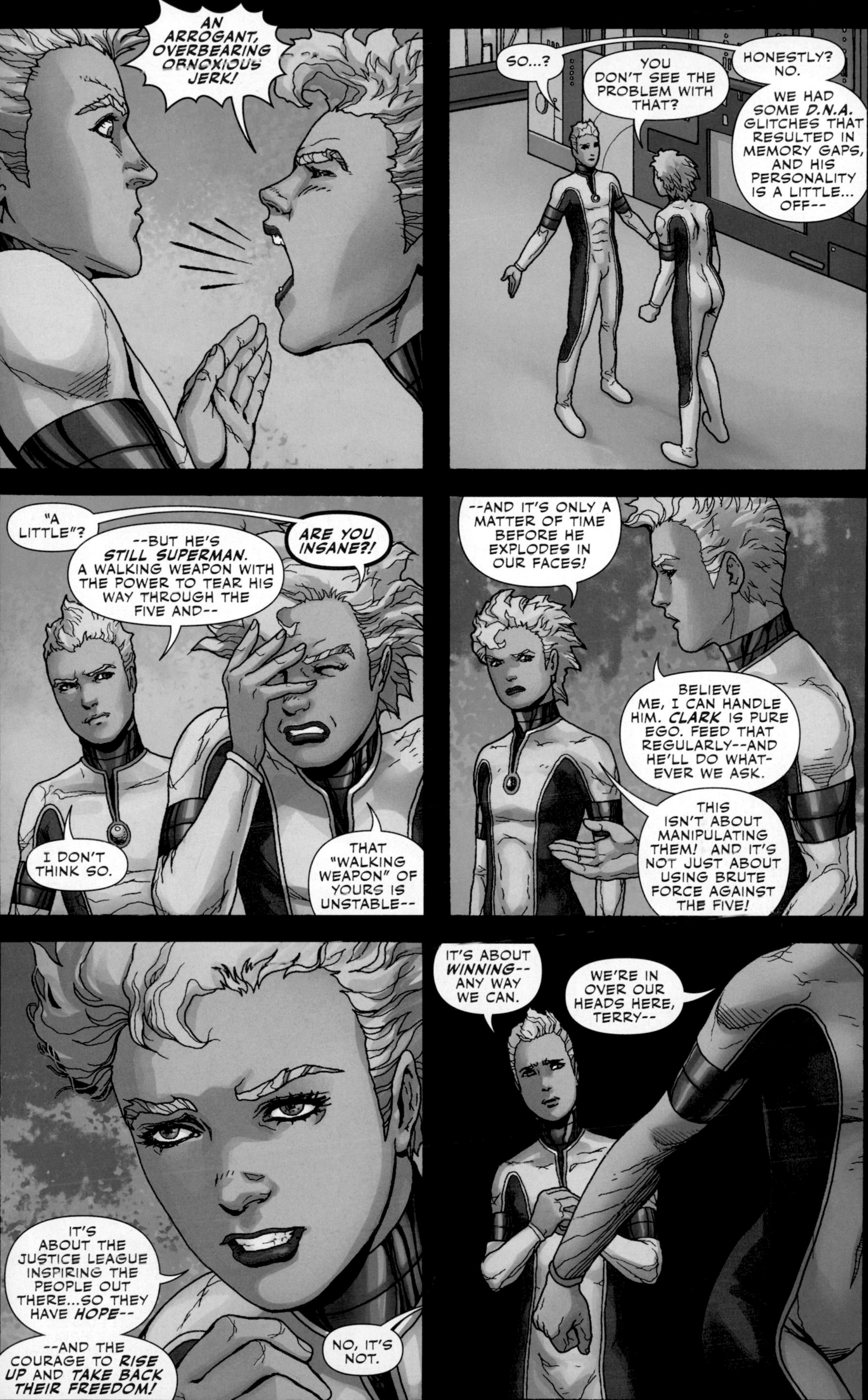
AN ARROGANT, OVERBEARING ORNOXIOUS JERK!
SO...?
YOU DON'T SEE THE PROBLEM WITH THAT?
HONESTLY? NO.
WE HAD SOME D.N.A. GLITCHES THAT RESULTED IN MEMORY GAPS, AND HIS PERSONALITY IS A LITTLE... OFF--
"A LITTLE"?
ARE YOU INSANE?!
--BUT HE'S STILL SUPERMAN. A WALKING WEAPON WITH THE POWER TO TEAR HIS WAY THROUGH THE FIVE AND--
I DON'T THINK SO.
THAT "WALKING WEAPON" OF YOURS IS UNSTABLE--
--AND IT'S ONLY A MATTER OF TIME BEFORE HE EXPLODES IN OUR FACES!
BELIEVE ME, I CAN HANDLE HIM. CLARK IS PURE EGO. FEED THAT REGULARLY--AND HE'LL DO WHATEVER WE ASK.
THIS ISN'T ABOUT MANIPULATING THEM! AND IT'S NOT JUST ABOUT USING BRUTE FORCE AGAINST THE FIVE!
IT'S ABOUT THE JUSTICE LEAGUE INSPIRING THE PEOPLE OUT THERE...SO THEY HAVE HOPE--
--AND THE COURAGE TO RISE UP AND TAKE BACK THEIR FREEDOM!
NO, IT'S NOT.
IT'S ABOUT WINNING-- ANY WAY WE CAN.
WE'RE IN OVER OUR HEADS HERE, TERRY--

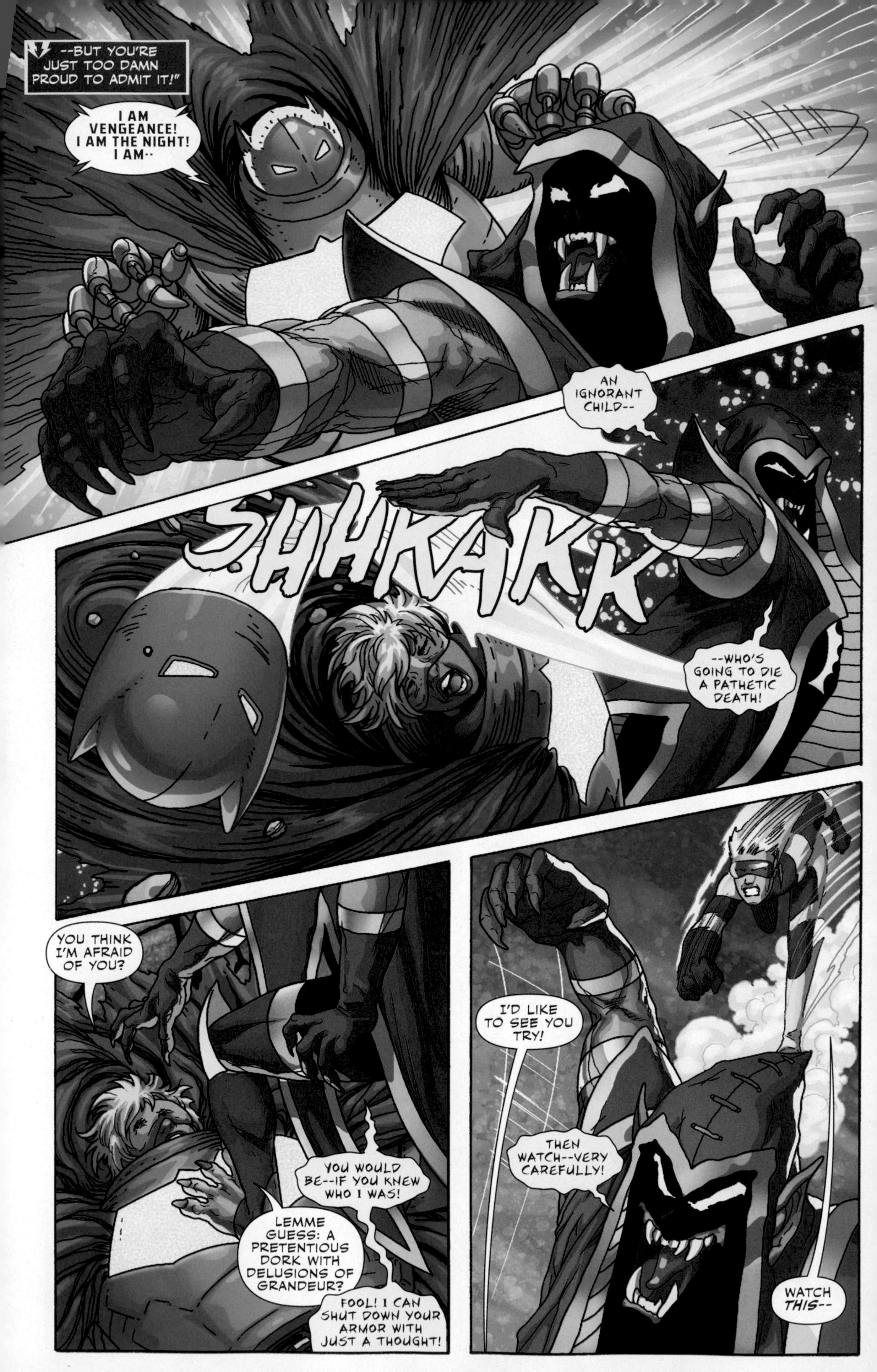
--BUT YOU'RE JUST TOO DAMN PROUD TO ADMIT IT!"
I AM VENGEANCE! I AM THE NIGHT! I AM--
AN IGNORANT CHILD--
SHHKAKK
--WHO'S GOING TO DIE A PATHETIC DEATH!
YOU THINK I'M AFRAID OF YOU?
YOU WOULD BE--IF YOU KNEW WHO I WAS!
LEMME GUESS: A PRETENTIOUS DORK WITH DELUSIONS OF GRANDEUR?
FOOL! I CAN SHUT DOWN YOUR ARMOR WITH JUST A THOUGHT!
I'D LIKE TO SEE YOU TRY!
THEN WATCH--VERY CAREFULLY!
WATCH THIS--

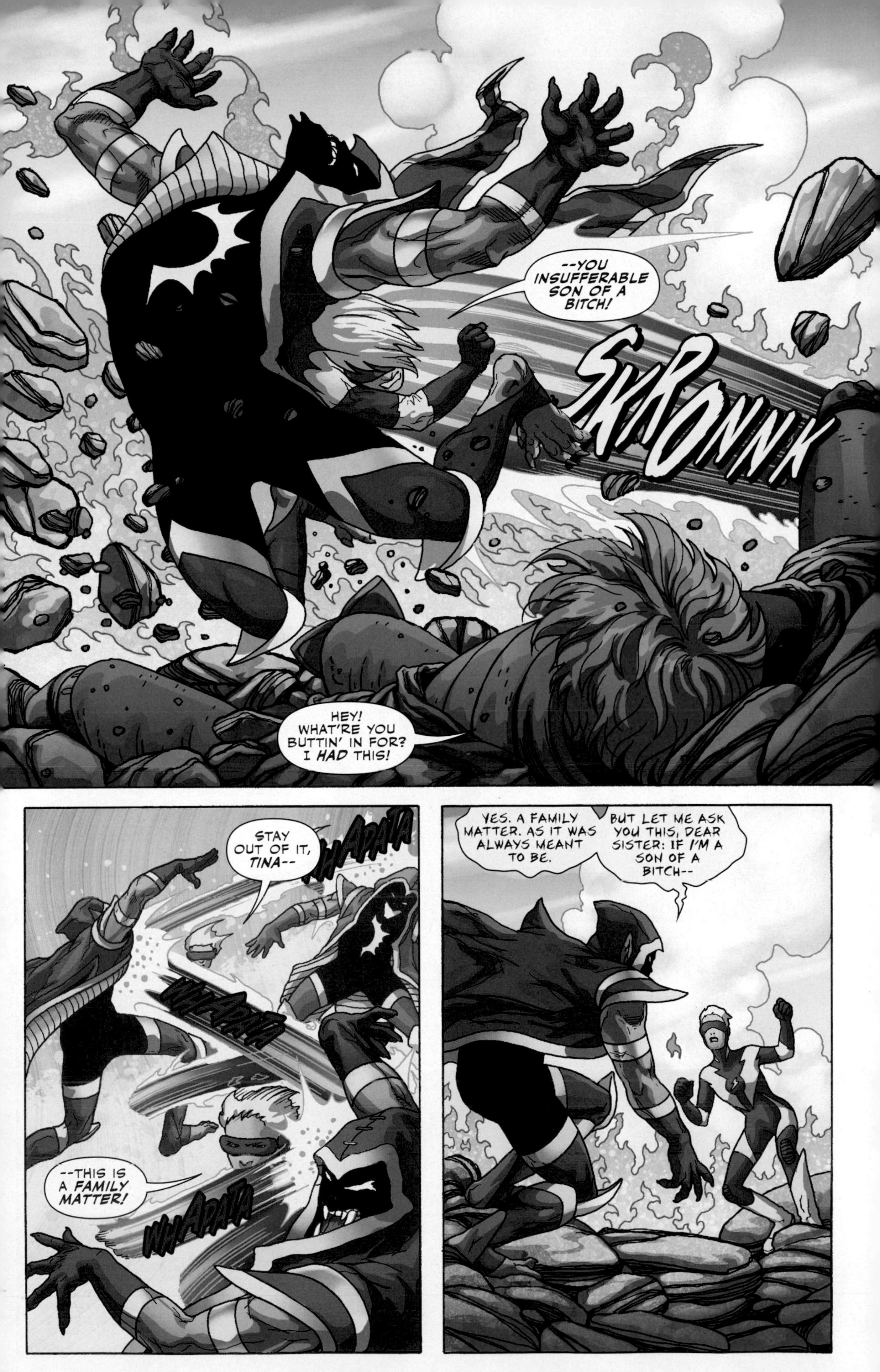
--YOU INSUFFERABLE SON OF A BITCH!
SKRONNK
HEY! WHAT'RE YOU BUTTIN' IN FOR? I *HAD* THIS!
STAY OUT OF IT, *TINA*--
WHAPATA
WHAPATA
--THIS IS A *FAMILY MATTER!*
WHAPATA
YES. A FAMILY MATTER. AS IT WAS ALWAYS MEANT TO BE.
BUT LET ME ASK YOU THIS, DEAR SISTER: IF *I'M* A SON OF A BITCH--

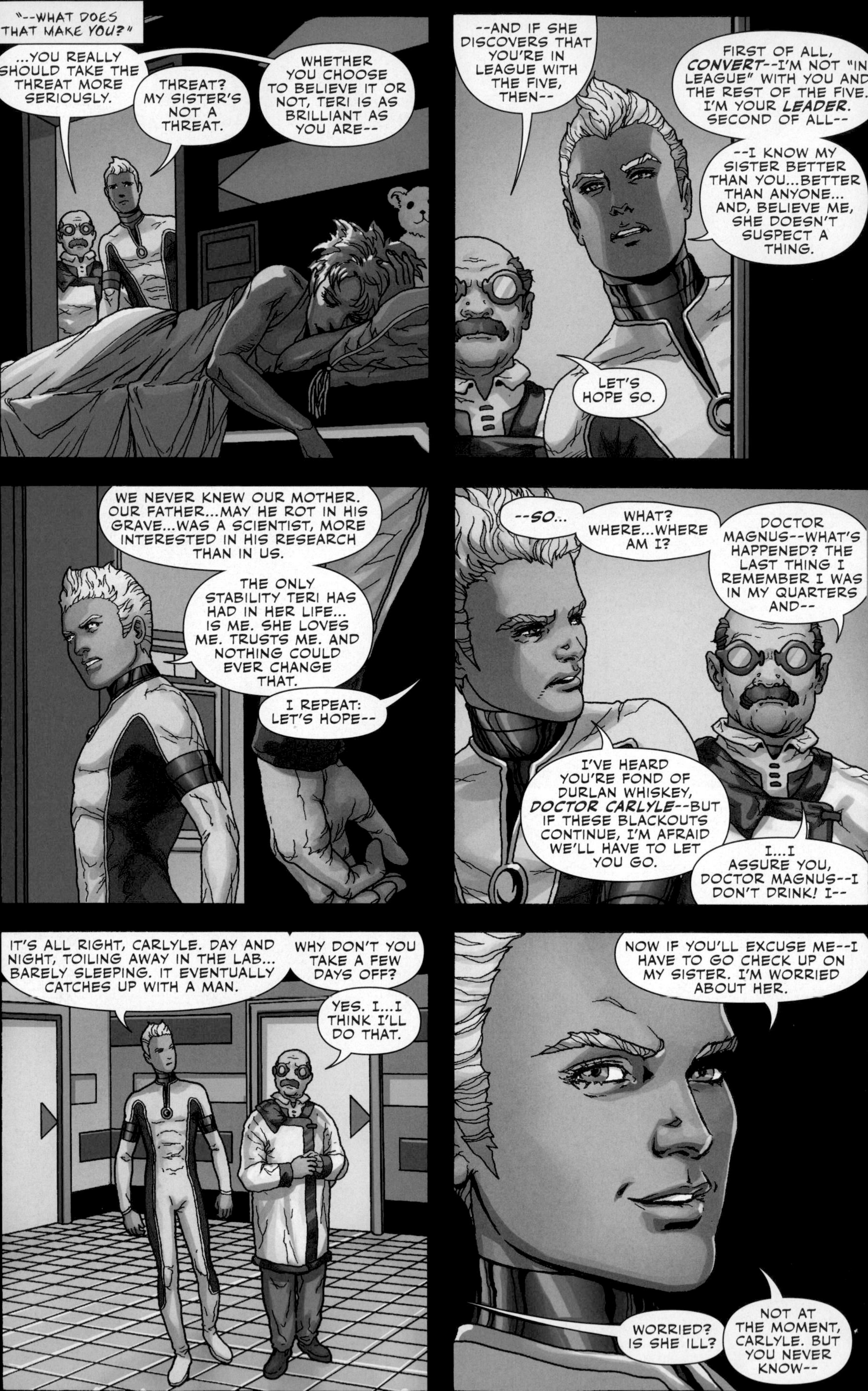
"--WHAT DOES THAT MAKE *YOU?*"
...YOU REALLY SHOULD TAKE THE THREAT MORE SERIOUSLY.
THREAT? MY SISTER'S NOT A THREAT.
WHETHER YOU CHOOSE TO BELIEVE IT OR NOT, TERI IS AS BRILLIANT AS YOU ARE--
--AND IF SHE DISCOVERS THAT YOU'RE IN LEAGUE WITH THE FIVE, THEN--
FIRST OF ALL, ***CONVERT***--I'M NOT "IN LEAGUE" WITH YOU AND THE REST OF THE FIVE. I'M YOUR ***LEADER***. SECOND OF ALL--
--I KNOW MY SISTER BETTER THAN YOU...BETTER THAN ANYONE... AND, BELIEVE ME, SHE DOESN'T SUSPECT A THING.
LET'S HOPE SO.
WE NEVER KNEW OUR MOTHER. OUR FATHER...MAY HE ROT IN HIS GRAVE...WAS A SCIENTIST, MORE INTERESTED IN HIS RESEARCH THAN IN US.
THE ONLY STABILITY TERI HAS HAD IN HER LIFE... IS ME. SHE LOVES ME. TRUSTS ME. AND NOTHING COULD EVER CHANGE THAT.
I REPEAT: LET'S HOPE--
--SO...
WHAT? WHERE...WHERE AM I?
DOCTOR MAGNUS--WHAT'S HAPPENED? THE LAST THING I REMEMBER I WAS IN MY QUARTERS AND--
I'VE HEARD YOU'RE FOND OF DURLAN WHISKEY, ***DOCTOR CARLYLE***--BUT IF THESE BLACKOUTS CONTINUE, I'M AFRAID WE'LL HAVE TO LET YOU GO.
I...I ASSURE YOU, DOCTOR MAGNUS--I DON'T DRINK! I--
IT'S ALL RIGHT, CARLYLE. DAY AND NIGHT, TOILING AWAY IN THE LAB... BARELY SLEEPING. IT EVENTUALLY CATCHES UP WITH A MAN.
WHY DON'T YOU TAKE A FEW DAYS OFF?
YES. I...I THINK I'LL DO THAT.
NOW IF YOU'LL EXCUSE ME--I HAVE TO GO CHECK UP ON MY SISTER. I'M WORRIED ABOUT HER.
WORRIED? IS SHE ILL?
NOT AT THE MOMENT, CARLYLE. BUT YOU NEVER KNOW--

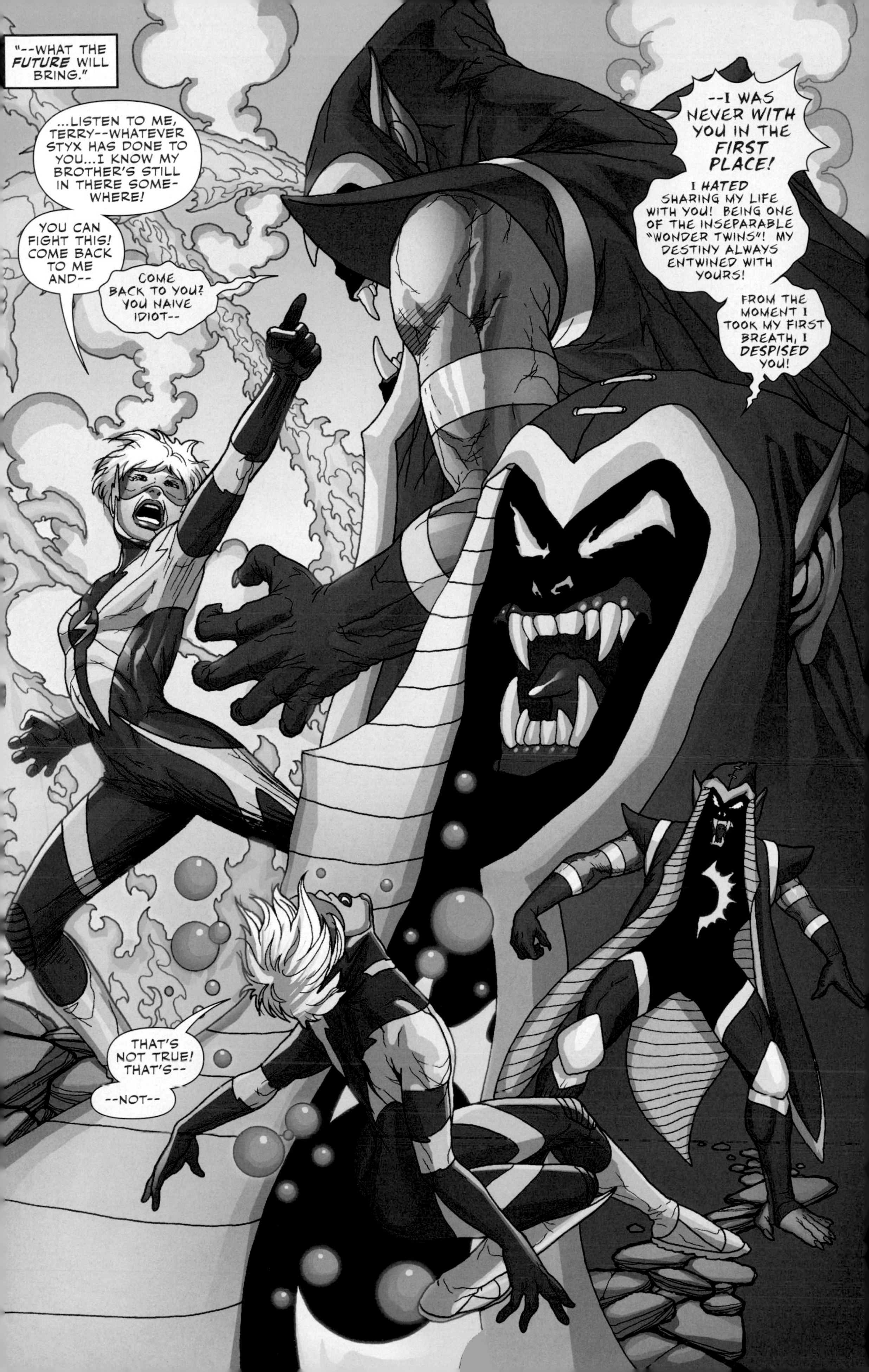
"--WHAT THE FUTURE WILL BRING."
...LISTEN TO ME, TERRY--WHATEVER STYX HAS DONE TO YOU...I KNOW MY BROTHER'S STILL IN THERE SOME-WHERE!
YOU CAN FIGHT THIS! COME BACK TO ME AND--
COME BACK TO YOU? YOU NAIVE IDIOT--
--I WAS NEVER WITH YOU IN THE FIRST PLACE!
I HATED SHARING MY LIFE WITH YOU! BEING ONE OF THE INSEPARABLE "WONDER TWINS"! MY DESTINY ALWAYS ENTWINED WITH YOURS!
FROM THE MOMENT I TOOK MY FIRST BREATH, I DESPISED YOU!
THAT'S NOT TRUE! THAT'S--
--NOT--

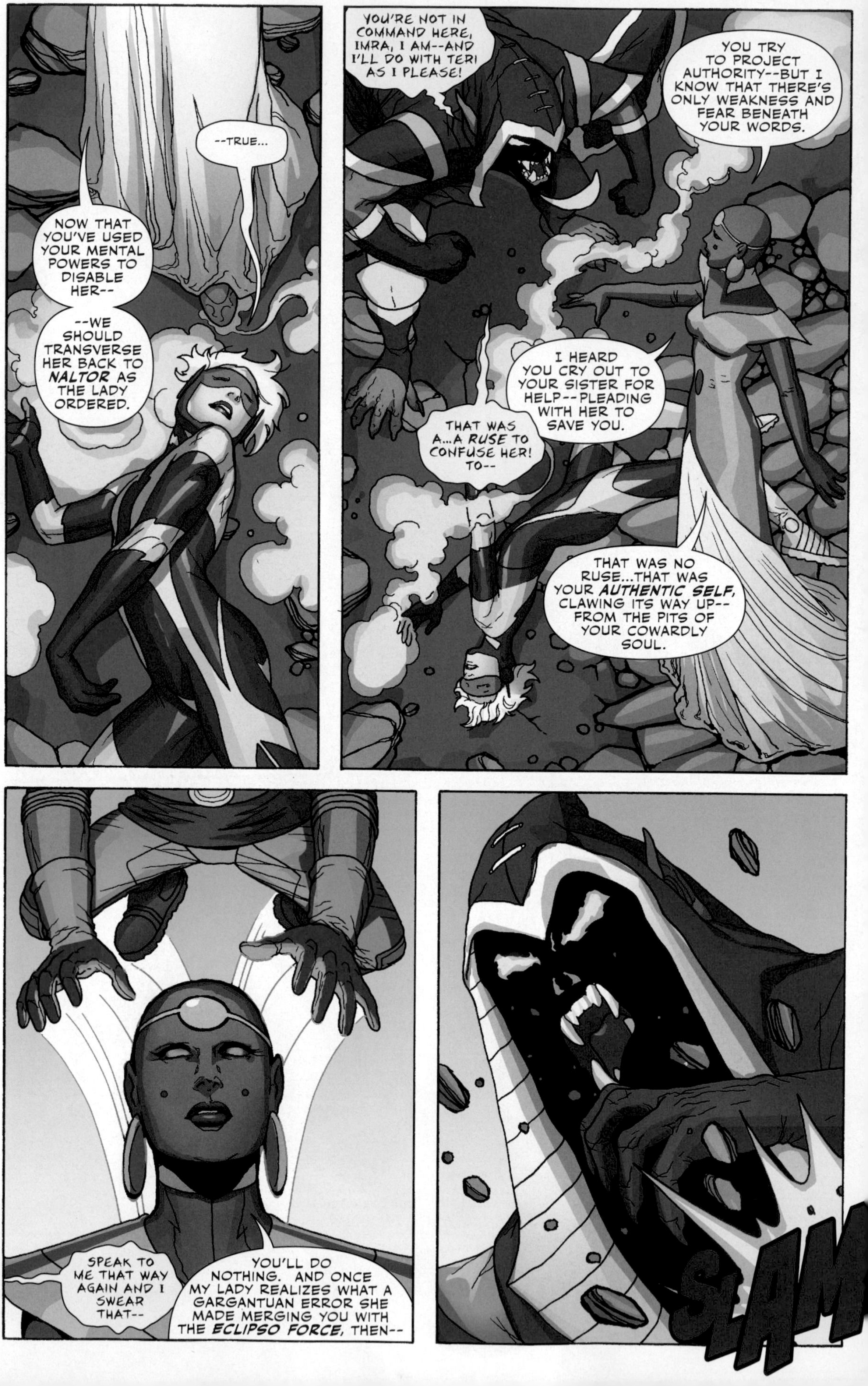
--TRUE...
NOW THAT YOU'VE USED YOUR MENTAL POWERS TO DISABLE HER--
--WE SHOULD TRANSVERSE HER BACK TO *NALTOR* AS THE LADY ORDERED.
YOU'RE NOT IN COMMAND HERE, IMRA, I AM--AND I'LL DO WITH TERI AS I PLEASE!
YOU TRY TO PROJECT AUTHORITY--BUT I KNOW THAT THERE'S ONLY WEAKNESS AND FEAR BENEATH YOUR WORDS.
I HEARD YOU CRY OUT TO YOUR SISTER FOR HELP--PLEADING WITH HER TO SAVE YOU.
THAT WAS A...A *RUSE* TO CONFUSE HER! TO--
THAT WAS NO RUSE...THAT WAS YOUR *AUTHENTIC SELF,* CLAWING ITS WAY UP-- FROM THE PITS OF YOUR COWARDLY SOUL.
SPEAK TO ME THAT WAY AGAIN AND I SWEAR THAT--
YOU'LL DO NOTHING. AND ONCE MY LADY REALIZES WHAT A GARGANTUAN ERROR SHE MADE MERGING YOU WITH THE *ECLIPSO FORCE,* THEN--
SLAM

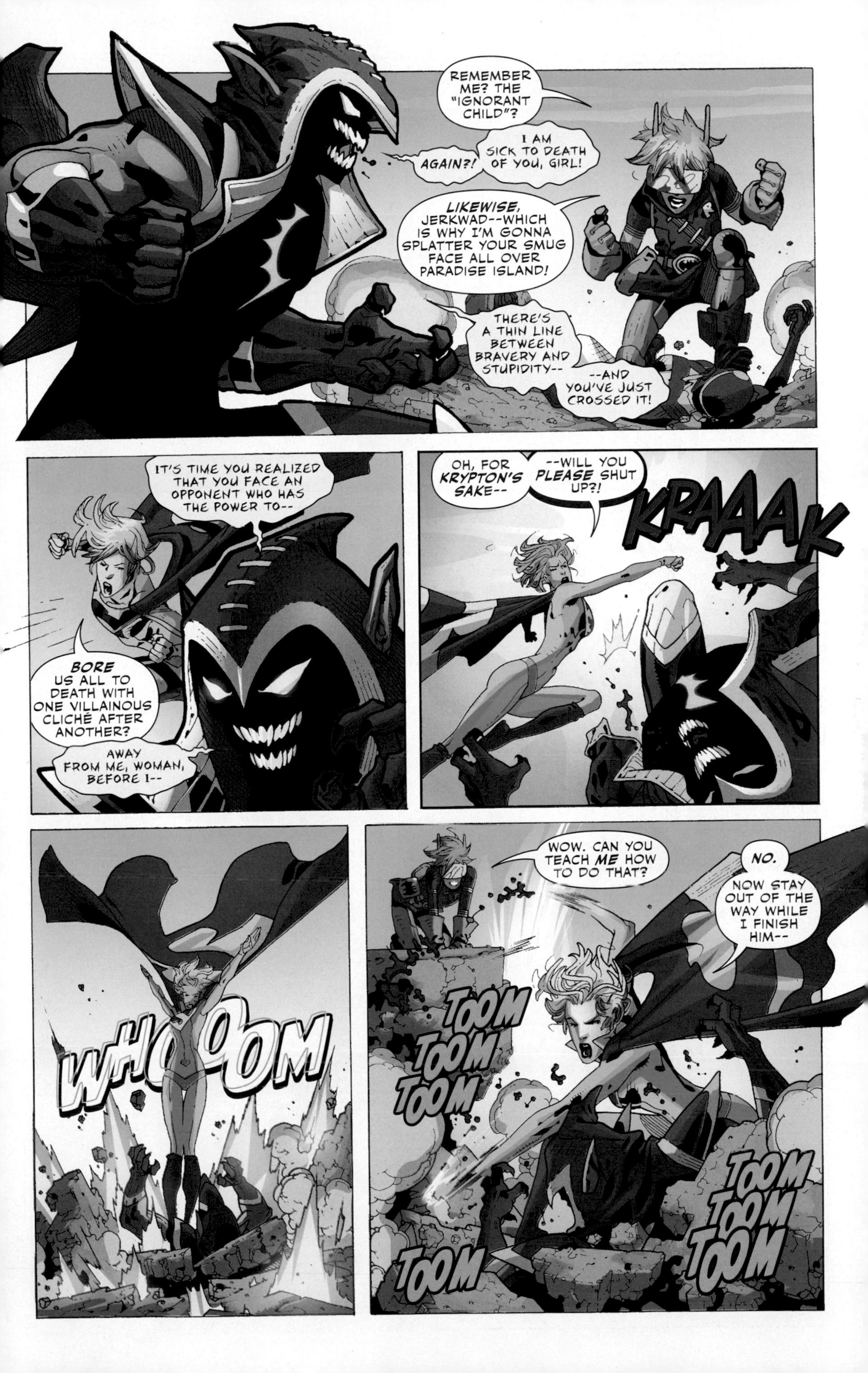
REMEMBER ME? THE "IGNORANT CHILD"?
AGAIN?!
I AM SICK TO DEATH OF YOU, GIRL!
LIKEWISE, JERKWAD--WHICH IS WHY I'M GONNA SPLATTER YOUR SMUG FACE ALL OVER PARADISE ISLAND!
THERE'S A THIN LINE BETWEEN BRAVERY AND STUPIDITY--
--AND YOU'VE JUST CROSSED IT!
IT'S TIME YOU REALIZED THAT YOU FACE AN OPPONENT WHO HAS THE POWER TO--
BORE US ALL TO DEATH WITH ONE VILLAINOUS CLICHÉ AFTER ANOTHER?
AWAY FROM ME, WOMAN, BEFORE I--
OH, FOR KRYPTON'S SAKE--
--WILL YOU PLEASE SHUT UP?!
KRAAAK
WHOOOOM
WOW. CAN YOU TEACH ME HOW TO DO THAT?
NO.
NOW STAY OUT OF THE WAY WHILE I FINISH HIM--
TOOM TOOM TOOM
TOOM
TOOM TOOM TOOM

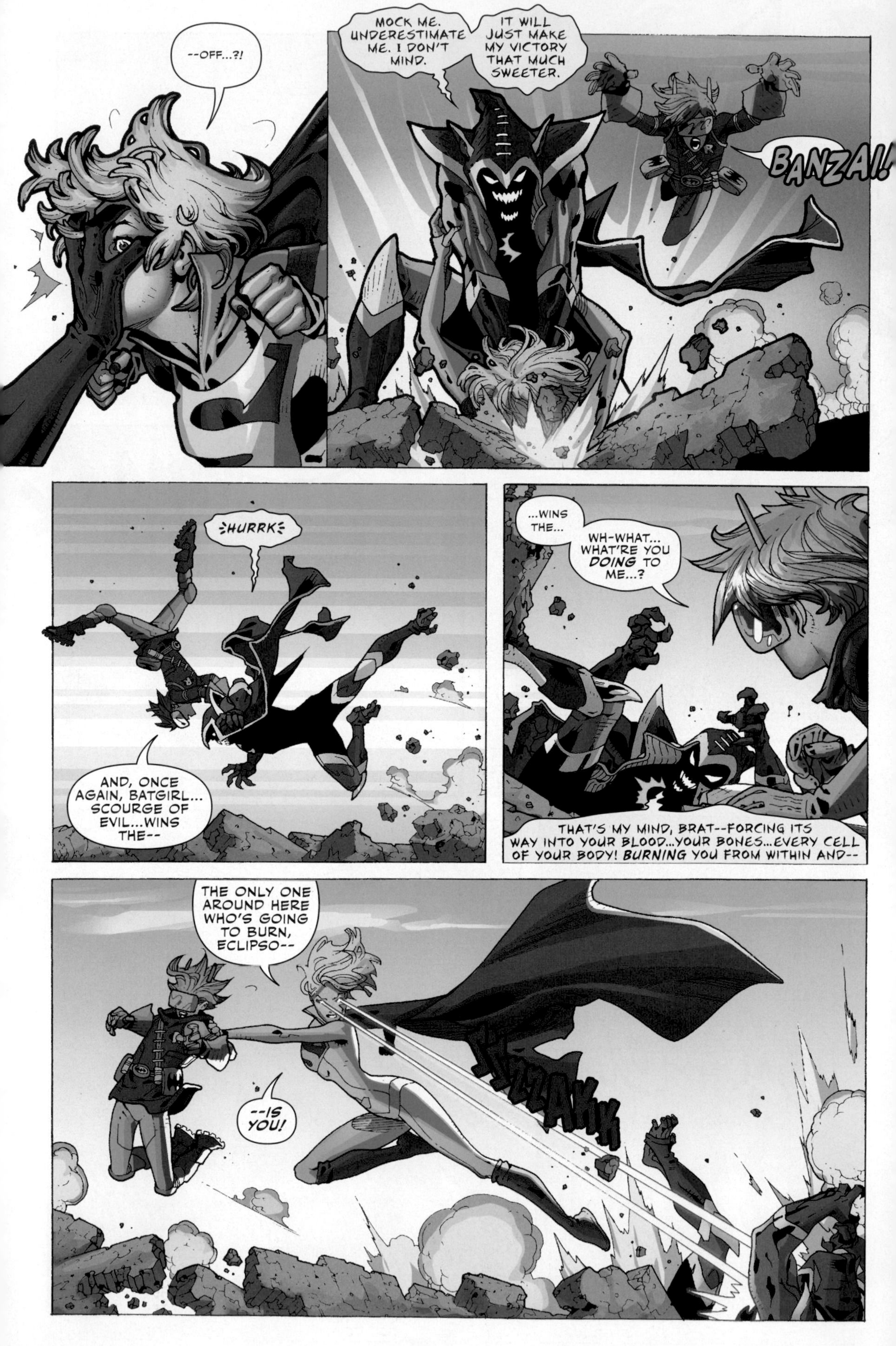
--OFF...?!
MOCK ME. UNDERESTIMATE ME. I DON'T MIND.
IT WILL JUST MAKE MY VICTORY THAT MUCH SWEETER.
BANZAI!
HURRK
AND, ONCE AGAIN, BATGIRL... SCOURGE OF EVIL...WINS THE--
...WINS THE...
WH-WHAT... WHAT'RE YOU DOING TO ME...?
THAT'S MY MIND, BRAT--FORCING ITS WAY INTO YOUR BLOOD...YOUR BONES...EVERY CELL OF YOUR BODY! BURNING YOU FROM WITHIN AND--
THE ONLY ONE AROUND HERE WHO'S GOING TO BURN, ECLIPSO--
--IS YOU!

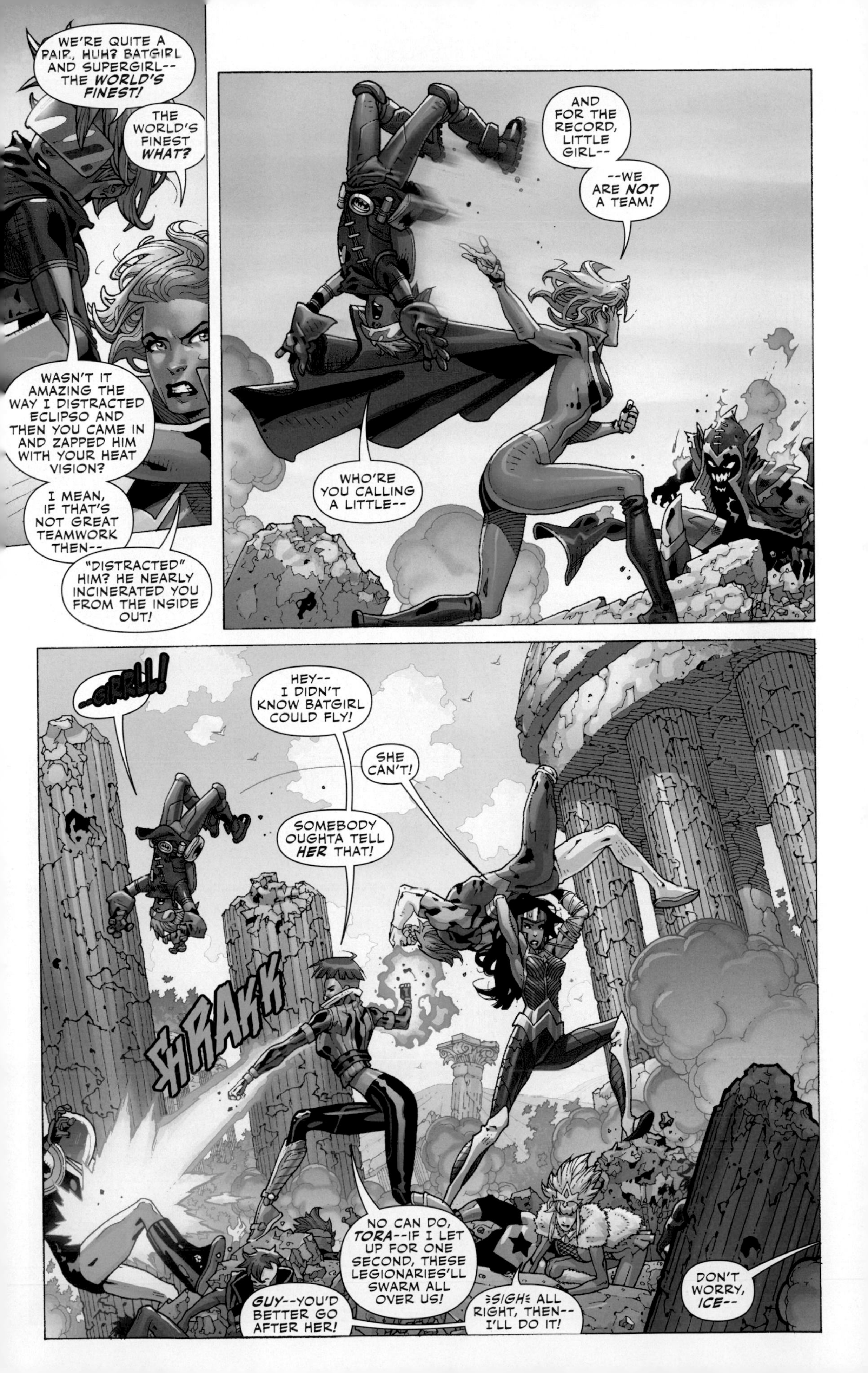
WE'RE QUITE A PAIR, HUH? BATGIRL AND SUPERGIRL-- THE WORLD'S FINEST!
THE WORLD'S FINEST WHAT?
WASN'T IT AMAZING THE WAY I DISTRACTED ECLIPSO AND THEN YOU CAME IN AND ZAPPED HIM WITH YOUR HEAT VISION?
I MEAN, IF THAT'S NOT GREAT TEAMWORK THEN--
"DISTRACTED" HIM? HE NEARLY INCINERATED YOU FROM THE INSIDE OUT!
AND FOR THE RECORD, LITTLE GIRL--
--WE ARE NOT A TEAM!
WHO'RE YOU CALLING A LITTLE--
--GIRRLL!
HEY-- I DIDN'T KNOW BATGIRL COULD FLY!
SHE CAN'T!
SOMEBODY OUGHTA TELL HER THAT!
SHRAKK
GUY--YOU'D BETTER GO AFTER HER!
NO CAN DO, TORA--IF I LET UP FOR ONE SECOND, THESE LEGIONARIES'LL SWARM ALL OVER US!
SIGH ALL RIGHT, THEN-- I'LL DO IT!
DON'T WORRY, ICE--

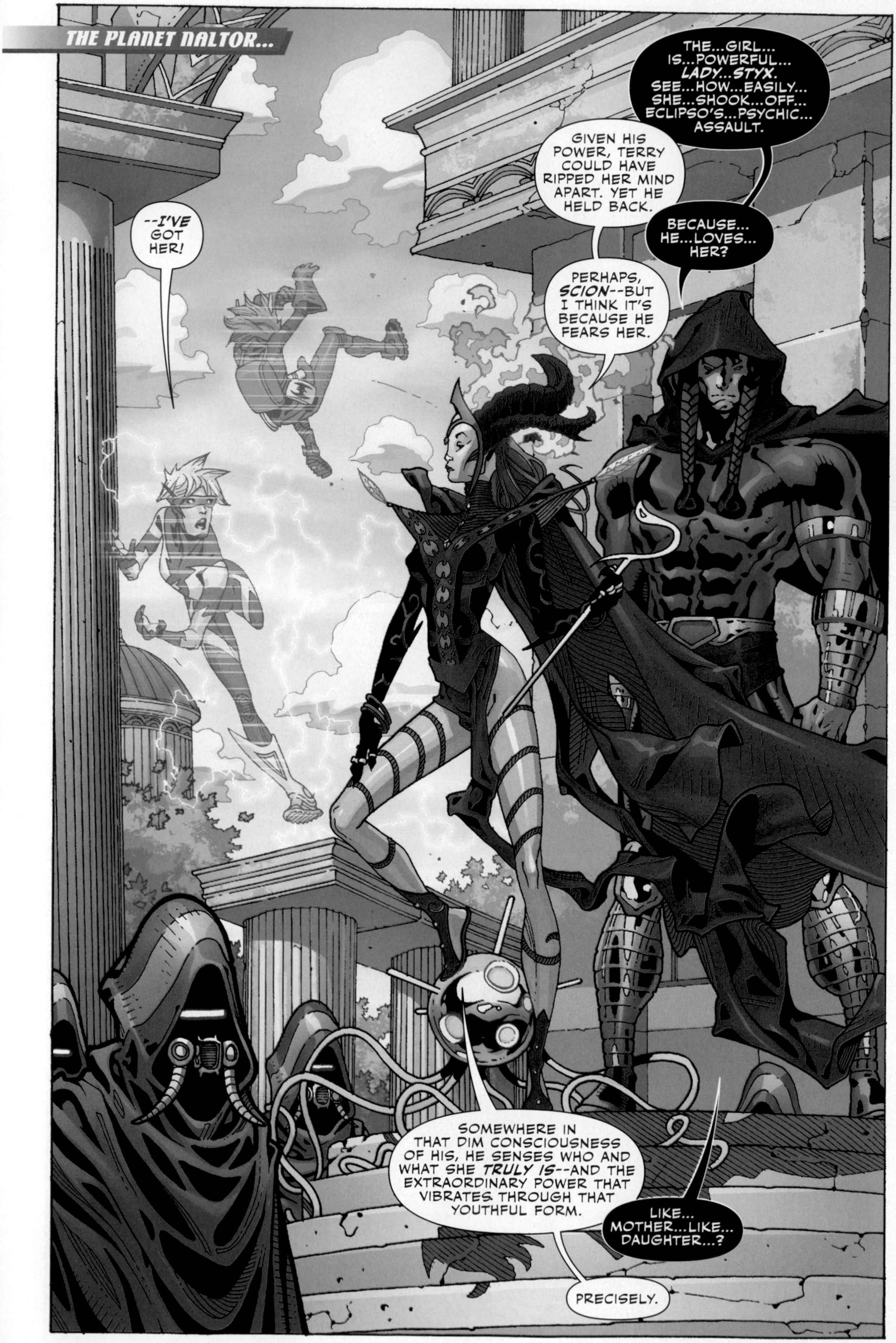
THE PLANET NALTOR...
THE...GIRL... IS...POWERFUL... LADY...STYX. SEE...HOW...EASILY... SHE...SHOOK...OFF... ECLIPSO'S...PSYCHIC... ASSAULT.
GIVEN HIS POWER, TERRY COULD HAVE RIPPED HER MIND APART. YET HE HELD BACK.
BECAUSE... HE...LOVES... HER?
PERHAPS, SCION--BUT I THINK IT'S BECAUSE HE FEARS HER.
--I'VE GOT HER!
SOMEWHERE IN THAT DIM CONSCIOUSNESS OF HIS, HE SENSES WHO AND WHAT SHE TRULY IS--AND THE EXTRAORDINARY POWER THAT VIBRATES THROUGH THAT YOUTHFUL FORM.
LIKE... MOTHER...LIKE... DAUGHTER...?
PRECISELY.

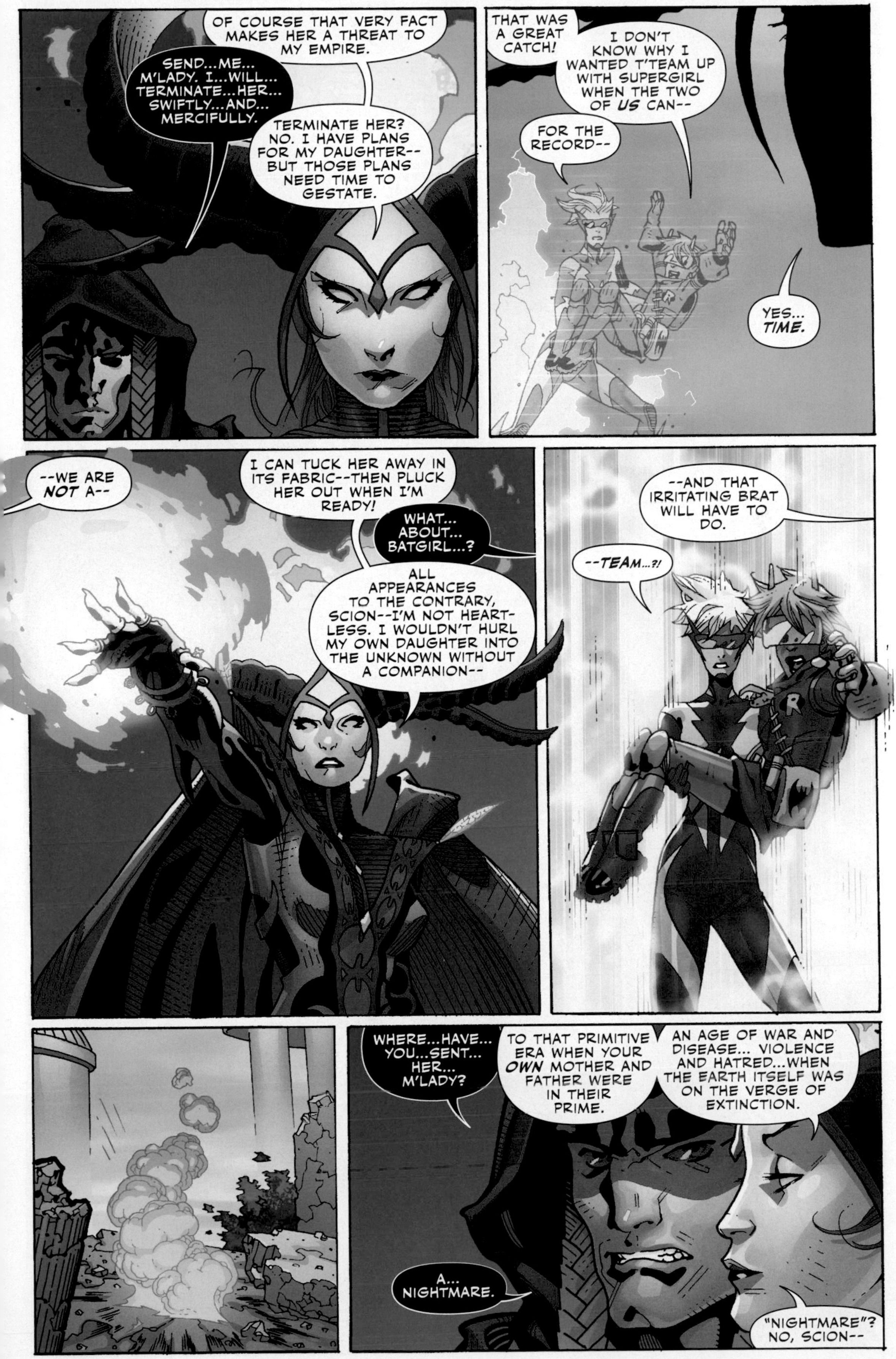
OF COURSE THAT VERY FACT MAKES HER A THREAT TO MY EMPIRE.
SEND...ME... M'LADY. I...WILL... TERMINATE...HER... SWIFTLY...AND... MERCIFULLY.
TERMINATE HER? NO. I HAVE PLANS FOR MY DAUGHTER--BUT THOSE PLANS NEED TIME TO GESTATE.
THAT WAS A GREAT CATCH!
I DON'T KNOW WHY I WANTED T'TEAM UP WITH SUPERGIRL WHEN THE TWO OF US CAN--
FOR THE RECORD--
YES... TIME.
--WE ARE NOT A--
I CAN TUCK HER AWAY IN ITS FABRIC--THEN PLUCK HER OUT WHEN I'M READY!
WHAT... ABOUT... BATGIRL...?
ALL APPEARANCES TO THE CONTRARY, SCION--I'M NOT HEARTLESS. I WOULDN'T HURL MY OWN DAUGHTER INTO THE UNKNOWN WITHOUT A COMPANION--
--AND THAT IRRITATING BRAT WILL HAVE TO DO.
--TEAM...?!
WHERE...HAVE... YOU...SENT... HER... M'LADY?
TO THAT PRIMITIVE ERA WHEN YOUR OWN MOTHER AND FATHER WERE IN THEIR PRIME.
AN AGE OF WAR AND DISEASE... VIOLENCE AND HATRED...WHEN THE EARTH ITSELF WAS ON THE VERGE OF EXTINCTION.
A... NIGHTMARE.
"NIGHTMARE"? NO, SCION--

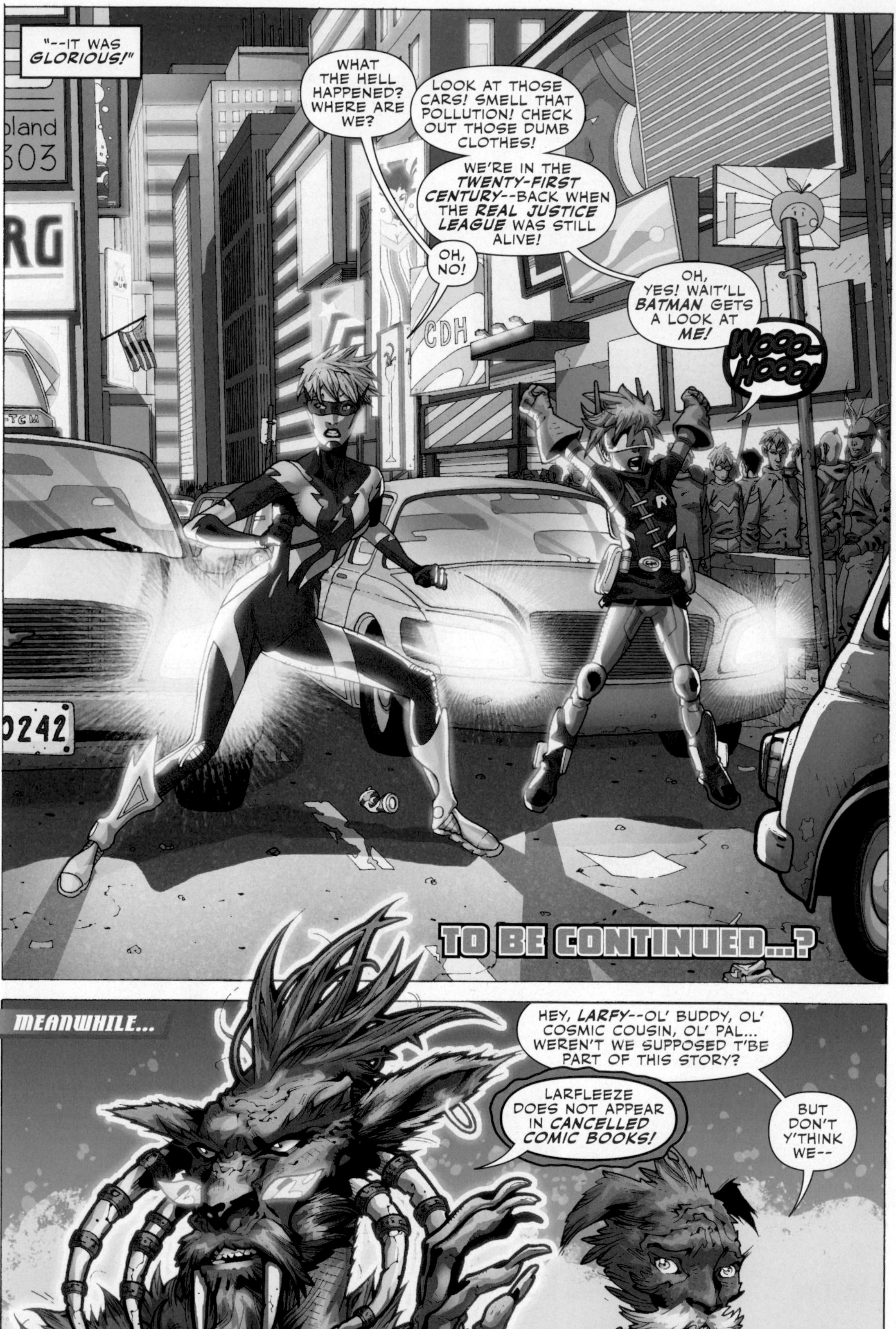
"--IT WAS GLORIOUS!"
WHAT THE HELL HAPPENED? WHERE ARE WE?
LOOK AT THOSE CARS! SMELL THAT POLLUTION! CHECK OUT THOSE DUMB CLOTHES!
WE'RE IN THE TWENTY-FIRST CENTURY--BACK WHEN THE REAL JUSTICE LEAGUE WAS STILL ALIVE!
OH, NO!
OH, YES! WAIT'LL BATMAN GETS A LOOK AT ME!
WOOO-HOOO!
CDH
TO BE CONTINUED...?
MEANWHILE...
HEY, LARFY--OL' BUDDY, OL' COSMIC COUSIN, OL' PAL... WEREN'T WE SUPPOSED T'BE PART OF THIS STORY?
LARFLEEZE DOES NOT APPEAR IN CANCELLED COMIC BOOKS!
BUT DON'T Y'THINK WE--
CASE CLOSED!

Unfinished Inventory Story for JUSTICE LEAGUE 3001

SCRIPT BY KEITH GIFFEN AND J.M. DEMATTEIS • PENCILS BY DOUG MAHNKE

INKS BY CHRISTIAN ALAMY

PAGE ONE

Unless otherwise noted, all captions are Green Lantern's.

PANEL ONE
(1) Cap: I was born on Earth...

(2) Cap:...but I found my destiny in the stars.

(3) Bot. Cap: Sometimes I think that Hal Jordan is just a fiction, a convenient mask...

PANEL TWO
(4) Cap: ...and that Green Lantern is who I truly am.
(classic 60's Green Lantern logo)

(5) Cap: Yes, I had a career, friends, family—but that was a thousand years ago.

(6) Cap: And the life I led back in the 21st century seems like a rapidly-fading dream.

PANEL THREE
(7) Cap: Of course the fact that our memories were damaged when Cadmus resurrected the League only adds to that feeling. There are holes in my past—miles wide.

NO #8

(9) Cap: I reach for a familiar face, a beloved place, the recollection of a mother, a brother, a lover...

PANEL FOUR
(10) Cap: ...and they just slip away. And maybe that's for the best.

(11) Cap: I am dying, after all: the green energy that gives me my power—is killing me.

(12) Cap: Or should I say what's left of me since that lunatic Locus reduced me to a miniature version of myself.

(13) Bot. Cap: *Back in Justice League 3000 #2—Harvey.

PANEL FIVE
(14) Cap: I project a full-grown form...an echo of the man I was... but, beneath that—I'm just a few inches tall.

(15) Cap: And the weird thing is I've gotten used to it.

(16) Cap: After you've died and been reborn by having your DNA injected into an unwilling host body, well...

PANEL SIX
(17) Cap:...I guess you can get accustomed to anything.

(18) Cap: That said, there's one thing I need to know before my green-cancer takes me out.

(19) Cap: And if that world down there is what I think it is...

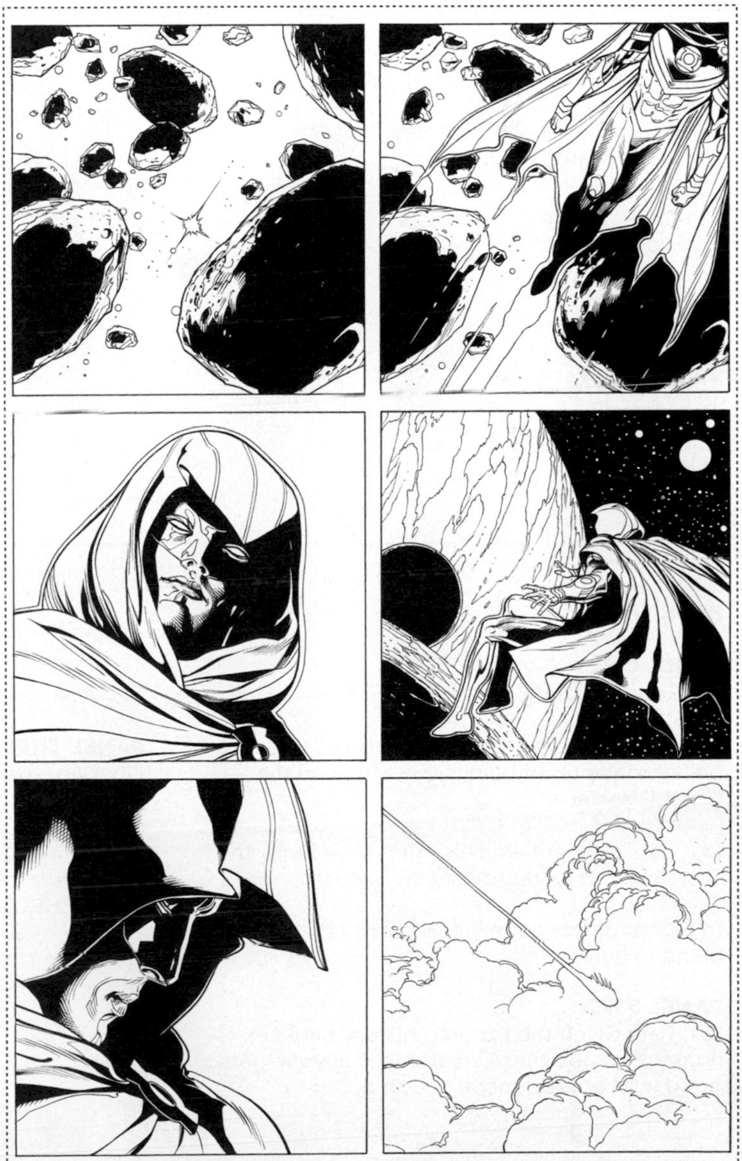

PAGE TWO

PANEL ONE
(1) Cap: ...I'll find my answer here.

(2) Cap: Concord Twelve.
(LOCATION CAP)

(3) Cap: An untold tale of JUSTICE
LEAGUE 3001 (logo) (NOT GL)

(4) Title: ANIMAL CRACKERS!

(5) Credits: Keith Giffen & J.M.
DeMatteis, writers
(Bottom of Page)

Dough Mahnke & Christian Alamy,
guest artists
Brian Cunningham, group editor
Harvey Richards, ringmaster

PAGE THREE

PANEL ONE
(1) Cap: Amazing!

(2) Cap: What Tora told us was true: an entire
planet made up of beings that survived the
Great Disaster.

(3) Cap: Sentient animals—that have built, and
sustained, an extraordinary civilization.

(4) Cap: Better get my hood up if I hope to
blend in here.

PANEL TWO
(5) Cap: Given the tortured history between
humankind and these creatures, if anyone gets a
good look at me, I might set off a...

(6) Ape 1: Holy jumpin' primates! (BURST)

PANEL THREE
(7) Cap:...panic.

(8) Ape 1: It's him!

(9) Ape 1: He's come back!
(ATTACHED)

(10) Ape 1: He's come back! (ATTACHED;
HEAVY BLACK BORDER)

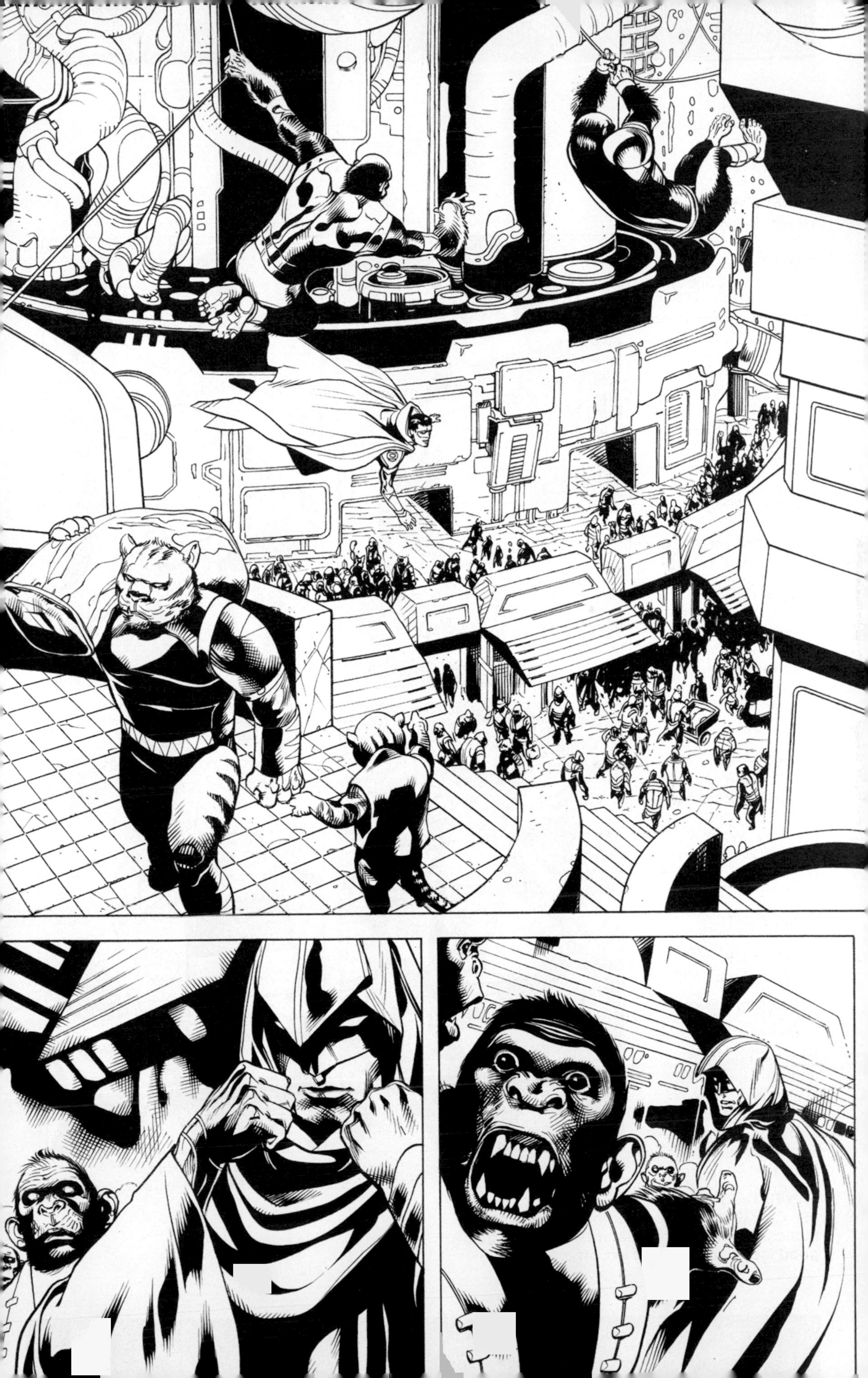

PAGE FOUR

PANEL ONE
NO COPY

PANEL TWO
(1) GL: Uh...there's clearly been a mistake.

(2) GL: Whoever you may think I am...I'm not! So, please—get up—

(3) GL: —because you're making me really uncomfortable. (ATTACHED)

(4) Captain (OS): ...don't tell me you people are at it again!

PANEL THREE
(5) Captain: I swear it seems like every other week there's a rumor that he's back—all you yokels get excited—and then—

PANEL FOUR
(6) Captain: Oh, you gotta be kiddin' me!

(7) Cop: What is that? A Halloween mask? (ATTACHED)

(8) GL: I assure you, officer—this is my face.

(9) Captain: Sure it is.

(10) Captain: Sigh. If I had a nickel for every time some delusional idiot pretends t'be Green Lantern, I wouldn't have t'be stuck in this dead-end job.

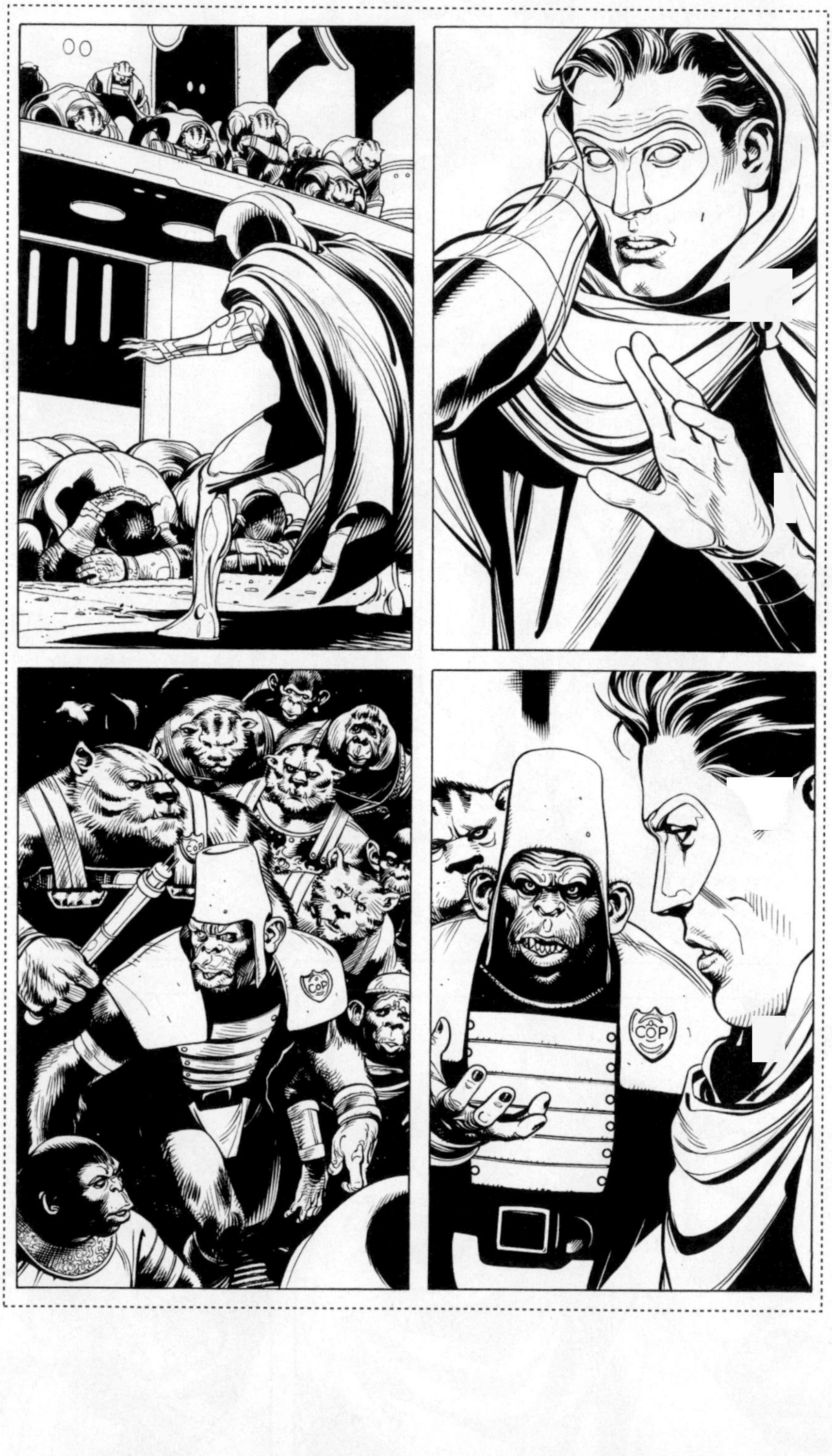

COP
COP

PAGE FIVE

PANEL ONE
(1) GL: It's not a mask, officer. And, for better or worse, I am a Green Lantern.

(2) GL: But why are these people reacting like this?

(3) TIger Cop (OP): Y'know, Captain—now that I'm gettin' a good look at it—I don't think that is a mask!

PANEL TWO
(4) Tiger: I mean, no one could make somethin' that ugly!

(5) GL (OP): Hey!

(6) Tiger: Uh...no offense.

(7) Captain: I think you're right, Tigrowski! I mean, that is one gruesome sight!

(8) GL (OP): Hey!

PANEL THREE
(9) Captain (OP): So you really are one o' them? The spectrum warriors?

(10) GL: Well, I was. Once.

(11) Captain (OP): An' what're you now?

(12) GL: Well, you see, I died in battle ten centuries ago...and then I was resurrected and shrunk... and then—

PANEL FOUR
(13) GL: Let's just say it's a long story.

(14) Captain: Yeah? Well, it's a story I wanna hear. So let's us head over t'the station...toss back a few cups of banana latte—

(15) Captain: —and get t'the bottom of this.
(ATTACHED)

(16) GL: I'll be happy to go with you, Sergeant—but, before we do—

PANEL FIVE
(17) GL: —could you please explain why everyone's gaping at me and acting like I'm the second coming!

(18) Captain: 'cause—according to them— you are!

(19) GL: Excuse me?

(20) Captain: You need glasses or somethin', pal?

PANEL SIX
(21) Captain: 'cause it would take a blind man t'miss that!

(22) GL: "That" what?

(23) Captain: "That"—

PAGE SIX

PANEL ONE
(1) Captain: —that!

(2) GL: Holy crap.

(3) Tiger: That's one way of puttin' it.

(4) Bot. Cap: "A temple—built in honor of the Corps?"

PAGE SEVEN

PANEL ONE
(1) GL: How is that possible?

(2) GL: I was under the impression that—in this century—the Green Lantern Corps is despised throughout the known universe.

(3) Captain (OP): Not around here.

PANEL TWO
(4) Captain: You're like gods t'most of those yokels out there.

(5) GL: Me—I never went in for all that religious claptrap. In fact, I always thought the lanterns were just a legend.

(6) Captain: Yet here you are. Or claim t'be.

PANEL THREE
(7) Captain: An' I can't help wonderin' why.

(8) Captain: An' if you tell me it's a long story, I'll lock you up an' (ATTACHED) throw away the key!

(9) GL (OP): It's not very complicated, Sergeant: I came to your world—

PANEL FOUR
(10) GL: —looking for answers.

(11) Captain: Care t'share the question?

(12) GL: The people of Concord Twelve survived the Great Disaster. Your history is intact. You know things that no one else in all the galaxy knows.

(13) GL: And before I die, I have to understand what happened.
(ATTACHED)

PANEL FIVE
(14) GL (OP): What did the Corps do—to become so hated in—

(15) Captain: Wait, wait, wait: Before you die?

(16) GL (OP): Another long story.

(17) Captain: You're just full of 'em.

PANEL SIX
(18) Captain: But you ain't kiddin', are you? I can see it in your eyes. Smell it on your skin.
You really are dyin'.

(19) GL (OP): I am.

(20) Captain: Geez.

(21) Captain: Ya got my sympathies, kid.

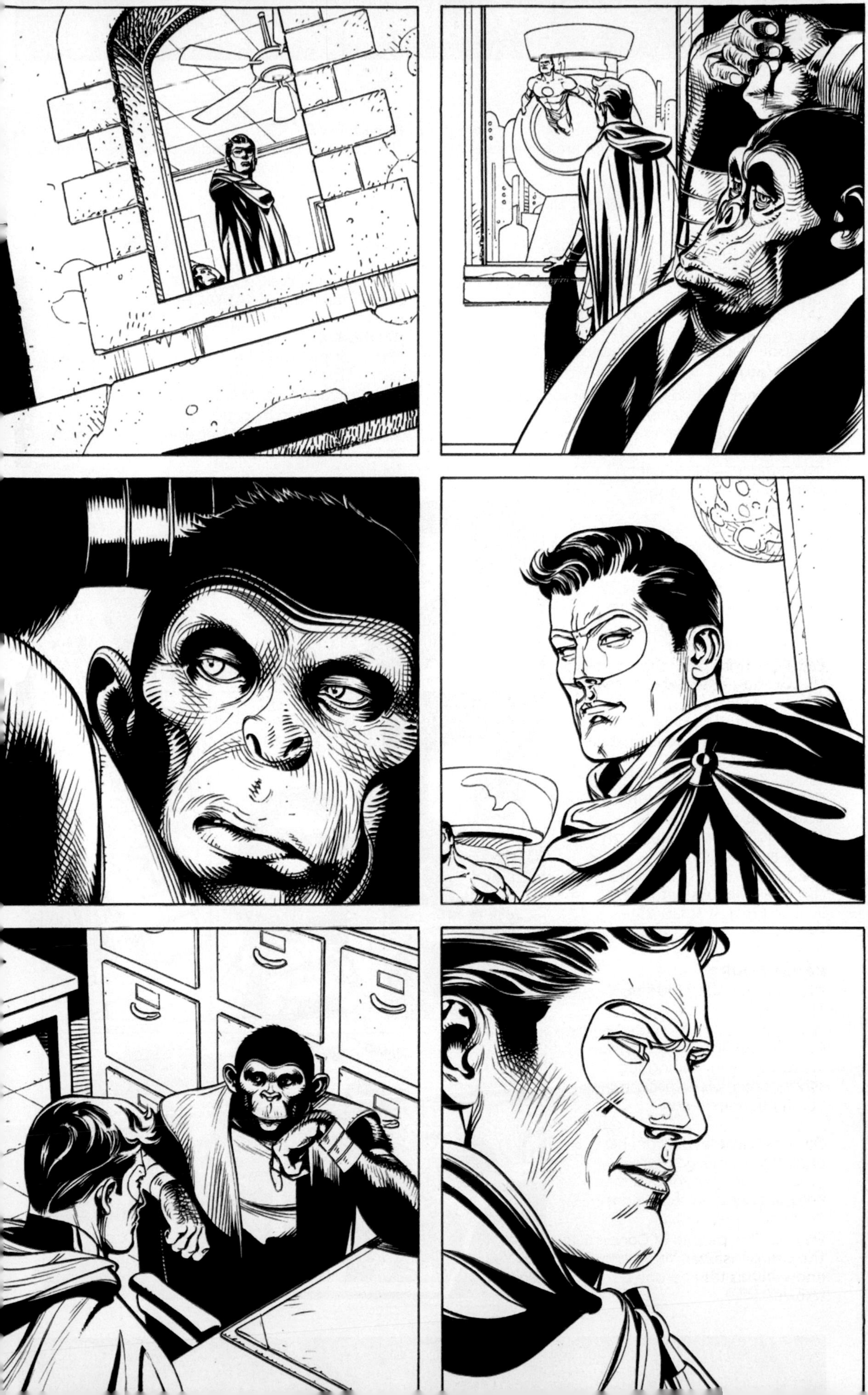

PAGE EIGHT

PANEL ONE
(1) Captain: What I haven't got are the answers you're lookin' for.

(2) GL: But I'd think that here, of all places, you'd know.

(3) GL: Your people...your history...made it through the Great (ATTACHED) Disaster intact and—

(4) Captain: Intact?

PANEL TWO
(5) Captain: Nobody made it through that holocaust intact. Maybe more fragments of our history survived than in some other places—

(6) Captain: —but most of it's full of myths and misinformation.

(7) GL: No oral tradition?

(8) Captain: You want me t'answer that with a straight face?

PANEL THREE
(9) GL: You know what I mean!

(10) Captain: The only oral history that survived is the tale of the Exodus.

(11) GL: Exodus? You mean when Tora...the, uh, ice goddess...led your people off Earth and into space?*

(12) Bot. Cap: *As detailed in Justice League 3000 #14— Harvey.

PANEL FOUR
(13) Captain: "Ice Goddess"? That's news t' me!

(14) GL: But Tora said she was instrumental in helping the sentient animals to escape the human genocide and—

(15) Captain: Maybe from her perspective she was some great savior. Everybody's the hero of their own story, right? From our perspective?

(16) Captain: She didn't even merit a footnote. (ATTACHED)

PANEL FIVE
(17) Captain: But the Exodus story does involve your green buddies.

(18) GL: The Corps?

(19) Captain: Piqued your interest, huh?

(20) Captain: Well, pull up a chair, pour another cup o' banana joe—(ATTACHED)

PANEL SIX
(21) Captain: —an I'll tell ya how it all happened.

(22) Captain: After the Disaster hit...an' don't ask me what caused it, 'cause nobody knows—the animal races came out better than the humans.

PAGE NINE

Unless otherwise stated, all quoted captions are Captain's.

PANEL ONE

(1) Cap: "Maybe it was our natural survival skills. Or maybe we're just tougher than you fleshies."

(2) Cap: "'Fleshies'? Don't you think that's a little offensive?" (GL)

(3) Cap: "Believe me, your people called us—an' did to us—a lot worse. An' after the Disaster, it was our turn to gain the upper hand.

PANEL TWO

(4) Cap: "I ain't proud of how we behaved—but we ruled for something like two hundred years. An' it was a peaceful couple of centuries—

(5) Cap: "—till you fleshies...humans...rose up again. After that it was a decade of war... then a fragile peace... then more war.

(6) Cap: "The humans eventually herded us onto reservations... then into concentration camps. By that time we'd had our fill of Men... and of Earth.

PANEL THREE

(7) Cap: "There was an animal uprising... more fighting, more death...and those of us that survived cobbled together a space ark from remnants that survived the G.D.

(8) Cap: "A group of sympathetic fleshies helped us put the ship together. Maybe your ice goddess was one o' them.

(9) Cap: "Problem was—

PANEL FOUR

(10) Cap: "—there wasn't room for our whole population on the ark. Some had to stay behind. Animals turned on animals then—an' the humans took advantage of the conflict to—

(11) Cap: "Well, calling it genocide doesn't do it justice.

(12) Bot. Cap: "A few thousand of us managed to get out.

PAGE TEN

Unless otherwise stated, all quoted captions are Captain's.

PANEL ONE

(1) Cap: "But where in the name of Boxer were they gonna go?

(2) Cap: "They travelled for years...some say more than a century...new generations bein' born on the ark. But time took its toll.

(3) Cap: "Supplies dwindled. Inter-species hatred began to rear its ugly head. And the ark—

PANEL TWO

(4) Cap: "Well, it became more of a flying coffin. Either the animals were gonna annihilate each other—

(5) Cap: "—or we'd all die of starvation, somewhere in deep space.

(6) Cap: "That's when a holy man appeared. Some say he was an ape, others say he was a giraffe. I don't know if he was even real.

(7) Cap: "But the story says he prophesied a great light that would appear in the cold void—

PANEL THREE

(8) Cap: "—an' lead us out of the darkness."

(9) Cap: "The light. Was it—?" (GL)

(10) Cap: "You got it, pal: it was green. One o' you Lanterns found us—

PANEL FOUR

(11) Cap: "—an' guided us to a new world.

(12) Bot. Cap: "Maybe it wasn't Eden."

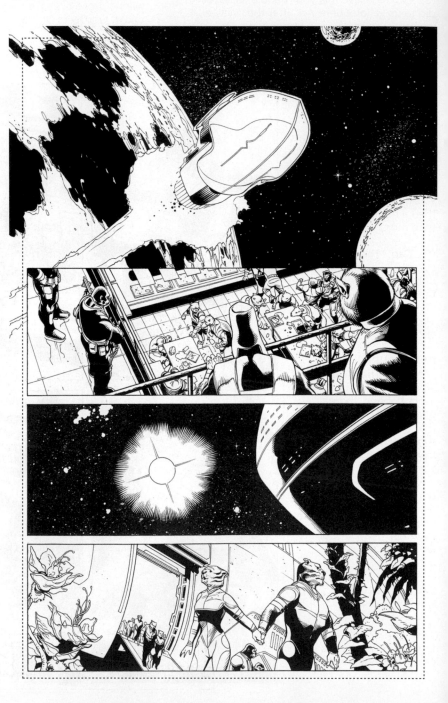

PAGE ELEVEN

PANEL ONE
(1) Captain (OP): —but it was home.

(2) GL: So I'm no closer to the truth than I was when I arrived here.

(3) GL: If the Corps had gone bad—if they'd done something so terrible that they were reviled on a thousand worlds—

PANEL TWO
(4) GL: —why would they have helped your people?

(5) Captain: Hey—maybe it happened or maybe someone just threw that in t'make the story more interesting. I tend t'favor the latter interpretation—

(6) Captain: —but, as that temple out there makes clear, I'm in the (ATTACHED) minority.

(7) GL: Well, thank you for taking the time to explain what you could, Sergeant. I'll be on my way now and—

(8) Captain: Right! Typical fleshie!

PANEL THREE
(9) Captain: Don't get what you want—so y'just abandon us.

(10) Captain: Shoulda known all that talk about you Lanterns bein' (ATTACHED) the greatest cops in the galaxy was just a load o' elephant turds.

(11) GL: We were the greatest! The Corps fought to protect the innocent! To fight injustice! To—

(12) Captain: Yeah? Well I'd like t'see you prove it!

PANEL FOUR
(13) GL (OP): Prove it? How?

(14) Captain: Hey—Tigrowsky!

(15) Tiger: Yeah, Cap?

(16) Captain: What's the latest on our serial killer?

(17) Tiger: Couple of beat cops had him cornered this morning—least they thought they did.

(18) Captain: Got away again?

(19) Tiger: Yeah—

PANEL FIVE
(20) Tiger (OP): —an' both our guys are in the hospital—fightin' for their lives. But we got three Beast Squads on the bastard's tail.

(21) Captain: So whaddaya say...Lantern? You wanna prove to those people out there that you're worthy of their worship?

(22) Captain: Or you wanna do it like most "gods"—and leave us to sink in our own stinkin' sewage?

(23) GL: Well, when you put it like that—

PANEL SIX
(24) GL: —how can I refuse?

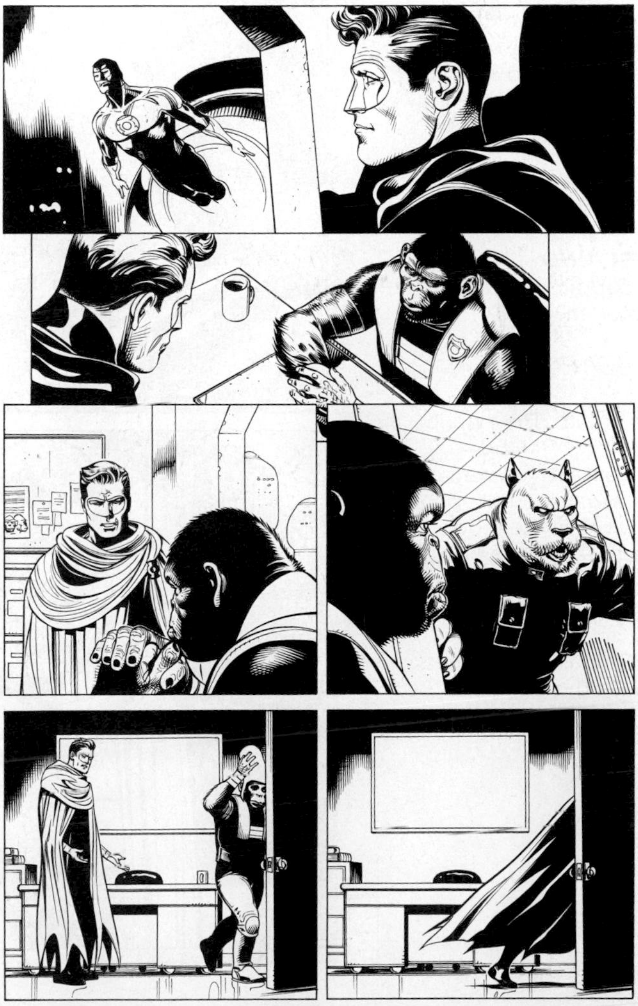

PAGE TWELVE

PANEL ONE
All balloons in this panel are floating, no tail.

(1) Captain: ...figures they'd track him here.

(2) GL: Wait. Is this a...meat processing plant?

(3) Sign: Sam's Yummy Meats!
From our slaughterhouse to your table!
You can't beat our meat!

(4) Captain: Yeah. So what?

(5) GL: But...but this is a world of animals. Don't tell me that you eat your own?

(6) Captain: Hey, jackass— we're carnivores, not cannibals!

(7) Captain: We genetically engineered a new breed of cattle—dumb as posts, like we used t'be before we evolved. Keep us all fat an' fed.

(8) GL: But—

PANEL TWO
(9) Captain: You a vegetarian?

(10) GL: No, but—

(11) Captain: Then zip it.

(12) Captain: Anyway, our killer always targets people that work in the food industry—might be a guy at the local market or the chef at a top restaurant.

(13) Captain: But he gets loose in there and hundreds of people could—
(ATTACHED)

PANEL THREE
(14) Tiger: Five employees are already dead, Captain—including the plant manager.

(15) Captain: Damn...

(15) Tiger: One of 'em managed to hit a silent alarm an' that's what brought the squads here.

PAGE THIRTEEN
Unless otherwise noted, all captions are GL's.

PANEL ONE
(1) GL: I've got this.

(2) Captain: You sure?

(3) GL: Your men go storming in there, who knows how many more will die?

(4) Captain: Guess you're gonna earn that temple, huh?

(5) GL: I don't need anybody's worship.

PANEL TWO
(6) Captain: Then why?

(7) GL: It's what I do, Captain. I can't help it. "Brightest day, blackest night" and all that.

(8) Captain: I don't know what the hell you're babblin' about—but best o' luck t'ya, fleshie—

PANEL THREE
(9) Cap: "—an' be careful in there." (CAPTAIN)

(10) Cap: The stench in this place—!

(11) Cap: Hope to God I don't upchuck all over my cloak.

PANEL FOUR
(12) Cap: I guess those creatures down there are the genetically engineered cows the captain was talking about.

(13) Cap: "Dumb as posts," he said. But what happens on the day when they...

PANEL FIVE
(14) Batcow: MOOOOOOOO!!!!
(OPEN LETTERS; NO BALLOON)

PANEL SIX
NO COPY

PAGE FOURTEEN

PANEL ONE
(1) Cap: ...evolve...?

(2) Batcow: Cowardly, superstitious criminal! Prepare to die—
at the hands of the—

(4) Batcow: BATCOW!
(ATTACHED; A VARIATION ON THE CLASSIC BATMAN LOGO)

(5) Bot. Cap: Batcow?!

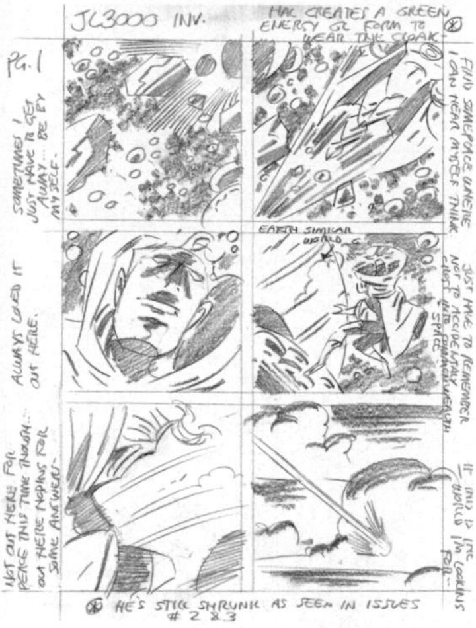
JL3000 INV.
PG. 1
HAL CREATES A GREEN ENERGY GL FORM TO WEAR THE CLOAK
HE'S STILL SHRUNK AS SEEN IN ISSUES #2 & 3

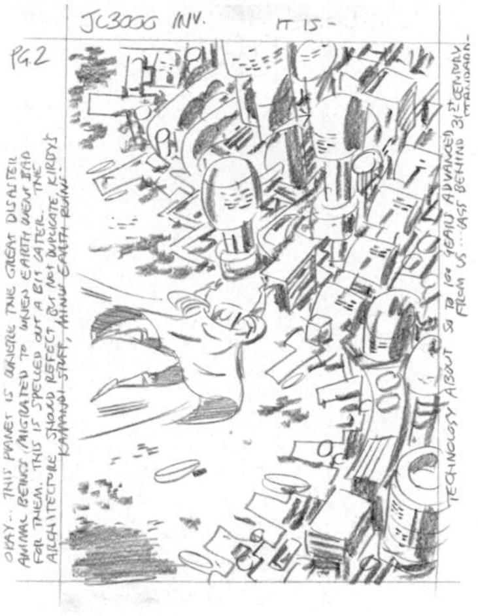
JL3000 INV.
PG. 2
IT IS-

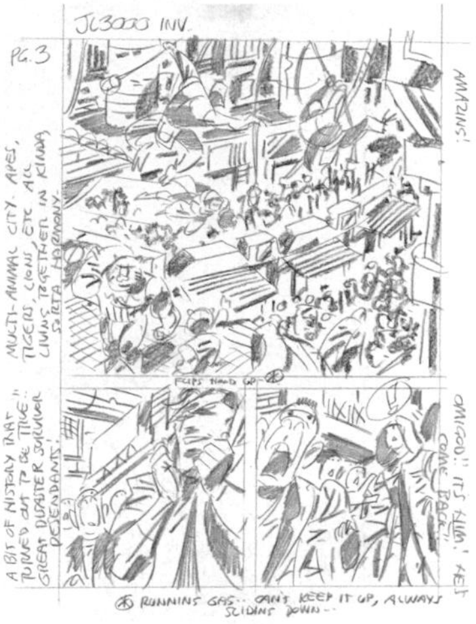
JL3000 INV.
PG. 3
RUNNING GAG... CAN'T KEEP IT UP, ALWAYS SLIDING DOWN-

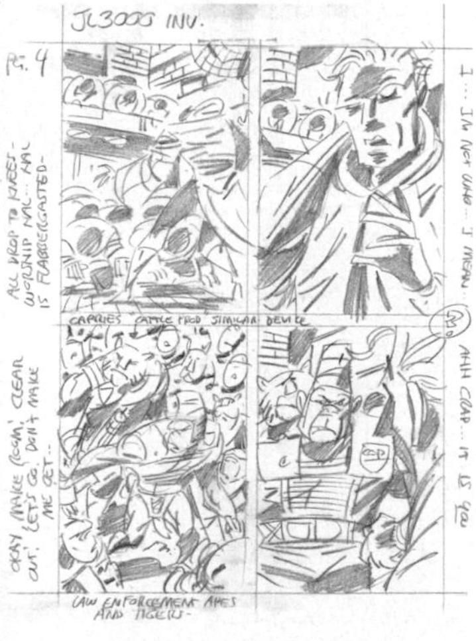
JL3000 INV.
PG. 4
LAW ENFORCEMENT APES AND TIGERS-

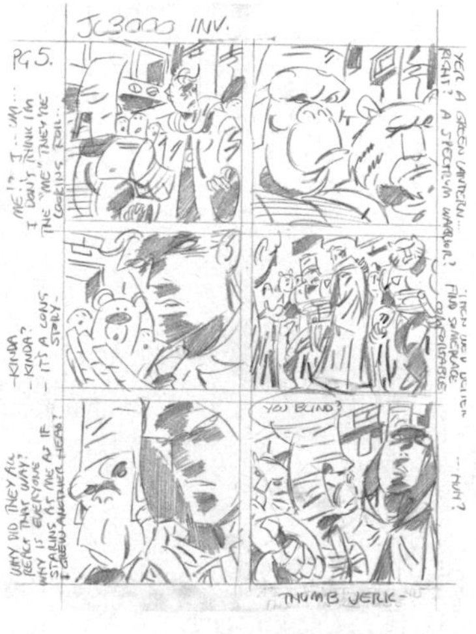
JL3000 INV.
PG. 5
YOU BLIND?
THUMB JERK-

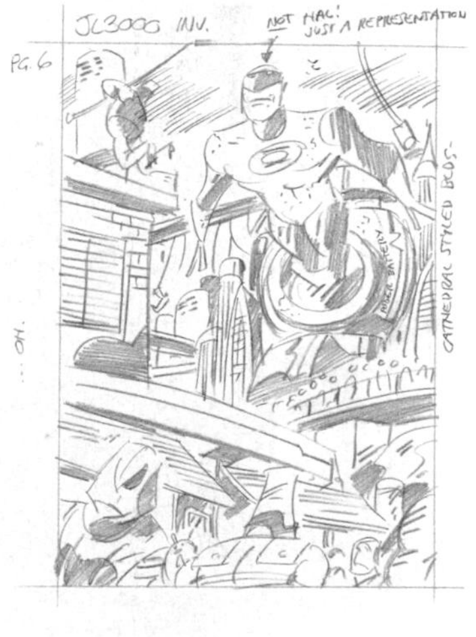
JL3000 INV.
PG. 6
NOT HAL!
JUST A REPRESENTATION

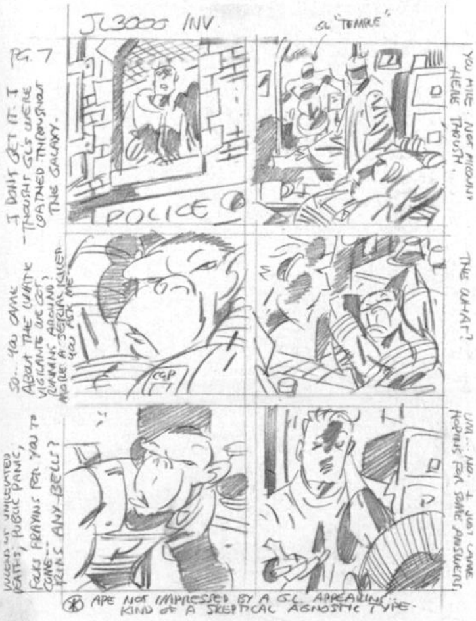
JL3000 INV.
PG. 7
POLICE
APE NOT IMPRESSED BY A G.L. APPEARING...
KIND OF A SKEPTICAL AGNOSTIC TYPE-

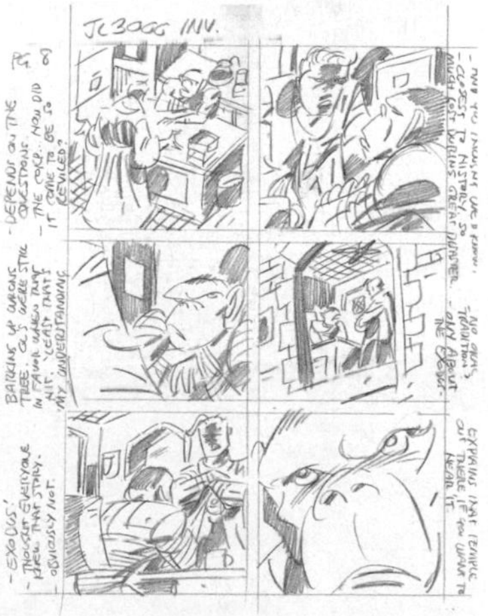
JL3000 INV.
PG. 8

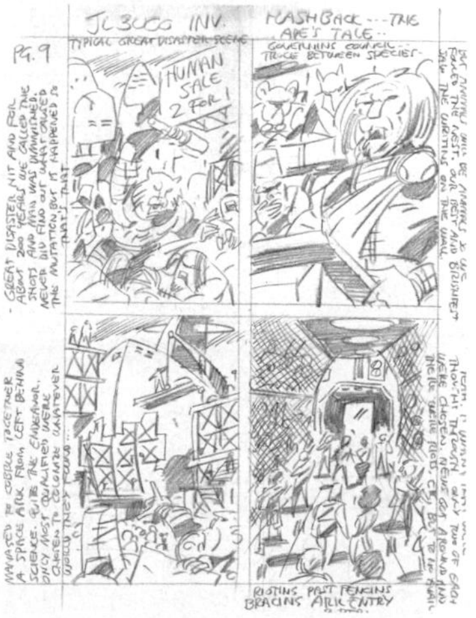
JL3000 INV.
PG. 9
FLASHBACK--- THE APE'S TALE-
TYPICAL GREAT DISASTER SCENE
HUMAN SALE 2 FOR 1

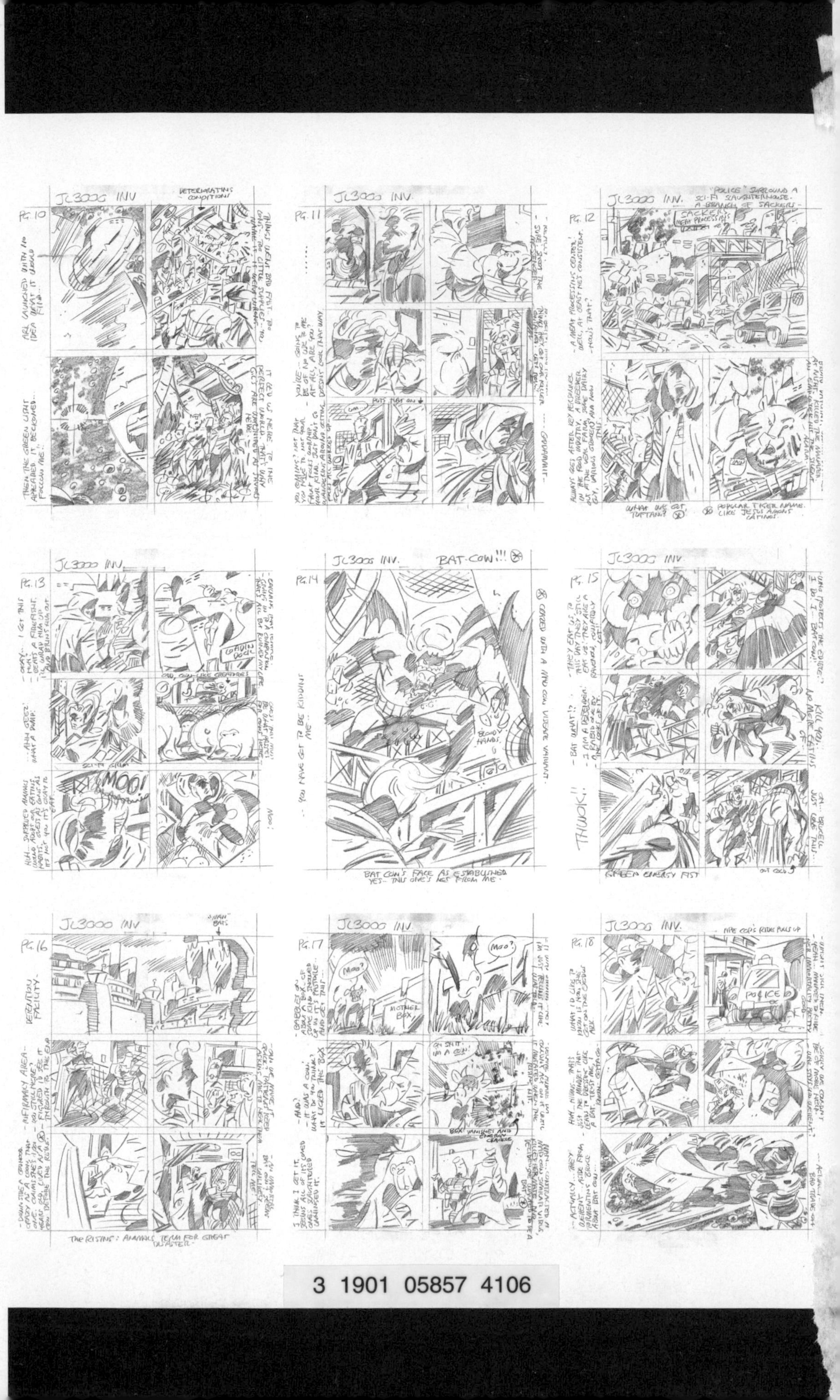

JL3000 INV.
PG. 10
PG. 11
JL3000 INV.
PG. 12
PG. 13
JL3000 INV.
BAT-COW!!!
PG. 14
JL3000 INV.
PG. 15
THUNK!!
GREEN ENERGY FIST
JL3000 INV.
PG. 16
DETENTION FACILITY.
JL3000 INV.
PG. 17
MOTHER BOX
JL3000 INV.
PG. 18
POLICE